Response
& Analysis

SECOND EDITION

Response & Analysis

SECOND EDITION

Teaching Literature in Secondary School

Robert E. Probst

HEINEMANN
Portsmouth, NH

Heinemann

361 Hanover Street
Portsmouth, NH 03801-3912
www.heinemann.com

Offices and agents throughout the world

The author and publisher wish to thank those who have generously given permission to reprint borrowed material:

Calvin and Hobbes cartoon by Bill Watterson. Copyright © 1995 by Bill Watterson. Reprinted by permission of Universal Press Syndicate. All rights reserved.

"Death of the Ball Turret Gunner" from *Complete Poems* by Randall Jarrell. Copyright © 1969, renewed 1997 by Mary von S. Jarrell. Reprinted by permission of Farrar, Straus, and Giroux, LLC.

(Credits continue on p. vi.)

Library of Congress Cataloging-in-Publication Data
Probst, Robert E.
  Response and analysis : teaching literature in secondary school / Robert E. Probst.—
2nd ed.
      p. cm.
  Includes bibliographical references and index.
   ISBN 0-325-00716-0 (alk. paper)
   1. Literature—Study and teaching (Secondary)—United States. I. Title.
PN70.P76 2004
807'.1'273—dc22   2004007824

Editors: Lisa Luedeke, Leigh Peake
Production: Lynne Reed
Cover design: Joni Doherty
Cover photograph: Pando Hall/Getty Images
Cover author photograph: Arnold Clark Studio
Typesetter: Argosy Publishing
Manufacturing: Steve Bernier

Printed in the United States of America on acid-free paper
08   VP   4   5

To my parents, Harry and Marian Probst.
And to my wife, Wendy, and my sons, Geoffrey and Bryan.

PREFACE

About ten years ago, Louise Rosenblatt, while sitting in Princeton, New Jersey, talked with fifty teachers and me as we huddled around a speakerphone in Anchorage, Alaska. During the conversation, Dr. Rosenblatt made the remark that she had written Literature as Exploration "as a defense of democracy." I wasn't sure what she meant at the time, and may not fully grasp it even now.

I think, though, that she meant that we have to learn to read both our texts and the world responsively and responsibly if we're to preserve democratic processes. That is to say, we must not simply submit to texts, accepting too easily what they offer us, following them too willingly wherever they would take us. Rather, we have to bring those texts to bear upon our lives, and our lives to bear upon the texts, reflecting conscientiously upon the experience, attitudes, and ideas that emerge from our reading, analyzing both the text and ourselves, continually rethinking who we are, what we believe and value, and where we stand in the world. Literature offers us the chance to do that thinking. If our students learn to read in that way, they may be able to exercise some control over their lives and participate in the free thought necessary for a democracy; if they don't, they're prepared only to follow, accepting someone else's decisions and judgments.

This book is an effort to figure out how we might teach that responsive and responsible reading in the secondary schools, grades six through twelve.

Whatever changes have found their way into this revised edition I owe to a great many people from whom I've learned, borrowed, and stolen. Louise Rosenblatt is still the foundation; her theory is as strong and vital now as it was when she first articulated it almost 70 years ago. Many others, however, have helped me explore it and have shown me, more clearly than I otherwise could have seen, what it means in the classroom and in a democratic society: R. Baird Shuman led me to first explore these ideas; Kylene Beers taught me everything I know (a small part of what she knows) about working with kids who have difficulty reading; Ken Holmes showed me skillful and sensitive teaching of less privileged students in an impoverished inner-city; Joan Wynne helped me tremendously to better understand African-American and Latino students; Hal Foster demonstrated for me how universities and schools can work together; and there are many others (too many to name), including the teachers studying at Georgia State University who put up with my experiments in the classroom and shared their own with me, and countless middle and high school students around the country who have helped immensely, although they may not know it.

I would also like to thank Lisa Luedeke, who diligently kept after me to get this revision completed—it would never have happened without her support and encouragement—and the others at Heinemann who work so hard to bring a book together. In many ways, it's been a group project, although I'm responsible for the misspelled words and other errors.

—Bob Probst
Marathon, Florida
July 2, 2004

CONTENTS

1

Three Readers Reading
Theoretical Foundations

was on my way to class early one Monday morning—it was about 7:45 A.M., long before I like to be awake, and I wasn't sure that I was in the right corridor or even, for that matter, in the right building—when a colleague of mine crossed the hallway, planted himself in front of me, stuck his finger in my face, and announced, "I only read trash." Even for that cranky old professor, it was an unusual greeting, more an accusation than a greeting, actually, and at that hour, without having had so much as a cup of coffee to give me false courage, I wasn't sure how to respond. "Good morning" didn't seem an adequate defense, but nor did I want to turn and run. I backed cautiously up against the wall while he glared at me, daring me to utter a word of self-justification or repentance, but all I could muster was a mumbled question. "Why," I asked, "are you sharing with me this fascinating insight into your intellectual history at this ungodly hour on a Monday morning when I am inoffensively searching for my classroom?"

He repeated and elaborated, "I only read trash, and it's because of what you guys did to me when I was in high school."

I knew then that I was a stand-in for his fondly remembered English teachers because I was, at that time, the only one in the department who worked with English teachers. I was, at that very moment, on my way to the Secondary English Methods class, wishing I had left the office a bit earlier that morning. He went on to explain, "You made me read all that stuff you loved, or at least you *claimed* to love it—I never could understand how you could like all that junk—and then you made me take quizzes about it, write papers explaining why it meant what you said it meant, take tests, do research, memorize names and dates and places. . . . Every day was just another opportunity for you to show me one more time how uneducable, unenlightenable, and unperceptive I was, how impenetrable, insensitive, and illiterate I was always doomed to be. So I read trash. I don't read that *Literature* (his snoring intonation both capitalized and italicized the word, and nearly underlined it, too) that you inflicted on me; I only read trash."

And with that, he stomped off down the hall, leaving me reeling and wondering if there was a safer route from my office to my class. I never did find out just what it was that had provoked that assault, but as I made my way to the safe harbor of my classroom, I reflected that I was, in fact, guilty of all his charges. Especially in the early days of my teaching, I *had* decided what my students would read, and it was almost always the great or near-great *Literature* (capitalized and italicized). I had either loved it or pretended to, I had given my students quizzes, tests, and term papers, and I had interrogated and explicated, assigned and judged. I suppose I must have had the same effect on some—I hope not all—of my students.

And so I made my contribution to the shelving scheme we find in so many bookstores today, with "Literature" in one section and "Fiction" in another. It was an arrangement that used to befuddle me. I could name, I thought every time I visited the nearby B. Dalton's, a whole list of books that were both fiction and literature—how were they making the distinction? And then one day I happened to follow a local businessman into that store and he taught me, inadvertently, what the distinction was. I was close behind him when we entered the store and we came to the "Literature" section first. He stopped dead in his tracks and I nearly ran into him.

He seemed to be gathering his courage, took a deep breath, and started down the aisle, taking quick, small steps, staying right in the center of the path, as far away from the books on either side as he could get. I followed him and noticed that it did not, in fact, seem a hospitable place. I began to understand why he was tiptoeing down the aisle, eyes fixed on the floor ahead of him, measuring the distance to safety, shoulders hunched, arms clutched across his chest in a futile effort to slow his rapid, shallow breathing. There was Dostoevsky, staring out at him from the cover of one massive tome, with his beady, penetrating eyes and his dark, bushy, unkempt beard; there was Milton, pensive and morose; and many others, all of them in four shades of dull brown, all of them appearing to say, "There is no way you're going to grasp the nearly incomprehensible ideas I've buried in these 1,300 pages of small print." Halfway down the aisle, he turned up the collar of his coat, as if chilled by the cold breath of some former English teacher on the back of his neck, and I felt the room grow colder, too. Probably in sympathy.

He came at last to end of the "Literature" section, passed into the "Fiction" shelves, and there he took a deep breath, turned his coat collar back down, wiped the sweat from his brow, muttered a short prayer of gratitude that he had not, God forbid, strayed into the "Poetry" section (where he knew he would have been irretrievably lost), and began to browse in the books. Here he felt more comfortable. In this section the author was no longer on the front covers in dull, dark, dreary colors, peering intently into the seamy recesses of his unsatisfactory soul, silently promising tests and term papers. Here he was on the back of a bright, multi-colored cover, smiling, in jeans and a flannel shirt, kneeling in a modest backyard, arms around the neck of a Labrador retriever, promising only a good story.

The distinction between "Literature" and "Fiction" was, I realized, obvious. "Fiction" is what you want to read. It's what you pick up at the airport bookstore before a long flight, what you buy to take with you to the beach, what you read in bed before turning out the lights. It's what you want to read tonight, though you may not remember having read it tomorrow (or admit to your colleagues that you did).

"Literature," on the other hand, is what you want to *have read*, but you don't particularly want to read it tonight. You want it to become part of your past without ever burdening your present. You want to *have read* Shakespeare and Tolstoy and Emerson, but tonight, well, there's the new Grisham novel you bought on impulse the other day, and *NYPD Blue* is on. . . .

This was not what I became an English teacher to accomplish. I was not enduring hall duty, bus duty, and lunch duty just so that I could drive my students away from literature for the rest of their lives and justify a shelving system whose sole purpose is to make it easier for people to avoid the very texts I hoped to encourage them to read. I watched the gentleman browsing happily through the mysteries (I was looking for one, too, since I had a long flight that afternoon and *Ulysses* weighed so much) and thought I'd be much happier to think that I had turned out students who thought more like the woman who had been sitting next to me on an earlier flight.

We'd struck up a conversation that ultimately got around to the work we did. When I told her that I was an English teacher, fearing that worries about grammar would now silence her, she surprised me by responding happily. "English was my favorite subject," she said. "I went into marketing, but I loved literature. I still remember my American Lit professor. We read Hawthorne and Melville," she reminisced. "Melville was the greatest writer; I loved his books. Not that big one," she said, "the one about that big white fish, but that short book. . . . What was it? Ah, I remember now—*Billy Bob*. I loved *Billy Bob*."

I had leaned forward, but I restrained myself. After all, we've all confused titles or names at one time or another, and I thought that the echo would return from the back of the plane and she'd hear it and correct herself. I didn't want to be the stereotypic hypercorrect English teacher those students who had trouble with "between he and I" fear meeting. She never heard the echo, however, and we chatted about *Billy Bob* for a while before wandering off to other topics.

Her professor must have done something right, I thought, because it was far better for her to love *Billy Bob* than to hate *Billy Budd*. She could always find the book again if she wanted to—it wasn't that much further down in the alphabetical listing, and she had remembered the author's name correctly in any case. Far better that she think kindly of *Literature*, even if she had ended up in marketing.

I'd have been happier still, however, to think I'd sent off students who would say what a passenger on another trip once said to me in a similar conversation. He was a pilot, hitching a ride home, and when he heard that I taught English, he told me that he'd flown Intruders over Vietnam during the war, and that he'd spent some time on the ground in a combat zone, probably serving as the military equivalent of an air-traffic controller for other fighter pilots. As a result of that, he said, there had been a book about the infantry experience in Vietnam that had mattered a great deal to him. "DelVecchio's *Thirteenth Valley*," he said, "was the most important book I ever read because it helped me make sense of my time in Vietnam."

When he dozed off, I made a note of his remark because it seemed to represent so compactly what was possible with literature. He was not happy because he had passed a hard test on the book, or because he had written an A+ paper on it; rather, he valued the book because it had helped him make sense of experience. It was interesting, too, that in his phrasing he retained a great deal of responsibility for what had transpired with the text. He did not say that the book explained things for him, that DelVecchio told him what it all meant, or that the book had answered all his questions and resolved all his doubts; rather, he said, the book "helped me make sense of my time in Vietnam." He did the work of understanding, but the book helped.

That, I thought, is what I hoped literature would offer my students. I wanted to hear one of them say, one Friday after class, "*Romeo and Juliet* helped me make sense of my parents' controlling ways," or something like that. I did not want to hear them whine, "We had Shakespeare last year—do we have to have him again?" But I hadn't had, either in my training or in the models of teaching I'd seen, anything to help me figure out how to help my students toward that sort of experience with literature.

My teaching was, of course, shaped principally by the teaching I'd received, by the models provided by my own literature teachers in high school and college. These models, I was gradually coming to realize, had been largely shaped by the school of thought that was dubbed "New Criticism." The pedagogy inspired by New Critical theories had emphasized the single text, "the autonomous and autotelic nature of the single, lonely poem,"[1] and it was a pedagogy in which students and their views were of little significance in the scholarly pursuit of the best reading, the correct reading, the authoritative reading. Robert Scholes summarizes the consequences of New Critical domination in the schools:

> This New Critical privileging of the integrity of the work in literary study led to a whole series of interpretive, pedagogical, and editorial gestures. Students were given poems to interpret with their titles removed, their author's names concealed, and their dates ignored. Anthologies were produced with the works ordered not by chronology but by the alphabet, with biographical information omitted or hidden in appendices, with no visible clues as to country or date of origin. In the name of improved interpretation, reading was turned into a mystery and the literature classroom into a chapel where the priestly instructor (who knows the authors, dates, titles, biographies, and general provenance of the texts) astounded the faithful with miracles of interpretation. The scandal at the heart of the New Criticism—and the source of its power—was this use of cultural codes by instructors who officially asserted that such material was irrelevant to the interpretive process. I am not suggesting conscious fraud, of course, but a myth of pedagogy that was believed because it gratified the pedagogues who believed in it. And the whole position was grounded in the notion of the bounded, self-sufficient work.[2]

Many of us have been in classrooms where performing miracles of interpretation upon bounded, self-sufficient works was the daily task. We were to deduce what the author meant, what the text had to tell us. We were to extract from the print whatever the writer had hidden there. Who we were and what we thought, felt, remembered, valued, rejected, and wondered about were more or less irrelevant. The meaning was in the text—our job was to dig it out. And so, if we paid attention, if we wanted to become good readers of literature as the New Critics and many of our teachers conceived of good readers, we became the student Louise Rosenblatt would describe:

> Instead of plunging into the work and permitting its full impact, he is aware that he must prepare for certain questions, that his remarks on the work must satisfy the teacher's already crystallized ideas about it.
>
> The teacher of college freshmen literature courses is often perturbed to find this attitude affecting the work of even the most verbally proficient students. They read literary histories and biographies, criticism, introductions to editions, so-called study guides, and then, if there is time, they read the works.[3]

Rosenblatt is the most important and influential (especially for teachers in the public schools) of the theorists who objected to the constraints of New Critical approaches. She objects here to instruction that steals the literary experience from students, driving them to replace it with the experience offered by study guides. Other theorists have expressed similar concern with some approaches to teaching literature. Scholes, for instance, objects to the profession's focus on the self-sufficient work and its neglect of the "cultural codes," suggesting that he sees instruction in literature hiding the art of reading from students by failing to teach them anything about the shaping influence of history, society, and culture. David Bleich also reacts strongly to the New Critical concentration on the single work, but he does so principally because it neglects the shaping influence of the individual reader's psyche. The goal of Bleich's work, as Steven Mailloux describes it, is:

> to reinscribe the organized discussion of literature within a discourse that aggressively advocates the freedom of the individual self in a pedagogical community. Bleich's approach to teaching places the individual student and his subjective response at the center of literary study.[4]

These scholars all suggest that we need to pay more attention to the role of the reader, that "individual self," than New Critical theory encourages. Presumably, had my cranky colleague met with a teacher influenced by Rosenblatt, Scholes, or Bleich, he might not have felt so disenfranchised, so alienated from literature.

All three of these theorists exemplify the heightened interest in the role of the individual reader and her responses to a text, though there are, of course, differences between their theories and consequently different implications for readers Bleich, with his stress on the freedom of the individual reader, represents the school of thought that seeks to understand the literary act by examining how the unique individual makes sense out of literary works. His emphasis falls heavily upon the reader—sometimes, we might fear, to the neglect of the text. Scholes, on the other hand, places less emphasis on the uniqueness of individual readers, concentrating instead on the larger patterns and conventions in literature and culture that enable the work to communicate meaning. Rosenblatt, perhaps the most moderate and balanced of them all, focuses on the meeting of reader and text, the event that transpires while a reader and a book are together.

Although the differences among the various critics may at times seem trifling and unimportant, they do represent different ways of looking at the work and the reader, and different aspects of literary studies that might be emphasized. The critics and theorists differ in the relative stress they place on three elements: the reader, the text, and the relationship between text and world. Thus they may suggest different teaching practices for those of us hoping to brighten the prospects of readers like my disenchanted colleague. Let's briefly examine some of the differences of opinion to see what possibilities they open up for literature teachers in the secondary schools.

Subjective Criticism

Bleich locates the source of meaning in the individual reader, and his method of study demands close attention to the actual readings of students. In his major theoretical work, *Subjective Criticism*, he insists on a revision of the epistemological base for the study of literature. Knowledge is made rather than found, he argues; all but the simplest acts of perception are in fact intellectual acts of making symbols and then interpreting them.

He illustrates the point by noting that if we observe a beautiful landscape—Mount Rainier, in his example—and if the observation yields a moment of reflection, the perception itself was evaluative. We focus our attention on the mountain because "it was not simply 'Mt. Rainier' that I saw, but it was 'the magnificent Mt. Rainier.'" When this happens, he says, we have "peremptorily converted the real mountain into a symbolic mountain," and then evaluated our symbolization, our "perceptual experience of the mountain," and not the actual, tree-covered, snow-capped granite object.[5] That is to say, when we talk about the mountain we aren't really talking about the mountain, we're talking about our perception. We are talking about some aspect of ourselves.

It is the same with literature, Bleich asserts; we read, we transform the text into symbols as our emotions and intellect direct us, and we interpret the symbols we have created. Thus the study of literature must begin with response, with our act of evaluative perception. The literary work exists in the mind of the reader, just as the "magnificent Mt. Rainier" exists in the mind of the viewer. True, there is a huge rock lying out there, but it is our perception of it and our reaction to it that makes it worthy of observation and reflection. If we don't see the magnificence, it's just a rock pile—who cares? The text, too, is there, physically existing apart from the reader. But by itself it is simply ink on paper—again, who cares? Not until it is read, and thus reformulated in the reader's mind, does it become literature. And when we talk about it, again, we're talking about our perception. We are talking about some aspect of ourselves.

Bleich places heavy emphasis on the act of reformulation, so much so that he seems almost to deny the text an active role:

> The subjective paradigm, in emphasizing the distinction between real objects, symbolic objects, and subjects (i. e., people), holds that only subjects are capable of initiating action.[6]

Thus the text, an object, cannot act. It cannot constrain and direct the reader; the reader alone directs himself in the activity of reading. It's an unsettling notion for teachers confronting thirty students, particularly if we have come to depend on the stable foundation a text seems to promise. When I was leading my students to the *right reading*, when I knew what my quizzes and tests were going to ask, at least I knew where we were going. I had good notes from my college courses and the teacher's guide to give me confidence and courage, but Bleich took all that away from me. Each of your students is going to make symbols of the text, he said, each in his or her own unique way, just as the observer makes a symbol of the mountain and in making those symbols creates meanings, each one unique and personal. What could I do with my college notes if all my students were going to be off on their own creating their own unique meanings out of last night's homework assignment, without a hint of gratitude for the care with which I had long ago captured Professor DeMott's lectures?

Bleich's conception of reading must seem frighteningly alien to those trained in New Criticism, which postulates the stable text in which meaning resides. Bleich rejects that stability and security. Relocating meaning in the reader's subjective response and reflection on that response seems to suggest that there can be no standard of correct interpretation, no way of asserting anything at all that is not a statement only about the self. Nonetheless, despite our uneasiness, the subjectivity of the individual reader has to be taken into account. Consider trying the following short experiment.

ASSOCIATIONS AND READINGS

Assign one individual to conduct this activity with your classmates if you're in a course, or conduct the experiment yourself with your own class if you're teaching.

Choose a word (preferably a short, simple word referring to something in the world with which everyone in the group would be familiar). Ask the participants to have a piece of paper and a pencil handy and then to close their eyes, breathe deeply, and clear their minds. Tell them that in a minute or two, after everyone seems to be calm but before too many fall asleep, you're going to say a word, and that when you do you'd like them to jot down the first association, thought, or feeling, whatever it may be, that comes to mind.

Wait until the room is quiet, say the word once, and then wait while they write. Some will grab their pencils and write immediately, some will ponder for a few moments before writing, others will write one word or will jot down a phrase, and still others may begin a more extended statement. One or two will stare at you wondering what the correct answer is, but we'll ignore them for the moment.

When everyone seems ready to go on, ask them what they jotted down and make a note of each response on the board or a blank transparency. Then take a look at them:

What differences do you see in the responses?

Do the different responses suggest different perspectives, different individual histories, different concerns?

Are there similarities among any of the responses?

Do those similarities suggest common experiences or shared values?

Do any of the responses hint at a story or anecdote that might be developed further or that might have shaped the individual's reaction to the word you used?

Did any of the responses evoke from another member of the group a comment like "Ah, I never would have thought of that," or "Yes, that's exactly how I feel"? Did that comment lead to further conversation?

Let the conversation go as long as there's energy for it, and then ask, "Which of your various responses was right?" The absurdity of the question should be apparent to all. Ask, "What does this suggest about how we read? Here we have twenty (or maybe forty) different responses to one simple word from thirty people. What does that suggest about the readings we might have of a couplet, a sonnet, or a novel? What does it suggest about questions of validity or correctness in literary experience?"

Here, for example, is the result of such an exercise with a small group of graduate students. The word *car* elicited the following responses from about fifteen students:

Old, junk, David's

Question authority

Tires

Speed

Leather

Stick shift

Air blowing through hair

Freedom

Shiny paint

Accident

Transmission

Backseat

Messy trunk

Convertible

Necessity

Motion sickness

Solitude/place for thought

Love in the backseat

Monthly payments/ necessary expense

Dust baby blue

Theft

Beep beep my horn went beep beep

Four-wheel drive

Shopping

Oh no! My son turns sixteen in February!

Red, black, fast—a dream realized

Gone

Assembly line manu- facturing

Groceries

Crash test

Dummies

Air bags

Tire pressure

Oil change

Polish

Jimmy Carter

Carnivore

Car phone

Love to drive

Sporty

Toyota

New

Old

Rust

Japan makes them cheaper

That's an average of roughly three responses for each participant, though they were asked for only one. Notice the range of associations, each person drawing upon her own history, making her own connections. Some are very similar: "Red, black, fast—a dream realized," "Speed," and "Air blowing through hair" are all probably recalling the sensual pleasure of rolling along a country road slightly faster than the law allows. "Rust" and "Old, junk, David's" are concerned with other issues. "Japan makes them cheaper" and "Monthly payments" are worried about the bills. Some are very different. "Love in the backseat" and "Oh no! My son turns sixteen in February" obviously associate the word "car" with two very different memories or concerns. Or perhaps not, but we were too discreet to probe. . . .

Next, take a short poem. Not too short. Consider this one if it's appropriate for your students:

The Journey[7]

One day you finally knew
what you had to do, and began,
though the voices around you
kept shouting
their bad advice —
though the whole house
began to tremble
and you felt the old tug
at your ankles.
"Mend my life!"
each voice cried.
But you didn't stop.
You knew what you had to do,
though the wind pried
with its stiff fingers
at the very foundations —
though their melancholy
was terrible.
It was already late
enough, and a wild night,
and the road full of fallen
branches and stones.
But little by little,
as you left their voices behind,
the stars began to burn
through the sheets of clouds,
and there was a new voice,
which you slowly
recognized as your own,
that kept you company
as you strode deeper and deeper
into the world,
determined to do
the only thing you could do —
determined to save
the only life you could save.

—Mary Oliver

Give a copy to each student and read it aloud. Ask the students to read through the poem again and then circle the most important word in it. Don't define *important*, even if they demand it. Next ask them to look back over the poem and identify the most important phrase. If you can get away with it, try to get them to glance through the poem yet again just to make sure they're content with their choices. Re-reading is a powerful strategy for improving understanding, though students resist it. This task, however, with its slightly changing focus for each reading, might veil the request to "read it again" and evoke less indignation than those words typically get from students who see re-reading as little short of abuse.

Next divide the class into groups of four and talk about the choices the students have made. Suggest some general structure for the discussion, but encourage your students to explore the ideas that arise, not to just answer the questions hastily and move on. Throughout the discussion, try to be aware not only of your own thoughts and associations, but those of other readers, too—what do you share and how are you different?

What word was most important? Why?

What phrase was most important? Again, why?

What, in your own experience (your memories, associations, hopes, and fears) influenced your choices?

Finally, what did you learn about one another through the discussion?

After sufficient time, which will vary with the maturity and sophistication of the group, bring everyone back together and open the floor to a discussion of the implications of the experience for the reading and teaching of literature. Does the experience confirm or refute the notion that "the subjective syntheses of the reader" are, at the very least, a significant element to be considered by teachers of literature?

Bleich suggests that although the "subjective syntheses" are the heart of a discussion of a work, and that we are essentially discussing not the work but our perceptions of it, the situation is not so grim as it may seem. We aren't necessarily condemned to isolation within our own mental world. If we cannot appeal to objective criteria for the validation of knowledge, we do have ways to reach or approach agreement, or at least to have a good conversation.

He calls the process "negotiation," and it is dependent on his notion of an "interpretive community." If we cannot directly grasp the literary work, we can at least respond to it, "resymbolize" it, and communicate our personal re-creation of the work to other readers. We can then see what is shared and what is not. Knowledge is thus the result of sharing responses. Readers declare their responses to the work and then are enabled, presumably by a common cultural background, to discuss those individual re-creations, seek similarities and differences, and to construct a consensus that—for them, at that time, in those circumstances—is knowledge. Knowledge, in Bleich's critical theory, is what is declared to be so by the community. It emerges from a pooling of our individual perceptions, and a reconsideration of them.

This concept leaves us with a problem. Bleich denies that the text can act on the reader, it is an object, and "only subjects are capable of initiating action." Bleich says that:

> . . . there is often an illusion that a text acts on a reader, but it can hardly be the case that a text actually does act on the reader. . . . Therefore, discussion of the work must refer to the subjective syntheses of the reader and not to the reader's interaction with the text.[8]

That is to say, when we talk about the work, we are really talking not about the work, nor even about the individual's reading of the work, but about something still further removed from the text: the reader's "subjective syntheses," his unique vision. The reader seems to be left solitary—alone in his subjectivity, his sensibilities awakened by the text, but otherwise untouched. There seems, in Bleich's view, no hope of communication with the text, in the usual sense that suggests some understanding of another's meaning. The literature is not a source of knowledge, but only a stimulus to subjective meditation; the knowledge is formulated later, in the interchange among readers. Communication, for Bleich, resides not in the act of reading, but only in the aftermath, the discussion of the reading with others:

> The practice of formulating response statements is a means for making a language experience (hearing, speaking, reading, or writing) available for conversion into knowledge. A response can acquire meaning only in the context of a predecided community (two or more people) interest in knowledge.[9]

Two or more readers come together, with a common interest in knowledge of something they have read, and talk in such a way that knowledge is the result. Bleich is unclear about the criteria by which that knowledge is to be judged—

presumably, agreement is the deciding factor. If a community agrees on some proposition, then that proposition *is* knowledge for that community. Bleich points out that even when some principle is disputed by a member of the community, the accepted "knowledge" of the group establishes the context in which the dispute takes place:

> Like the infantile processes of language acquisition, subsequent contexts of knowledge formation are always communal, even if a particular individual forms knowledge in opposition to his community.[10]

So, when everyone thought the world was flat, it was, for all practical purposes, flat. The community declared it to be flat and it remained flat, until a few rebels saw it differently and risked sailing over the edge. The difficulty with the theory of literature Bleich proposes, for English teachers, is that it doesn't seem to encourage anyone to sail up to the edge and peer over. Instead, it encourages them to focus on their "subjective syntheses"—that is to say, on their perceptions of flatness. Bleich's emphasis on the subjective nature of reading risks losing the text. Granted, the text is inert and lies placidly on the desk until we do something with it. In that sense it does not act on the reader, as Bleich has argued. But if it is little more than a catalyst for our own meditations, if *all* of the value in literary experience lies in the "language experience (hearing, speaking, reading, or writing) available for conversion into knowledge," then the text itself appears to recede into insignificance. Anything that will get us talking will do.

Such a theory seems to give the teacher little guidance and tempts us toward a conception of teaching as the endless repetition of "How do you feel? What do you think? Isn't that nice? What shall we do now?" We want the text to matter more than that. We may accept Bleich's corrective emphasis on the subjective reader and approve his respect for each reader's uniqueness, but we still want the reader to sail up to the edge and peer intently and respectfully at the text itself.

There is, perhaps, another source of discomfort for us in this conception of literature and literary experience. If we are unwilling to let the text slip too far into the background, we may also be uneasy about the overwhelming importance of the interpretive community. Bleich has said, "A response can acquire meaning only in the context of a predecided community (two or more people) interest in knowledge."[11] Is my response meaningless, then, if I have no one to talk with about it? We are fortunate, as teachers, to have that community provided for us, but we know, too, that much literary experience is solitary. A friend recommends a book and by the time we've read it she has moved on through several others; we pass it on to another friend, but by the time he's read it we've changed schools, moved to another city, and forgotten that it's missing from our shelves. Does that mean that our reading of the book was a waste of time?

Could we not, on the other hand, learn to engage in something like an internal dialog, speculating about the possible responses of other imagined readers and weighing them against our own, or perhaps considering our responses to a re-reading and weighing those against our initial reactions? And couldn't we engage in something like an imaginative dialog with the author or with a character? It seems that there ought to be some possibilities for the reader alone with her book.

After all, the oral exchange between members of a community (or a classroom) is no less verbal than the act of reading. When we meet to discuss our responses to a literary work, we speak; that is, we interact linguistically. An individual participating in the discussion is thus confronted with the words of his comrades. This is almost exactly the same situation he finds himself in when he reads a literary work. In both cases, the individual confronts a text. He then has the words of the text before him. If those words on the page are inert, if they have meaning only insofar as he "resymbolizes" or reconstitutes them, then surely the spoken and written words of those in his community are also inert until resymbolized or reconstituted. The difference between the reader sitting down with a novel and the student reading a classmate's response paper or hearing her comments is surely not so great that we may consider one but not the other to be a source of knowledge. The listener must, after all, act on the words of his colleagues just as the reader acts on the words of the text. In both cases, if we accept Bleich's premises, he must resymbolize and then work with the images and thoughts he has created. Like the text, the spoken word is inert and immobile; it must be heard by an active, thinking listener to become anything more than vibrations in the air. If the immediate verbal exchanges within the community, governed as they must be by the rules of language, can yield knowledge, then surely the verbal exchange between writer and reader might also yield knowledge. And if it can, then we must not let the text slide too far from the center in our effort to respect the individual reader.

The point to be made in this discussion of Bleich is that the uniqueness of the reader *must* be respected. It cannot be casually set aside, as it has been in other, perhaps more traditional approaches. Bleich's epistemology is a problem, but his critical theory does have the great virtue of focusing attention on individual readers. It would have readers respond to a work, consider each other's responses, and finally assess the work and their comprehension of it as a community. Consider for a moment how different this vision of the classroom is from, for example, that suggested by a New Critical emphasis on the text or a literary historian's emphasis on dates and influences. The courses and curricula arising out of those schools of thought would not give a great deal of attention to the nature of the exchanges among students, to the flow of discourse in the classroom. In some ways, Bleich seems to be at the opposite end of the spectrum from the New Critics. If they emphasize the text itself, the autotelic text, Bleich emphasizes the reader, the group of readers who come together in the classroom, and the exchanges in which they are able to engage.

This perspective is likely to lead to a pedagogy that respects students. The teacher working from such a base will not fall into the patterns for which Scholes criticized the New Critical professors. Rather than performing miracles of interpretation for the class, such a teacher will more likely invite the students themselves to perform. And that performance might not be restricted to interpretation alone if individual responses lead elsewhere. They might, for instance, lead to the student telling her own story—personal narrative rather than interpretation, just as the responses to the word *car* hinted at the stories behind them. The teacher might be expected to respect the uniqueness of the individual student, invite her responses to texts, and encourage her to enter into the resulting dialog or storytelling.

Further, the teacher is likely to value learning about the self as highly as learning about the literature. In fact, he may not see the two as distinct. Learning about literature without learning about the self would be pointless or impossible in a program founded on the principles Bleich develops. One of the undeniable implications of his theory is that students and their thoughts are the center of the curriculum.

But, although Bleich's critical theory and the sort of research and teaching that emerge from it may give us some insight into the student's role in her own literary experiences, they do not tell us as much as we might like about the contributions of the literary work itself. More moderate critics and teachers, however much they respect the reader's perspective, will feel uncomfortable with a theory that places so much weight on the students' shoulders, especially in the secondary schools. On the one hand, such an approach is likely to appeal to students. It does, after all, grant them and their opinions a central place in the classroom, and thus it might motivate them to participate. On the other hand, too many students are inclined to value their own unconsidered opinions too highly already, and teachers may fear the potential for misunderstanding the subjective approach. If students assume that the invitation to express and examine their own feelings and thoughts is, in fact, an invitation to say whatever they please without bothering to think, then the classroom will become unmanageable and the discourse unreasoning and unproductive. Although Bleich suggests some techniques for directing the work of the class, teachers' uneasiness with this vision of literature instruction is likely to persist.

Bleich's critical theory also seems to offer little guidance for developing the literature curriculum. The directions a class will take are presumably to be found in the course of reading and discussion. Although that notion is exciting and potentially powerful, since it suggests a natural movement for the course that would allow real growth and exploration, it offers little security and imprecise notions about the structure of a course or a program. It requires the teacher to be unfailingly conscious of students' responses to the literature and each other, always looking for the next step. The prospect of maintaining that degree of vigilance would be intimidating enough under ideal circumstances, with smaller and fewer classes. For a teacher faced with 150 students of widely differing backgrounds and abilities, it may be overwhelming.

We may want to keep a firmer grip on the text itself than we find in Bleich's ideas, and perhaps seek a bit more structure for our courses and curriculum than his notions suggest.

Transactional Theory

Rosenblatt suggests a vision of literary experience that neglects neither the reader nor the text:

"The poem" cannot be equated solely with *either* the text *or* the experience of a reader. Something encapsulated in a reader's mind without relevance to a text may be a wonderful fantasy, but the term "poem" or "literary work," in transactional terminology, would not be applicable to such a "mental experience" any more than to an entity apart from a reader.[12]

Rosenblatt's view of reading as an interaction or transaction between the reader and text is more moderate than Bleich's and is shared by other theorists such as Wolfgang Iser and Hans Robert Jauss, both from the German school of critical thought known as Reception Aesthetics. They, too, seem to maintain a balance, recognizing that the reader's unique perspective will greatly influence the shape a literary work takes in her mind but also granting that the work itself has the power to affect the reader's responses, guiding her in some directions and steering her away from others. Still, Rosenblatt agrees that the unique reader must be respected:

What each reader makes of the text is, indeed, *for him* the poem, in the sense that this is his only direct perception of it. No one else can read it for him. He may learn indirectly about others' experiences with the text; he may come to see that his own was confused or impoverished, and he may then be stimulated to attempt to call forth from the text a better poem. But this he must do himself, and only what he himself experiences in relation to the text is—again let us underline— for *him*, the work.[13]

The little experiment with free-associations to a single word and then with the reading of Oliver's "The Journey," if successful, should have demonstrated the validity of these statements. Those forty different responses to the word *car* gave some hints about the range of experiences it evoked from the members of the group, and perhaps about their personalities and circumstances. The person who said "Oh no! My son turns sixteen in February!" revealed her anxiety about turning over the key. Whoever said "Monthly payments" was thinking about her checkbook; "Love in the backseat" was reminiscing or regretting; "Question authority" was meditating about something else. None of these readers offered a pure, precise, dictionary definition of the word. We learn very few words through dictionaries; we learn them by associating them with things and events, and then those prior experiences become inextricably interwoven with the word, and they shape our reactions to it and our understandings of it each time we meet the word again. And if the simple, referential word *car* so obviously brings to mind different associations, memories, feelings, and images, how much more complex must the transaction be when that word is placed in a sentence with ten other words, equally evocative and imprecise, and that sentence in a stanza or paragraph, and that stanza or paragraph in a poem or an essay. . . .

Still, the word itself clearly matters. Without it there would be nothing holding us on the ground, establishing some parameters for the discussion so that we would have the opportunity to share experiences and explore differences and similarities. If I am the fifteen year old who thinks of speed and freedom when he hears the word *car*, then I'll have the chance to see that the mother of another fifteen year old may have a very different perspective. Neither the word nor a poem made with it can be "equated solely with either the text or the experience of a reader."

And so Rosenblatt does not diminish the reader's role, but she insists that the reader must accommodate herself to the text. She must be in some ways guided, or she is fantasizing rather than reading. Iser makes a similar case. For him, also, the text is more controlling and confining than it is for Bleich, who views the reader as the source of meaning. The text, Iser says, does several things. It establishes a perspective, it arouses—and frustrates—expectations, it guides the reader's imagination through the creative act of reading, and it provides gaps and uncertainties that the reader must fill in. The text, for Iser, is a much more active agent than it is for Bleich. Still, all of these actions imply equal participation by the reader. The text guides, but the reader realizes:

> [A] literary text contains intersubjectively verifiable instructions for meaning-production, but the meaning produced may then lead to a whole variety of different experiences and hence subjective judgments.[14]

The text supplies much, but not everything. Were it to offer everything, Iser argues, the reader would be bored and dissatisfied. Her imagination and intellect must have work to do—details to sketch in, implications to elaborate, questions to answer—or she will find reading a monotonous and unchallenging activity. The fictional world, Iser insists, must leave much to the reader. He says, in his discussion of conflict:

> Generally, the nature of these conflicts is such that although possible solutions are adumbrated in the text, they are not explicitly formulated there. The formulation will take place through the guided activity stimulated in the reader, for only in this way can it become part of the reader's own experience.[15]

Iser speculates that the emptiness of much escape literature results from the usurping of the reader's role:

> The more explicit the text, the less involved he will be, and in passing one might remark that this accounts in great measure for the feeling of anticlimax that accompanies so much of what is called "light reading."[16]

It is also possible, of course, for the text to demand too much and offer too little, frustrating the reader:

> In this process the text may either not go far enough, or may go too far, so we may say that boredom and overstrain form the boundaries beyond which the reader will leave the field of play.[17]

We may note that Rosenblatt's and Iser's conception of the literary text is slightly different from that of either Bleich or the group we have so casually categorized as New Critics. The New Critics see the text as the repository of meaning. Bleich sees the individual reader as the source of meaning. Rosenblatt and Iser, on the other hand, see the exchange between text and reader as the process that creates meaning. The potential richness of the literary work thus exceeds its contents, because the work initiates emotional and intellectual responses that cannot be predicted from the text and cannot be said to reside in the text, but neither are they purely and simply within the readers.

Reading is thus neither a search for "the meaning" of the work, a meaning residing in the text, as in the New Critical approaches, nor a self-contained journey into one's own mind, as in subjective criticism, but an opportunity to explore and create. The task is not finding clues and solving problems, but realizing potential. The question becomes not so much "What does the work mean?" as "What can we do with the work?"

This can be a very productive question for literature teachers to raise, for it forces them to consider the perspective of their students and look on them as potentially active, thinking, creative individuals. Further, it broadens the possibilities for teaching because it respects the potential of the work to generate thought that goes beyond the work itself. Students need not, in other words, be confined to interpretation, to discussing meaning or the author's techniques and intentions. Rather, they may explore the possibilities of transforming the work of fiction into a poem, or the poem into a play, or they may find that a work stimulates them to introspection that leads elsewhere. Rosenblatt and Iser imply respect for all these possible directions. The field in which the reader may play is larger in their conception of literature than it is in the New Critics', and the range of possibilities for the classroom is thus significantly broadened.

Still, despite these possibilities, the reader is not totally outside the control of the text. As Iser is careful to point out, the work structures and directs, and it is this fact that gives the work its significance. It provides a "structure that enables the reader to break out of his accustomed framework of conventions, so allowing him to formulate that which has been unleashed by the text."[18] The answer to our subjective isolation is clearer in Rosenblatt and Iser than in Bleich. It lies not solely in negotiation among readers, but in the direct exchange between reader and text. The text takes its reader beyond the confines of her own prior experience, and it does so not by giving her new information but by providing her with material and experience from which to formulate the new. That material *is* new; it is something other than either the text or the reader, herself, before confronting the text. In the process of reading, responding, articulating questions, and contemplating possible answers, the reader may gradually define herself. The knowledge she gains is not something that the literary work has given her—it is something of her own that the work has enabled her to create. As she reads and thinks, she inscribes herself upon the world, declaring what she believes and what she denies, what she values, and what she rejects. Try this short experiment.

ONE TEXT, TWO POEMS

In pairs, preferably male and female, choose one of the following two poems after glancing through both quickly, or perhaps having them read aloud. When you've established pairs and chosen the poem, please read it reflectively, without any concerted effort to interpret or judge it. Read through it once or twice more—it's not that long—allowing it to evoke, if it has the power to do so, memories or stories of your own. There's no need to analyze or explain this poem—simply relax with it if you can, and let it lead you to your own thoughts, however far afield they may seem. Search in the experience of reading for some memory of your own, an incident it calls to mind, perhaps a person or place from your past.

If you are fortunate enough to find that the poem calls forth a memory, concentrate on that memory, trying to recall it as fully as you can. If you wish, write briefly about it:

Sign for My Father, Who Stressed the Bunt[19]

On the rough diamond,
the hand-cut field below the dog lot and barn,
we rehearsed the strict technique
of bunting. I watched from the infield,
the mound, the backstop
as your left hand climbed the bat, your legs
and shoulders squared toward the pitcher.
You could drop it like a seed
down either base line. I admired your style,
but not enough to take my eyes off the bank
that served as our center-field fence.

Years passed, three leagues of organized ball,
no few lives. I could homer
into the garden beyond the bank,

into the left-field lot of Carmichael Motors,
and still you stressed the same technique,
the crouch and spring, the lead arm absorbing
just enough impact. That whole tiresome pitch
about basics never changing,
and I never learned what you were laying down.

Like a hand brushed across the bill of a cap,
let this be the sign
I'm getting a grip on the sacrifice.

—David Bottoms

Pockets[20]

The point of clothes was line,
a shallow fall of cotton over childish hips
or a coat ruled sharply, shoulder to hem,

but that line was marred by hands
and all the most amazing things
that traveled in them to one's pockets
goitering the shape of grace with gifts—

a puffball only slightly burst
five links of watch chain passed secretly in class
a scrap of fur almost as soft as one's own skin.

Offended at my pouching of her Singer stitch
my mother sewed my pockets up
with an overcast tight as her mouth
forbidding all but the line.

I've lived for years in her seams—
falls of fabric smooth as slide rules
my hands exposed and folded from all gifts.

And it is only recently, with raw fingers
which still recall the warmth and texture of presents,
that I've plucked out stitches sharp as urchin spines
to find both hands and pockets empty.

—Karen Swenson

After you've taken a few minutes to read and reflect on the poem you've chosen, address the following questions:

1. Insofar as you wish, share with your partner the memory or story the poem evoked. Share as much or as little as you like. Feel free to ask each other questions, but feel free also to decide how much or how little you'll share. Be sure that each of you has the opportunity to talk.

2. Reflect for a moment on the stories you've heard and told, those in the poem and those of your partner. What do they have in common? How do they differ? With what aspect of human experience do they all deal?

3. Did the recalling and sharing of your own stories shed any light on the poem? Did you see anything more clearly in the poem as a result of telling and hearing the other stories? Did the discussion change your feelings about the poem in any way?

4. What were the pleasures or pains of the reading, the storytelling, and the subsequent discussion? Did you observe anything new about yourself, or if not new, then more clearly or in a new light?

5. Did the activity provide you with any insight into the poem? Did you find any satisfaction or pleasure in what you have learned about your partner(s)?

6. If time permits, as a pair, share your readings of the poem, your stories, and your discussion with another pair of readers. Do you observe any similarities or differences in the paths the two discussions followed?

7. Finally, what inferences can you draw about the role of the reader in creating meaning from a text?

I hope that the reading and the discussion lead you to see some of the possibilities for readers and texts. Each poem was easily identified as either a "male" or a "female" poem, and thus the reader's gender is likely to have influenced the reading and the discussion. Furthermore, the poems, despite their distinctiveness, are nonetheless accessible to all readers. Some women have commented, for example, that they responded much more strongly to Bottoms' poem because they remember so clearly someone, whom they didn't think wise at the time, teaching them something of great significance in their lives. And there have been men who bristled at memories of confinement and restraint when they read Swenson's poem.

The main point of the activity, however, is to make concrete the notion that what we get out of a text is more than or different from what the author put into it. Bottoms does not know your old baseball coach; Swenson does not know whether your mother sewed up your pockets. But those stories are there, in you, and may well emerge if the literature class respects the notion that meaning is made and not found, that the significance of the literary work emerges in the transaction between reader and text, and among readers.

Rosenblatt and Iser would argue that it is in the exchange between the reader and the work that knowledge is produced. Iser, for instance, describes the loss of self in reading. The reader thinks, for a time, the thoughts of another, abandoning her own perspectives, attitudes, and ideas. It is in that temporary loss of self that the individual profits from reading, for through it she is able to reformulate and see freshly:

> [T]here occurs a kind of artificial division as the reader brings into his own fore-ground something which he is not. This does not mean, though, that his own ori-entations disappear completely. However much they may recede into the past, they still form the background against which the prevailing thoughts of the author take on thematic significance. In reading, then, there are always two levels, and despite the multifarious ways in which they may be related they can never be totally kept apart. Indeed, we can only bring another person's thoughts into our foreground if they are in some way related to the virtual background of our own orientations (for otherwise they would be totally incomprehensible).[21]

The confrontation with the new, in the form of the literary text, allows the reader to see aspects of herself that were previously hidden. Thus, much of the learn-ing that results from the literary experience is, in Iser's vision, learning about the self:

> [A] layer of the reader's personality is brought to light which had hitherto remained hidden in the shadows. . . . The significance of the work, then, does not lie in the meaning sealed within the text, but in the fact that that meaning brings out what had previously been sealed within us.[22]

The process is not just inference. It is not, that is, simply the task of tracking down the thoughts and perceptions underlying the text. It is instead the process of discovering the self by introducing into it the alien thoughts and perceptions offered by the literary work, by submitting—momentarily and partially—to the control and direction of the text. And by bringing to bear upon the text the relevant thoughts and experiences of our own, just as you likely brought to bear upon the text, either Swenson's or Bottoms', the memories it evoked.

Reconceiving the Act of Reading

Iser's discussion suggests an interesting point about the act of reading. It reminds us that a literary work is not a thing, but a process. Often, perhaps especially in the secondary school classroom, the work is treated as a single unchanging entity. The actual experience of reading, however, refutes that. As we read, we find ourselves changing perspective, revising impressions, accumulating information and insight, and passing through a series of emotional states. Iser would have us consider the flux and movement of reading, something the less sophisticated reader may have difficulty doing.

Stanley Fish, who is perhaps even more interested in the temporal nature of reading than is Iser, demonstrates the idea with a subtle analysis of several disputed points in Milton scholarship. He shows that one reading is possible, even probable, up to a certain point in the poem, but at that point another reading must be admitted into the picture. Traditional scholarship has disputed which meaning is the more likely, revealing its view of the literary work as a stable, meaning-bearing entity. Fish, however, argues that it is less appropriate to treat the work as a thing, with a demonstrable meaning, than as an experience with life and movement. He argues that the reader should observe the shift, accept it, and consider it part of the effect—and thus the meaning—of the poem:

> This moment of hesitation, of semantic or syntactic slide, is crucial to the experience the verse provides, but, in a formalist analysis, that moment will disappear, either because it has been flattened out and made into an (insoluble) interpretive crux, or because it has been eliminated in the course of a procedure that is incapable of finding value in temporal phenomena.[23]

Although the subtleties of Milton may be beyond most secondary school students, they can still gain from observing the evolution of their perspective as they read. In even so simple a work as *Killing Mr. Griffin*, a young adult novel we'll return to later in the book, the shift in perspective is important. If we attend to Iser and Fish in our classrooms, we'll look for a way to make students aware of that moment of "semantic or syntactic slide." The first several chapters are told from the point of view of the students. For these characters, and thus quite likely for the reader, Mr. Griffin is harsh, demanding, and unfriendly. In the fourth or fifth chapter, the reader is shown Mr. Griffin more directly, unfiltered by the minds of the students. Seen that way, he is a much more likable fellow, whose humor and goodwill are for the first time in clear view.

This shift in perspective almost demands an accommodation by the reader. He cannot fully retain his earlier sense of identification with the students. He must at the very least examine the new evidence, and likely his view of Mr. Griffin will be softened for the remainder of the book. Mr. Griffin is neither good nor bad, flattened out and disposed of by a formalist analysis that concentrates on the aftermath of reading rather than on the temporal process. Instead he is a character toward whom our feelings are likely to change as we move through the novel. That movement is crucial. The effect of the novel is to arouse an expectation and then frustrate it, to borrow Iser's terminology, and the reader is thus invited to participate in the process of learning, which is the process of continually revising one's perceptions and beliefs.

Fish would argue that the work's meaning lies in the process, not in a final, neat, completed statement that immobilizes it. We need not debate to a conclusion whether Mr. Griffin is vicious or kind. Rather, we might notice what effect the change in stance has on us as readers. We may feel chastened and cautioned, realizing that we have been comfortable with a premature judgment. If so, then that feeling, and perhaps a resolution to judge less hastily, will be part of the meaning of the novel for us. "It is the experience of an utterance—*all* of it and not anything that could be said about it, including anything I could say—that *is* its meaning."[24]

Awareness of the temporal nature of literature could have an obviously invigorating effect in the classroom, primarily because it raises interesting and provocative questions besides "What does it mean?" It may stimulate teachers to consider techniques for helping students watch themselves in the process of reading. It may suggest the simple virtue of changing one's mind, and reward that act above the rather dubious accomplishment of being "right." And it of course suggests the value of literature as experience, as an analog of life itself, not simply a means to an obscure end like "appreciation of the cultural heritage."

Here we have a vision of literature as communication. The literary work is, or at least represents, another consciousness, giving the reader access to insights, experiences, and perceptions that would otherwise lie beyond her reach, thus allowing her to reformulate her own consciousness. In Bleich's conception that communication seems possible only within a group actively conversing. In Rosenblatt's and Iser's, it is possible in the encounter of reader and text. Both views acknowledge and respect the uniqueness of the reader. Bleich sees that uniqueness as almost inviolable; the individual is trapped within his subjectivity, freed from it only slightly through knowledge-producing discourse with friends or classmates. Iser has the individual overcome her isolation not only through discussion, but also through reading, which invites the reshaping of perceptions:

> The efficacy of a literary text is brought about by the apparent evocation and subsequent negation of the familiar. What at first seemed to be an affirmation of our assumptions leads to our own rejection of them, thus tending to prepare us for a re-orientation. And it is only when we have outstripped our preconceptions and left the shelter of the familiar that we are in a position to gather new experiences. As the literary text involves the reader in the formation of illusion and the simultaneous formation of the means whereby the illusion is punctured, reading reflects the process by which we gain experience.[25]

Clearly Iser believes the reader has contact with the visions offered by the text and can profit from them. We may go a step further, however, from the relationship between the reader and the text to that between the reader and the culture. We've mentioned the idiosyncratic element in language and literature. You and I can't ever know precisely what the other means by a word. No word, even the simplest concrete noun like *dog* or *house*, will evoke identical thoughts in the minds of two people. But linguistic activity is not totally idiosyncratic. It also has a social dimension, we must share something, or language is no longer language, but simply random utterances that communicate nothing. That social dimension, other speakers and other texts, enables us to refine our understanding. As we use language—if we haven't grown too rigid—our understanding of these terms evolves. The young child who applied *dog* to all friendly, furry creatures comes to learn that it applies only to some and that *cat* is more appropriate for others.

What we're concerned with in our literature classes is, of course, not the meaning of simple referential terms like *dog* and *cat* (and *car*, to recall the earlier workshop and what it revealed about the subtleties of language), but the much more complicated—though usually short, even monosyllabic—terms about which the great literature circles: love and hate, justice and revenge, good and evil, right and wrong. It's to those questions about human nature that literature speaks, and about which Rosenblatt cautions:

> The danger is in the unquestioning adoption of the general attitudes toward human nature and conduct that permeate the very atmosphere we live in. Unfortunately, the ideas that are taken most for granted are often the ones that merit the most skeptical scrutiny.[26]

As we read, if we read thoughtfully, we refine our conceptions of human nature and conduct. *Macbeth* invites us to reflect on power and ambition, redefining those terms as we go; *Invisible Man* demands that we consider what it was to be black in America in the 1940s; *Saving Private Ryan* encourages us to reconsider the glories of war; other books and poems and plays and movies invite us to reflect on other issues.

It is our immersion in literature that gives us the greatest hope of identifying, understanding, and perhaps challenging and reformulating those ideas that we tend to absorb from the culture:

> The more conscious the individual is of the nature of the cultural forces with which he is interacting, the more intelligently can he accept or resist them, and the more intelligently can he modify their power and their direction.[27]

The power of books like *To Kill a Mockingbird* or *Huckleberry Finn* lies in their questioning of the general "attitudes toward human nature and conduct" that permeated the society at the time they were written, and that still contaminate it, and their ability to make readers more conscious of those cultural forces so that they might reshape them.

So it is with all great literature. Although we have emphasized individual responses and have argued that response and interpretation cannot be adequately discussed without considering the reader, literature also serves a social purpose. It integrates the reader into the culture, inviting her to define herself against the background of cultural expectations and to modify that background as she does so. Jauss argues that the reader:

> does not first have to bump into a new obstacle to gain a new experience of reality. The experience of reading can liberate one from adaptations, prejudices, and predicaments of a lived praxis in that it compels one to a new perception of things. The horizon of expectations of literature distinguishes itself before the horizon of expectations of historical lived praxis in that it not only preserves actual experiences,

but also anticipates unrealized possibility, broadens the limited space of social behavior for new desires, claims, and goals, and thereby opens paths of future experience.[28]

Literature thus has a "socially formative function"—it both shapes the individual so that he fits the culture and reshapes the culture in response to new visions. Annie Dillard writes, "The mind fits the world and shapes it as a river fits and shapes its own banks."[29] The idiosyncratic and the social are, then, the two aspects of literature's function. It trains the reader in the conventions of meaning peculiar to the society, giving the members of the group a common conceptual framework, and it reshapes that framework by bringing to bear on it what is unique in the writer and in the reader. Thus it forms the reader to fit her culture and reforms the culture to fit the reader.

This is a much more complete vision of the "cultural heritage" than that offered by the traditional literature curriculum, which often seems to see the cultural heritage as a stack of books or a list of great names. Here we begin to develop a sense of the dynamic relationship between the individual—reader or writer—and the culture. The individual assimilates the culture into himself, defines himself in relation to the norms of the culture, and presses for a redefinition of those norms. In the traditional curriculum, the task is much simpler and less interesting; it simply involves learning the culture, remembering its rough outlines and its major events and names, and accepting its values and customs. Jauss and others suggest a much more vigorous and healthy role for literature. They point out that its primary task is defining reality—clarifying and enriching our understanding of "love," "justice," "good," "right," "happiness," and the other great cultural issues.

The emerging changes in our view of the text, of the reader's role, of the act of reading, and of literature's place in the culture raise a related question about the nature of interpretation. Despite all the turmoil in criticism, as several theorists have observed, interpretation has remained the unquestioned goal of literary studies. Jonathan Culler, more strongly than anyone else, condemns this tendency:

> There are many tasks that confront criticism, many things we need to advance our understanding of literature, but one thing we do not need is more interpretations of literary works. It is not at all difficult to list in a general way critical projects which would be of compelling interest if carried through to some measure of completion; and such a list is in itself the best illustration of the potential fecundity of other ways of writing about literature. We have no convincing account of the role or function of literature in society or social consciousness. We have only fragmentary or anecdotal histories of literature as an institution: we need a fuller exploration of its historical relation to the other forms of discourse through which the world is organized and human activities are given meaning. We need a more sophisticated and apposite account of the role of literature in the psychological economies of both writers and readers; and in particular we ought to understand much more than we do about the effects of fictional discourse. . . . What are the ways of moving between life and art?[30]

Treating literature as experience, rather than simply as meaning-bearing text, requires us at least to reassess the nature of interpretation. Fish would redefine interpretation *as* experience. Culler would go further and have us abandon the notion that interpretation is the only critical task, or even the most valuable. The needs he lists for literary studies suggest the range of possibilities. Clearly, some have been and are being addressed—Fish deals with literature's effects, Bleich and others with the "psychological economies," Jauss with its function in social consciousness. All of these approaches could begin to influence and reshape the literature curriculum in the secondary schools, offering us new structures, goals, and activities. This text will explore some of the changes inspired by the work of Rosenblatt and others.

In subsequent chapters we'll continue to discuss the relationships we've discussed here—that of the reader and the text, the reader and other readers, the text and other texts—and the discussion inevitably will lead us to consider the broadest spectrum of relationships, those that constitute the culture. Ultimately, literature is the reservoir of humankind's efforts to cope with life, to impose some order on the chaos of experience. It allows the intelligent reader access to herself by giving her access to others, all those others who have written in a language she can read.

The studies of literature and literary theory touched on here reinstate the reader at the center of the literary experience, thus redefining literature's place in the culture. It becomes once again the possession of everyone rather than of the scholarly elite, and it provides us with a touchstone by which to judge and revise our own conceptions of the world and our place in it. It thus merits a place at the center of the curriculum, as the most fundamental and significant of all the disciplines, for it is in the study of literature that we each build the conceptual world in which we live.

Endnotes

1. Frank Lentricchia, *After the New Criticism* (Chicago: University of Chicago Press, 1980), p. 3.

2. Robert Scholes, *Semiotics and Interpretation* (New Haven, CT: Yale University Press, 1982), p. 15.

3. Louise M. Rosenblatt, *Literature as Exploration*, Fifth Edition (New York: Modern Language Association, 1995), p. 63.

4. Steven Mailloux, *Interpretive Conventions: The Reader in the Study of American Fiction* (Ithaca, NY: Cornell University Press, 1982), p. 43.

5. David Bleich, *Subjective Criticism* (Baltimore, MD: Johns Hopkins University Press, 1978), p. 98.

6. Ibid., pp. 110–111.

7. Mary Oliver, "The Journey," in *Dream Work* (New York: Atlantic Monthly Press, 1986), p. 38.

8. Bleich, p. 111.

9. Ibid., p. 132.

10. Ibid., p. 133.

11. Ibid., p. 132.

12. Louise M. Rosenblatt, *The Reader, the Text, the Poem: The Transactional Theory of the Literary Work* (Carbondale, IL: Southern Illinois University Press, 1978), p. 105.

13. Ibid.

14. Wolfgang Iser, *The Act of Reading: A Theory of Aesthetic Response* (Baltimore, MD: Johns Hopkins University Press, 1978), p. 25.

15. Ibid., p. 46.

16. Ibid.

17. Wolfgang Iser, "The Reading Process: A Phenomenological Approach," in *New Literary History*, Volume 3, No. 2 (Winter 1972), 280.

18. Iser, *The Act of Reading*, p. 50.

19. David Bottoms, "Sign for My Father, Who Stressed the Bunt," in *In a U-Haul North of Damascus* (New York: William Morrow, 1983), p. 22.

20. Karen Swenson, "Pockets," in *A Daughter's Latitude: New and Selected Poems* (Townsend, WA: Copper Canyon Press, 1999), p. 88.

21. Iser, *The Act of Reading*, p. 155.

22. Iser, *The Act of Reading*, p. 157.

23. Stanley Fish, "Interpreting the Variorum," in *Is There a Text in This Class?* (Cambridge, MA: Harvard University Press, 1980), pp. 154–155.

24. Fish, "Literature in the Reader: Affective Stylistics," in *Is There a Text in This Class?* p. 32.

25. Iser, "The Reading Process," p. 295.

26. Louise M. Rosenblatt, *Literature as Exploration*, Fifth Edition (New York: Modern Language Association, 1995), p. 15.

27. Ibid., pp. 155–156.

28. Hans Robert Jauss, *Toward an Aesthetic of Reception*, Timothy Bahti, Trans. (Minneapolis, MN: University of Minnesota Press, 1982), p. 41.

29. Annie Dillard, *Living by Fiction* (New York: Harper & Row, Publishers, 1982), p. 15.

30. Jonathan Culler, *The Pursuit of Signs: Semiotics, Literature, Deconstruction* (Ithaca, NY: Cornell University Press, 1981), p. 6.

2

The Reader and the Text

W hen your mother first read you *Mother Goose*, you weren't worried about the quiz she was going to give you on Friday, you weren't taking careful notes just in case you'd have to write an essay about character development, symbolism, or historical influences, and you weren't dreading the prospects of a research paper on the author's life. You just curled up in her arms and listened....

The pleasures that first drew us to literature were not those of the literary scholar. When our parents read us nursery rhymes, we listened for the rhythms of the language and the stories they told without analyzing the rhyme scheme or the metrical pattern, without exploring their political or social significance, without learning about their history or their authorship. Later, we listened to "Little Red Riding Hood," not to identify characteristics of the fairy tale, but to find out whether the wolf ate the little girl for dinner. And still later, we read *Catcher in the Rye*, not to investigate Salinger's style and trace the literary influences of his book, but to see how Holden Caulfield coped with adolescence.

Typical middle or high school students are likely to seek similar rewards in reading. They are not, and are not likely to become, professional literary scholars. When they finish school, they're going to perform surgery, drive cabs, run banks, rob banks, wait on tables, build houses, design bridges, or sell real estate. To assume casually that what is of interest to Kittredge and Brooks and Frye is also of paramount importance to a typical secondary school student is to make a rash leap of faith. If we begin to plan programs by investigating literary scholarship, listing major writers and writings, cataloging techniques and outlining history, we make that leap. Scholarly questions are not irrelevant, but other questions may take precedence; they have to do with the interests and satisfactions of the average reader.

What, then, are the reasons for reading a work of literature, and why do we attempt to teach it? If, as I have suggested, students are unlikely to come to literature class with a scholarly passion for information about the sources of Shakespeare's plays or the social context of the early American fire-and-brimstone sermons, they nonetheless bring with them experiences, interests, and a lengthy agenda of ideas, problems, worries, and attitudes, all of which concern and preoccupy them. If literature is enjoyable or if it touches upon some of those preoccupations, then students will have a reason to read. They will read because they are interested in themselves, and because in the reading they may themselves become the focus of attention. They will read for the pleasures and rewards implicit in the vision of literature and literary experience suggested by Louise Rosenblatt and others.

In other words, their reason for reading is the same as that of an independent adult or a younger child: self-indulgence. That self-indulgence may take many forms. Its most common form is a harmless pursuit of diversion and simple pleasure, the escape into a good story that entertains and distracts us from other worries. At its worst, the self-indulgence is a search for confirmation of distorted visions, a vicarious exercise of hatreds and biases that cannot be safely indulged elsewhere in a civilized society. But at its best, it is the self-indulgence of one hoping to see more clearly and understand more fully who one is and where one stands. Great literature demands reflection upon one's own attitudes and beliefs. The unique claim of imaginative literature at its best is that it is about me. And, of course, about you.

When the literature is *read*, rather than worked upon, it draws us into events and invites us to reflect upon our perceptions of them. It is not at that point a subject to be studied as an artifact illustrating an age or a product representing an artist; it is rather an experience to be entered into. "Entering into" literature, however, may be different from most of our other experiences. The literary work invites us in not only as participants, but also as spectators. It freezes events, scenes, thoughts, and emotions so that they hold still for examination. Few other moments in our lives allow us that time for thought. Events move too quickly, and we are too deeply and thoroughly involved. The work of literature, however, allows us both to experience and to reflect upon experience, and in so doing it gives us a unique opportunity to come to understand ourselves and the world around us.

Adolescents, characteristically preoccupied with the self, should be ideal readers. That is not to say that they *will* read well, nor even that they will read at all. They may despise literature, the literature classroom, and the literature teacher. They may even express great pride in their inability to make sense out of the written word. But, unless they are very unusual, they have the one characteristic that is essential for the reader of literature: an interest in themselves. They are concerned about their relationships with peers, their gradual assumption of responsibility for themselves, their evolving relationships with their parents. They are growing more vividly aware of important decisions whose time is rapidly approaching. They want to understand work, love, hate, war, death, vengeance, responsibility, good, evil—in other words, they are interested in the themes of the literature that has established itself as worth reading and discussing. They are not—or at least we should hope that they are not—beyond caring about those matters, someone whose most serious thoughts are of Sunday's football scores, current hairstyles, and next week's episode of the soap operas.

Adolescents should not yet be content with their conception of the world, with their understanding of themselves and their society. They should not grow rigid and unchanging, working as hard to avoid learning as the young child does to learn.

Literature should strike a responsive chord in them, offering the substance to keep alive questions and interests, feeding them so that continual re-examination is rewarded with some sense of growth or progress.

Preoccupation with the self should make adolescents uniquely receptive to literature, for literature invites their participation and judgment. It gives them the opportunity to test perceptions against those of the author, characters, and other readers, and in that testing to see more clearly who they are and how they feel, react, and think. To provide that opportunity is the purpose for teaching literature. Reading is, after all, something we do in one way or another virtually every waking minute:

> The readers of books, into whose family I was unknowingly entering (we always think that we are alone in each discovery, and that every experience, from death to birth, is terrifyingly unique), extend or concentrate a function common to us all. Reading letters on a page is only one of its many guises. The astronomer reading a map of stars that no longer exist; the Japanese architect reading the land on which a house is to be built so as to guard it from evil forces; the zoologist reading the spoor of animals in the forest; the card-player reading her partner's gestures before playing the winning card; the dancer reading the choreographer's notations, and the public reading the dancer's movements on the stage; the weaver reading the intricate design of a carpet being woven; the organ-player reading various simultaneous strands of music orchestrated on the page; the parent reading the baby's face for signs of joy or fright, or wonder; the Chinese fortune-teller reading the ancient marks on the shell of a tortoise; the lover blindly reading the loved one's body at night, under the sheets; the psychiatrist helping patients read their own bewildering dreams; the Hawaiian fisherman reading the ocean currents by plunging a hand into the water; the farmer reading the weather in the sky—all these share with book-readers the craft of deciphering and translating signs. Some of these readings are coloured by the knowledge that the thing read was created for this specific purpose by other human beings—music notation or road signs, for instance—or by the gods—the tortoise shell, the sky at night. Others belong to chance.

> And yet, in every case, it is the reader who reads the sense; it is the reader who grants or recognizes in an object, place, or event a certain possible readability; it is the reader who must attribute meaning to a system of signs, and then decipher it. We all read ourselves and the world around us in order to glimpse what and where we are. We read to understand, or to begin to understand. We cannot do but read. Reading, almost as much as breathing, is our essential function.[1]

Students read literature to know themselves, and, insofar as they each are a composite of their ideas, attitudes, beliefs, and emotions, to create themselves, for reading will enable them to refine and sharpen their conceptions of the world and the people in it. It is those conceptions that make them who they are. As we read, we write (and speak) ourselves into existence.

Purpose in the Teaching of Literature

To begin by discussing the interaction of reader and literary work may seem odd. Wouldn't it make more sense to begin with the substance to be taught, the content of the literature courses? We could list the appropriate works and compile the relevant information about authors, historical events, literary periods, and genres. We could identify the terminology that might prove useful in the classroom and specify the literary concepts that students should master during their school years. Then, having laid this foundation of information about literature, we could discuss what we know about adolescent students and their interests, skills, inclinations, habits, and problems. We could analyze their psychological and linguistic development and consider the results of reading-interest studies. We could then make some assertions about what we wanted to teach—the literature—and whom we wanted to teach—the adolescent—and from those assertions we might expect a pedagogy to emerge.

This strategy has an undeniable appeal. Moving logically and plausibly down the journalist's checklist from "what" to "whom" to "how" and, presumably, sooner or later, to "why," it seems a manageable procedure. Moreover, we could easily subdivide the lists of texts, names, concepts, terms, and dates into the years, semesters or quarters, units, and lessons, the building blocks of the school curriculum. Furthermore, these lists should suggest some organizing principles so that not only would we have the information to be presented, but we would have it neatly arranged. Our list of literary genres, for example, might suggest that part of the curriculum be arranged generically—a few weeks on poetry, followed by a stretch on the short story, a drama unit, a couple of months on a novel or two, and whatever time is left over on the essay. Literary history, of course, suggests a chronological pattern that is easily developed into a full curriculum, especially if we restrict our attention to the literature of one national group, the seventh century is followed by the eighth, the eighth by the ninth, and so on until we run out of either centuries or school days.

Such structures are reassuring. They give shape and substance to the work of the literature classroom, helping us specify objectives, design instruction, and evaluate our results. Starting with the literature itself, and then moving along one of the several trails, cleared and marked, until we have sufficient guidelines for a course, seems to be a rational and practical approach to instruction in literature. To wander from those trails would be to stray into unmapped regions with no assurance that we will emerge where we hope to be.

But that raises real and fundamental questions: Where do we hope to be? What do we want the student of literature to experience and learn in our classes? These questions are neglected if we start with the accumulated body of information about the literature and allow it to set directions. If knowledge of genres is the essence of the literary experience, it's difficult to argue with spending a year investigating the differences between poems and plays, plays and novels, novels and movies. If literary history is the model, we should begin with *Gilgamesh* and dutifully work our way toward the twenty-first century. If author study is the model, we can list the great writers, alphabetize them, and start to work on *Aesop's Fables.* But the question remains: Does genre study, or literary history, or any of several other approaches offer the experience of literature that we seek for students in the secondary schools?

Is technical and historical knowledge what the student needs or wants from the study of literature? It is, clearly, what many of the professionals are interested in studying; a cursory examination of the prominent journals in literary studies indicates that exegesis, history, technical analysis, and other such matters are the major preoccupations of scholars. But are they major (or even minor) interests of most students in secondary English classes? Should students in secondary schools be asked to adopt the professional stance of the literary scholar in their reading of literary works? The appealing strategy of using literary knowledge accumulated over the centuries to generate curriculum and instructional procedures has the virtue of efficiency, but it does not consider purpose. By failing to ask what we hope to accomplish in the secondary school English program, we assume that the goals of the professional literature student are also the goals of the middle and secondary school literature student, though instinct, common sense, and one short afternoon in the classroom all tell us that this is not a safe assumption. Some of the notions we've touched upon in the first chapter may suggest alternatives.

The Uniqueness of the Discipline

Literature is unique as a discipline. In a very important sense, literature does not exist outside the individual reader in the same way as do the physical phenomena studied by the biologists, chemists, and other scientists. A volcano is there regardless of who sees it or fails to see it, and it will erupt or lie dormant for reasons of its own whether anyone cares or not. But a literary work is inevitably dormant until it is read. True, the *text* is there, but the ink on the paper amounts to little until a reader picks up the page, reads and responds to it, and thereby transforms it into an event. It is the experience that the text invites and enables the reader to have that makes it literature. The text becomes literature by virtue of what the reader is able to do with it. If the reader can't do anything with it, it remains ink and paper. Pick up a text in, let's say, Russian (assuming that you don't read Russian—if you do, then try Japanese). Does anything remotely resembling your experience with *Mother Goose* or *Catcher in the Rye* happen while you flip through those pages and stare at those strange shapes? Walter Slatoff, commenting on the uniqueness of literary works as objects of study, remarks:

> The objects we study are curious also in that they assume their full or significant form and being only in active conjunction with a human mind. To some extent, of course, this is true of all objects. Whatever one's theory of perception, one has to agree that some qualities of any object are dependent on human perception. But works of literature have scarcely any important qualities apart from those that take shape in minds.[2]

Literature, in other words, is written for readers rather than for scholars. That doesn't mean that specialists can't study it, but if they neglect to consider the fact that they are not the primary or intended audience, they stray from center. It's clearly possible to distinguish between Petrarchan and Shakespearean sonnet forms, to argue whether a certain Coleridge poem is or is not one of his "conversational" poems, or to quarrel over the authorship of Shakespeare's plays, but it's unlikely that any of the authors originally conceived of their works as subjects for that sort of treatment. If the literature curriculum gives students that misimpression, it does them a serious disservice, teaching them that they are not sufficiently prepared, that they do not have the background, the credentials, and the scholarly disposition to be readers. Shakespeare's audience, those standing in the pits munching oranges, would not have been so intimidated. They would have come to the play for the experience it offered, as our students now go to movies, and would not have doubted their competence to enjoy that experience, despite their lack of professional literary training.

Literature isn't the private domain of an intellectual elite. It is instead the reservoir of all humankind's concerns. Although it may be studied in scholarly and professional ways, it wasn't written to be the subject of such study, to provide intellectual exercises for academics. In the middle and secondary schools, we are not dealing with an intellectual elite, but with a representative group from the local community. We must keep clearly in mind that the literary experience is fundamentally an unmediated, private exchange between a text and a reader, and that literary history and scholarship are supplemental. Studying them may or may not contribute significantly to our understanding of the private exchange, but it cannot be substituted for it. As Rosenblatt says:

> all the student's knowledge about literary history, about authors and periods and literary types, will be so much useless baggage if he has not been led primarily to seek in literature a vital personal experience.[3]

When we substitute historical or critical questions for the direct experience of reading and reflecting, we are on the periphery. We are like baseball statisticians discussing batting averages—the discussion has to do with the game, but it is not the same as playing the game. No doubt some people will prefer the statistics to the game, but it is nonetheless important to perceive the distinction between the two and to avoid confusing them in our teaching. The ball player and the statistician require different training. So do the reader and the literary scholar.

Our literature programs must provide the experience that the typical reader requires. If we can also satisfy those rare students whose interest in literature extends to literary scholarship, then by all means we should do so, but we must not neglect those students who will be readers and not scholars. Such negligence has been a fault of most of the literature programs that evolve from cataloging information about literature. Arthur Applebee, in his history of the teaching of English, points out that "[t]eachers of English have never successfully resisted the pressure to formulate their subject as a body of knowledge to be imparted."[4] He continues,

Part of the uneasiness which teachers have felt with attempts to define their subject matter as a body of knowledge results from an awareness, often unarticulated, that the goals which they seek to accomplish through the teaching of literature are ultimately not defined by such knowledge, but rather are questions of values and perspective—the kinds of goals usually summed up as those of a "liberal" or "humanistic" education.... Only rarely have they considered, however, the implications of such an emphasis for the way their subject should be taught, being for the most part content to assume that the humanistic benefits would follow naturally from exposure to the proper content....[5]

Rosenblatt, many years earlier, had criticized the results of that assumption:

The adolescent can be easily led into an artificial relationship with literature. Year after year as freshmen come into college, one finds that even the most verbally proficient of them, often those most intimately drawn to literature, have already acquired a hard veneer, a pseudo-professional approach. They are anxious to have the correct labels—the right period, the biographical background, the correct evaluation. They read literary histories and biographies, critical essays, and then, if they have the time, they read the work.[6]

That, sadly, is what we were sometimes encouraged, almost ordered, to do in our English courses. It was what was expected, for example, by the professor who began his course by saying, "We're going to be studying the short fiction of Herman Melville this semester" (the big book about the fish would come later), "and these are the critical works you must know." He handed out a list of books and essays—the authoritative pronouncements about Melville's short fiction—and of course, as good students, we knew what we were to do. It would be inefficient to read Melville's short stories on our own, burdening ourselves with the confusions that would inevitably result, and then have to struggle through the critics to undo the damage our deficient intellects had wreaked upon our comprehension. No sense wasting all that time and effort. Far wiser to read those critics first, find out what it was we were supposed to think, and then read Melville and think those thoughts. One student in the class, older and more experienced, counseled us to not jeopardize our grade point averages with *any* direct contact with Melville at all. Reading his fiction would just muddy the water. After all, he pointed out wisely, there would be plenty of time to read Melville after the course was over if we wanted to. I gathered, from the enviable grade he earned in the course, that his understanding of Melville was unmatched. Whether he ever actually read Melville, I don't know.

As Rosenblatt suggests, the literature program devised to present information about literature deprives us of the fundamental experience with literature, encouraging us to bypass a crucial step in reading. Rosenblatt's criticism is confirmed by the popularity in the schools of the commercial study guides, short summaries of literary works with critical and historical commentary appended. Even for students who do not literally bypass the work, Rosenblatt's comment may be metaphorically accurate. If they read with no other purpose in mind than to find and recall information, we may legitimately wonder whether they have had a literary experience more significant than that of the student who reads only a summary.

We are suggesting, then, that we look first at the actual reading. Interest in the other approaches to literary works will come, if it comes, from this first step, but if that step is ignored, imposing those other studies on the students is likely to lead to distaste for literature and to the artificiality or pseudo-professionalism about which Rosenblatt warns us. Programs developed to teach a body of information about literature tend, unfortunately, to attempt to create literary historians and critics before they have created readers.

Let's see, then, what sort of literature teaching may result from considering that neglected step, the actual reading of the work, but first consider the short experiment presented in Workshop #3.

MARGINALIA

It's easy to read without reading, to spend an hour with a text and lose all that transpired during that time. We've all experienced a wandering mind while working through *Fun and Games with Multiple Regression Analysis*, when our eyes continue to pass mechanically down the page while our thoughts stray to problems at home or to next Saturday's party. Suddenly we realize that we've turned three or four pages and have absolutely no idea what might have been on them.

But we might also lose much of our more pleasurable reading. We found a good book for the flight to Baltimore and passed the trip absorbed, but then we disembark, elbow our way through the airport, arrange to have our luggage returned from Buenos Aires, find a cab, check in at the hotel, and then realize (or perhaps not) that much of that reading is gone. We wondered at one point just why the character might have done that, why the author had let that conversation stray to those issues; at another we thought how amused our Democratic friends would have been at this scene, and how outraged the Republicans; at another we remembered something similar happening to us long ago and resolved to call the old friend who was there; at another. . . and so on. But after the airport, the baggage, the traffic, the line at hotel registration, all of that is gone, vanished, evaporated like mist in the morning sun, and all that's left of our literary experience, our transaction with this text, is a rough outline of the plot, the names of some of the characters, and the vague notion that it was a good book.

That's an unfortunate and common loss. If, as Rosenblatt argues, the essence of literature is in the transaction, then we are left only with miscellany, a few bits and pieces of prose, the sort of nonsense that finds its way into such silliness as the *Accelerated Reader* tests.

CAPTURING OUR READINGS

To try instead to capture your responses, associations, memories, questions, and thoughts as you read so that you may become more alert to what's going on in your mind as you move through a text, consider preparing a story so that it has a large right margin, as in the stories on the following pages. If you want to use a story in your textbook, and you don't wish to scan, reformat, print, and copy, grab a pack of Post-It notes and use them. Read through the story, annotating the text in the expanded margin or on the Post-Its as you go, and then discuss. Here are the sort of instructions you might follow (or give a class), and two texts to experiment with, one easy and one fairly challenging, in case you don't want to find your own:

Instructions

Please read the story, occasionally stopping to write notes in the margin. You might jot down a question, capture a memory, or express your surprise, annoyance, or other reaction.

When you've finished reading, pair up with another reader and look over your annotations. Lay the texts side by side and glance down the page until you come to the first point at which someone wrote a comment and focus on that. Discuss the reaction, criticism, question, memory—whatever it was—for as long as it merits attention, and then move on to the next annotation. If the annotations point to questions, try to answer (or explore) them; if the annotations point to your own stories, tell them; if they point to strong emotion, try to figure out why. Be alert to the similarities and differences in the way each of you read the piece.

After you've talked for a while, try to articulate any issues or questions that are suitable for the entire class to discuss. Were you able to see similarities and differences in the way you approached the text? Could you capture responses, thoughts, and associations? Did your conversation with another reader sharpen at all your understanding of how you read the story?

You'll find on the next few pages two formatted stories. The first is suitable for a middle school class, whereas the second is challenging even for the best seniors and adult readers:

Eleven[7]
Sandra Cisneros

What they don't understand about birthdays and what they never tell you is that when you're eleven, you're also ten, and nine, and eight, and seven, and six, and five, and four, and three, and two, and one. And when you wake up on your eleventh birthday you expect to feel eleven, but you don't. You open your eyes and everything's just like yesterday, only it's today. And you don't feel eleven at all. You feel like you're still ten. And you are—underneath the year that makes you eleven.

Like some days you might say something stupid, and that's the part of you that's still ten. Or maybe some days you might need to sit on your mama's lap because you're scared, and that's the part of you that's five. And maybe one day when you're all grown up maybe you will need to cry like if you're three, and that's okay. That's what I tell Mama when she's sad and needs to cry. Maybe she's feeling three.

Because the way you grow old is kind of like an onion or like the rings inside a tree trunk or like my little wooden dolls that fit one inside the other, each year inside the next one. That's how being eleven years old is.

You don't feel eleven. Not right away. It takes a few days, weeks even, sometimes even months before you say Eleven when they ask you. And you don't feel smart eleven, not until you're almost twelve. That's the way it is.

Only today I wish I didn't have only eleven years rattling inside me like pennies in a tin Band-Aid box. Today I wish I was one hundred and two instead of eleven because if I was one hundred and two I'd have known what to say when Mrs. Price put the red sweater on my desk. I would've known how to tell her it wasn't mine instead of just sitting there with that look on my face and nothing coming out of my mouth.

"Whose is this?" Mrs. Price says, and she holds the red sweater up in the air for all the class to see. "Whose? It's been sitting in the coatroom for a month."

"Not mine," says everybody. "Not me."

"It has to belong to somebody," Mrs. Price keeps saying, but nobody can remember. It's an ugly sweater with red plastic buttons and a collar and sleeves all stretched out like you could use it for a jump-rope. It's maybe a thousand years old and even if it belonged to me I wouldn't say so.

Maybe because I'm skinny, maybe because she doesn't like me, that stupid Sylvia Saldivar says, "I think it belongs to Rachel." An ugly sweater like that, all raggedy and old, but Mrs. Price believes her. Mrs. Price takes the sweater and puts it right on my desk, but when I open my mouth nothing comes out.

"That's not, I don't, you're not . . . Not mine," I finally say in a little voice that was maybe me when I was four.

"Of course it's yours," Mrs. Price says. "I remember you wearing it once." Because she's older and the teacher, she's right and I'm not. Not mine, not mine, not mine, but Mrs. Price is already turning to page thirty-two, and math problem number four. I don't know why but all of a sudden I'm feeling sick inside, like the part of me that's three wants to come out of my eyes, only I squeeze them shut tight and bite down on my teeth real hard and try to remember today I am eleven, eleven. Mama is making a cake for me for tonight, and when Papa comes home everybody will sing Happy birthday, happy birthday to you.

But when the sick feeling goes away and I open my eyes, the red sweater's still sitting there like a big red mountain. I move the red sweater to the corner of my desk with my ruler. I move my pencil and books and eraser as far from it as possible. I even move my chair a little to the right. Not mine, not mine, not mine.

In my head I'm thinking how long till lunchtime, how long till I can take the red sweater and throw it over the schoolyard fence, or leave it hanging on a parking meter, or bunch it up into a little ball and toss it in the alley. Except when math period ends Mrs. Price says loud and in front of everybody, "Now, Rachel, that's enough," because she sees I've shoved the red sweater to the tippytip corner of my desk and it's hanging all over the edge like a waterfall, but I don't care.

"Rachel," Mrs. Price says. She says it like she's getting mad. "You put that sweater on right now and no more nonsense."

"But it's not—"

"Now!" Mrs. Price says.

This is when I wish I wasn't eleven, because all the years inside of me— ten, nine, eight, seven, six, five, four, three, two, and one—are pushing at the back of my eyes when I put one arm through one sleeve of the sweater that smells like cottage cheese, and then the other arm through the other and stand there with my arms apart like if the sweater hurts me and it does, all itchy and full of germs that aren't even mine.

That's when everything I've been holding in since this morning, since when Mrs. Price put the sweater on my desk, finally lets go, and all of a sudden I'm crying in front of everybody. I wish I was invisible but I'm not. I'm eleven and it's my birthday today and I'm crying like I'm three in front of everybody. I put my head down on the desk and bury my face in my stupid clown-sweater arms. My face all hot and spit coming out of my mouth because I can't stop the little animal noises from coming out of me, until there aren't any more tears left in my eyes, and it's just my body shaking like when you have the hiccups and my whole head hurts like when you drink milk too fast.

But the worst part is right before the bell rings for lunch. That stupid Phyllis Lopez, who is even dumber than Sylvia Saldivar, says she remembers the red sweater is hers! I take it off right away and give it to her, only Mrs. Price pretends like everything's okay.

Today I'm eleven. There's a cake Mama's making for tonight, and when Papa comes home from work we'll eat it. There'll be candles and presents and everybody will sing Happy birthday, happy birthday to you, Rachel, only it's too late.

I'm eleven today. I'm eleven, ten, nine, eight, seven, six, five, four, three, two, and one, but I wish I was one hundred and two. I wish I was anything but eleven, because I want today to be far away already, far away like a runaway balloon, like a tiny *o* in the sky, so tiny-tiny you have to close your eyes to see it.

She Unnames Them[8]
Ursula K. LeGuin

Most of them accepted namelessness with the perfect indifference with which they had so long accepted and ignored their names. Whales and dolphins, seals and sea otters consented with particular grace and alacrity, sliding into anonymity as into their element. A faction of yaks, however, protested. They said that "yak" sounded right, and that almost everyone who knew they existed called them that. Unlike the ubiquitous creatures such as rats and fleas, who had been called by hundreds or thousands of different names since Babel, the yaks could truly say, they said, that they had a *name*. They discussed the matter all summer. The councils of the elderly females finally agreed that though the name might be useful to others it was so redundant from the yak point of view that they never spoke it themselves and hence might as well dispense with it. After they presented the argument in this light to their bulls, a full consensus was delayed only by the onset of severe early blizzards. Soon after the beginning of the thaw, their agreement was reached and designation "yak" was returned to the donor.

Among the domestic animals, few horses had cared what anybody called them since the failure of Dean Swift's attempt to name them from their own vocabulary. Cattle, sheep, swine, asses, mules, and goats, along with chickens, geese, and turkeys, all agreed enthusiastically to give their names back to the people to whom—as they put it—they belonged.

A couple of problems did come up with the pets. The cats, of course, steadfastly denied ever having had any name other than those self-given, unspoken, ineffably personal names which, as the poet Eliot said, they spend long hours daily contemplating—though none of the contemplators has ever admitted that what they contemplate is their names and some onlookers have wondered if the object of that meditative gaze might not in fact be the Perfect, or Platonic, Mouse. In any case, it is a moot point now. It was with the dogs, and with some parrots, lovebirds, ravens, and mynahs, that the trouble arose. These verbally talented individuals insisted that their names were important to them, and flatly refused to part with them. But as soon as they understood that the issue was precisely one of individual choice, and that anybody who wanted to be called Rover, or Froufrou, or Polly, or even Birdie in the personal sense, was perfectly free to do so, not one of them had the least objection to parting with the lowercase (or as regards German creatures, uppercase) generic appellations "poodle," "parrot," "dog," or "bird," and all the Linnaean qualifiers that had trailed along behind them for two hundred years like tin cans tied to a tail.

The insects parted with their names in vast clouds and swarms of ephemeral syllables buzzing and stinging and humming and flitting and crawling and tunnelling away.

As for the fish of the sea, their names dispersed from them in silence throughout the oceans like faint, dark blurs of cuttlefish ink, and drifted off on the currents without a trace.

None were left now to unname, and yet how close I felt to them when I saw one of them swim or fly or trot or crawl across my way or over my skin, or stalk me in the night, or go along beside me for a while in the day. They seemed far closer than when their names had stood between myself and them like a clear barrier: so close that my fear of them and their fear of me became one same fear. And the attraction that many of us felt, the desire to smell one another's smells, feel or rub or caress one another's scales or skin or feathers or fur, taste one another's blood or flesh, keep one another warm—that attraction was now all one with the fear, and the hunter could not be told from the hunted, nor the eater from the food.

This was more or less the effect I had been after. It was somewhat more powerful than I had anticipated, but I could not now, in all conscience, make an exception for myself. I resolutely put anxiety away, went to Adam, and said, "You and your father lent me this—gave it to me, actually. It's been really useful, but it doesn't exactly seem to fit very well lately. But thanks very much! It's really been very useful."

It is hard to give back a gift without sounding peevish or ungrateful, and I did not want to leave him with that impression of me. He was not paying much attention, as it happened, and said only, "Put it down over there, O.K.?" and went on with what he was doing.

One of my reasons for doing what I did was that talk was getting us nowhere, but all the same I felt a little let down. I had been prepared to defend my decision. And I thought that perhaps when he did notice he might be upset and want to talk. I put some things away and fiddled around a little, but he continued to do what he was doing and to take no notice of anything else. At last I said, "Well, goodbye, dear. I hope the garden key turns up."

He was fitting parts together, and said, without looking around, "O.K., fine, dear. When's dinner?"

"I'm not sure," I said. "I'm going now. With the—" I hesitated, and finally said, "With them, you know," and went on out. In fact, I had only just then realized how hard it would have been to explain myself. I could not chatter away as I used to do, taking it all for granted. My words now must be slow, as new, as single, as tentative as the steps I took going down the path away from the house, between the dark-branched, tall dancers motionless against the winter shining.

This was an effort to make an informal record of your transaction with a text. If you did it conscientiously, you might be able to make some observations about how you read. One pair of students, for example, in trying this activity with another story ("Kong at the Seaside," by Arnold Zweig), reported an interesting contrast. One of the two readers commented, "I was so annoyed at having to stop reading to write down my thoughts that I just couldn't do it. I tried, I really did, but I was so irritated I was getting angry, so I just quit trying to write. I read through to the end of the story and then I went back and tried to remember what I was thinking at several places. My partner, on the other hand. . . ." And here her classmate interrupted in a tone that expressed her surprise at what had happened, "I started writing while I was in the first paragraph and got so interested in what I had to say that I never got back to the story. I wrote the whole time and when you asked us to stop annotating and talk with one another I still hadn't even finished reading the first paragraph."

Each was startled at the other's experience, and the activity highlighted for each some aspect of her approach to a text. Now that you have read the text, made notes on it, and discussed your experience with another reader, try to make any observations you can about your own way of reading this story.

The Reading Act

We suggested earlier that it was self-indulgence that drove readers to books, self-indulgence of the lazy sort that seeks momentary release from work or worry, of the destructive sort that seeks confirmation of biases and opinions, or of the constructive sort that seeks experience yielding clearer understanding of the self and of the world. The first sort does not concern us—idleness is only a venial sin—and the second is perhaps best confronted by close attention to the third. This third form of self-indulgence is introspective; it involves reflection on one's own values, attitudes, beliefs, and ideas. It can be like a conversation between writer and reader, as the reader tests perceptions and understandings against the writer's. The conversation is not easy; the writer's work is done and the reader now bears the burden. To make sense of the work, she must find connections with it. The reader cannot become the writer, seeing with the writer's eyes, thinking with the writer's mind. Instead, she gathers and refines her own impressions, and interprets, tentatively at first, then with more assurance, shaping the meaning and significance of the work. History, biography, and rhyme scheme are peripheral matters at this point; the focus of attention is the interchange between reader and text.

Let's consider some possible transactions with one text. Consider yourself a student, read the poem that follows, and ask yourself what you have experienced:

As Best She Could[9]

Old widow crazed with hunger, you came in crippled,
your backcountry eyes bright and furtive, your voice

careening between a whimper and wild thin laughter.
I saw you take the edge of the chair and cower
as the social worker cut through your explanations,
your patches of self-respect, with her curt queries.

Terrible your smile when asked about your holdings
in bonds, in bank accounts, in property,
your look when reminded of life insurance lapsed.

She wouldn't believe you lived as best you could
on the meager uncertain amount your daughters sent you
and paid no rent to an old and kindly landlord.

She took your naked terror of death for greed
and probable fraud, denied you, sent you off
for written proofs from daughters out of state.

Their misspelt notes came in some three weeks later,
your card for medical care went out, but soon
came back from Public Health a cancellation.

No blame attached, the regulations followed,
your death quite likely in any case, but still
I see you rise and quiver away, your stiff heart
pounding with baffled rage, with stifled pride.

—Donald Jones

Reflect for a moment.

If nothing comes to mind, consider: What does the poem make you feel? If nothing, can you tell why? If something, then what, precisely? Does it remind you of anyone you know, anyone that you have ever seen, any experience you have had? Does it call to mind thoughts, ideas, or attitudes, even if they seem tangential? Is there any word in the poem that you think is particularly important?

Responses vary, perhaps more widely than might be expected of what may seem at first a rather straightforward narrative poem. One group of students reports feeling anger at the social worker. The old woman, they point out, is doing the best she can—she is uneducated, ill, inarticulate, and scared of a bureaucracy she doesn't understand. The social worker should have more compassion, they insist, should be a bit more sympathetic, a bit more like the kindly landlord who has allowed the widow to live rent-free. After all, it isn't her own money the social worker is dispensing; it doesn't hurt her to approve the widow's request.

Some students in this faction begin to speak of the evils of big business and big government, which, they assert, have no soul, no feeling for individuals. Agencies like the one depicted here exist for the purpose of giving soft jobs to irresponsible people like the social worker, who want simply to collect their paychecks and go home. Some students have had conflicts with institutions—insurance companies, the Department of Motor Vehicles, or perhaps the school—and have stories of their own to tell, stories called to mind by reading the poem.

Others may even create stories to account for the events in the poem. One student speculated (though "speculate" is too weak a term, for the student insisted that her reading was absolute, incontrovertible truth) that the social worker and the widow's daughters had conspired in a scheme to obtain the widow's welfare money.

Let us not concern ourselves here with accuracy or defensibility of each response, or even with its proximity to the text. Clearly, the student who compared the social worker with the generous landlord had made a statement more easily traced to the text than that of the student who invented a complex conspiracy to defraud the widow of her pittance. In the early stages of discussion we hope to elicit, not to judge, the students' responses. It isn't important to identify who is right and who is wrong; in fact, except on some relatively simple and uninteresting points, it probably isn't possible to determine right and wrong in the reading of a poem. Rather, we are simply trying to find out what the responses are. We will then be able to look more closely at the readings to discover what we can about the readers, the text, and the process of reading.

Although anger with the social worker and sympathy with the widow are the most frequent first responses to the text, there are others. A second group, for instance, reports indifference to the widow's unfortunate situation. She should have planned better, these students say, and besides, she is not a very appealing character: she is crazy, her eyes are sneaky like a rat's eyes, her voice that of a witch, and her smile "terrible." No wonder the social worker distrusts her and demands that she provide some proof for her claims. Everyone cheats the welfare system, anyway, and someone should put a stop to it. The trouble with too many people, they moralize, is that they want something for nothing.

Again, we may for the moment overlook the casual transformation of "crazed" into "crazy," and the acrobatic leap from the old widow to "everyone" and "too many people."

A third group of students reports a less partisan reading. They suggest that in a sense the social worker, as well as the old widow, did "as best she could." The ambiguity in the title suggests to them that neither of the two can really be blamed. The old widow may be trapped by her ignorance and her lack of bureaucratic sophistication, but the social worker is also trapped, by the regulations and procedures of the bureaucracy for which she works. These students say that the problem, larger than one welfare client or one social worker, is with the whole system. Circumstances are at fault, not either of the two people. "No blame attached," they cite, and agree that no one is to be blamed, that the widow's death *is* quite likely in any case. They point out that regulations do have to be followed, or we have anarchy.

Even when regulations are followed, the welfare system, so the papers tell them, is rife with fraud and mismanagement.

Often, the students in the last group cited seem more disturbed by the poem than do others. The students who respond with anger have a target for that emotion, and those who are indifferent to the widow have, they feel, justification for that lack of concern; but those who think that neither the widow nor the social worker can be held fully accountable are frustrated and annoyed by their inability to find someone to blame.

The three readings of the poem presented here are, of course, rough generalities, a composite of responses from several classes; individual student responses will be as varied as the students themselves. But these serve to indicate the possible range of response to "As Best She Could." We might perceive a still broader range of possible readings by imagining the widely varying audiences this poem may find in the schools across the country, and predicting their responses (keeping in mind that such predictions are rash and unreliable). What, for instance, would be the likely response from students whose parents are on welfare; from students whose parents are unable to obtain welfare; from those whose parents are fraudulently obtaining welfare; from those who work after school and whose parents both hold two jobs to avoid having to take welfare; from those whose family income exceeds $100,000 or $1,000,000 a year; from those students who perform some sort of part-time social work; from those living in the middle of the largest cities; or from those living in remote rural areas?

Consider also the variations that may arise from the special circumstances in which the poem is encountered. Might not a student's response on reading the poem in December, as Christmas approaches, differ somewhat from his response to the same poem in April, as income-tax deadlines begin to make his parents more irritable than usual? It is at least conceivable that he may tend more toward generosity at one time, and more toward stinginess at another. Would responses perhaps be affected if the papers had recently featured stories in which welfare recipients had been cheated of much-needed money by dishonest government employees? Or if the story had been of recipients cheating the government and therefore the taxpayers?

Considering the infinite number of possible readers and circumstances in which they may read, the responses described above may not seem to do justice to the vast number of readings the poem may support. But the point is not to attempt to identify all possible reactions to the text. Rather, it is to suggest that variations are inevitable, and that they are legitimate. Coming to the text from different backgrounds, with different attitudes, under different circumstances, students must naturally have different readings. Perhaps you observed that in your discussion of "Eleven" or "She Unnames Them."

Without speculating further about why students respond as they do, we can nonetheless see some justification or explanation for each of these responses. The first response, for instance, in which the dominant feeling is anger toward the social worker, may be seen to reflect a natural sympathy for the victims of society. We may quarrel with the students' portrayal of the social worker and the vehemence of their condemnation, and we may doubt the efficacy of the action they say she should have taken, but we are probably able to accept the students' sympathy and compassion for the widow. In any event, if the text has awakened those feelings in a student, they cannot be readily ignored; if the students themselves ignore them, they deny their own readings and must substitute someone else's, presumably the teacher's. This is good note-taking instead of good reading.

Similarly, there is some justification for the responses of those students whose immediate dislike of the widow or those who cheat the welfare system causes them to approve the social worker's handling of the situation as cautious and professional. Again, we may quarrel with some aspects of their reading, possibly with their insensitivity to suffering, or with their assumption that the widow is cheating the system, but we must admit that the widow is not an attractive character, that some people do cheat the welfare system, and that a government employee is obligated to handle funds responsibly.

Those students who respond neither by blaming the widow nor by criticizing the social worker but by rising to a higher level of abstraction and finding fault with "conditions" also have a point. The title of the poem is ambiguous, allowing us to see both the widow and the social worker as doing the best they can. Further, it is surely possible for bureaucracies to grow so large that they become unmanageable and ineffective, trapping their employees in unproductive routines. We may be critical of the students' shift of focus from this situation, these people, to the more abstract topic of "bureaucracies," and may guess that they are avoiding the issue raised by the poem, but the reading is nonetheless plausible.

We have, then, several different readings of the same text, each connected in some way to the words on the pages, each linked to past experience or accumulated attitudes, and each exhibiting imaginative leaps or, perhaps, errors. I suggested disregarding these leaps or errors for the moment in order to explore the basis of the responses, and identified some foundation for each reading, either in the text itself or in the background of the reader. The poem could arouse anger in students inclined toward sympathy for society's defeated, leave indifferent those inclined to demand that people accept the consequences of their own failures, and drive to higher levels of abstraction those able to see both sides of an issue or unwilling to commit themselves. In other words, the poem does support at least some aspects of each reading—some, but not all, for clearly several of the students' comments were dubious.

Some critics and teachers would view this collection of responses as lying on a continuum at greater or lesser distance from a hypothetical perfect reading. That perfect reading is most closely approached by the most perfect reader, presumably the one most experienced and best able to suppress his or her individuality in the interest of pure, objective, uncontaminated reading. In this view, the students' readings are, of course, wrong, some more so than others. Those who adopt this perspective see the teaching of literature as a process of purging the elements that interfere with achieving a pure reading, usually the elements of personal perspective.

But those personal elements matter. Michael Dirda, reminiscing about his childhood, tells of his visits to his uncle's home and their significance in his reading, years later:

Anything, absolutely anything in the world might be found on my Uncle Henry's property and when, half a lifetime later, I read the description of a wonder-filled Parisian junk shop in Balzac's gothicky novel *The Fatal Skin*, I recognized the place immediately.[10]

His pleasure in that link is obvious. It would not have made him a better reader, a more enthusiastic reader, to have told him to ignore those memories, as I once was told. I still remember the moment, if not the seminar or the professor's name or even the day's text. We were studying Milton and I made the mistake of mentioning some memory that a passage had called to mind for me. The professor barely raised his head, peered at me over his wire-rimmed glasses, and said something like "Mr. Probst. John Milton didn't know your grandfather and wouldn't have given a damn about him if he had, so while you're in my class, let's not indulge in irrelevant nostalgia and bore one another with stories about our relatives. Try to keep your attention on the text and the work at hand, if you please."

"Keep out of it," he was saying. "Neither you, your grandfather, nor the horse you rode in on matter an iota. Do not taint this text by even thinking about, much less mentioning in *my* seminar, anything that emerges from within your inadequate self. Suppress with a vengeance whatever might slither out from the murky depths of your sordid, seamy, idiosyncratic soul."

Presumably, he would have said much the same to Dirda if he had carelessly dared to mention Uncle Henry. Perhaps Dirda would have had more courage or insight than I and would have muttered under his breath, "No. Regardless what you say and your years of Milton scholarship, my Uncle Henry *does* matter." I, on the other hand, aspiring as all young English majors do to be the perfect reader, kicked myself in the shin beneath that ancient, oaken seminar table and resolved never to let *my* thoughts, *my* memories, *my* feelings, *my* life intrude again on my scholarship. I banished my grandfather from the classroom, forbidding his memory to ever set foot on campus again, and reminded myself that when the professor and I read differently, that difference was evidence of deficiency, and the deficiency was, of course, mine.

It took some time to realize that the difference might be just that—difference and not necessarily deficiency. A clarified reading may be achieved, Rosenblatt showed me, not by rejecting the uniqueness of the individual, but by accepting it and using it as a point of entry into the literary work. We may, in other words, view these three different readings of "As Best She Could" not as misreadings to be corrected, but as three different perceptions of one event, arising from the transaction of text and reader, each perception having the potential to tell us something about the text, the event, and the perceiver. The past experiences and acquired attitudes that shape these perceptions need not be seen as contaminants, but simply as the characteristics of the individual and therefore unique reader. If, in discussing these readings, we can identify demonstrable errors, then we may correct them. If, on the other hand, we discover that one reader's focus and interest are different from those of another, then we may wish to accept those differences and refrain from enforcing a conformity opposed to any serious intellectual tradition.

The poem gives each of us an opportunity to look at ourselves, putting our ideas and attitudes into perspective. The poem is, in a sense, something that we have created as we read. We bring to the text our understandings of the words, our expectations of the behavior of people, our ingrained biases and predilections, and from that create the experience that becomes for us the poem. Rosenblatt explains,

> What each reader makes of the text is, indeed, *for him* the poem, in the sense that this is his only direct perception of it. No one else can read it for him. He may learn indirectly about others' experiences with the text; he may come to see that his own was confused or impoverished, and he may then be stimulated to attempt to call forth from the text a better poem. But this he must do himself, and only what he himself experiences in relation to the text is—again let us underline—*for him*, the work.[11]

To learn to read more perceptively and intelligently, we must reflect on our own perceptions of a work to see what they reveal both about us and about the text. Sympathetic readers of the Jones poem, for instance, may feel some satisfaction in observing that they care about the victimized widow, that they respond to this distress with sympathy. Or they could decide that their intense sympathy is too emotional and thoughtless, and that it would be more reasonable to recognize the constraints upon the social worker, taking a less hostile, more sympathetic view of her. They may even come to think that their initial feelings of sympathy for the widow were false—that they had responded in that way out of a sense of moral obligation dictated by the poem, but that they would not have felt anything at all, except perhaps revulsion or fear, if they had actually encountered such a person on the street. The reading of a poem provides the opportunity to observe oneself reacting, to reflect upon those reactions, and thus to learn about oneself.

Similarly, readers who felt no initial sympathy for the widow and thought the social worker wise to act cautiously with her have the opportunity to consider this reaction. It would be dangerous to analyze too closely why one response emerges rather than another—dangerous, at least, for anyone other than the readers themselves. But the teacher can note the response and invite reflection upon it. The students might confirm the original response or they might decide that it was too hardhearted. Even though the social welfare system must be governed by rules, not whim or passion, they might still feel some sorrow for those whom the system cannot help. They may conclude that their first response derived from a childish distaste for people who seem different—deformed, aged, crippled, uneducated, or different in some other dimension—and that they must not indulge what seems now, upon reflection, to be an immoral prejudice. Thus they may reverse their position and utterly change their understanding of the poem and their ways of reading it.

Let's not judge which of these various possible outcomes to reflection on the poem would be the best. Presumably, our own reading of the poem will predispose us to think of one as better than another. If we feel great sympathy for the widow, we are likely to think of those who do not as insensitive, unfeeling, perhaps coldly rational people. In that case we may see the reversal in our last hypothetical student as a desirable conversion, a literary experience that had yielded insight and an enrichment of the student's conceptions and attitudes. If, however, we favor a reading of the poem that holds in mind the necessary and desirable constraints upon the social worker, we may see that reversal as a weak-minded surrender to emotionalism. Our job is not shaping students to either viewpoint, but assisting them to read so that they may shape themselves. To force them to take a stand they don't believe in would be as immoral as to preach the virtues of Christianity over atheism, or of atheism over Buddhism; these are private decisions that the teacher must not attempt to control. The task in the teaching of literature is to help students think, not to tell them *what* to think.

Three points are at issue here. *The first is that the reader makes the poem in reading it.* She makes it as she does because she is who she is. She understands or misunderstands words in certain unique ways, she has had certain experiences and has not had others, and she holds certain biases, preferences, attitudes, beliefs, and interests. These factors, among others, contribute in subtle ways to the reading that emerges. It is the only reading of which she is capable at the time. She is trapped by her own history, her own perspective. A high school student cannot read "As Best She Could" from the perspective of an ill, impoverished, aged widow, because he is not in that position. He can read it from the perspective of a young adult envisioning himself as aged and impoverished; he can call to mind older relatives; he may himself be poor, but he is not the old widow, with her history, her suffering, her nearness to death. His ability to envision that situation may be great or poor, but the act of envisioning remains one of imagination and is therefore circumscribed by his intellect and experience. Because the reader is not the character, he must call upon his own resources to imagine what the character is like; he cannot call upon resources and experiences he has not had.

The second point is that the reader sees herself in the poem she has made. Other readings are possible, as the divergence within any group will demonstrate. The fact that the reader has read the poem one way rather than another reveals something about her. The reading is a reflection of the self, enabling the reader to stand back and observe aspects of her own mind, in much the same way as a writer might read his drafts, to discover what it is that he has thought or imagined. It objectifies those elusive elements of the self—attitudes, values, beliefs—in the form of feelings or thoughts that may then be examined. The student reads the poem, responds, and then looks at that response as a clue to what is happening within the poem and within herself. Intelligent reading is thus a process of revision.

The third point is that reading is itself experience—potentially a transforming experience. Thus, that student who discovered himself to be hardhearted and unfeeling has had an experience in reflecting on the poem that may incline him, in the future, to take a somewhat more sympathetic stance. Whether the effect is long-lasting is not the question; it will last at least as long as his re-reading of the poem, and it is, consequently, an experience upon which his re-reading will be based, and one without which his new reading would be impossible. In that sense, the student, through reshaping his conceptions and attitudes, creates himself as he reads.

We should perhaps pause here to reiterate that we are speaking of possibilities, of potential relationships between reader and text. They are not automatically or easily achieved. Perhaps they are rare, even for the best readers. But to forge these significant relationships, in which the self is defined and reshaped, is the primary goal of literature.

Two Problems

ERRORS IN READING Our discussion of Jones' "As Best She Could" has so far ignored two obvious problems: errors in reading, and authorial intent. The first is the easier to deal with. It is clearly possible to make errors in reading a text. Our insistence upon beginning with a reader's response is not an assertion that that response is good or right, but simply that it is the place one must begin. It is quite possible for the response to betray a careless or thoughtless reading of the text, with words misunderstood, sections of the work ignored, stock responses substituting for real ones, the reader's personal associations and memories imputed to the text or the writer. Good readers learn to distinguish between what is in the text and what comes from associations with it, but young readers may not yet know the difference between the influence exerted by the words on the page and that of their own background and the context of the reading. Still, regardless of the influences upon students' readings, one must begin with their responses.

Discussion has the potential for refining responses either at the fairly sophisticated level of thought we have been examining or at a more primitive level. Consider two instances of error in the reading of the Jones poem. In the first, one young student responded to the poem with some disgust. "Her husband should take care of her; we shouldn't have to." Another student protested that she didn't have a husband to take care of her, to which the young critic replied, "She has to have a husband—she has three daughters, doesn't she?" (presumably borrowing the "three" from the "three weeks" mentioned in the sixth stanza). When other students pointed out that she was a widow, he replied, "So what?" The problem was then obvious. He didn't know the meaning of the word "widow," interpreting it as "old woman." The discovery that it meant something different compelled him to change his reading of the poem. The process of correcting the error was fairly natural and unthreatening. His response to the poem was not condemned; rather, the discussion revealed a misreading, which he then changed. It happens to us all.

The conspiracy theory is also an example of an error in reading. The student who proposed that the social worker and the widow's daughters had conspired to steal the welfare money ultimately saw that there was no real evidence for that reading. She had invented it and thought it would make a good story, but the words of the poem didn't indicate that anything of the sort had happened. The reader had used the poem to stimulate her own imagination—a perfectly valid activity, but not quite the same thing as close reading. Confronted with this student, a teacher would have to decide between two possible responses: either invite her to pursue the thoughts stimulated by the poem, however irrelevant to the text itself, or ask her to suspend those thoughts for the moment and try to read the poem again. As Rosenblatt has said, the poem is not solely either the text or the reader's response. The reader's experience falls somewhere on a continuum. At one extreme is a reading highly responsive to and closely controlled by the text, and at the other a reading triggered by the text but otherwise responsive to and controlled by the psyche of the reader. The conspiracy theory falls at the latter end of the continuum. As long as the reader isn't deceived into thinking that her invention is actually part of the text, there's nothing wrong with that sort of response—it may, in fact, lead to artistic creation by the reader. If it is habitual with an individual, however, we may doubt that she is learning to exercise control in her reading. The student should be encouraged to observe the differences between close reading and free association and should not confuse the two.

When the investigation of responses leads to the discovery of errors in reading, the errors may be gently corrected and the discussion continued, but two extremes are to be avoided. The reading of literature must not become an exercise in avoiding errors, as is likely if comprehension questions dominate the discussions, if the teacher emphasizes some notion of "right" or "correct" reading, or if an error is considered an embarrassing blunder rather than a natural and desirable step in learning. Error-avoidance strategies will make students cautious, timid, and chronically unsure of their perceptions, damaging them as much here as such strategies typically do in composition work. Nor, on the other hand, should errors be ignored on the ridiculous premise that all is a matter of opinion to which everyone is entitled, regardless of how foolish and unsubstantiated. Although words may be imprecise, they stand for a range of possibilities, calling to mind references, images, or relationships similar to some degree in all who know them. To disregard those shared understandings is to deny the possibility of any communication at all.

We may see finding and correcting reading errors as part of the general process of refining one's perceptions of the text. In essence, there is little difference between discovering that a word means something other than what we had thought and finding that our attitudes on an issue are slightly different from those we would have expected. In both cases, linguistic control is improved. The child who discovers that the word *dog* refers not to any four-legged animal, but only to those with certain characteristics, and the adult who, reading *All Quiet on the Western Front,* refines his understanding of the emotions of war, are both going through the same intellectual process, though at different levels of sophistication. The one sharpens his understanding of *dog;* the other refines his understanding of *war.* If students can be encouraged to think of the reading of literature as an opportunity to refine and clarify their ideas, rather than as a test of their ability to read accurately and recall details, they may come to accept errors as a natural part of the process and become less inhibited and defensive about them.

AUTHORIAL INTENT   The question of authorial intent often gives rise to discussion of error in literature classes. Presumably, much of the labor in reading literature is in trying to determine what the writer hopes to say, what effect she hopes to create in the reader. Those are, of course, perfectly legitimate questions. But should they dominate? I've suggested that the class deal first with student responses, trying to determine whether they derive from the text itself, associations it calls to mind, or from something else. The students, in discussing these issues, will be making statements about themselves: "I think . . . ," "I feel . . .," "I believe. . . ." When the students begin to say, "The writer thinks . . ." or "The writer feels . . .," they commit themselves to a different kind of discussion. They are no longer concerned simply with expressing themselves, but have assumed the task of marshaling evidence for their inferences. Both expressing the self and analyzing the writer's intent are important; neither should dominate, and neither should be neglected.

Consider "As Best She Could." It is quite possible to explain the reaction of the student who thinks the social worker is justified in her skeptical and suspicious treatment of the widow. Is it equally possible to ascribe that attitude to the author? Can we say that Jones, too, feels that the social worker is doing her best, constrained by the regulations of the agency for which she works, and is therefore blameless? The poem offers little support for that contention. The social worker is described as "curt"—she "cut through your explanations, your patches of self-respect"—she refuses to believe the widow, interpreting fear as greed and fraud—she "denied you, sent you off." There is little there to suggest that Jones, or to speak more accurately, the persona Jones adopts in this poem, approves of the behavior he has depicted. The evidence indicates that he sympathizes strongly with the widow.

It is important that students who sympathize with the social worker have enough perspective not to confuse their response to the poem with interpretation of the writer's intention. That is not to say they should repress their response; they should simply not assume the writer shares it. Nor, if their response reveals a radical difference between their attitude and that of the writer, should they necessarily revise their opinions to conform to the writer's. They should be encouraged to reconsider their attitude, but they need not feel obligated to submit to the writer's presumed authority.

The move from response to interpretation involves, then, a shift in focus. In the beginning we are less concerned with the writer's intent than with the actual effect of the work. That is to say, the reader is first simply responding, without trying to impose a direction on that response. Whether it is visceral, emotional, or intellectual, it is as far as possible not manipulated, not "produced" to satisfy some self-imposed (or teacher-imposed) task, as it would be if the reader came to the text thinking, "I must devise some proposition about this work that I can then demonstrate" or "I must generate some feeling about this work, to show that I am a sensitive person." At this stage, the reader is receptive rather than aggressive. If any task or question governs this first encounter with the text, it is, "What does this poem do to me—what does it make me feel or think or wonder?" Identifying the effect of the work leads naturally to the question, "What is the source of that effect?" As we have seen, the source lies partially in the text and partially in the reader's experience. Distinguishing between the two demands both introspection and analysis, resulting in the act of interpretation, which can be defined for now as drawing inferences about the meaning and significance of a work or about its intended effect.

Having abandoned the basic tenet of the New Critics—that there is an absolute and perfect reading of a work—we are left with a view of reading in which inferences about authorial intent are only one piece in a larger mosaic. We can't be satisfied, then, with submission to the work, suppressing or forgetting ourselves so that we are assimilated into the world of the text; such a way of reading shows too little regard for the reader. Nor can we accept the submission of text to self, for which the governing principle is "it's my opinion and I'm entitled to it." Such a view betrays indifference to the literary work. Teachers have too often found themselves in an unfortunate conflict in which they held the former position and their students the latter. But the matter is not a simple either/or question as Slatoff, discussing the critical literature on the topic of "belief," suggests:

> This discussion of "belief" has been valuable in many ways, but almost all of it focuses only on major conflicts or discrepancies between beliefs and implies that such conflicts are special cases or deviations from a norm of nearly complete harmony between author and reader. I would argue that such conflicts are merely extreme forms of a condition that obtains to one degree or another in all our literary experiences and that a complete correspondence of attitudes is not a norm but another extreme, one which may, in fact, interfere with a judicious or even adequate response as much as a violent opposition of values.... Our usual experience, it seems to me, involves a curiously complex set of adjustments and maladjustments between our own views and ways of feeling and those which inform the work, a set of adjustments much more like those in a successful marriage than in, say, a dream or brainwashing. As in any relation that is not completely harmonious, we will sometimes defer to the author, sometimes accept things for the sake of the argument, sometimes entertain notions indulgently and give the benefit of the doubt, sometimes suspend judgment temporarily, sometimes mutter or grumble or give a tolerant smile, sometimes view with distaste, suspicion, alarm, or dismay, sometimes revise an impression eagerly, sometimes begrudgingly, sometimes rise fiercely up in arms, sometimes wonder anxiously where the author stands, and so on. The critical discussion of the matter so far seems to envision only two sorts of marriages—blissful and miserable.[12]

As Slatoff suggests, the interpreting process is neither one of submission nor one of tyranny; rather, it is an attempt to see clearly, giving both the author and the self their due. Interpretation, although it is an effort to say something about the meaning of the text, must keep the reader clearly in mind. There is always an "I" in the picture, speculating about the meaning of the words and the significance of their arrangement.

The question of author's intent is not negligible, then, nor is it the most important question; rather, it is an issue that enables us to identify more clearly where we stand. Attention to the author's intent allows us to consider also the adjustments Slatoff spoke of that arise between reader and writer. As we see ourselves sometimes agreeing, sometimes tolerating, sometimes rising fiercely up in arms, we have the opportunity to watch aspects of our belief and thought manifest themselves. We have, in a sense, the opportunity to view ourselves as objects—not only to participate, but to observe, reflecting on our own minds and discovering how we feel about what we find there. The literary work represents another consciousness, which, by its contrast with our own, enables us to refine ourselves, confirming, clarifying, modifying, or refuting perceptions, attitudes, and ideas.

Self-Definition

Thus exchange with the text can become for the reader a process of self-creation. The entire process—responding, correcting errors, searching for the sources of the response, speculating about the author's intent, and weighing the author's values and ideas against one's own—culminates in a sharpened, heightened sense of self. Some part of the reader's conception of the world is confirmed, modified, or refuted, and that changes the reader. If literature has the potential for contributing so much to the conceptual filter through which we receive the world, then we must teach it in such a way that the student, while retaining full authority for her moral and philosophical stance, nonetheless is given the opportunity to see the consequences of those attitudes. The student is changed by her responses to "As Best She Could" and to all the other poems, plays, and novels she reads. She needs the opportunity to see, judge, and reshape those responses, consulting her own heart and mind as she does so, since she is the one ultimately responsible for what she becomes.

Autonomy of the Reader

The teaching that postulates one perfect reading toward which all must strive comes from an autocratic tradition viewing the student as shaped by the wisdom of the great authors, molded by the influence of teachers. It sees him as clay to be sculpted or as the *tabula rasa* on which author and teacher will write. This vision assigns too little authority to the student, who must, regardless of strengths or deficiencies, see things through his own eyes and construct his own image of the world, and too much responsibility and clarity of vision to the writer and the teacher, who are, after all, fallible.

J. Mitchell Morse cautions readers about the dangers of submitting unthinkingly to representations of the world in the works of even the great writers. In an essay entitled "Prejudice and Literature," he offers examples of "vulgarities" in some of the most respected literature:

> Let us observe some cases, minor and major: the inadvertent offenders Valery Larbaud, James Joyce and Charles Lamb, the doubtful case of Charles Dickens, and the deliberate offenders T. S. Eliot, Ezra Pound and William Shakespeare. The result in each case is literary vulgarity.[13]

He explains each one's offense against reason—Joyce's prejudice against women, Eliot's racism and anti-Semitism, Pound's fascist sympathies, and Shakespeare's anti-Semitism, for instance—and then concludes:

> Let us not be overawed, even by Shakespeare, so far that we can't recognize vulgarity for what it is when it solicits our participation like a whore on a street corner.[14]

His point is that the reader is responsible: "Let us not be overawed." We, as readers, must be individually responsible for what we make of the literature, always willing to resist if resistance is appropriate. Absorbing the prejudices of great writers is little better than absorbing those of poorer writers; in both cases we are guilty of mindless submission to the text. What teachers should seek is not submission, but intelligent interaction. We should not, as Morse has said, be overawed by anyone, for to accept values, attitudes, and ideas without question is to decline responsibility for one's own mind, becoming at best the lucky disciple of someone wise, at worst the unfortunate pawn of a manipulator. Whether the unreflective reader falls under the sway of a prophet or a predator is, of course, a matter of sheerest luck, since, in his uncritically receptive state, he exercises no control over his thoughts and emotions, allowing himself to be shaped and molded, and thus is incapable of choosing whom to follow.

The schools should not encourage such receptivity. Teachers do not necessarily know what students should think or feel or do, and should not be tempted to relieve them of the burden of their own intellectual decisions. Although we are older, more experienced in some ways, and probably more skillful, educated readers than our students, we must nonetheless exercise restraint. If we keep in mind that the poem we create as we read is one of many possibilities, shaped by our experiences and attitudes as well as by the words on the page, we'll recognize that our readings have no special claim to authority. Our students are different people, with different backgrounds and proclivities. They must not be molded in our image, but encouraged to grow along lines natural to them, modified and shaped by reason and the necessity for compromise in a society.

Essential Points

Our discussion of the reading act has made several points. The first and most basic is that the reader makes the poem as she reads. She doesn't seek an unalterable meaning that lies within the text for anyone with the wit and will to ferret it out; instead, bringing to bear upon the text whatever perspective and knowledge she has accumulated over the years, she creates meaning from the confrontation. We've tried to forestall charges of permissiveness or anti-intellectualism by arguing that this view does not reduce reading to the simple task of reacting and emoting. Instead, it complicates it by requiring the reader to consider her personal investment in the experience and not to pretend to suppress her own perspective—an impossibility—in a futile effort to achieve total objectivity and purity in interpretation. The value of clear, accurate, correct reading is not denied, but affirmed. Such reading is achieved, however, only through careful attention to both text and self, through conscientious reflection on the thoughts and emotions called forth by the work.

The second point is that the reader has the opportunity to see herself in her reading. Literature invites the reader to observe her own responses, to see herself as if in a photograph, some aspect of her emotional or intellectual self captured and awaiting inspection; thus it rewards the reader with sharpened understanding of herself.

For the moment, she can be both a participant, feeling and thinking, and an observer, watching herself feel and think.

Literature therefore enables the reader to remake herself, and that is the third point. Reading is an experience that shapes, perhaps confirming attitudes and ideas, perhaps modifying or even refuting them. The student creates herself intellectually as she reads.

Thus, fourth, the reader must be active and responsible. She cannot be simply receptive, waiting to be provided with interpretations, to have significances pointed out and implications developed for her. To do so is to accept someone else's reading uncritically, adopting another's feelings and thoughts as one's own. Encouraging that docility makes for placid, malleable, lazy students, and places the English teacher in an untenable position, diminishing his role from that of teacher to that of spiritual leader, charged with the unethical task of molding his students.

We must qualify these four points about the reading of literature by acknowledging that we are speaking of its potential. We may seldom see this potential achieved in the classroom, may seldom achieve it in our own reading, but it remains, nonetheless, a goal. Let's turn our attention now to a practical question: What does the teacher do to encourage students to read in this way? Although the pattern is natural, it is also hard work, demanding thought, which is seldom easy.

Conditions for Response-Based Teaching

We have looked fairly closely at some of the possible readings of one poem. Let's briefly consider the conditions necessary in a classroom for obtaining those readings and then speculate about the teaching of another poem to see what principles of instruction may emerge.

Receptivity

If discussions are to invite the responses and perceptions of students, it's necessary that we welcome these responses and perceptions. We must let students know that we seek their comments and will give them consideration. Pseudo-inductive teaching,

in which, under pretense of open discussion, we lead the class to a preordained conclusion, will show students that we don't seriously consider their opinions and that
we have asked them to speak only to contribute bits and pieces of an argument
we've already formulated and outlined in our lesson plan. This is Socratic practice
at its worst.

A delicate balance is required. We must establish an atmosphere in which students feel secure enough to respond openly, but must not deceive them into believing that initial responses are sufficient. Nor, on the other hand, should we make
students think their responses are invited to provide clay pigeons to shoot at. If we
ridicule student responses, there will soon be few responses left to ridicule. This is
not to say that response-based teaching demands the intimacy of a sensitivity session and that students should be required to lay bare their souls, but it does require
reasonable freedom from fear of castigation or mockery, and from obsequious submission to the authority of the teacher or author. The classroom must be cooperative, not combative, with students and teachers building on one another's ideas,
using rather than disputing them. Debate is an unsuitable model.

Tentativeness

Hence the second condition: Students must be willing to be tentative, to express
thoughts and feelings they are unsure of, to change their minds. In other words, we
must treat initial response as a draft, as something to build upon, modify, or perhaps
reject. A teacher who encourages the students' desire to be right—probably a desire
that most of their previous schooling has carefully inculcated—is likely to find them
holding back from the discussion, waiting for clues from the teacher or from stronger
students, or resorting to commercial study guides for borrowed insights. Students
should not be afraid to change their minds; revising one's opinions is a normal part
of intellectual activity. In fact, changing one's mind should be encouraged, since it
is evidence of thought.

Rigor

The third condition follows from the second: Students must be willing to think.
Unconsidered, unexamined response is simply the first step in reading. What must
follow is rigorous analysis—searching for one's assumptions, drawing inferences about
one's own attitudes and those expressed in the text, and considering other points
of view offered by the teacher, other students, and sometimes critical works. Such
study is more demanding than the comprehension and recall many reading programs require, more demanding than memorizing of information about literature.
Further, it seldom reaches closure, at least for the group as a whole. The final step
in this sort of reading is a personal statement: "I, because of who I am, conclude
this about the work, myself, and the other students in the class. . . ."

Achieving such results is not simple. As Rosenblatt says:

> A situation conducive to free exchange of ideas by no means represents a
> passive or negative attitude on the part of the teacher. To create an atmosphere of

self-confident interchange he must be ready to draw out the more timid students and to keep the more aggressive from monopolizing the conversation. He must be on the alert to show pleased interest in comments that have possibilities and to help the students clarify or elaborate their ideas. He must keep the discussion moving along consistent lines by eliciting the points of contact between different students' opinions. His own flexible command of the text and understanding of the reading skills it requires will be called into play throughout.[16]

Rigor is demanded, then, of the teacher as well as the student. But rigorous scrutiny of the work and the responses shouldn't obliterate the personal element of reading. It may, to the contrary, change the reader's awareness of the personal, or even sharpen it. As they develop a tolerance for ambiguity and uncertainty, coming to accept the idea that meaning and understanding are private creations, not absolutes to be discovered, students may less often plead with you, pens poised to capture your every word, "Now that we've shot the bull for an hour, will you please just tell us what it means?" Unfortunately, the premise of much early schooling has been that there *are* right answers and it is important to find them. This is a false hope from which we should free our students.

Cooperation

The fourth condition depends on the preceding three: The class must work reasonably well as a group. It must achieve a level of trust that will allow discussion of response, which is discussion of the self; it must accept tentative, groping statements and the necessarily uncertain progress of the talk; and it must respect both individuality and the constraints of logic and reason. Students must come to realize that others will often pursue lines of thought that they themselves consider uninteresting or irrelevant, and they must learn to tolerate the occasional blind alleys into which they themselves stray. They must come to see that no discussion involving twenty or thirty people can be equally satisfying and interesting to all, and accept the responsibility for exerting some influence on the direction the class takes so that their own concerns are attended to. And they must learn to accept, as opportunities to learn about classmates, those moments when the discussion takes another tack, pursuing a question that bores them.

Suitable Literature

The fifth condition, one that will occupy a chapter later in the book, is that the literature provide some substance—ideas, style, language, attitude, whatever—worthy of reflection. This condition is difficult to meet because it involves matching student with text when there may be 150 to 200 students to consider, and either a limited collection of texts, in situations that restrict the teacher's choices, or an unmanageably large number, when the teacher is free to select almost any appropriate paperback. The matching involves careful analysis of the group, broad knowledge of the available literature, and luck. It can never be perfect, even when there is time to assign different works to individual students. Still, the pattern of instruction invites students to talk first about themselves and their responses, and thus even works that don't inspire instant love may nonetheless provoke sufficient reaction to start discussion.

None of these five conditions will ever be perfectly achieved in a classroom. They are not prerequisites to response-based teaching. In fact, class sessions dealing with literature should help cultivate the desired conditions. Still, however imperfectly realized, they represent the classroom atmosphere toward which we might strive. In subsequent chapters we will consider some of the techniques for achieving this tone in the class.

Teaching a Work

Let's consider now how we might teach the following poem to a class of high school students. Begin by distributing copies and reading it aloud:

A View of a Pig[17]

The pig lay on a barrow dead.
It weighed, they said, as much as three men.
Its closed, pink, white eyelashes,
Its trotters stuck straight out.

Such weight and thick pink bulk
Set in death seemed not just dead.
It was less than lifeless, further off.
It was like a sack of wheat.

I thumped it without feeling remorse.
One feels guilty insulting the dead,
Walking on graves, but this pig
Did not seem able to accuse.
It was too dead. Just so much

A poundage of lard and pork.
Its last dignity had entirely gone.
It was not a figure of fun.
Too dead now to pity.

To remember its life, din, stronghold
Of earthly pleasure as it had been,
Seemed a false effort, and off the point.
Too deadly factual. Its weight

Oppressed me—how could it be moved?
And the trouble of cutting it up!
The gash in its throat was shocking, but not pathetic.

Once I ran at a fair in the noise
To catch a greased piglet
That was faster and nimbler than a cat.
Its squeal was the rending of metal.

Pigs must have hot blood, they feel like ovens,
Their bite is worse than a horse's—
They chop a half-moon clean out,
They eat cinders, dead cats.

Distinctions and admirations such
As this one was long finished with.
I stared at it a long time. They were going to scald it,
Scald it and scour it like a doorstep.

—Ted Hughes

You might try giving them five minutes to write freely. Tell them, "After I've read the poem aloud, read it over again, and then begin writing. Write whatever comes to mind—reactions, complaints, questions, memories, anything. But keep writing for five minutes. Don't stop. Follow your thoughts wherever they take you." Most students will have had some experience with free-writes. You can then ask for several students to read theirs aloud to the class and use them to identify issues to discuss.

Or, after you've read the poem, skip the writing and just ask students for their reactions, urging them to say whatever comes to mind. Their comments will vary:

"That's disgusting."

"I like the part about the greased piglet at the fair."

"What did he mean by 'distinctions and admirations'?"

"I've seen animals slaughtered on the farm—it's no big deal."

"Gross. Why would anyone write about something so unpleasant?"

"He doesn't seem to feel any sympathy at all—why does he bother to write on something he doesn't care about?"

"It's silly for someone to care so much about a dead pig."

The most common response of all is "*Ycchh*" or a similar expression of distaste. The poem is useful for experiments with response-based teaching primarily because it does elicit revulsion from so many students, giving you the opportunity to smile in acceptance (and, if it happens to be true, to acknowledge sharing the feeling). The class is thus informed that it is not necessary to like everything the teacher offers, nor to disguise their reactions.

The students' comments may seem simple—a few questions, a few remarks about what they like and dislike or the feelings the poem has aroused. But despite their brevity, they provide an excellent starting point for the discussion. Even the semi-verbal expression of disgust is a place to begin.

Ask students to comment on both themselves and the text: "Why do you feel so disgusted by the poem?" They may reply with some comment about the text, perhaps citing a particularly repugnant image, or with an anecdote from their own experience, perhaps about seeing a dead animal or watching one die. Any of these responses is an opening into the poem and the students' readings of it.

If, for instance, a student expresses disgust at certain images in the text—let's say those of stanza eight—you may ask if other students react the same way to the lines, or if they find different parts of the poem that disgust them. Or you may ask, if others report that stanza eight doesn't affect them in the same way, what effect it does have. The questions, although they still require personal statements rather than interpretation, begin to reveal differences in reading that may later lead into close analysis.

Consider another example. Perhaps a student has recalled coming upon a dead animal. In this case, noting that the comment isn't about images in the text but about personal experience, you might ask slightly different questions:

What details do you recall about the experience?

What do you remember seeing, feeling, thinking?

Did your experience seem similar to that of the speaker in the poem, or were there differences?

The responses, although again they'll be personal and anecdotal, will nonetheless move the class further along toward a close analysis of the text.

Three Responses

Suppose a student reports disgust at the images of the dead pig and, when asked which lines she finds most unpleasant, cites stanza eight. The teacher or, preferably, other students may then point out that the images in stanza eight are of the living pig, not the dead pig, and ask if it is really the images of death that disgust her. The student is then driven back to the text and may discover that her feelings derive from associations of her own—ideas or memories of death from other experiences— and that it is not actually the images of death in the poem that call forth her distaste. Or she may decide that, curiously, it is those images of the live pig that disgust her, though he'd thought it was the idea of death. In either case she has the beginnings of an insight. She may see that the narrator in the poem seems not disgusted by the dead pig, but almost indifferent to it. In the first stanzas it is like an object: "less than lifeless, further off," and "Just so much a poundage of lard and pork." Those observations may yield further questions: Why does the speaker remain so indifferent to the dead animal, yet stand there staring at it? Why does he present us with such an unpleasant picture of the living pig?

The last two questions move the discussion from the student's feelings to the text, but the student's perspective remains a central issue, since we've identified a contrast between her reaction to the images of death and that of the speaker. We have also identified two different possible sources for the student's disgust: her own past experience and the images of the living animal. But without pursuing those questions at the moment, let's look at another starting point and see where it takes us.

Many students are irritated at the speaker's indifference toward the dead creature, asking, "How can he be so unfeeling and callous?" Or they'll raise a similar question, revealing an inference about the author's purpose: "If the writer wanted us to feel sorry for an animal, why didn't he write about a horse or a dog? No one can feel sorry for a pig." The students either detect indifference on the part of the writer or find it in themselves and sense that it is inappropriate, suspecting that the writer would not want them to feel that way. These questions open a second pathway into the poem, especially if some other student objects that the speaker is not at all unfeeling, but instead cares more than any sensible person would.

If two or more students provide such disparate views of the speaker, the line of questioning is obvious. Pointing out the difference, you might call for elaboration, asking, "What accounts for your view of the speaker's attitude?" Those who see him as callous may point out that he says as much: "I thumped it without feeling remorse"; the pig is "Too dead now to pity"; to remember its life is a "false effort and off the point." Those who think the speaker is sensitive may point out that many terms suggesting feelings creep into his account. They may point to stanza three and note the words "remorse," "guilty," "insulting," and "accuse." True, he denies all the feelings those terms suggest, but if he did not either feel them or note their absence, would he mention them at all? Either he feels some remorse, the students may argue, or he thinks that he *should* feel it.

Once again, close attention to the text is called for. Both points of view are defensible: There is evidence that the speaker feels, and there is evidence that he does not. Neither student is clearly right or wrong, though their statements indicate that they have responded more to some aspects of the text than to others. Again, let us for the moment abandon this line of thought and consider a third point of entry into the poem.

Our first path began with an expression of feeling, our second with an inference about the intent of the poem. The third will begin with what seems to be a digression. One student, after reading the poem, told the class about an experience it had called to mind. She had at one time been interested in medicine and had, in an anatomy class she arranged to attend, participated in dissecting a cadaver. She began with what was going to be an endless apology—"I know this is off the point and I have no idea why I thought of it and it probably isn't relevant at all and I know you won't want to hear about it and I shouldn't take up the class time. . . ." When we finally broke in to urge her on with her story, she reported that the students in that lab had at first been very uncomfortable, laughing and joking awkwardly, but the uneasiness had gradually passed away, to be replaced, for her, by sorrow for this corpse that had recently been a living person. "When we got close to the gurney I saw that he didn't look that old, but he was very thin and had about a three-day growth of beard, and I think maybe he was a wino and I got to wondering about who he had been and if he had any family. . . ." In her eyes he was gradually changing from *cadaver* to *person*. But those reflections had to be dismissed quickly—"Then the doctor came in with his scalpels and the pans for his heart and liver and spleen and everything else and I couldn't think about that anymore." So she settled down to the work at hand, but she could never completely suppress a tinge of sadness.

She told of the incident briefly and simply, concluding with more apologies for the digression, and without understanding why she had thought of it.

This story, although not a statement about the text, nonetheless suggests some questions that return us to it: Why do you think the poem called to mind that incident? Do you see any connections between that memory and the incident recounted in the poem? Here again we are looking at the text and asking for close reading, but motivated by the desire to explore a response. We are brought, almost regardless of where we begin, back to the text. The first response, the expression of disgust, leads us to an examination of the speaker's attitude and the intent behind the images of the poem. The second response, an inference about the speaker's attitude, leads us to investigate how the poem presents that attitude. The third response, the anecdote, takes us into comparisons with the incident of the poem. As we discuss the comparisons, an interpretation of the poem begins to take shape.

Comparing the poem and the incident in the laboratory should focus attention on the attitudes of the student and the persona in the poem. In the poem, students may note a tension between sensitive and callous, introspective and objective. As they note the objectivity in the beginning and near the end, and the sense of sorrow beginning in about the third stanza and culminating around the seventh, where the speaker wanders off into reverie, they may begin to see that the poem moves between these two poles. They may suggest that the poet begins coldly and objectively, then gradually comes to feel accused by the corpse, remembers that it was once a living thing with some dignity, and begins to feel something like sorrow, despite asserting that such thoughts are off the point. A question might arise about the strangely unpleasant imagery of the eighth stanza—the "hot blood," the bite "worse than a horse's," the eating of "dead cats." Asked to consider why the poet might turn to such repellent images at that point, the students may come to see the stanza as an effort to make the corpse disgusting, reducing it once again to a lifeless object, so that the speaker may comfortably retreat from the involvement he has begun to feel. One cannot, after all, sustain sorrow for something as insignificant and unpleasant as a slaughtered pig; that would be silly sentimentality. Thus, the poet conjures the distasteful images to justify ceasing to care; he reduces the pig to nothing more than a doorstep, something less than lifeless and thus not to be mourned.

The movement in the poem, then, is much like that of the student's anatomy class. There, too, we had a sense of diminishing distance as the student moved from indifference to sorrow for the lost life, then a shift back to objectivity, though tinged with feeling, as she began to work. The cadaver was less than lifeless; then its dignity was remembered; then it again became an object. You can't wonder about the man's family when his internal organs are being removed and employed as visual aids in an anatomy lesson.

Another reader took us through a similar experience. He, too, failed at first to see any relevance at all in his response, yet it, too, followed the structure of the poem.

The night before we addressed "As Best She Could" in class he had been fixing dinner and happened to pass by his TV when the news was reporting the day's events in Vietnam. As it often did, the report gave body counts—so many American soldiers killed, so many Viet Cong bodies collected, so many missing and unaccounted for. He paused for a moment and the thought occurred to him that each man represented on that scorecard was a person just like himself, dead in the mud, that for each there were parents and children and wives and friends whose lives had been ripped apart irreparably that afternoon, and that it seemed, well, inadequate to reduce all that to something like the sports report. But, he said, his hamburger was burning and later he had all those chapters I'd asked him to read so he flipped the channel to a ball game, grabbed another beer, and got on with things.

So, from the students' initial responses, whether the student recognizes their relevance or not and from the discussion they stimulate, a reading of the poem emerges. This is an oversimplification, of course, for no reading is likely to be agreed upon by all unless some suppress their own thoughts or are too lazy to try to discover what they are. The reading proposed here is simply one possibility. It is a common ground that many readers have found in the poem, to which they add much that is their own. For some, the poem will be dominated by the associations it calls forth, as with the student who remembered the anatomy class. For others, it confirms the belief that emotions must be respected but controlled. The speaker, they think, is wise to pause and reflect on the dead pig, but wiser still to assert his rationality at the end and prepare to pass on to other matters. And others have a nagging sense that death has not been adequately dealt with in the poem, where it is briefly moving and then simply forgotten. Death, they believe, requires more explanation, or at least more ritual. They themselves would not want to be so quickly forgotten.

Within such a discussion the teacher should allow the students' unique perspectives, yet also help them read more accurately, fostering awareness both of the text and of individual differences in viewpoint. What may result is a keener understanding of both the work and the self, for neither is lost sight of during the discussion, and neither dominates for long. The teacher's questions should call for clarification and elaboration, always keeping in mind both self and text.

Preparing for Teaching

It is difficult to describe how to formulate appropriate questions, although our three approaches to the Hughes poem may suggest a way to begin. Careful reading of the text will help you predict some of the responses that you may encounter in the class. In "A View of a Pig," the tension between indifference and concern will alert you to one possible line of inquiry. The class may, of course, respond unpredictably and follow some unforeseen path. In that case you have to react quickly, but your careful reading of the poem, if you are not too tightly bound to one perspective, should enable you to follow the lead of the group.

Sometimes you might experiment with teaching a work that you have not carefully read in advance, perhaps inviting the students to submit works for the class to discuss, or, if you don't trust their judgment and discretion, asking a colleague to run off thirty copies of a good poem or a very short story for you. Have her seal them in an envelope and then take them into class and pass them out before you've even glanced at the text. Lacking the insight that careful preparation would have given you, you're then forced to rely on the very process you are espousing for your students. Such an experiment, terrifying as it may be, gives you the opportunity to model some of the behavior you hope to elicit from them. Perhaps most important, it allows you to be wrong, to make mistakes, to be convinced by the sharper insights of someone else—in other words to engage in the natural activities associated with learning and thinking. Kids see a great deal of *meaning already made* in the classroom—our textbooks are full of it; but too seldom do they get to see *meaning being made*, to see a teacher wrestling with a challenging text, wondering about lines, dealing with memories, suggesting interpretations, rejecting some and confirming others. Teaching something you haven't previously read brings you into the class as someone who *is learning*, not as one who already *has learned* and who means to dispense wisdom without acquiring any more in the process.

The discussion of the Hughes poem suggests several ways to begin and some questions that might lead the students to further reflection and analysis. Although no rigid pattern for teaching literature presents itself, several principles might be suggested.

Principles of Response-Based Teaching

There are several thoughts we might keep in mind if we hope to encourage and respect students' responses, and use those responses to encourage students to reflect on and analyze their reading.

SELECTION   First of all, we should choose literature for its potential to interest students. We'll discuss what this means at greater length in later chapters, but for now we may say that selecting literature simply because it illustrates a genre, exemplifies a period of history, or demonstrates certain literary techniques is less likely to be successful than selecting it because it is appropriate to the students who will read it. It must not be too difficult or easy, either syntactically or conceptually, although that is hard to judge and much more complicated than applying readability formulas to several paragraphs of text. Nor, on the other hand, must it necessarily be relevant, as that term is commonly misconstrued. It need not deal specifically with the students' age group, locale, or the personal problems that preoccupy them. *Beowulf* may be more relevant than some of the contemporary fiction directed to the adolescent reader, although much young adult literature is excellent and useful.

RESPONSES AND QUESTIONS   Second, the discussion should concentrate, at least at first, on the students' responses. They should be encouraged to accept those responses, whatever form they take, and move from there to a closer analysis. The talk about response is, in essence, discussion of the poem, since it is about what the student has created from the text. As the discussion proceeds, of course, we'll want to help students distinguish between what they have brought to the text and what they find in it, so that they see the difference between having feelings and inferring those of writer or character.

In general, we should try not to shape responses with our questions, not to predispose students to follow our own line of thought. The ambiguous "Well?" or "Any thoughts or feelings?"—once students become familiar with our intention to open discussion with their responses—may be sufficient to start the discussion.

ATMOSPHERE   Third, we should try to cultivate an atmosphere that is cooperative rather than competitive. Debate is an inappropriate model, since it assumes that someone is right and someone is wrong, that someone wins and someone loses. The discussions should build, one idea feeding the next, with participants gradually acquiring sharper insights, changing their minds, and adding the observations of others to their own, broadening their perspectives on the work. Students should see no merit in taking a position and holding to it stubbornly. Such intransigence is doctrinaire, authoritarian, and unsuitable in an academic environment.

Consequently, we should encourage students to make tentative statements, aware that they are not bound to them and that they may later be withdrawn or revised. We should encourage them not to wait until they are sure or until they have divined our thoughts and those of the rest of the class. To do this is to refuse an opportunity to see into themselves.

RELATIVITY   Fourth, there are no absolutes; the poem is made by each reader individually and by the class collaboratively. Nonetheless, it is possible to have foolish or incorrect readings. The reader who insists that the word *infer* means what the word *imply* means is simply, flatly, incontrovertibly wrong. The student who thinks that *widow* means *old woman* is not entitled to that unique, individual point of view—again, it is wrong. The rejection of absolutes does not mean that everything is a matter of opinion. Individuals and society continually negotiate language; it is held in common and can be shaped by the individual only within limits, beyond which it is no longer language. Respect for response in the teaching of literature is based on the idea that intelligent reflection upon one's responses leads to understanding, but that doesn't mean that unconsidered response is all. A balance is necessary. The teacher, while respecting the individuality of her students and the difficulties of seeing clearly into their minds, and deprived of the clear and absolute standards that the New Criticism attempts to offer, must gently pull students toward intelligent examination of their responses to the literature.

FORMS OF RESPONSE   Fifth, the form of student responses will vary. Interpretation will not be the only, or even necessarily the best, culmination to the discussion. It is possible, for instance, for a student to be carried by a work into a line of thought far afield from the text itself. "A View of a Pig" might stimulate a student who had recently experienced the death of a friend or relative to reflect upon that death in a way that was not tied to the text, but might nonetheless be valuable for the student. He should not, of course, confuse reflecting upon other experience with reading, and the teacher might be suspicious if a student were invariably to find some digression crucial to the health of his psyche. Still, who is to say that the sincere digression, one that is not concocted to avoid the work of close reading, is less important than the text itself? Just as we may value a song because it reminds us of a distant friend, so a literary work may serve us by bringing some non-literary experience to mind.

The purpose of this chapter has been to explore the nature of the relationship between reader and text: I've suggested that the act of reading is fairly complex, drawing in subtle and unpredictable ways on the experience and the attitude of the reader, and we have begun to establish some principles for instruction that will encourage the student to read more intelligently than she otherwise might. The next chapter will discuss in greater detail the work in the classroom.

Endnotes

1. Alberto Manguel, *A History of Reading* (New York: Viking, 1996), pp. 6–7.

2. Walter I. Slatoff, *With Respect to Readers: Dimensions of Literary Response* (Ithaca, NY: Cornell University Press, 1970, p. 23.

3. Louise M. Rosenblatt, *Literature as Exploration* (New York: Modern Language Association, 1995), p. 59.

4. Arthur N. Applebee, *Tradition and Reform in the Teaching of English: A History* (Urbana, IL: National Council of Teachers of English, 1974), p. 245.

5. Ibid., p. 246.

6. Louise M. Rosenblatt, "The Acid Test in Teaching Literature," *English Journal*, 45 (February 1956), p. 71.

7. Sandra Cisneros, "Eleven," in *Woman Hollering Creek and Other Stories* (New York: Vintage, 1992), pp. 6–9.

8. Ursula K. LeGuin, "She Unnames Them," in *The New Yorker*, January 21, 1985, (Found in *We Are the Stories We Tell*, Wendy Martin, Ed., New York: Pantheon, 1990, pp. 270–273. Rights held by LeGuin and agent, Virginia Kidd.)

9. Donald Jones. *Medical Aid and Other Poems* (Lincoln, NE: University of Nebraska Press, 1967).

10. Michael Dirda, *An Open Book: Coming of Age in the Heartland* (New York: Norton, 2003), p. 83.

11. Louise M. Rosenblatt, *The Reader, the Text, the Poem: The Transactional Theory of the Literary Work* (Carbondale, IL: Southern Illinois University Press, 1978), p. 105.

12. Slatoff, pp. 69–70.

13. J. Mitchell Morse, *Prejudice and Literature* (Philadelphia, PA: Temple University Press, 1976), p. 154.

14. Morse, p. 193

15. Bill Watterson, Calvin and Hobbes, Universal Press Syndicate.

16. Rosenblatt, *Literature as Exploration*, p. 71.

17. Ted Hughes, "A View of a Pig," in *New and Selected Poems* (New York: Harper & Row, 1960), p. 27.

3 *The Reader and Other Readers*

Y ou usually don't go to a movie alone. Not, in any case, if there's someone else around who'd like to see it, too. It's just more fun to share the popcorn and to have someone else to talk with about the movie afterwards. If it's a good movie, you'll have much to say, questions to ask, scenes to talk about; if it isn't, you'll have complaints you'll want to share with someone. You'd rather not go to a movie, watch it, and then go home, take out the trash, wash the dishes, and pay your bills. A great movie, even just a good movie—even a bad movie, for that matter—demands discussion. You need to sit down and talk about it.

Talk is called for. You don't walk out of the theater thinking, "I sure wish my old English teacher, Ms. Riley, was (or did she say it should be *were*?) here to give me one of those devious ten-question multiple-choice or true-false or fill-in-the-blank quizzes she used to give us every other day to make sure we'd done our homework, because I know I'd knock it—I paid attention; I caught every nuance, every detail; I know the plot, the characters, the cinematic techniques, the pacing, the tone, the theme, the style, everything about this movie. I'd get 100 percent, an A+. She'd be so proud of me she'd write a note home telling my parents that I was a model student and that they should raise my allowance and give me back my driver's license. She'd start drafting my letters of recommendation to Oxford and the Sorbonne." No, you don't think those thoughts. Nor, on the other hand, if it were (or was?) a confusing movie—something like *Memento*, with its recursive structure, starting and backing up, retracing its steps, going over the same events again and again—do you walk into the lobby and call out, "Is there an English teacher in the house?" hoping that one will step forward proudly and proclaim, "I am here! What is it you need dissected, vivisected, analyzed, explicated, and made crystal clear?"

No, what you do is head to the nearest coffeehouse, sit down with your friend or friends, order a drink, and talk, just talk. You compare notes, tell them what you liked, ask them about what confused you, argue about whether Bruce Willis or Anthony Hopkins might have been better in that role than Hal Foster (probably not). Good movies, and good books, want to be talked about.

But it doesn't usually happen. Not outside of the classroom, in any case. Kylene may give me a book that she loved, but by the time I've read it and get back to Houston she's moved on and read twelve other books. I pass it along to Hal, but he goes off to Akron and we don't talk until I'm deep into something Kathleen sent me so I can't remember the issues he'd like to discuss. There aren't enough people reading the same thing at the same time.

Except in English classes. There you have a rare opportunity. You have thirty kids and a book. You can talk.

Chapter 2 was about what happens when someone reads and reflects upon a literary work; it focused on the individual response to a text. Good reading, it was argued, is neither submission nor arrogance. That is to say, it is not simply a matter of absorbing the work, receiving it as one receives the comfort of a warm shower. Nor, on the other hand, is it an opportunity either to loose one's unconsidered opinions upon others or to indulge in quiet self-deception. Rather, it is a matter of responding to the text and of thinking carefully about both the response and the words on the page in order to understand both oneself and the work better. This notion of good reading recognizes limitations to any one person's knowledge and experience, and asserts that those limitations, that particular point of view, necessarily shape the understanding of the text. In this chapter we'll look at the relationships among readers.

In the discussion of the Jones poem, "As Best She Could," we examined how various readers' points of view might shape their readings of the poem and how reading the poem might in turn shape the points of view. People will read the poem differently, and if they read carefully and thoughtfully, they will be slightly different people when they finish reading. The Hughes poem "A View of a Pig" provided an illustration of the transition from response to analysis, showing how the responses of students could raise questions that compel them to look closely at the words on the page for answers. So far, the discussion has concentrated on the individual's private reading of the work, her transaction, as Louise Rosenblatt calls it, with the text.

Once students are beyond the schools' reach, their reading is likely to be not only private, but also independent and solitary, unassisted by any other readers. They probably will not search out book discussion groups or critical essays to help them think through their experiences with literature. While in school, however, they have the opportunity to invite others into the private exchange between work and self. Other readers can help tremendously by calling attention to different readings, alternatives they might not otherwise have noticed. It is with this opportunity that this chapter is concerned.

The opportunity to read in company with others is not without its drawbacks. Though the group provides a variety of insights and responses to work with, it demands tolerance of occasional digressions and ramblings; though it provides a forum for your own thoughts, it demands that you share the platform with others; though it provides feedback for those who speak, it allows a retreat into anonymity for the timid ones; and though it may provide much stimulation for thought, it may also intrude disruptively into the private meditations that are part of the personal and solitary act of reading. Individual students may find themselves lost in the crowd, with little chance to express their thoughts, or perhaps even to think them. With other subjects the problem may not be so acute, but the teaching of literature must be grounded in the students' responses to the text, so they need the opportunity to articulate those responses. The ideas and concepts in the literature classroom do not have identity and substance independent of the students; rather, they are produced by the students as they interact with the text. Unless students read and respond, there is no literature to teach—only texts and information about texts. The unresponsive student of algebra may grasp its basic principles, and the indifferent student of history may begin to comprehend the sequence and the rationale of events, but the student of literature who hides in the crowd or parrots the thinking of classmates, who learns only to paraphrase the critical judgments of scholars or to memorize peripheral information about authors' lives and historical periods, has not begun to learn the literature. Those parroted observations and memorized judgments reflect not less learning, but no learning whatsoever. They indicate that the student has failed to confront the literature and test himself against it. Insofar as the classroom permits students to avoid dealing with responses, it permits them to ignore the literature.

So the classroom may help or hurt, and the teacher's job is to manage it in such a way that it helps more than it hurts. We may begin by considering how reading in a group differs from reading alone. What differences does it make to a reader to have twenty-five or thirty other readers around, all dealing with the same text? Perhaps the most significant difference is the group's pressure on the individual student to respond to the text aloud. Reading without anyone else to talk to, a student too easily puts a work aside without articulating her thoughts, and thus without fully digesting it. Without the talking or the writing that might follow reading, the student's reaction to the work remains undefined, unspecified. George Henry describes the typical act of reading:

> We read at our own pace, finish with an inchoate lump of meaning unformed by language, and then go on to other reading or non-reading activity. Only when we try to communicate the ideas of the passage to ourselves or to others or to relate it to another work or passage do we determine what meaning is really ours. . . . In short, we must conceptualize it—join it to something. That is, we must synthesize it, which always entails bringing something of ourselves to it. The conclusion for teaching, it would seem, is that reading is inextricably tied up with both oral and written composition, with experience, with other concepts inside us, and with other reading.[1]

The group, because it consists of others whose inchoate lumps are different from mine, compels me to define my own more carefully, and thus see how I differ from those around me. Students who can be brought to sense their uniqueness can be encouraged to take interest in and explore it further. It is the group that gives one the sense of uniqueness; without others, the individual remains indistinguishable, an image without a contrasting background. The varying perspectives that may emerge in discussing a literary work with a class fill in that background for the individual, helping him to see more precisely where he himself stands; in other words, the group supplements his imagination by showing him alternatives that he might not have envisioned as he read the work. Recognizing those alternative readings assists and encourages him to clarify his own and thus to understand himself. And—equally important—the discourse about readings may enable him to come to understand his fellow students better.

This testing of oneself against others may occur infrequently. Students are likely to resist it. Followers are, after all, more numerous than leaders; buying is easier than creating. Given the opportunity, students may simply accept, and even seek, some-one else's reading. It's much easier, after all, to wait until the class star has spoken and then say "I think what she said" than it is to think something yourself. Teachers who try to encourage students to think independently, to reason out their own understanding of a text, soon come to hear in their dreams the constant refrain "But tell us what it means." The students want something they can jot down in their notes, if they take notes, with assurance that these notes will be both *right* and *important*—that is to say, that they'll be on the test. The teacher, after all, is the one with answers—the answers that count, at least, on important things like tests. Raised on a diet of multiple-choice questions, students come to view thinking as a process of choosing from among several statements, one of which is right and four of which are wrong. If occasionally intellection is complicated by a choice that reads "all (or none) of the above," they suspect that someone has been careless or lazy, allowing ambiguity to creep in and muddy the processes of thought.

Such students, given the chance, will agree with the teacher's reading. If you withhold your own interpretation, they will fall back on the second line of defense and accept the reading offered by that student whom they know to be most often right. Only when all else fails will they consider the desperate and frightening course of thinking for themselves. The pain that labor inflicts is likely to discourage them from ever attempting it again.

Finding Responsibilities

The testing of self against others isn't natural or easy. Overcoming the inertia of the group and breaking down students' resistance to the work of thinking require some ingenuity on the part of the teacher. This problem is solved in part by careful selection of works, an issue we'll discuss more fully in later chapters. If a work touches upon matters in which students have a vital interest, and if the students can read it with enough ease to be able to grasp the fundamental issues, then they may react strongly enough to the text to feel the need to speak. Yet it's also surprising how often works that seem to have little relevance to the students will nonetheless sustain a long and energetic discussion. The energy for these discussions often seems to come not so much from the work itself as from the lucky appearance of a difference in the readings of several students. It is as though the literary work has served as the catalyst for an examination of oneself and one's friends in the classroom.

Those moments are hard to predict and harder still to arrange, but the teacher who seeks them can do several things to increase their frequency. First of all, we can demonstrate that they are welcome, which we may do by inviting and accepting personal response and by encouraging attention to the statements made by students in the class. Using them simply as building blocks in an argument of our own, as steps to a predetermined reading to which we will lead the class regardless of its inclinations, tells the class that their insights and questions are valuable only insofar as they contribute to our labors. On the other hand, listening to them and dealing with them indicates that we consider them significant and worth investigating. In such an atmosphere students are more likely to make statements interesting enough to stimulate thought and discusssion.

Response Statements

Further, you can find ways to put mild pressure on students to think and to formulate their reactions to what they have read. For instance, you may deprive the students of the opportunity to seize upon someone else's reading by asking them, immediately after they have finished reading a work, to take five or ten minutes to note their first responses to it. Without dictating a form for the notes, suggest that they jot down questions, observations about the worth of the piece, memories it calls to mind, speculations about the writer, or condemnation or approval of the ideas presented. Required to verbalize in solitude, however briefly, students will be forced at least to begin to make sense of their impressions of the text. No one else will have said anything with which they can simply agree; they will have to begin, by themselves, the labor of conceptualizing. Having begun it, they may feel some commitment to develop or explore it, since it is their own.

Thus those brief notes may yield the substance of the discussion. Depending on the group, you may want to allow discussion to begin informally, when one of the short statements read aloud elicits a reaction from students, or you may prefer to use the first several minutes of discussion to select from among the statements several that you can arrange as an agenda for the session. You might ask for several students to volunteer to read or paraphrase their notes, jotting down the essence on the board to serve as a rough agenda for subsequent talk, or else collect the papers from the class and, looking through them, read out loud several that you think may be provocative, preserving the anonymity of the writer if that seems desirable.

Another alternative is to collect the five-minute responses and sort them into groups. You might tell the class, "I need about five or ten minutes to arrange these responses according to the issues or ideas they address. Please just look over the text again quietly so that I can do that" (a slightly disguised request to re-read, pleading *your* necessity, not theirs). Then sort them quickly so that you have groups of three to six, rearrange the students accordingly, and invite them to talk about their various readings. Once, feeling either bold or lazy (or both), I called for their responses, telling them that I was going to quickly sort them thematically. I took up the papers and then, poring intently over them as if studying every nuance to be sure that my grouping was carefully done, I randomly divided them into five or six stacks. Then I rearranged the class and asked each group to study the collection of responses they'd had to the text and try to figure out what it was about their brief papers that had led me to put them together in a group. Several groups successfully articulated some idea that bound them together; a few struggled fruitlessly to find a common thread. But the point, of course, was simply to get them talking.

If you're discussing these free-writes with an active, alert, outspoken group, the students might be content to listen, as the responses are read, for the ones that arouse their interest. On the other hand, if the students are too outspoken or eager, then submitting them to the discipline of working by an agenda to ensure that all of the worthy statements are considered may be more effective. A more reticent group, happy to let you read all the remarks without commenting at all, may need more than a casual invitation to comment on whatever statement appears interesting. For that group, the formality of an established agenda may be more productive.

The complexity of the work under consideration may also influence your choice of method. A work complex enough to elicit a wide range of response, touching several different themes, might be better handled in the more orderly fashion, again, to ensure that the various issues raised by the students are all given time. Regardless of the technique, you should keep in mind that the brief writing period is intended to force the students into solitary, unassisted thought about the work read and to obtain that thought from them so the group can discuss it. The justification for isolating them at first is that the students' responses will more likely be their own and that the collection of responses will be more varied and wide-ranging. Thus we need to demonstrate our respect for that variety by refraining from criticism of the statements and by managing the discussion with some discretion. If we too blatantly select statements we either like or disagree with, or those of particular students, either good or bad, it will soon become clear to the students that we are not using the statements to begin a discussion of their responses and concerns, but that the statements are simply the hooks upon which we can hang our own views.

That is not to say that we should completely avoid guiding the discussion; the excesses of the overly indulgent teacher who confuses freedom and anarchy do the student little good. There is nothing wrong, for instance, with suggesting that the class pursue certain questions before it undertakes the discussion of others. For instance, a poem might elicit the following two hypothetical responses from two students in the class:

> "I like the character in this poem. She seems to me to be a bit confused, but good-natured and kind."

> "This poem represents everything that is wrong with twentieth-century poetry. It's the worst of Dylan Thomas and Bob Dylan wrapped up in one."

The teacher would, of course, have to take the class into consideration, but if the class is typical, beginning discussion with the first response rather than the second may yield more lively talk. The first response focuses on something fairly specific—the character—and comments on it in a personal, subjective manner. The remark could easily lead to further talk about what the student, and other students, find appealing or unappealing in people, and to observations about the specifics in the poem that develop an impression of the character. The second response, on the other hand, tends toward the abstract, the formal, and the scholarly, and it makes broad statements that would be difficult for most high school groups to handle very well. What, for instance, does the speaker mean by "twentieth-century poetry"? And to what characteristics of Thomas and Dylan is she referring?

This second response, if dealt with early on, seems likely to impede the discussion. First, it will probably intimidate or annoy those students who feel uncomfortable with the vast concepts to which the speaker has so casually referred. A high school student who can easily sum up all twentieth-century poetry and test this particular poem against that summation either has an imposing intellect or is a pompous fraud. Even if such a response does not antagonize the rest of the class, it is likely to lead to vague talk that, by avoiding specifics, manages to sound impressive without saying much at all. A discussion of twentieth-century poetry presumes knowledge of twentieth-century poetry, and most students don't have the background to handle such a large and slippery concept.

The first response will draw more students into the conversation. It does not pretend to great scholarship, breadth of reading, or depth of insight; it simply comments on the person created by the poem. More students are likely to feel capable of discussing such a mundane, human issue. The talk is also more likely to lead to specifics:

Who is the character?

How is she represented to the reader?

What is the source of her confusion?

Why does she seem kind?

All of these questions direct attention to the poem, calling upon the students to refer to and draw inferences from the text.

The first response may also lead to reflection upon one's own perceptions or values: What characteristics do you consider desirable or attractive in people? What features do you share with the character in the poem? These reflections, too, might lead back to the poem: Does this character actually have those virtues you have said are desirable, and if so, how are they shown? Such discussion is concrete, being built on specific observations and inferences that can be traced to the text. It demands actual thought, not simply manipulation of phrases likely to be encouraged by too hasty an effort to discuss "twentieth-century poetry."

After the concrete discussion the first response might promote, the class may be ready to deal with the more abstract second response. Students may be reminded of other poems as they talk, and thus may recall specific examples of twentieth-century poetry to compare with the poem before them. By replacing the generalization with examples, they can retain some of the concreteness of the earlier discussion. They may even arrive at a statement about twentieth-century poetry in general. Questions may also arise about the characteristics of Dylan and Thomas, and samples of their work may be presented for examination by the group. The second response is not, in other words, a useless statement to be discreetly avoided by the teacher. But it is more difficult to deal with effectively and therefore not a good place to begin. Start with the concrete and specific, and then move on.

After discussing the first statement about the poem, the class may sense the vagueness and ambiguity in its efforts to deal with the second. They may see that the second response brings up issues they are not yet ready to handle comfortably. That student who offered the second response may be gently led to qualify it. She may be compelled to reflect on the possibility that the response was not really a response to the poem, but an effort to impress the teacher and the class with insight and knowledge she did not possess. That, however, is a judgment for the student herself to make. Although the teacher may suspect such a possibility, she should not voice her suspicions too openly for fear students will hesitate to contribute in the future. The purpose of these response statements, after all, is to initiate discussion. They are not to be treated as the products of thorough, painstaking thought, but as guesses or suggestions to be explored. If the exploration leads nowhere, nothing is lost but a little time, and the class may turn its attention to other possibilities, one of which may lead to insight.

On the other hand, our second student might really be on to something. She may not simply be trying to impress the class and the teacher, and might be encouraged to find a poem by Thomas and a song by Dylan and show us just what she means. How do these texts compare with one another? What are their similarities? How do they all represent "twentieth-century poetry"?

The teacher may assist in finding the most productive route for the discussion to take, but should not deceive the students about the nature of thought by suggesting that it is all orderly, cumulative, and successful. Students must learn, largely by experience, that some beginnings are more likely to lead to productive discussions than others, and they must also learn to tolerate uncertainties and failures. A lesson that moves logically, almost inexorably, from beginning to end may give the teacher a satisfying sense of craftsmanship, but it does not accurately reflect the process of thinking any more than a research report accurately reflects the process of scientific experimentation. The classroom should, as often as possible, demonstrate the process of thinking as well as its results.

Patterns of Discussion

Brief responses, jotted down in the five or ten minutes after reading, may serve as the basis for a variety of patterns of discussion. As we have noted, you may read them aloud, with pauses for discussion when one of them provokes a reaction; you may call on volunteers to present their statements to the class; or you may list the statements on the board and rearrange them into a formal agenda for the class session. There are other possibilities as well. For instance, the teacher may wish to pair students initially, asking them to read one another's statements and react to them. The pairing for this activity could be purposeful; you might place together two students whose views are radically different, so that under your watchful eye they could learn to listen more attentively and tactfully to opposing viewpoints. You might even prescribe that students must first find something in their partner's statement to agree with or commend, if only the neatness of the handwriting, to begin the conversation on a more pleasant, less adversarial note.

After discussing in pairs, the class might combine pairs into groups of four, and perhaps later into still larger groups. Discussion in these small groups will be easier for students to handle than discussion with the full class. The talk will be less likely to jump from one issue to another, but may instead be progressive, allowing the students to build upon and come to understand one another's ideas. After the groups have reached a certain size, perhaps four or eight, the entire class may come together again to hear the ideas the smaller groups developed.

Discussion first in pairs and then in slightly larger groups serves a purpose like that of the brief writing period following the reading. It allows ideas to germinate and grow enough so that they can't be ignored. In the full class, the ideas of the more vocal students are likely to command attention, whereas equally valuable ideas of more timid students may wither away unnoticed. If, however, those fragile thoughts grow for a few minutes in the more comfortable setting of small groups, they may root firmly enough that students will be willing to present them to the class. As the short writing period discourages students from simply waiting for someone else's ideas about the reading, so the small group discussion nurtures ideas until they can stand on their own before the full class.

The talk will wander far from the original statements, and when discussion has concluded, those first statements may again become useful. You may ask the students to look at their first notes, reflect upon them, and again write briefly:

Have their original ideas changed?

Have they seen the poem from other perspectives?

Have their first responses been confirmed?

Has anything been revealed to them about their classmates or themselves?

The original statements may serve the students as a journal might, to remind them of how they felt and what they thought. Reviewing those notes may help to show them what they have learned in the discussion. They may even grow less eager for your explanations of works and less dependent on the narcotic of grades for their sense of accomplishment.

These notes will also give you an excellent way to judge the effectiveness of discussion and the appropriateness of the literature. If the notes show that the students have been thinking and listening to others respectfully but not submissively, then they are likely to be enjoying the work. If the responses remain arid and detached, and if the notes written after discussion indicate that little or nothing has happened, then you can reconsider the material or the way you are managing the class.

One of our goals for the literature classroom is to invite students into the on-going dialogue about significant issues that is our culture. The guided discussions within the classroom should ultimately prepare them to take responsibility for themselves in all of those discussions they'll later enter without the aid of a teacher. Thus it's important to move them toward independence, gradually backing away and allowing them to take more and more control of the discussion. Consider the activity presented in Workshop #4.

DIALOG WITH A TEXT

Prepare a small booklet of prompts of questions (I'll suggest some below) that might guide the students through a conversation about a text. It's easily done by duplicating each prompt in each quadrant of a page as follows:

Dialog with a Text	Dialog with a Text
Dialog with a Text	Dialog with a Text

This way, when the sheets are copied (roughly one set for every four students in the class) and collated into sets, they can then be stapled and cut, each yielding four small booklets 5.5 inches by 4.25 inches.

Pass out whatever text you plan to use. A poem is suitable since you might be able to handle it satisfactorily within the class period, but even a short story, provided students can read it quickly (or the night before), would also work. If you're about to begin work on a longer work, perhaps a novel, then you

might select a passage that you find interesting or provocative. Then hand out the booklets, requesting that students not read through their booklet in advance, but rather take it page by page as discussion progresses. Tell them to read the text, or read it aloud to them, and then ask them to begin working their way through the booklet. Suggest that they spend a few minutes reflecting on the question or prompt, jotting down notes about it in the booklet itself, and then share their thoughts and talk as long as seems productive. If the discussion takes a path of its own, urge them to follow it, even if it strays from the text or the question. Tell them that when the talk seems to flag, they should agree as a group that they're ready to move on, and then turn to the next prompt, read it, again reflect for a few moments, and then discuss. Let them continue for what seems to you an appropriate period, and then pull the entire group back together to consider the issues that have come up in the small groups.

Here's a set of prompts for you to use or consider (obviously they would have to be modified for students according to their maturity):

Instructions

Please read the poem and take a moment or two to reflect on it. Then turn to the next page and begin. Take a few minutes—as much as you need or want—with each question. Please reflect on each question for a moment or two, perhaps jotting down brief notes, before discussing it. Some may be more productive than others for you, and you may wish to give those more time. There is no rush, no need to finish them all. Please don't glance ahead in the booklet.

- Introduce yourself to your partner(s): Where are you from, what are your interests, and so on. Ask any questions you wish.

- What feeling or emotion did the text give you? Describe it briefly and explain why you think the text caused that reaction.

- What memory does the text call to mind—of people, places, events, sights, smells, or even of something more ambiguous, perhaps feelings or attitudes?

- What did you see happening in the text? Paraphrase it, retelling the event briefly. When you discuss it, see if there are differences in the paraphrasing among discussion partners.

- Did the text give you any ideas or cause you to think about anything in particular? Explain briefly what thoughts it led you to.

- What is the most important word in the text? Explain briefly why you think the word you've picked is the most important.

- What is the most important phrase in the text? Explain briefly why you think it's so important.

- What image or picture did you see as you read the text? It might be something you remember and not something in the text. Describe it briefly.

- What sort of person do you imagine the author of this text to be?

- How did your reading of the text differ from that of your discussion partner(s)? In what ways were they similar?

- How did your understanding of the text or your feelings about it change as you talked?

- Does this text make you think of another text, song, TV show, or literary work? What is it and what connection is there between the two pieces?

- What did you observe or learn about your discussion partner(s) as your discussion has progressed?

- If you were to write a few pages, maybe a letter, about your reading of the text, who would you write to and what would you write about?

If you're trying this activity, take your time with it. The objective is not to finish first, to rush through the questions and be done with them, but rather to start conversation and see where it takes you. Remember the movie and the coffeehouse discussion afterward—you aren't hoping that the cab gets there before you finish your drink; you're hoping the snowdrifts slow it down enough so that you can have one more and make this one other point you have to make or ask this one other question you just have to ask. Students think of questions as tasks to be accomplished. They can get through twenty discussion questions of the complexity of "What is the meaning of life?" in roughly five minutes. The problem is to slow them down, to encourage them to explore, to relax, to investigate, to speculate, to consider and reconsider, to tell stories, to ask more questions, to remember, to explain, to learn a bit more about the movie or the text and the friends who spent the evening with them.

Focused Writing

You might also vary the pattern by placing constraints on the written responses. Ask students to respond to a certain aspect of the work: the motivation of a character, the influence of the setting on the mood, the nature of the conflict between two characters, the values implicit in the choices characters make, or the values and beliefs of the writer as shown in the work. Or suggest that they respond from a particular perspective. If, for instance, you want students to compare the works of two authors, one of whom the class has recently read, have them read the first work of the new writer and respond as though they were the writer they have previously studied. Such an assignment is, of course, more complicated and demanding, and you have to judge the group carefully before making it.

Further, keep in mind that any restriction on student response sacrifices something. The virtue of the free response is that it identifies the student's most vivid connection with the text. It may be a memory, an interpretation, an image, or even a digression that seems entirely unrelated, but it is the immediate consequence of the encounter of reader and text, and is thus material from which meaning might be made. Constraints on the response diminish the chances that it will be so intimate a part of the reader. The constrained response is the result of the encounter of three forces—the reader, the text, and the assignment; that third variable will interfere with the interaction of the first two. Presumably, compensation lies in stretching students to new perceptions they might have missed, or in increased efficiency in teaching some element of literary art. We may decide that it's worth the sacrifice, but we shouldn't let the assignment dominate the literature itself. If students' responses are too frequently or severely constrained, the students may come to see the literature only as a basis for prescribed exercises and may find themselves taking the pseudo-professional approach to their reading that Rosenblatt decried. The essential feature of response-based literature teaching is that it makes every effort to ensure that students discover their own routes into the literature.

Longer Response Papers

Instruction may be further varied by expanding the brief writing period. Students may be asked to write a long response, perhaps several pages, identifying and elaborating on their reactions to a work and tracing them as far back into their own history and as deeply into the text as they can. A longer response statement is, of course, more than an effort to identify starting points for discussion; it demands that students sustain their thinking alone, without the support and questioning of other students or the teacher. In a sense, it asks them to discuss the work with themselves, to reduce the dialog of the classroom to an internal monolog. More difficult than the ten-minute response, it nonetheless has the virtue of allowing students the opportunity for uninterrupted reflection, at length, on their own perceptions. They need not suspend their thoughts to consider those of their classmates, or compete for the time to voice opinions; they can follow their own thoughts wherever they lead.

As is the case with shorter writing assignments, you may constrain long response papers in some way if it seems desirable. In fact, constraint may be of more value to the students in longer papers than in the shorter response statements since it helps sustain and focus their thoughts. Responses longer than a page or two, however, may be difficult for students not yet used to the technique and aware of what to expect. The self-reliance demanded by a longer paper will quickly drain those unpracticed in pursuing their own thoughts, so it may be wise to begin with very brief writing assignments and only gradually ask for more extensive statements.

You can also assign response papers so that only limited direction is given. Richard Adler proposes a technique that he calls "answering the unanswered question." Observing that "[f]or too long we have tended to ask students questions, bypassing their questions," Adler suggests inviting students to identify the unanswered questions in a work of literature and propose answers to them. He points out:

> As readers, all of us have found gaps in stories wherein we wish the author had supplied us with more information. For example, if we read in a story that a character did something after discussing a situation with a friend, we wonder what the dialogue between them might have included, or how the two persons conducted that dialogue.[3]

The student seeking the question or questions that remain, for her, unanswered, or at least not explicitly answered, will look closely at the text and at herself. The assignment does not neglect the student or declare her to be irrelevant, but forces her to ask herself, "What is it that *I* do not understand in this work?" The question is general enough to allow the student's individuality to surface, and yet may inspire a bit more confidence and sense of direction than the instruction simply to respond.

Assignments like Adler's may help make longer response papers more palatable to the class. David Bleich, in *Readings and Feelings,* offers several more strategies for eliciting responses from students. He proposes a sequence that "begins by asking for the most important word in the work, then the most important passage, and then the most important feature, whatever it may turn out to be."[4] As one might predict, Bleich asserts that it is "immediately clear that each person has a different sense of what 'importance' means."[5]

Those different notions of importance indicate unique readings of the work. The statements made are often specific enough to discuss intelligently, and the very presence of the word "importance" seems to compel people to offer reasons. "This word is the most important because. . . ." What follows the "because" is the substance of the discussion.

You might plan one or more class sessions around Bleich's sequence. The discussion might, for instance, be divided into three sections. First, you would ask students to read the work and answer the question "What is the most important word in the text and why?" After giving them several minutes to reflect on the question and jot down brief notes, you could call on several students for their comments, and use them to begin a discussion. If the resulting talk seems energetic and productive, it can be pursued. It might be exhaustive enough that no further impetus is necessary. On the other hand, if talk begins to fade, you may revive it by means of the next question, "What is the most important passage in the text, and why?" Again, several minutes of reflection and writing might precede the discussion, which may in turn be interrupted for the third question, asking for the most important feature of the work.

The technique, like Adler's, provides a task, thus giving direction and purpose to the students' thinking, but the questions are sufficiently open to allow students their own responses. The shifts in focus, although minor, may be enough to refresh a discussion and reawaken the flow of ideas. The technique is a compromise between freedom and control, directing the students but encouraging them to look inside themselves as well.

Like the brief written response, Bleich's teaching pattern may be varied in several ways. For instance, you might vary the length of time for reflection. At one extreme, you may wish to raise the question as soon as reading is completed and encourage the students to respond with their first thoughts. The spur-of-the-moment choice of most important word might be different from the choices they would make if given a leisurely period for contemplation. That rash choice may lead them to a surprising discovery. Or students may reject their choice after they have had several minutes to think, and thus learn something about the difference between instinct and thought.

At the other extreme, you might ask students to prepare three- to five-page papers answering *one* of the three questions. These longer papers, explaining the student's choice of most important word, passage, or aspect, require the student to look at both the text and himself and examine the transaction that has taken place between the two. The assignment allows the student a fair amount of latitude. His choice may spring from his own concern with a particular issue, conceivably one of minor importance to the author, or it may be an exercise in close textual analysis, an effort to identify a key to the writer's intentions. Ideally, a student will encounter a diverse enough collection of literary works during his years in school that his papers will fall at both ends of the spectrum, some dominated by an interest in self-understanding and some by a fascination for the workings of the writer's mind. The virtue of teaching literature with attention to student responses is that it allows this latitude; the challenge for the teacher lies in the difficult judgments such teaching demands, for he must look for patterns in the students' responses and encourage them to try new things, not cling to one approach or the other.

Dealing with Longer Response Papers

Both the spontaneous, unconsidered choice and the fully developed paper can promote the exchange of ideas within the classroom. Discussion after long written response, however, may be somewhat more difficult to manage than that following brief periods of writing. Those hastier responses are fragments or kernels of thought, and are fairly easy to handle. The longer statements, on the other hand, are likely to be not fragments of ideas but full logical chains. They are more difficult to discuss because they are more complicated, because they are themselves "works," or literary essays. You might respond to them in several ways.

One way, of course, is to reply in private, either in conference or through notes returned with the papers. Both are time-consuming. Notes, because they are easily ignored, are of questionable value, although they are traditional and students may feel neglected if nothing is written on their papers. A brief note is probably a good idea, if only to reassure students that their efforts have been given a serious reading.

Too often, however, students come to view papers as exercises in avoiding errors or predicting the teacher's views, perhaps as a result of too many futile lessons on grammar and usage or too many comprehension questions in basal readers. When comments on papers consist of little more than approbation or correction, students come to see them not as part of a dialog about their writing progress, but as a final, authoritative judgment of their work. This misapprehension is reinforced by the absurdity of grading; if there is both a grade and a comment written on the paper, most students will look first, and perhaps last, at the grade. And the comments, regardless of their content or motivation, are likely to be taken as judgments or corrections.

Teachers who wish to participate with students in thinking about the literature may have to shake them loose from some of their preconceptions about the teacher's role, and that may be easier in short private conferences than in lengthy notes on the students' essays.

CONFERENCES   Conferences allow the teacher to speculate with the student, and to make remarks that in writing would require careful phrasing too time-consuming to undertake regularly. You might, for instance, think that a student's response is facile and evasive, skirting a difficult issue in the literature. To explain this might require a lengthy analysis of the student's paper, carefully worded to find the right tone. Such a comment might more easily be made orally, where your tone and bearing can demonstrate that you hope to understand, not accuse, to help the student think, not tell her what to think. In conference, you can observe the effect of your remarks on the student and can adjust and correct.

In these conferences teachers might strive for several goals. The first is a sense of shared purpose with the student, as people working together for a better understanding of the literature and of themselves. We should neither represent ourselves as absolute authority on the literature nor deny the sharpened insight that broader experience and fuller knowledge will have given us. On the other hand, students too have a rich background of experience that provides the context for their reading and shapes their response. In a conference, we have to demonstrate respect for both the perceptions of the student and the words of the text. We must convey somehow that we are not the final authority, the one who decides what the text means; meaning is created by the individual reader through the subtle process of reasoning about one's own responses to the words. The conference is a cooperative venture in which student and teacher reason together. The student contributes what he knows of himself and his responses, while the teacher contributes what she knows of the work, the process of reading, and the student. Again, as with all aspects of instruction in literature, a delicate balance is required.

A second goal for the conferences, and one that might be made explicit, is to model in miniature the kinds of exchanges hoped for in the full class. First of all, the talk is cooperative rather than competitive; the point is to understand, not to win arguments. Students should learn to suspend their own thoughts momentarily for the purpose of listening to another's. They should maintain respect for differing points of view, but also for reason, logic, and evidence. And they should consider both the reader and the text. These criteria are more easily met in discussions with two or three than in a group of thirty. If they can be modeled, even occasionally, in the smaller groups, then they are more likely to be met in the large group.

A third goal is to evaluate the student's work. The seriousness of the student's efforts to understand the literature and deal rationally with her responses to it may be more readily judged in a private conference than in the aftermath of full class sessions. Furthermore, the student herself will be involved in the evaluation. She is, after all, the only one who can know with any assurance whether she is thinking conscientiously about her reading. Others, including the teacher, are too easily fooled. The final judgments upon her work are the student's; if she is to continue to learn from her reading in the years after school, she must begin to assume responsibility for those evaluations rather than leave them in the hands of others. In private conferences the teacher may be frank, asking more penetrating questions, encouraging the student to take responsibility for self-examination.

GROUP DISCUSSION   Dealing with long written responses in groups and in the full class, although it will be made easier by conferences, remains a difficult task. Patterns similar to those used with the very brief writing periods are possible, but the work is complicated by the greater length of the papers. One alternative is to provide an outline for the discussions, divide the class into the appropriate size groups, and ask them to follow it. For instance, students may be paired and given a set of instructions like the following:

1. Read your partner's paper, taking careful notes on:
   any questions you have about his or her ideas
   any points you think need to be explained more completely
   any disagreement you have with his or her interpretation of the text
2. Discuss your notes with the author of the paper, encouraging him or her to elaborate and explain as much as he or she wishes. Keep in mind that your purpose is to help your partner to think, not to change his or her mind. If you disagree with points your partner has made, you might express those disagreements, but only to show her another perspective or another reading, not to persuade your partner to accept it. After discussing one paper, reverse roles.

3. When you have discussed both papers, add a paragraph or two of postscript to your own paper in which you record any additions, clarifications, or changes in your thinking that your conference has yielded.

Groups may need either more or less guidance than this brief outline provides. For example, they may need time limits for each step. The purpose of the outline is simply to provide security and direction for students who may not feel comfortable finding their own way through a discussion of one another's papers. Ideally, the time will come when you can discard such outlines and give students the freedom of the open request, "Discuss each other's papers." That time may not come quickly, however, and shallow, perfunctory efforts to discuss one another's works may be discouraging in the meantime.

VARIATIONS Other patterns for discussing longer responses are worth experimenting with. For example, placing students in groups of three, ask students to discuss the third student's paper. While they talk, the writer should remain silent, taking notes on the conversation. After a specified time, the writer should join the discussion to reply to points the other students made and questions they raised. In larger groups of perhaps four or five, students might read the papers written by group members; identify one major issue, question, or idea that the group seems either to share or to disagree on; and then discuss that issue. The group might then summarize its discussion for the entire class so that the class can discuss it.

Even if the students' papers are not discussed directly, they can serve as a source of ideas for discussion. We can abstract interesting issues from the papers; the students, having written them, are likely to have opinions about which issues they want to discuss. It is also possible for the papers to suggest by their neglect of an issue that it might be appropriate for the discussion. For example, if all the students have commented on the events of a story but have failed to consider the motivations of the characters, you may want to give time to that issue. That is not to say that the response statements should be ignored, but neither should they be allowed to dictate the topics treated in the classroom. Having given thought to the papers, the students may be expected to discuss more intelligently whatever arises in class, whether it is drawn directly from those papers or not.

Of course, the teacher may devote class sessions to analyzing the students' writing problems and accomplishments as well as to exploring the literature. Our concern in this chapter is promoting interactions among students, so we've concentrated on the usefulness of the response statements in stimulating thought and discussion, but they may also serve in other ways. For instance, we might display them, if that seems a desirable way to reward performance or make the students' thoughts available to one another (and if, of course, the writers are willing). Or we might compile them into a journal that we can distribute within the class, perhaps near the end of a unit, as a sampling of the students' reflections on the material. They might also serve as the basis for long papers of other kinds. If, for example, a student's response to a work speculates about the author, you might encourage the student to undertake a research paper on that writer. Or if the response suggests other possible outcomes of a story or reminisces about characters the student has either encountered or envisioned, you might be able to persuade the student to try writing fiction of her own. If the student speculates about the intentions of the author, she might work on a critical essay, binding herself to careful analysis of the text, and perhaps undertake the study of other critical statements about the work. Other possibilities will suggest themselves as the work proceeds.

At the very least, response papers will serve as a source of some insight into the students themselves. That insight might be the discouraging revelation that a student is barely comprehending, or that he is comprehending but remains unmoved by the literature, but even that may help you to reconsider your selections, teaching, or both. At best, the responses afford a privileged glance into the mind, allowing teachers to understand aspects of the student's thought and personality that might surface in no other way. Revealing or not, the response papers should indicate clearly to the students that their feelings and thoughts are important in the classroom.

These papers provide teachers with an excellent opportunity to move the writing process all the way through to publication. In recent English Methods classes, for instance, we invited responses to the Cisneros piece "Eleven." The class was asked to read and reflect briefly on the story, writing for about ten minutes to catch responses to the text, any thoughts, memories, or emotions it awakens. They then divided into small groups—about four in each—to discuss those brief essays and the issues that came up. Predictably, since the story was about a classroom incident and these were students working to become teachers, there were memories of classrooms, incidents in schools, former teachers, and the like.

We then pulled the whole class back together to see what the various groups had discussed. We talked for awhile, deciding that many of the responses had to do with memories of English classes. So I asked them to write again for several minutes using the following assignment:

> Recall an experience as a student in an English class, perhaps a very good or very bad lesson, or a particular teacher, again perhaps exceptionally good or bad, or maybe an unusual collection of students in a class or group within the class. Write briefly about it—ten or fifteen minutes—a few paragraphs to capture the rough sketch of the person or the crude outline of the event.

Again, when they finished writing we went into small groups to talk. I encouraged them to read aloud what they had written, but didn't demand it, since these were obviously going to be very rough drafts and I didn't want to embarrass anyone. Still, I wanted them to begin sharing responses and collaborating on their work, taking a few risks if they could muster the courage.

After some time in groups we came back together as a full class once again to see what had transpired, and finally, I sent them off with the assignment to expand their two short responses—the first an unmediated reaction to "Eleven" and the second their reflection on a memory of some previous English class—into something longer and more polished. The specific assignment was the following:

Take your draft and spend some time expanding it into a longer piece, polishing and revising it in the light of both the small-group and the full-group discussions. Make of this short essay whatever you want it to be. You might simply write a story or an anecdote from the classroom; you may prefer to explicitly analyze the memory, pointing out the principles of teaching that you think are revealed; or you may wish to write an essay on teaching practice. Do whatever you wish.

On subsequent days students reviewed the drafts with one another, helping to revise and polish them, and then put them together in a small booklet, printing copies for each member of the class. The computer makes that easy, enabling us to combine all the essays into one file, format everything consistently, print it out in booklet form, copy, and staple. Within a week or so we were able to move from initial response to publication.

The purposes for this activity were, of course, specific to the English Methods class. I wanted the students to begin their study of teaching with reflections on their own prior experiences, to see how individual responses to a work of literature— sometimes dramatically different—might lead to coherent and interesting discussion, to see how literature and composition instruction might be integrated, to show them that there might be some pleasure in publication, even on the small scale of the classroom, and to begin to develop some sort of community within a group of students who had come together for the first time. Your purposes will, of course, be different, but your design might be similar, moving back and forth among reading, writing, and talking.

The Teacher's Role: As Teacher and as Learner

It may seem that this emphasis on the responses of students, whether they are visceral and ill-considered or carefully reasoned, diminishes the authority and stature of the teacher. In a sense it does, for by choosing to view reading as an act of creation rather than a search for one true meaning, the teacher relinquishes the traditional authority of the pedagogue. The abdication is not complete, however, for he has to assume a different responsibility: to counsel his students through the difficult act of thinking. The attention to students' first reactions is not meant to substitute for thought, but to precede and prepare for it. As Bleich says, "feeling precedes knowledge";[6] a student must desire to know before he will undertake the labor that results in knowing. The literature teacher encourages students to feel and then to think about what they feel in hopes that the thinking will then matter and the students will give more effort to it. If this succeeds, and the students begin to discover that the literature *does* raise questions that matter to them, it might become easier to encourage and demand careful thought.

In so doing, the teacher may find herself talking about her own responses, lecturing about the work or the writer, or arguing with the students about their interpretations. But that isn't out of place in a style of teaching that emphasizes student participation. If a class begins to work well, the students may accept the teacher as a participant in the same processes of responding and thinking, able to contribute as another learner. The teacher who has achieved this stature with her class may find that she slides easily back and forth between the roles of teacher and student. At one moment she may be managing the class, assuming all the responsibility and authority that implies, and at another moment she may be seated in discussion, joining the group as an equal, shown no more and no less deference than anyone else.

Authority

A teacher who achieves that relationship with her students has a rare opportunity to influence their thinking. Having abandoned the authority of power—the threat of grades and tests—she may retain the authority of reason. Rather than present the result of her thought, she joins in the process of thinking, giving the class the opportunity both to challenge her and to observe her. In other words, the demand that the teacher respect student responses is not a demand that she ignore her own. She should refrain from imposing her perceptions on the students, but if the class has matured enough to accept her views without holding them sacred, it will be useful to present them. They may broaden the discussion, showing the class how an older person, with more experience of the world and of books, reacts to the work. The students should receive her opinions as they would receive those of a published critic—not as the final word, but as the reflections of an experienced reader. In an untrained class that expects a great deal of telling and explaining, the teacher must move cautiously, withholding her own thoughts to give the students room for theirs. But when the class comes to understand the process of responding and building on responses, and sees that differences in readings are not only expected but desired, we may state opinions with less fear that they will be taken as the final word.

In such circumstances, our responses and thoughts may even serve as models for the class—not because they are right or correct or best, but because they may demonstrate interesting lines of inquiry that the class has not discovered for itself. In one class, for instance, many students had recently watched a film entitled *Death Wish,* the story of a man whose wife and daughter are raped and beaten, one of them dying and the other left in a catatonic state, by housebreakers. The courts fail to convict the killers, and the hero decides to seek justice by setting himself up as a potential victim for the sort of spontaneous crime that took his family. Then, when assaulted, he summarily executes his attacker. He becomes a vigilante wandering the streets, apparently vulnerable to anyone looking for an easy victim.

The students, almost without exception, heartily approved. They agreed that crimes against the defenseless were inexcusable, that the courts and the police were inefficient, that punishment for violent crime was too mild, and that the efficiency and finality of the hero's method were laudable. He was, in their eyes, a modern-day Robin Hood, a little soiled by his surroundings—his city was grimier than Sherwood Forest—and by the brutality of his method, but nonetheless a hero, defending the weak against predators.

On the other hand, although I shared the students' vicarious satisfaction with the rapid and well-deserved executions of the criminals, I was not so pleased with the movie, and said so. I told the class I thought the film had exploited my natural anger at stupid and violent crimes, moving me to applaud a form of justice I really didn't condone. Leaving justice in the hands of either victims or vigilantes was likely to lead to some terrifying abuses. The hero had made no mistakes, but would all who modeled themselves on him be so lucky? Might they not shoot someone running from the scene of a crime and then discover that she was a frightened bystander rather than the criminal? Further, the crimes the hero dealt with were all clear-cut cases of violent aggression, many of which could be stopped by violence. But if vigilante justice were approved and accepted, it might be exercised in situations of less clear and obvious crime, perhaps when someone felt deceived in a business arrangement that was not quite illegal but not completely upright. In short, I worried about the film because it seemed to promote a dangerous conception of justice by playing upon natural feelings of rage and impotence and using incidents carefully conceived to support its principles.

The discussion of the film was a digression from other class work, and I wasn't attempting to lead an analytical attack on the movie. I was simply expressing an opinion, and intended to return quickly to the work at hand. The observations, however, suggested a line of thought the students had not recognized. They had been caught up in the emotional satisfaction of vicarious revenge, but a more complicated response to the film, one that involved reflecting on the implications of its notion of justice, was also possible. The students accepted these thoughts not as the voice of authority, but as an interesting alternative to their view. Some were annoyed, apparently because my reservations about the film diminished the pleasure they could take from it, and some seemed almost chastened, perhaps by the discovery that they had neglected to consider the implications of what they felt. In any event, my reflections seemed to contribute to the students' thinking about the film, even though I had presented them directly, perhaps even didactically, without making any subtle effort to raise doubts or elicit further thought.

In other words, I wasn't trying to teach in the sense that teaching is leading students in their own thinking; nonetheless the students seemed to be learning. I had for the moment been accepted as one of the class members; my opinions were neither jotted down to be returned on the next test, nor disregarded as the irrelevancies of an academic. It was a lucky happenstance, of course; both students and teacher had seen the same film and wanted to talk about it, interested in the film and in each other's responses. The incident may serve as a model of the sort of relationship between student and teacher toward which the procedures outlined in this chapter strive. When such a relationship is achieved, when students talk for the sake of the literature and themselves and not for the teacher or the grade, then the teacher may feel more comfortable joining in the discussion.

Range of Response

I have suggested several techniques for encouraging students to respond and work with their responses. It might be appropriate now to consider what kinds of responses the literature and discussions might provoke and how these will influence the course of the conversation. The range of response is, of course, infinite; each reader is unique and will react differently from day to day depending upon the circumstances. Still, the responses seem to fall into rough categories, which are useful as a crude checklist for observing what takes place in the classroom and judging how best to intervene.

PERSONAL   Some responses are comments about oneself. They may express feelings produced by the work read or describe incidents or individuals it called to mind. These responses may draw heavily upon the text, but they are more likely to depart from it or abandon it completely, as the reader explores memories awakened by the work. Although such responses may seem to offer little potential for teaching, the teacher might use them in several ways. You might simply encourage the student to follow his own thoughts and see where they lead. If the reading has generated enough enthusiasm and energy, this process may be very satisfying, even if it does not reflect the goals traditionally associated with literature instruction.

If the student is unable to elaborate on his thoughts without assistance, the teacher might suggest exploring their connection with the work. What, she may ask, are the similarities and differences between the incident you recall and that presented in the story? Or, how does the person you remember differ from the character in the play who called her to mind? Such questions provide the student with a small task that may help him to think further. The questions may be appropriately dealt with either in class or in writing; in the classroom, however, the teacher must keep in mind her obligation to the group. Other students may or may not be interested in the comparison between a story and the memory it brings to one student. The teacher might remind the class that discussion will not do justice to all possible issues and that they should make a note of questions that interest them so that they can either consider them in private, use them as topics for future papers or journal entries, raise them again later in the class session, or talk them over in private conference with the teacher or with friends. In class, it may often be necessary to move the discussion on to other matters.

Personal responses are unquestionably desirable in the literature class, but the teacher might be alert for three possible problems. One is the possibility that students will use personal digressions as a way of avoiding serious thought about the work. Responding with opinions and feelings is not the sum total of reading. Students also need to learn to analyze, to interpret, and to seek evidence for their conclusions.

The second possible problem is that the classroom may become for some students an orgy of self-expression and for others an exercise in voyeurism. There are occasional students who cannot resist the temptation to bare their souls and who are likely, when invited to respond to a literary work, to embarrass the class, the teacher, and perhaps themselves with vehement outbursts or intimate revelations. The teacher needs to defend both the class and such students themselves from that sort of behavior. That is perhaps best done by gently guiding the discussion into other paths or by encouraging others to speak, but it may also be necessary to speak privately with a student who is too outspoken, both to find out why and to recommend greater discretion or restraint in the future.

3   The third possible danger, the most subtle, is the tendency of personal comments to invite amateur psychoanalysis. Neither the class nor the teacher is qualified to analyze a student's psyche on the basis of her response to a literary work. To do so is to become badly distracted from the task at hand, which is to deal with a literary work and the responses to it. The student's *response* may be examined and analyzed, but the student should not be, except insofar as she wishes to do so herself.

TOPICAL   Some responses are *topical,* focusing on the issue raised by the literary work. A book like *Go Ask Alice* may encourage some students to talk about their own encounters with drugs or about friends who have run into difficulties like those Alice faced, but it may also elicit more general discussion of the issue of drugs or of parent-child relationships. Responses in which the issue is the most prominent concern may also digress widely from the text. In the discussion of *Go Ask Alice,* some students may bring up the hypocrisy of a generation that can devote time at a smoke-filled cocktail party to condemning marijuana, or they may lament the ineptness of the police and the courts in enforcing the drug laws. They may, in other words, have a backlog of thought on the issue that they can call forth at will, with little or no regard for the text.

The teacher's charge in that case is to direct the energy of the students to the work at hand. If students are interested in the issues raised by the text, they may be led to take an interest in the attitudes it expresses toward those issues. The teacher might encourage them to compare their opinions with those offered by characters in the story or by the author. When the responses focus on issues, the teacher is likely to have little problem getting the students to speak out—the difficulty may instead lie in persuading them to pause long enough to hear what the writer has to say.

INTERPRETIVE   The third form the response may take is *interpretive,* an effort to judge the significance of the literary work. Here the reader focuses mainly on the text, intrigued by what it says and does. Thus students may respond to *Go Ask Alice* by wondering, "Is that really what it is like to be addicted to drugs and run away from home?" They may be reminded of no similar person or incident, and may not previously have considered the larger issue of the availability of drugs, but the work may still capture them and make them want to understand it. Of course, students need not be indifferent to the subject to want to interpret. Those with strong opinions may seek both the opportunity to express them and the chance to hear someone else's views. They, too, may wish to understand, as accurately and thoroughly as possible, what the writer has said. Many of those students who responded so strongly to *Deathwish,* although they were at first satisfied with their vicarious revenge, quickly became interested in interpreting the movie, in determining the implications of acting as the hero did and the significance of the narrow range of incidents the screenwriter had selected for his story.

Skill in interpretation has been a prominent goal of most literature instruction, and although our concern with response may reduce the emphasis on this skill, interpretation remains crucially important. The responses of the reader establish a basis upon which interpretive statements may be made and judged. An interpretation is, after all, the statement of one person, and thus, although bound to the text, it is still idiosyncratic. Nonetheless, students need to distinguish between expressive and attributive statements, recognizing that a statement that attributes some characteristic to a character or a text, or infers some belief on the part of a writer, requires us to offer some evidence for its validity. When we simply express our feelings, we may assume that we are the authoritative voice on the subject, but an inference requires proof. In an expressive statement, the student is restrained only by the demands of honesty—his feelings are his own and don't need proof or defense. An attribution or inference, however, does require demonstration. Thus, when a student says, "The author means . . . ," he obligates himself to a clause beginning with "because" and containing evidence for his conclusion. Marshaling such evidence is an extremely important skill that deserves a significant place in the literature classroom.

FORMAL   A fourth possible topic for the response is *form*. Young children take great pleasure in the repetition and rhythm of nursery rhymes and other children's poems. They seem to feel no void when the meaning remains obscure or simple, as it frequently is in children's verse. Their pleasure derives from the formal elements—the sound, the rhythm, and perhaps the images evoked. Although adolescents seem less patient with works that lack a strong narrative line, they too respond to formal elements, whether consciously or not, when they read. The reader who speaks of the suspense in a mystery or the buildup of fear in a novel of the occult is noting effects created by careful manipulations of form. Interested students should be encouraged to discuss those elements and even analyze them if the question, "How did the writer accomplish this effect?" arises. Such analysis should not be overemphasized. If it is, the students may see the text as something to work on rather than an experience to live through, and reading will no longer be an aesthetic experience. Rosenblatt cautions against the tendency to:

> hurry the student away from any personal aesthetic experience, in order to satisfy the efferent purposes of categorizing the genre, paraphrasing the "objective" meaning or analyzing the techniques represented by the text.[7]

Rushed into the scientist's role, students are likely to bypass the literary experience:

> The great problem, as I see it, in many school and college literature classrooms today is that the picture—the aesthetic experience, the work—is missing, yet students are being called upon to build an analytic or critical frame for it.[8]

So the talk about form should not be purely analytical. There are, of course, works that call conscious attention to their form and almost demand that it be analyzed. Henry Reed's "Naming of Parts" (which we'll discuss later), with two voices, the drill sergeant's and the bored recruit's, sliding back and forth into one another, seems to compel the reader to look at technique. So does a work like Robert Cormier's *I Am the Cheese* (1977, Dell), a young adult novel sufficiently complex and disturbing to capture the interest of the most sophisticated adult reader. Cormier's book tells about a terrifying event in the words of a child whose mind has been disturbed by it. The story itself is intriguing, but more intriguing is the author's skillful management of form. Readers will want to examine what he has revealed, what he has concealed, and how he manages to do both. The analysis of form in such instances can be very productive and satisfying; it comes as a natural part of the reading, answering questions that the reading inspires. But when it is imposed as an exercise, rather than to answer questions raised by the text, it can supplant rather than support the aesthetic literary experience.

✭ **BROADER LITERARY CONCERNS**   Finally, the reader may address *broader literary concerns*. These include interest in biography, literary periods, the working habits of the writer, and the history of the times portrayed. Mary Renault's novels may inspire an interest in early Greece and Rome, Poe's short stories may stimulate curiosity about his unhappy life, *The Night Thoreau Spent in Jail* may lead some students to read *Walden* and perhaps Emerson's essays, the movie *One Flew over the Cuckoo's Nest* may be compared with the book, and *2001* may arouse an interest in computers and artificial intelligence. Such interests are to be encouraged; they are the lucky events of teaching. A teacher with several good bibliographies (like *Books for You* and *Your Reading*—see the end of Chapter 5) or a helpful librarian can entice a student into a great deal of independent and valuable reading when she discovers that a literary work has awakened curiosity.

Using the Catalog of Responses

This list of responses, with its five crudely drawn and overlapping forms, has proved useful for some teachers in observing class discussions. They have found it helpful to note, for instance, those classes in which one form of response predominates. Some classes make little effort to do anything but interpret the works read. Raised on comprehension and interpretation questions, they seem to have allowed their capacity for emotional response or personal involvement to atrophy. In such cases the teacher may wish to encourage a more personal interchange with the text using the techniques discussed in this chapter.

The list is more likely to be of help, however, in judging the performance of individual students. Students tend to stick with the response modes they are used to, fearing to venture into new territory, and the teacher should adjust his instruction accordingly, encouraging the patterns each student neglects. The range of responses is broad, and students are better off learning a whole scale rather than restricting themselves to one note.

Variations

One problem that may have become apparent as this chapter progressed is that many of the techniques presented here are demanding, both for teacher and students. Response papers demand concentration and careful reading, and analyzing and discussing the responses may be even more rigorous. To teach in these patterns every day, five periods a day, may well be too exhausting. You'll find that when things go well in the classroom—when students do respond enthusiastically to the text, and the discussion is active, with most participants enjoying it and learning from it— the lessons may generate energy rather than drain it. Nonetheless, there will be days when it seems desirable to plan something simpler.

Strategies will suggest themselves in the course of other lessons. If, for instance, students develop an interest in the life and times of the writer they are studying, a session or two on that topic would be appropriate. I've discouraged substituting such information for direct experience with the literary text, but if the direct experience sparks historical or biographical interest, there is no reason not to satisfy it. The teacher might either lecture herself or ask students to prepare lectures or short papers to deliver to the class. Both experiences can be valuable, retaining the focus on the literature but providing some respite from the more severe demands of response-based discussion.

Class sessions devoted simply to quiet reading may also be beneficial. They are first of all pleasant, allowing students a small island of solitude in the middle of a day filled with other voices. They may also be used, if further justification is necessary, for private conferences, conducted quietly off to one side so as to distract as little as possible. The good results of sustained-silent-reading programs, in which everyone in the school suspends other work for a certain time each day to read, provide evidence for the virtues of this simple activity.

The strategies of creative drama might also be applied in literature teaching. It may take time for the class to grow comfortable with pantomime, improvisation, and role-playing, depending on previous experience and how comfortable the students are with one another, but once used to the techniques, students may find they provide insights into the literature that are inaccessible through other approaches. Students regularly asked to read and analyze literature may become cold-blooded in their judgments, showing no empathy for the characters portrayed. Acting out a scene from the work may help these students sense the feelings of the characters more clearly than they otherwise would. For instance, pairs of students might act out the confrontation between the old woman and the social worker in "As Best She Could." One student would imagine the thoughts and emotions of the old woman. She could be asked, in that role, to think about such questions as:

How do you feel about asking for welfare?

What do you know about the welfare system?

Do the conditions of your life make you confident or pessimistic?

How do you feel about your daughters and about the social worker?

The other student could imagine herself as the social worker:

How many clients have you seen today?

How have they treated you?

Are you well paid for what you do?

Are you compassionate and eager to help, or are you tired and bored?

How often have you been deceived by welfare clients?

Then the students could play out the scene.

After the improvisation they would be asked what they felt and thought as they acted out the scene. Many students report feeling emotions they had not anticipated, or feeling expected emotions more strongly than they had anticipated. The social worker, for instance, may report real anger toward the client. Simulating the experience produces some of the emotions and insights the actual experience might have yielded, giving students a perspective they couldn't attain through the more intellectual and distant process of analysis. It is one thing to say, "Well, she might be angry at having to deal with someone without the necessary forms who seems to want all the rules bent just for her," and quite another to shout, "*I* was furious!"

Students may also find through improvisation that things need not have worked out as the author arranged them. The student playing the old woman may grow so angry with the social worker that instead of walking away, she erupts in an angry tirade. Or the social worker may sympathize with the old woman and decide to bend the rules for her. If improvisations vary from the text, so much the better, for this demonstrates that the poem is the result of the author's choices, and that other choices could have been made, revealing different values and ideas and resulting in different poems. Just as varying response statements yield discussion by showing alternative readings of a poem, so might varying improvisations reveal the alternatives from which the writer has selected.

The premise of the first chapter was that students should be encouraged to experience the literary work, allowing it to stimulate images, feelings, associations, and thoughts, so that reading might be personally significant. The premise of this chapter has been that discussion will yield insight into varied readings and perspectives, and will both deepen the capacity to respond to literature and sharpen the powers of analysis. Toward that end, students should be encouraged to speak with one another about their readings and analyze them together. Chapter 4 will introduce the third element—other texts—and attempt to show how a collection of literary works can be compiled and taught so as to further broaden response and sharpen analysis.

Endnotes

1. George Henry, *Teaching Reading as Concept Development: Emphasis on Affective Thinking* (Newark, DE: International Reading Association, 1974), p. 17.

2. Robert E. Probst, "Dialogue with a Text," *The English Journal*, Vol. 78, No.1 (January, 1988), 32–38.

3. Richard Adler, "Answering the Unanswered Question," in *Re-Vision: Classroom Practices in Teaching English, 1974–1975*, Allen Berger and Blanche Hope Smith, Eds. (Urbana, IL: National Council of Teachers of English, 1974), pp. 74–75.

4. David Bleich, *Readings and Feelings: An Introduction to Subjective Criticism* (Urbana, IL: National Council of Teachers of English, 1975), p. 50.

5. Ibid.

6. Ibid., p. 3.

7. Louise M. Rosenblatt, "What Facts Does This Poem Teach You?" *Language Arts*, Vol. 57, No. 4 (April 1980), pp. 391–392.

8. Ibid., pp. 393–394.

4

The Text and Other Texts

W e approach books with preconceptions, memories, biases, beliefs, and attitudes; if we read well and have been lucky enough to find a book with substance, we encounter other conceptions, beliefs, and attitudes. While we read, we think, looking for new perceptions, or perhaps for the similar, the old, the usual, made more noticeable by the text. We may begin to reshape our thoughts, finding some confirmed, some refuted, and some modified. We change as we read, perhaps in subtle ways, finishing the book slightly different from what we were before.

We then talk about our reading, bringing with us perceptions of ourselves, the book, and the world, and finding in others still different perceptions and attitudes. Again, if we are intelligent and lucky, the confrontation allows us to grow and learn by reshaping our thoughts. Similarly, we may read other books and find further variations in thoughts and attitudes that may lead us to still another reconsideration, helping us to understand not only ourselves and others but the first text as well. In the interchange between reader and work, some would argue that the text should predominate. They would expect us to be accurate and thorough in our reading, to do justice to the text. We are, in a sense, expected to submit to it and be guided by it. This notion of literature and of the reader's experience is expressed by Rene Wellek and Austin Warren:

> [T]he real poem must be conceived as a structure of norms, realized only partially in the actual experience of its readers. Every single experience (reading, reciting, and so forth) is only an attempt—more or less successful and complete—to grasp this set of norms or standards.[1]

Somewhere in the text lies meaning, pure and clean, waiting to be grasped by the perfect reader. There is, of course, no perfect reader, but he is approximated by the preeminent critic, whose reading becomes the norm. We read well insofar as we approach his reading, poorly when we depart from it, and thus our individual points of view are sources only of confusion. The accuracy of our reading depends on our ability to suppress or ignore our unique experiences and perceptions.

In this view, the students' readings are inevitably imperfect, and the teacher's goal is to help them move toward the approved interpretation. To achieve that perfect reading, unblemished by the subjectivity of the individual, the teacher naturally encourages, with each new work, a concentration upon that text, and that narrowed focus may isolate the work. Each time, the perfect reading of the single text, always beyond reach, is the goal. Since the students can never read one work adequately, what point is there, one may argue, in trying to comprehend groups of works?

The conception of reading I'm arguing for in this book is different. As the first chapters state, I see the reader not as submissive, bending to the author's will, but as creative, making meaning rather than finding it. Thus the text is not the only element that matters. The reader's task is to build meaning out of the confrontation of past and present experience, and each work read should be seen as part of this process: not only a valuable experience in itself, but a contribution to something larger.

What that something larger is depends primarily upon the students themselves. It may involve the refinement of a particular concept. Students who read and reflect upon "A View of a Pig" may find their notion of death changed slightly as a result. They may find it easier to accept their own detachment about the deaths they hear of, concluding that some distance is necessary, as it was for the speaker in the poem. Or they may find themselves thinking more frequently and painfully about the disasters of others. If the poem affects them at all, it is likely to contribute in some degree to a reshaping of their views.

In broader terms, literature contributes to shaping who they are. As students' ideas shift and their experience broadens, they themselves evolve and change. Literary works contribute significantly to this evolution. The literature class should help the students make connections between the books and their experience, continually revising their conception of the world and their place in it.

This view of both the reader and the process of reading suggests a more aggressive, self-affirming approach to the text. Rather than submit to the work, seeking only to find its "structure of norms," the reader instead forces the work to submit to her. That is to say, she uses it, incorporating it into herself. She tests its perceptions against her own, not to bend to the vision it offers, but rather to take what she can from that vision in clarifying or enlarging her own. She approaches the text not as a disciple looking for answers, but as a thinker looking for possibilities. The individual work, then, is not an end in itself, but part of an ongoing process of building one's own picture of the world, a process that involves many books and many other experiences.

Unfortunately, too few people continue to revise their notions about the world. We grow rigid. Our tendency to remain with the political party of our parents, to continue in the religions imposed upon us as children, and to retain our prejudices despite evidence that might accumulate against them suggests a willingness to settle comfortably into patterns of thoughts and behavior. Albert Ellis points out that man achieves so-called free will almost in direct inverse ratio to his becoming a socialized human being. The mere fact that one has, and early in one's life is raised by, duly conditioned and biased parents reduces one's possible free will to [a] meag[er] amount; the fact that one, additionally, is raised among hundreds of other human beings, and among humans who have a long history and an intrenched culture, further reduces one's potential free will to near-zero proportions.[2]

Culturally established norms become so deeply ingrained in consciousness that they come to seem as substantial and immutable as the laws governing the physical universe.

The creative and thoughtful person tries to assimilate and comprehend his culture without being trapped by it so completely that he can no longer see in other ways. He reflects and questions, attempting to see through to his assumptions and reconsider them, to absorb new information and insight even when it contradicts the notions he holds at the moment, and to modify his conceptions to accommodate the new experience. He is, in other words, unwilling to grow too complacent with the way he sees the world at the moment—it's the best he can do now, but he is unwilling to presume himself infallible, knowing that he might, sometime in the future, see more clearly and understand more completely.

He is also unwilling to presume that anyone else can have perfect and complete understanding. As a result, he is less likely to labor endlessly in pursuit of the one perfect reading that some would assume lies beneath the surface of the literary work. A critic's reading will matter, then, not as a norm or standard for his own, but as another perspective to consider. Likewise, the author's vision of the world may be important to the thinking reader, but again not simply as an end in itself. It matters insofar as it contributes to his pleasure and understanding—that is to say, to his own vision. He himself, rather than the author, is of primary importance in his reading. He reads not to satisfy an obligation to the writer, but to satisfy an obligation to himself.

Good readers revise their perceptions on their own. They are questioners, researchers; unwilling to be led by one source, they weigh one item against another, comparing, balancing, and seeking their own formulations. For such readers, the concept of power in *Macbeth* may be fascinating and worthy of contemplation, but it is not complete. Their own concept of power will be a thoughtful distillation of power as seen in *Macbeth,* in *All the King's Men,* and in their encounters with teachers, police, employers, and others who hold some form of power. They will agree with Newton that we see further than our predecessors by standing on their shoulders, neither rejecting them casually nor accepting them uncritically. For such readers, the text is not more important than the self. They don't submit to the authority of the printed word—not, at least, until they have thought about it long enough to decide that its ideas are their own. Unwilling to be indoctrinated, they prefer to reflect; they seek the insights of others not as answers to their questions but as the raw material from which to construct their own answers.

The comparison between literature and research may seem strange. Researchers start with a problem or question and look for information and ideas to help them solve it, but the reading of fiction and poetry is not quite so purposeful. Usually people pick up a novel not to help with a specific problem but to pass the time, to entertain themselves, to relax after the worries of the day. Researchers are more organized and methodical, selecting the materials they find most useful and studying them in an efficient pattern, but readers of literature, unless they are professional literary scholars, are likely to select their reading somewhat more haphazardly. They may know that they prefer mysteries, or romances, or stories by a particular writer. Or they may know only that they like books recommended by a certain friend. Those preferences will impose a casual organization on their reading, but few readers are likely to plan more thoroughly.

Still, there are some similarities between ordinary reading and scholarly research. Both scholars and readers formulate ideas based on the material they have read. Both research and reading lead to the same sort of cumulative product: a vision created by words. Our cultural vision itself, with its infinite personal variations, is essentially a creation, pieced together over centuries of reflecting, observing, reading, and talking. Part of the experience that yields such visions, a greater or lesser part depending on the individual, is reading. We may imagine an intelligent reader engrossed in a story of political intrigue, wondering if people really do behave that way, pausing occasionally to compare the characters with those of other works on a political theme, perhaps again *Macbeth* or *Advise and Consent,* or reflecting on what she learned from the Iran-Contra scandal or from all of the reports of corruption and deceit concerning the war on Iraq. If she makes such connections between previous experience and the current experience of the story, the thought stimulated will have contributed in some way to her vision of the world. Not research, exactly, but similar in the kind of thinking involved.

Sometimes the effect of the text is subtle, barely observable, but other times it may be dramatic and obvious. In a small school on the outskirts of San Juan, Costa Rica, several years ago, about the time Kosovo was coming apart at the seams, I was with a teacher and his class of eleventh-graders when the conversation turned for some unremembered reason to the news. A student had, I believe, brought in an account from the newspaper or one of the news magazines and had some questions about what was going on over there. We talked about it for awhile, reasonably and calmly, and as we were about to put the issue to rest and move on to the day's tasks someone mentioned the *Diary of Anne Frank* and suddenly the tone of the conversation changed.

They'd read the book the previous year, or perhaps earlier, and something in the conversation called it to mind. As they talked they noted some of the obvious similarities between the present suffering in Kosova and the sad history of Europe in the 1930s and '40s. Voices became somewhat more muted and faces more serious. It was as if they were no longer talking about distant events, but about real people, individuals, children like themselves, parents like their parents. Anne Frank seemed to put a face on the horrors for them, transforming what had been mere stick figures marching across an alien landscape in a distant country on a CNN newsclip into real, live, suffering people. The remembered book reshaped their reading of the day's news.

And, presumably, though we didn't discuss it, the news must have reshaped their understanding of the *Diary*. At the very least, it must have transformed it from a historical document to something current and contemporary. They must have realized that we haven't left the misery of Nazi Germany behind us. It was an interesting moment in the classroom, attesting to the power of texts to interact with one another and to bind us together in powerful ways. The *Diary*, at the moment, called to mind by a short news article, had brought together into one community the Jews suffering in northern Europe some sixty years ago, the disenfranchised and powerless people on both sides of the dispute suffering at that moment in Kosovo, and this small group of students in a rural school in Central America—a community that spanned six or seven decades and thousands of miles.

These were sharp kids with a good teacher, patient enough to allow the at first rambling conversation about current events and alert enough to see the possibilities when someone mentioned the *Diary*. But what of less skillful or intelligent readers? Not quite so alert to the pleasures of reflecting and to the links among texts, they will probably find the *Diary*, or *Macbeth*, or whatever story they happen to be reading less rewarding. They may read uncritically, as if a novel were a factual report from a trustworthy source, or they may be surprised by some unexpected event and reject the entire work as unrealistic. But they are less likely to make a conscious effort to assimilate it, to fit it into their own scheme of things. Unaware that reality is less a concrete world of things and events than a *conception* of those things and events, they are not likely to be interested in the prospect of reshaping their ideas. They may not realize that it can be done, and must be done, if they are to remain intellectually alive. Instead, a work may lie undigested in their minds, unconnected with anything else in their experience, read but unread, touching them momentarily if at all.

Such readers as these—and we may assume that many readers in the secondary school classroom will be of this sort—require some help in seeing the possibilities in their reading. If they are ever to approximate the behavior of thinking readers who seek connections between the text before them and other works, they must be helped to see those connections. Their reading must be organized for them, at least in part, to show how one work may affect the reading of another and to provide a variety of points of view. If works are selected in this way and students are encouraged to test the works against one another, they may come to expect and seek out lines of thought that bind single texts together into a cultural fabric.

Pairing Texts

Selecting works to be paired, and then to be joined together in still larger groups, requires compromise. If the teacher chooses as haphazardly and casually as the typical reader might choose his books, she may have to struggle to find connections between them. On the other hand, choosing works that fit together, either because they deal with similar situations or because they reveal similar or contrasting attitudes, is likely to predispose the teacher toward a certain line of inquiry. For instance, she may choose two works that seem to her to deal with the issue of responsibility. Perhaps, however, the students see in the first work reflections on the idea of freedom and autonomy and have little if anything to say about the notion of responsibility. How, then, does the teacher make the connection between the two works? If she is committed to pursuing the responses of the students, she will discuss the notion of freedom with them. She may then have trouble finding a link between that first work and the second. If she forces the discussion to the issue of responsibility, regardless of the students' concerns, she may be able to make the connection, but it will be with *her* reading of the work, not with theirs.

And so she compromises. She must predict possible student reactions to the works, and choose texts that seem related in some way. But she must also remain flexible and responsive to the group, taking care not to neglect their responses in trying to direct the talk down the paths she has mapped.

Consider the possibilities in two simple poems, suitable for a middle school class. The first, Henry Wadsworth Longfellow's "The Children's Hour," may lead to discussion about the relations between parent and child:

The Children's Hour[3]

Between the dark and the daylight,
    When the night is beginning to lower,
Comes a pause in the day's occupations,
    That is known as the Children's Hour.

I hear in the chamber above me
    The patter of little feet,
The sound of a door that is opened,
    And voices soft and sweet.

From my study I see in the lamplight,
    Descending the broad hall stair,
Grave Alice, and laughing Allegra,
    And Edith with golden hair.

A whisper, and then a silence:
    Yet I know by their merry eyes
They are plotting and planning together
    To take me by surprise.

A sudden rush from the stairway,
    A sudden raid from the hall!
By three doors left unguarded
    They enter my castle wall!

They climb up into my turret
    O'er the arms and back of my chair;
If I try to escape, they surround me;
    They seem to be everywhere.

They almost devour me with kisses,
    Their arms about me entwine,
Till I think of the Bishop of Bingen
    In his Mouse-Tower on the Rhine!

Do you think, O blue-eyed banditti,
    Because you have scaled the wall,
Such an old mustache as I am
    Is not a match for you all!

I have you fast in my fortress,
    And will not let you depart,
But put you down into the dungeon
    In the round-tower of my heart.

And there will I keep you forever,
    Yes, forever and a day,
Till the walls shall crumble to ruin,
    And moulder in dust away!

                —Henry Wadsworth Longfellow

The homey, comfortable picture may strike some students as archaic and funny, and the comparison between the rush of the three little girls and the assault of bandits on a castle may seem forced and unnatural. But students may also have a stronger reaction, a hostile reaction, to the father's possessiveness, especially if they themselves are at a stage where they want more freedom than their parents are willing to allow them. Students may feel that they should not be considered possessions to be locked up in the roundtower, but should be turned loose to make their own decisions. The attitude they may see in the father is that of the parent who owns, and therefore controls, his child. He is kindly, but superior, nonetheless; he presumes to see and understand what the children cannot:

Do you think, O blue-eyed banditti,
Because you have scaled the wall,
Such an old mustache as I am
Is not a match for you all!

I am more than a match for you, he asserts, though you don't see it. He claims further to be their captor:

I have you fast in my fortress,
And will not let you depart.

The tone is good-natured and light, but the imagery is that of prisons, prisoners and captors, and the relationship between the powerful and the weak. The students, identifying with the children in the poem, may resent their captivity, despite the affection the lines clearly display. If they are chafing under the restrictions of parents, loving or otherwise, they may well be annoyed by Longfellow's portrayal of the children as pleasant, simple baubles, owned by their father.

Thus, in discussing the poem, the class may want to talk first about the relationship between parent and child, focusing on associations called to mind by the reading rather than on the text itself. The students may want to tell about times in their own lives when their desire for independence conflicted with their parents' wish for control. Although the poem is written from the point of view of the father, it may not lead the students to adopt that view, and may in fact bring into sharper focus their own struggle for independence.

The second poem in this pair offers another angle on the issue. Kahlil Gibran's "On Children," from *The Prophet,* begins with a mother asking a question of the prophet:

On Children[4]

And a woman who held a babe against her bosom said, speak to us of children.
And he said:
Your children are not your children.
They are the sons and daughters of Life's longing for itself.
They come through you but not from you,
And though they are with you yet they belong not to you.
You may give them your love but not your thoughts,
You may house their bodies but not their souls,
For their souls dwell in the house of tomorrow, which you cannot visit, not even in your dreams.
You may strive to be like them, but seek not to make them like you
For life goes not backward nor tarries with yesterday.
You are the bows from which your children as living arrows are sent forth.
The archer sees the mark upon the path of the infinite, and He bends you with His might that His arrows may go swift and far.
Let your bending in the archer's hand be for gladness;
For even as He loves the arrow that flies, so He loves also the bow that is stable.

—Kahlil Gibran

Although the speaker is not a child, the poem represents the child's viewpoint in some ways. Most interesting, perhaps, is that it puts the parent in the child's position. The mother is being instructed by the prophet just as children are often instructed by their parents. She is not the authority, the figure of power, the source of guidance or rules; instead, she is submitting to the wisdom of someone else. In "The Children's Hour" the adult knows all that he needs to know; here, the adult is asking for guidance.

"On Children" invites a more sympathetic view of the parent. Portraying the mother as the questioner, and suggesting, through the prophet's advice, some of her doubts and unhappiness, Gibran invites the reader to understand the dilemma of the parent. She naturally feels possessive toward her children, but she must allow them their own thoughts and lives. They will live in the future, which is beyond her reach, and she must accept this, even though it is painful to let them go.

So the two poems present different views of parents, inviting the students to modify their own notions about that role in life. The first poem may encourage talk about the domination of parents, about their unwillingness to undo the bonds and recognize their children as individuals with their own thoughts and feelings. The second, the Gibran poem, may suggest that this domination and control could arise from worthy motives—love, the desire to protect, or perhaps the wish to preserve a relationship to which the parents have given much time and energy. It suggests also, of course, that the child must ultimately be released. The two poems, by providing two perspectives, should lead students to clarify their own views, and may help them put their own thoughts into words.

One student proposed that parents can both hold and free their children. They free them by allowing them to grow, releasing them as the archer releases the arrow, and at the same time they hold them by capturing them in memory, as the man in the Longfellow poem did. That student saw no conflict between the two poems; they offered, he thought, complementary visions of the parent-child relationship. This interpretation raises an important point. The poems are not chosen to represent a "right" and a "wrong" view, although of course individual readers may see them in that light. The goal is not that the students adopt one perspective or the other, but that they use both to clarify their own ideas. The teacher would not want to convince his students that all parents try to control their children because they love them—numerous cases of child abuse suggest that other factors may be involved. Similarly, students should not be encouraged to believe that only by freeing children completely can a parent demonstrate love. Students should not be catechized; they should be invited to reflect and judge for themselves.

The poems may help them do that reflecting and judging, but the ultimate responsibility is theirs. They must assimilate the poems into their own experience with their parents, using them to derive and articulate their own notions about parents and children, rather than simply accept the visions offered by Longfellow or Gibran.

Teachers will naturally find it hard to keep from expressing their judgments about the comparative worth of two works. One story may seem profound, the other trivial, one character realistic and the other stereotypic, one poem lyrical and the other clumsy, one essay moral and intelligent and the other unethical and stupid. It will seem negligent to allow students to persist in unenlightened readings when it would be so easy to inform and direct them. In the ideal class, one that accepted the teacher as another reader, she would feel comfortable participating fully, expressing her opinions, arguing her points, and passing her judgment on the works. In classes less than ideal, however, a teacher who is free with her opinions may encourage students to depend on her for "right" answers, lazily waiting for her to explain. Students will come to see the literary work not as an experience to think about but as a puzzle to be solved by someone who knows more than they do. When that happens, they are not learning to read literature, but to follow blindly and unthinkingly.

Thus our decision about how much to say will be a compromise. On the one hand, our job is to teach—to help students think and reason—and that helping calls upon our strongest resources. If we think one essay is well-reasoned and another is foolish, then in teaching our students to read critically we'll try to help them see the reason in one and the foolishness in the other. On the other hand, we must not encourage dependence, and must be alert for legitimate but unexpected readings that reflect a perspective different from our own. The uniqueness of each student must be recognized, and the demands of logic and reason must also be admitted, though sometimes the two create an awkward conflict for the teacher.

Neither the Longfellow nor the Gibran poem is especially difficult. Perhaps neither is a great poem. Still, because they treat similar subjects from different points of view, each can stimulate thought and help the reader clarify his attitudes about parent-child relationships. That clarification might take the form of agreement with the stance of one poet or the other, reconciliation of the two poems, or rejection of both in favor of some other view.

We've discussed the two poems to demonstrate how they might illuminate each other and contribute to the reader's thinking. The lines of thought that connect the two poems might clearly be extended to other works. Let's consider a few possibilities to show that the teaching of literature can be organic, evolving in response to both texts and students.

Routes Through the Literature

After reading the Longfellow and Gibran poems, the class might become interested in particular aspects of the discussion. One student might like to read more of Longfellow's poetry (though Longfellow isn't very popular these days); another might want to read and talk further about parent-child relations. Some students' readings might take them outside the realm of literature into psychological or sociological works. They may want to read about the increase in adolescent suicide and speculate about its connection with the rising divorce rate or about the evolution of the family as a basic social unit. Others, thinking about their own family experiences, may be stimulated to try producing literary works of their own—a short play, perhaps, with an autobiographical basis. The teacher might encourage all of those students to pursue their interests, allowing time in class for some of the work. If she is fortunate, the interests will fall into groups, making it simpler to organize the students and evaluate their work.

Perhaps a large enough group of students to justify including the entire class will express an interest in Gibran, or more specifically in *The Prophet,* the text from which the Gibran poem is taken. A brief explanation of the format of the book— a wise man being questioned about roughly twenty-five issues—might awaken curiosity about the ideas expressed. The teacher could read aloud the table of contents, stopping when students seem interested, or identify some promising sections and prepare them for distribution the next day. Several might provoke curiosity: "On Love," "On Work," "On Joy and Sorrow," "On Good and Evil," and "On Death" are good choices.

Let's assume that students want to read Gibran's brief essay "On Love." Since they have recently read his "On Children," we might ask the students to speculate about "On Love" before they read it. What might Gibran have to say about love? This question requires students to make a bridge from the preceding poem to this one, not from the theme, as they did with the Longfellow and the first Gibran poem, but from inferences about the author. The poem "On Children," now part of their background, is used to prepare them for "On Love." What would the man who wrote "On Children" have to say about love?

It may be objected that raising preliminary questions confines the students' responses and channels their thoughts. Clearly it does not leave them as free as would simply placing the poem before them. On the other hand, readers come to literary works in various ways—they stumble on some, have others recommended by friends, see films made from still others, read reviews of new books, or have them assigned in classes—and the source, whatever it is, will likely have an influence, however subtle, on the reading. Students need to be aware of that influence and learn to use it. Coming to a text without premeditation can be valuable, but so can coming to it with expectations and predictions in mind, as long as those expectations do not prevent one from seeing the text itself. In this situation, moving from one Gibran poem to the next, the students have simply been asked to form their own ideas. They have not been offered a judgment of the poem to agree with, nor have they been forced to deal with issues in which they have no interest. Rather, the teacher has responded to their curiosity about Gibran and has posed questions that any good reader might ask in approaching the second poem. All teaching requires compromise.

After speculating about the poem aloud or on paper, the students would read it:

On Love[5]

Then said Almitra, Speak to us of Love.
　　And he raised his head and looked upon the people, and there fell a stillness upon them. And with a great voice he said:
　　　When love beckons to you, follow him,
　　　Though his ways are hard and steep.
　　　And when his wings enfold you yield to him,
　　　Though the sword hidden among his pinions may wound you.
　　　And when he speaks to you believe in him,
　　　Though his voice may shatter your dreams as the north wind lays waste the garden.
　　　For even as love crowns you so shall he crucify you. Even as he is for your growth so is he for your pruning.
　　　Even as he ascends to your height and caresses your tenderest branches that quiver in the sun,
　　　So shall he descend to your roots and shake them in their clinging to the earth.

Like sheaves of corn he gathers you unto himself. He threshes you to make you naked.

He sifts you to free you from your husks. He grinds you to whiteness.

He kneads you until you are pliant;

And then he assigns you to his sacred fire, that you may become sacred bread for God's sacred feast.

All these things shall love do unto you that you may know the secrets of your heart and in that knowledge become a fragment of Life's heart.

But if in your fear you would seek only love's peace and love's pleasure,

Then it is better for you that you cover your nakedness and pass out of love's threshing-floor,

Into the seasonless world where you shall laugh, but not all of your laughter, and weep, but not all of your tears.

Love gives naught but itself and takes naught but from itself. Love possesses not nor would it be possessed; For love is sufficient unto love.

When you love you should not say, "God is in my heart," but rather, "I am in the heart of God."

And think not you can direct the course of love, for love, if it finds you worthy, directs your course.

Love has no other desire but to fulfill itself.

But if you love and must needs have desires, let these be your desires:

To melt and be like a running brook that sings its melody to the night.

To know the pain of too much tenderness.

To be wounded by your own understanding of love; And to bleed willingly and joyfully.

To wake at dawn with a winged heart and give thanks for another day of loving;

To rest at the noon hour and meditate love's ecstasy; To return home at eventide with gratitude;

And then to sleep with a prayer for the beloved in your heart and a song of praise upon your lips.

—Kahlil Gibran

You might ask the students to discuss their responses to the poem, the accuracy of their predictions, the correspondences they find between "On Love" and "On Children," and their judgments of Gibran's notion of love. Do they agree, for instance, that love is something to submit to? Does it give both pleasure and pain? Do you have to expect both, or can the pain be avoided? Is the pain in the failure of love rather than in love itself? Gibran portrays love as a force, almost a being, external to humans. Is that view helpful, or is love better seen as something that humans develop and cultivate rather than as something outside ourselves to which we submit? Such questions as these, selected and worded to fit the class, might provide a transition from the poems read earlier and help the students to investigate this one.

Where to from here? Perhaps to other selections from *The Prophet,* if the class is so inclined; perhaps to other poems, stories, or plays about love; perhaps even to nonfiction. James A. Gould and John J. Iorio's *Love, Sex, and Identity* contains, along with imaginative literature on the topic, a collection of essays on love. The first, by Albert Ellis, argues that our culture's notion of romantic love, which he describes in terms somewhat similar to those in the Gibran poem, is inadequate and even dangerous. Ellis suggests that by thinking of love as something we submit to, rather than something we build and cultivate, we become less able to control our lives.[6] In a class sophisticated enough to handle it, such an essay might expand the discussion, providing a viewpoint that contrasts with Gibran's and thus invites thought. Confronted with one idea, it is easy to shrug and submit. If it is well-expressed and seems reasonable, we tend to accept it rather than undertake the hard work of thinking about it ourselves. But confronted with two different ideas, we have to choose— or, in the process of deciding, create instead a third idea more palatable than either of the first two.

The routes through the literature may develop naturally; that is, you might watch carefully as the students discuss works to see what concepts, writers, and genres seem to capture their imagination, and then follow the leads you find. Or you can gently manage the routes, keeping in mind the need to respect students' responses. Few teachers will have the luxury of teaching a literature course without some sort of syllabus. They may have some freedom of choice, but they will usually have to teach certain specified works. Composition teachers may find themselves in a better position for teaching literature. Since their task is to teach writing, they can select literature to support the composition work—literature that offers ideas the students wish to write about. With no obligation to cover the Romantic poets or twentieth-century American playwrights, or whatever, teachers can select works to which their students will respond, so they may find themselves teaching, along with the composition, a very interesting literature course.

Teachers in an established literature curriculum, however, have less freedom, and their transitions from one work to the next may not be quite as smooth. Let us suppose, for instance, that the teacher who presented "The Children's Hour" and "On Children" to his class was beginning a unit on "The Family," a topic that might conceivably appear at some point in a middle or high school English program. The digression to Gibran's "On Love," although it focuses on romantic love, might provide a path back into the prescribed content, even to such an unusual story as Gina Berriault's "The Stone Boy." In this story, one of the questions that might be raised is, "How does one behave if one loves another person?" The young boy, who accidentally shoots and kills his brother, is outwardly unemotional. Shocked almost into immobility, he acts as though untouched by the accident, and his inability to show grief or remorse angers and frightens those around him.

There may be few obvious connections between "On Love" and "The Stone Boy," but the larger context established by the two poems on children might enable students to explore not only the ties between parent and child or between man and woman, but also between brothers or friends. The teacher might ask the class whether siblings typically feel love for one another. Is love the appropriate term? Is it too broad, applied to too many different sorts of relationships? Does love motivate predictable behavior; that is, can we observe someone's behavior and confidently say that it does or does not indicate love? Questions like these might lead the class relatively smoothly into "The Stone Boy."

Of course, the teacher also has the option of not making a transition. She may prefer simply to begin the new work, allowing the students to respond to it without the channeling that comes from transitional questions. Each method has its virtues and its defects. When a transition is made, students are more likely to see a direction in the work and feel that they are making progress. On the other hand, the transition limits responses. In the example of "The Stone Boy," the questions raised may predispose the class to think of the story as a statement about love. When transitions are not made, new lines of discussion may open up. But the students may also feel that their work is fragmented, jumping at random from one thing to another. Perhaps the best answer is first to discuss one work, then leave it to deal as openly as possible with another, then recall the first work and compare it with the second. Thus the students have the benefit of undirected response to each of the works as well as the intellectual challenge of bringing the two together.

Thematic Teaching

Clearly, we are moving toward larger collections of related works. Whether they are all by the same author, from the same period, on the same theme, or in the same genre, a relationship can be developed among them, and out of that relationship may come a sharpened understanding of literature or life. Works carefully selected for their diverse points of view can lead to sustained thinking about a topic.

As we have seen, though, arranging works into related groups can narrow the possibilities of response. George Henry, whose book *Teaching Reading as Concept Development* is the most thorough explanation of the rationale and procedures for teaching groups of literary works, discusses this problem:

> Some reading texts prefabricate the structure and lead the pupil through it by the hand, so to speak, still calling it discovery and invention. But the teacher using such texts has taken the relations and the structure from the text or its workbook. There is little discovery or invention for the pupil in such a case or when the relations and structures are relayed from a borrowed unit or perhaps a set of questions from an anthology. This process is not concept development because the pupil does not himself seek a relation or himself build a structure of relations.[7]

The danger is that the teacher's attempts to relate the various works will inhibit honest response to the text. Students may try to predict the teacher's thoughts, to follow her reasoning rather than develop their own.

This danger simply has to be admitted. The teacher cannot afford complete freedom in the literature class; to follow the interests and inclinations of the students all the time would be inefficient and exhausting. You would never know for certain what you might be reading and teaching in two days. You'd have very little time to find and prepare material for the class; books could not even be purchased in advance because the discussion might lead into unforeseen areas. For some issues you might not know of appropriate works and would have to do hasty and tiring research to follow the students' leads.

Thus some freedom must be traded for control and organization. But throughout her teaching the instructor must keep in mind the obligation to let students react to the work and test themselves against it. The goal is to involve students in building ideas as they read and talk, becoming thinkers, not followers. The intelligent reader negotiates with the text. He comes to it hoping to sharpen his insight or understanding, reflects on what is there, and finds his visions confirmed, modified, or refuted by that reflection. He neither changes his views easily and casually nor holds stubbornly to them despite new information. If his vision of the world is confirmed, he has the satisfaction of finding his position strengthened; if it is modified, he can see progress toward a clearer view; and if refuted, then he has the pleasure of new discovery.

Expanded Circles

In Chapter 2 we looked at the relationship between reader and text, emphasizing the overwhelming importance of the reader and suggesting that what she brings to the work be respected in the literature class. In Chapter 3 we discussed the relationship between the reader and other readers, pointing out that one can broaden one's views through encountering the views of others. In this chapter we have discussed the possibility of juxtaposing texts, suggesting that concepts and perceptions can be expanded still further by comparing works that have some elements in common. The three relationships might be seen as sets of ripples on a pond, affecting each other as they meet.

These ripples can expand to encompass more and more. The other readers, for instance, could well include critics. Instead of giving them the authority the New Critics claim, students could view them as other students, other readers, and thus consider what they have to offer, allowing it to shape their own perceptions as reason and instinct dictate. Similarly, the other texts could include almost anything. Students who become interested in the author may wish to look into biographies, and that may lead to an interest in the history of the period in which the work was produced. Those who become intrigued by cultural differences might look into the imaginative literature of other groups or into sociological or anthropological studies. Bright and mature students may wander far afield from the poem or play with which they began, and they should be encouraged to do that exploring. Other students may not have the intellectual energy or interest to travel the same paths, but they, too, should be helped to pursue their ideas. A teacher sensitive to his class and willing to allow time for the work can elicit a great deal of reading and writing from some of his students. He must, of course, be flexible—he must not hope to keep all students moving at the same speed through the same material. But it is possible, if he respects both individuality and reason, for his teaching of literature to be personally significant and intellectually rigorous.

Endnotes

1. Rene Wellek and Austin Warren, *Theory of Literature* (New York: Harcourt, Brace and World, 1942), pp. 138–139.

2. Allert Ellis, *The American Sexual Tragedy* (New York: Twayne Publishers, 1954), p. 98.

3. Henry Wadsworth Longfellow. *Tales of a Wayside Inn* (Boston, MA: Ticknor and Fields), 1863, pp. 149–150.

4. Kahlil Gibran, *The Prophet* (New York: Alfred A. Knopf, Inc., 1923, renewed 1951), p. 72.

5. Ibid., p. 76.

6. Albert Ellis, in James A. Gould and John J. Iorio, Eds., *Love, Sex, and Identity* (San Francisco, CA: Boyd and Fraser, 1972).

7. George Henry, *Teaching Reading as Concept Development: Emphasis on Affective Thinking* (Newark, DE: International Reading Association, 1974), p. 14.

5 *The Nature of the Genres*

The emphasis on response in our discussions so far should not suggest that knowledge about literature is unnecessary. We've noted the dangers of artificial approaches to teaching that substitute information for actual reading. To avoid such approaches, we have focused on the essential experience with literature, the process of noting our reactions to the text, evaluating them, and creating meaning from the exchange. Still, we haven't rejected as irrelevant the vast bodies of information about writer, genre, history, and criticism. We've simply relocated them, and perhaps reduced their significance. We've suggested that they are not the primary reasons for teaching literature—not, at least, in the elementary and secondary schools, which have broader goals than the production of literary scholars.

Expectations

Nonetheless, information about literature can be both interesting and important, even though examining responses comes first. As the discussion of "A View of a Pig" shows, student responses can lead to questions about history, literary technique, cultural patterns, or the life of the author. Response-based teaching can, in other words, arouse an interest in things outside the literary work and the reader's psyche. Further, information that students may not seek out can nonetheless help them read more intelligently and with greater pleasure. A discussion of the various genres, for instance, may help them avoid the frustration of coming to a work with false ideas of what to expect.

The genres do differ significantly in their aims and methods. Students who, from a composition class that demands clear, precise, fully documented essays, come to the complex poetry of Gerard Manley Hopkins may feel they have been deceived. If good writing is clear and unambiguous, then why must they suffer through an obscure and confusing poem like "God's Grandeur"? If the poem and essay had similar goals and could be judged by similar standards, this objection would be well taken, but of course the two forms work differently. The essayist is arguing a point, hoping to convince her readers. She does not want to lose them in ambiguous references or convoluted logic. The poet, on the other hand, is not usually so direct; he may work through suggestion, allusion, and intentional ambiguity to invite readers into the poem, allowing them to shape their reading in unique ways. The poet may try to evoke moods, capture scenes, arouse emotions, but he is unlikely to attempt extended argument. The poetic mode is less suited to complicated reasoning than the essay, and students should learn to expect that difference between the two genres.

Similarly, there are differences between, say, historical novels and biography. In an historical novel the author can play with the facts, rearranging some, drawing bold inferences from others, and inventing still others to fill gaps in the historical record. The biographer is denied this freedom and held more strictly accountable for the accuracy of her work. Readers who come to an historical novel expecting an accurate account of historical events will be either disappointed or deceived. Likewise, readers who come to biography expecting the completeness and narrative flow characteristic of a novel are likely to be unhappy with the author's inability to fill in where details are not available. Each genre has its own requirements and makes its own promises.

Providing information about the purposes and methods of the various genres will help students know what to expect, reducing the chances of frustration and disappointment. Let us consider the genres most often encountered in secondary schools and see what each demands of the reader and offers in return. Several categories are reserved for later chapters. Literature for young adults, because it is a sprawling and important body of literature in almost all genres, will have a chapter of its own. The visual media—theater, television, and film—because they are watched and heard rather than read, will also be treated separately. The genres that traditionally dominate in the secondary school we'll discuss here, beginning with poetry.

The Poem

Poetry is many different things, of course. It ranges from Frost's two-line "The Secret" to Spenser's book-length *The Faerie Queene,* from Jarrell's simple and direct "Death of the Ball Turret Gunner" to Milton's complicated and allusive *Paradise Lost.* It includes both the private meditations of Keats' "On First Looking into Chapman's Homer" and the public satire of Pope's "The Dunciad." Poetry is at times sensual, and at other times lofty, at times dramatic, even violent, and at other times peaceful. It may be presumptuous to try to discuss any topic so large and varied as "the poem" or "poetry." Some theorists, Richard Lanham in particular, say that poetry differs not in kind but in degree from other modes of writing. The distinction between poetry and prose, he suggests, is not so simple as the textbooks would have us believe. Rather, prose and poetry are ranges along a spectrum. Poetry, he says, is language that calls attention to itself, inviting the reader to take pleasure in the words, rhythms, and sounds, as well as in the statements made. Prose, on the other hand, tends to be more transparent, directing the reader to elements of the world, the things outside that the words call to mind. But, he points out, good prose is also enjoyed for its sounds and rhythms, its poetic elements, and good poetry is seldom completely without referential meaning. The two, prose and poetry, run together, transcending simplistic distinctions about the layout of lines on the page.[1]

Compression

Nonetheless, there are observations we may make about "the poem," granting that we may often find our generalities refuted by particular poems. Perhaps the most important feature of poetry, the one likely to give young readers greatest difficulty, is its compression. Poems are typically compact, each word carrying a heavy burden. They rarely introduce and summarize in great detail, and often fail to tell the whole story. They are not explicit in the same way that we urge student writers to be explicit. Few poems begin by spelling out their purpose or delineating the ground to be covered, and few lay out their conclusions and implications, striving for clarity and completeness. They present rather than explain. They sketch a picture, recount an episode, portray a character, suggest a mood, and then stop. The following poem by Randall Jarrell is an example:

Death of the Ball Turret Gunner[2]

From my mother's sleep I fell into the State,
And I hunched in its belly till my wet fur froze.
Six miles from earth, loosed from its dream of life,
I woke to black flak and the nightmare fighters.
When I died they washed me out of the turret with a hose.

—Randall Jarrell

As an essay, this is lacking. Who is the "I?" Where and when does all this take place? The writer has failed to give us details that even a freshman journalism major would know to include. And what's the point? The writer does not tell us why this death is significant, what conclusions we should draw from it. What he is saying, what this means, is all left unclear.

But expecting that sort of clarity from a poem is unfair. Jarrell is not trying to write a news report of a recent battle, nor a philosophical essay on the ethics of modern warfare. Rather, he is presenting a set of images, inviting the reader to observe them and react to them. The poem encourages speculation about both the writer's notions and the reader's.

We might, for instance, speculate about the images of the speaker we find here. He falls into "the State," which then becomes a bomber, hunches in its belly, wakes, dies, and is washed away. He does not seem very powerful or important, he seems always to be controlled from above, apparently by "the State." Is Jarrell complaining about the power of the state? Possibly. Is he objecting to war in general, because it can reduce people to bloody messes to be cleaned up with a hose? Again, possibly, perhaps even probably. But the poem isn't an elaborate commentary on the powerlessness of the individual in "the State," nor is it a treatise on war; it may invite commentaries and treatises, but it is neither. It is, rather, a collection of images working together to create an effect, suggesting lines of thought but not outlining a detailed argument.

The image of the last line is especially powerful. That the human body can be reduced to a mess that can only be washed away, not picked up and carried off, is shocking, perhaps largely because the idea is stated in such simple, direct language. The reader is tempted to draw conclusions from this imagined scene, condemning war for its casual destruction of human lives and lamenting how easily we can be obliterated. But those would be the reader's conclusions—Jarrell has stopped short of making them for us. He has stopped with the image, the particular; the inferences you and I draw, the generalizations we make, are our own responsibility, though he has set us on the path. One of the pleasures of poetry is that it allows us that freedom. But the reader must expect it; she must know that poetry works by suggesting and directing, and often stops short, leaving the reader with raw material from which to create meaning. James Dickey says of his poetry, and of poetry in general, that he wants:

> words to come together into some kind of magical conjunction that will make the reader enter into a real experience of his own—*not* the poet's. I don't really believe what literary critics have believed from the beginning of time: that poetry is an attempt of the poet to create or recreate his own experience and to pass it on.... I believe it's an awakening of the sensibilities of someone else, the stranger.[3]

A poem is like any other of life's experiences; none of them comes with explanatory footnotes or critical commentary. They happen, and we make sense of them as best we can. So it is—almost—with the poem. It happens, and we make of it what we can. It isn't that simple, of course. The poem doesn't just happen; rather, it is written. Its patterns are a product of the poet's imagination and planning. A poem has shape and design. But it doesn't have an instruction manual.

So the teacher needs to help students adjust their expectations of the poem. She may do that, in part, by direct explanation. She may suggest that students pause when confused and look for suggestions of meaning through unusual comparisons, abrupt changes, and unexpected images. If, for example, students falter over the rapid transition in the first two lines of Jarrell's poem, they need to look closely at the source of confusion, aware that the poet has compressed his meaning into compact images. The speaker falls into "the State," hunches in its belly. Then suddenly the belly is that of an airplane "Six miles from earth." The change is abrupt, unannounced, and probably confusing. "The State" has become the bomber. Students should be encouraged to ask themselves why the poet would make this sudden change. Their speculations will help them to understand the comparison between "State" and plane, a comparison that Jarrell has created but left his reader to elaborate.

The poem is like a field to be played in rather than a path to be followed. It doesn't fully control and direct its readers. Instead, it sets us free to feel and think—

not completely free, for its patterns and themes must be recognized if we are to say that we have read the poem, but free within the bounds it marks off for us.

Evocation

Evocative, image-laden poems like Samuel Taylor Coleridge's "Kubla Khan" invite a different sort of appreciation. If Jarrell's poem leads almost inevitably into the realm of ideas, Coleridge's poem leads us into the realm of visions. Jarrell's poem is discussable, suggesting issues to consider; Coleridge's is less so. Its meaning has to be approached in a different way. It isn't easy to ask students to draw inferences from "Kubla Khan" as one might with Jarrell's "Death of the Ball Turret Gunner." What can they make of the images in "Kubla Khan"?

To make anything of them, students must first enjoy them as a performance. They must let the words conjure pictures for them, and then be willing to look at the pictures and allow their minds to wander in the scene. In "Kubla Khan" the scene is a fascinating mix: Bright, sunny hillsides are contrasted with deep, sunless caverns, cold and lifeless; the river erupts violently from the earth, spewing boulders about as though they were light as hailstones, and then wanders quietly through an idyllic landscape and finally disappears down into the earth. Where do these visions take us? What do they mean? Jarrell's poem is easily—perhaps too easily—taken as a condemnation of war; it leads us to discuss war as an issue. Coleridge's doesn't do anything like that. It presents us with images, with a picture, but not, apparently, with an idea. How, then, do we have students work with the poem?

We might first make the point that not all poetry is philosophical or ethical in its intent, and we need not assume that the poem has a message. We might instead compare it to a picture, which we enjoy or fail to enjoy for its shape and color, not for a meaning we abstract from it. "Kubla Khan" is a poem that might be enjoyed in the quiet mood that permeates a good museum. Looking at paintings, we notice whether they please us or not; only before certain ones do we stop to ask what they mean. We may listen to Beethoven's symphonies and enjoy them immensely without trying to explain them. "Kubla Khan," too, may be read or listened to without concern for interpretation and enjoyed for the simple pleasure of its sounds and imagery.

Students who insist on explanation (and who may be more interested in the teacher's than in their own) may become less adamant if you ask them to bring in a favorite poster or record. Some of these, at least, will defy interpretation. They may be photographs of movie stars or instrumental pieces that are beautiful but do not *mean* anything. Asked to explain them, the students will have to admit that it can't be done. A portrait of an actor doesn't mean—it just is. Similarly, a poem might not mean—it might just be. That doesn't necessarily mean that there's nothing to be done with it. It may be suggestive or celebratory, and may, if we let it, send our minds wandering on paths we might not otherwise have explored, but it may not present us with problems to solve. Consider, for instance, a beautiful and simple poem like the following by Stephen Dunn:

Insomnia[4]

What should be counted was counted
up to a hundred and back.

And sleep came by, I think,
sensed too much movement and left.

Now there's desire meeting absence,
the multiplication of zero,

the mind, as always, holding out
for a perfect convergence

like a diver entering water
without a splash. There's a part

of me terribly stilled and alert,
a silence that won't shut off.

And there's this need to put on the light,
to not sleep on sleep's terms, sleep

which is after all like you, love,
elsewhere and difficult.

—Stephen Dunn

There is much that we might do with this poem, but it's unlikely that extended arguments about explications will be among them.

To help students temporarily stop trying to interpret, you might have them listen to a poem like "Kubla Khan" with eyes closed and visualize the scene Coleridge paints. Or you might have them listen to a poem like "Insomnia," allowing the words to conjure whatever associations or thoughts they may awaken. Ask them to listen as though the poem were music and to observe how it affects them. Read it aloud once or twice, and then ask the students to consider the dominant impressions they have. These need not be interpretations—just impressions or feelings. With "Kubla Khan," some students may focus on the sunny gardens and be cheered; others may imagine the ominous caverns, the tumult, the prophecies of war, and find their mood darkened; some may notice the presence of both elements and be curious about the contrast. With "Insomnia," some students may think of lonely moments or absent friends. All of these responses can be discussed.

The discussion need not be prolonged, but if it begins to touch on memories and associations, so much the better. The poem will have provoked responses and feelings in much the same way as a painting reminds us of a person or a song recalls a scene. Students may find that they have made something significant out of the poem, that they have not found but created meaning for it. For one student, "Kubla

Khan" might come to represent the range of experience possible in the world, from the peace and beauty of the gardens to the violence and fearfulness of the caverns and lifeless ocean. Light and dark, sun and ice, peace and war—she would like a taste of them all, and the poem, when she finds herself too lazy to seek them, may remind her that she does not want to pass through the world without touching it. This may not be what Coleridge had in mind, but it may be one reader's playing out of the poem, her performance. It can be valuable and satisfying even if it departs from Coleridge's intent. Songs that remind us of old friends and other places were not intended by their writers to do that, but we are content to let them work that way. If students have similar experiences with poems—and not all of them will with "Kubla Khan" or any other poem we happen to choose, of course—then they may return to poetry with pleasure and perhaps with sharper perceptions.

This kind of reading requires close attention to the words of the poem. Although we aren't asking the students to analyze each line, we are asking them to visualize and imagine. These skills are as important in every sort of reading as the skills of analysis. If students cannot imagine the "twice five miles of fertile ground" and the "gardens bright with sinuous rills," they cannot read the poem. The teacher can, of course, make sure they understand all the words, but beyond that he can do little to help except invite and encourage, freeing students now and then from having to interpret the work and gather evidence for their statements. If students will accept the idea that poetic imagery might work as the sounds of music do, however, it may free their imagination and their thoughts so that they can read creatively.

Which approach to reading one chooses will depend on what the poem is like. If it works with ideas and seems to make a point, then students might profit from an intellectual approach. If, on the other hand, it seems to paint a picture or sing a song, they might do well to wander in the imaginary gardens or listen to the melody. They should learn to be open to the poem's potential, paying careful attention to the words and their own responses. They must listen and participate; the poem won't give them everything, even if it is a poem with a point. They must play the game it offers, but they must understand that reading is a creative act, much more than a simple matter of receiving something given.

In a sense, readers of poetry must balance between passivity and activity. They must allow themselves to be led, but they must not follow mindlessly. They have to let Coleridge show them the gardens and the caverns, or they have missed his poem. But what those gardens and caverns come to represent may be something other than what Coleridge had in mind. If they are nothing more than his land-scape, the poem will be soon forgotten, but if the reader finds personal significance in them, her work will be rewarded. Readers can choose how much to be led by a poem. If, like John Livingston Lowes, they are fascinated by the imagery and want to understand Coleridge better, they may follow the critical path that led Lowes to write *The Road to Xanadu*.[5] If the poem brings up personal associations, then they may prefer to let the imagery stimulate their own thoughts. They may follow, or lead, or do both. Students should know that they have that choice, that a poem need not be an exercise in interpretation.

Symbolism

We have noted that the language of poetry is compressed, with each word carrying a heavy burden of meaning, and that poets often work by suggesting rather than stating. More traditional language would have served us as well—we might have spoken of *metaphor* and *symbol* instead of *compression* and *suggestion*. But *metaphor* and *symbol* too often become technicalities for students to trip over, rather than statements about how the poem works. It is much more important that students understand the nature of metaphor than that they be able to distinguish between a metaphor and a simile. That distinction is among the most useless in the lexicon of literary criticism, but the general idea of both terms—the linking together of two images so that one sheds light on the other—is crucial. Students who fail to grasp it will remain bewildered by most poetry. "The road was a ribbon of moonlight" can only be nonsense or a ridiculous lie to them. Perhaps even worse off is the poor student who reads the line and worries because he can't remember if this is a metaphor or simile. If he wracks his brain trying to recall the definitions rather than pictures the sinuous silvery shape snaking off into the distance, we may wonder if his training is serving him well. But if he understands that the poet tries to suggest qualities and feelings by such comparisons and that those qualities and feelings demand active participation, then the poem can begin to work.

Similarly, if students come to see that a symbol is not just a substitution of one thing for another but an association that invests an image with new meaning, they will be more inclined to play with the symbol. Rather than dutifully search for and define it, reducing it to a simple-minded equation, they are more likely to toy with it, explore it, and wonder about its ambiguities. Students who can say, "The flag is the symbol of our country" have memorized a simplified definition of symbol and managed to apply it in one instance. It is near useless knowledge, but harmless enough, as long as they know that symbol and thing symbolized are not the same. But other students can play with the symbol, asking questions about it: Does the flag represent the country as envisioned by the writers of the constitution, or as it has evolved? Does it represent the place, the people, a system of government, or a set of values? Does it represent a vision of a possible, perhaps an ideal, society, or instead the society, less than ideal, that we have achieved? Such students comprehend that the symbol is not a neat equation, a closed system of meaning, but instead suggestive, open-ended, challenging them to explore the possibilities it presents. If they understand that about the poetic symbol, they will be able to think creatively about the poetry they read.

Problems

INVERTED WORD ORDER   Poems do pose problems. Although not unique to poetry, some of the following problems occur often enough in poems to be discussed here. One is inverted word order:

One morn before me were three figures seen.

—Keats, "Ode on Indolence"

Whan that April with his showres soote
The droughte of March hath perced to the roote,
And bathed every veine in swich licour,
Of which vertu engendred is the flowr. . . .

—Chaucer, "Prologue," *Canterbury Tales*

Students who have played sentence-combining games in composition or language study may have a sharp enough sense of the flexibility of English to face these uncommon constructions calmly. They might be asked to rephrase the lines in more familiar patterns and then consider the difference in style or effect. How, for instance, does "I saw three figures in front of me one morning" differ from Keats' phrasing? This sort of analysis is imprecise, and students should not get the impression that the poet has magically found the one and only way to state the thought. But different wordings do change the emphasis, rhythm, and tone, and thus alter the meaning slightly, yielding different impressions of the writer and evoking different responses from readers. Students should begin to consider the effects that can be achieved, even if they do so in vague and impressionistic terms.

For students unable to handle the peculiarities of the sentence structure, a technique suggested by Abraham Bernstein might be useful. He recommends offering the students a paraphrase before they confront the work.[6] His purpose is not to help students understand confusing word order, but to emphasize the nuances of the phrasing. Giving students the gist of the passage would no doubt help them to work more easily through the original.

Paraphrasing, by students if they can do it or by the teacher if they cannot, will also help with dialect, or, as in the example from Chaucer, archaic language. A teacher who has spent some time with her students may be able to judge how much help they'll need. If not, she might test their comprehension by offering them several lines from the poem they are to read as a trial run. Eight or twelve lines from Chaucer, for instance, given to the class with a request to try to translate them into contemporary English, would be enough to suggest how much help the students will need without being so frustrated that they come to dislike the work. If no one comes close to translating the test lines, the group will need assistance; the Middle English is beyond them. If most of the group does well with the trial run, then it might be appropriate to challenge them with the original.

The same issue is faced with a poet like Robert Burns:

To a Mouse

Wee, sleekit, cow'rin', tim'rous beastie,
O, what a panic's in thy breastie!
Thou need na start awa sae hasty,
    Wi' bickering brattle!
I wad be laith to rin an' chase thee
    Wi' murd'ring pattle!

—Robert Burns

This stanza would be impossible for some groups and reasonably easy for others. Some students would even be able to approximate the sense of "brattle" and "pattle," though they might not deduce their exact meaning. Some contemporary dialects may also pose a problem, though they are probably not so difficult as Middle English or Scottish dialect.

ALLUSIONS   Poems full of allusions will also be hard for students unfamiliar with the source of the allusions. It would be foolish to teach Yeats's "Leda and the Swan" without some explanation of the myth it draws on. That explanation can come before or after the reading, depending on what the teacher hopes to do with the poem. Contemporary poetry is almost as likely to contain unfamiliar allusions as that of the Neo-Classic poets. The middle stanzas from Frank Horne's "Nigger—A Chant for Children" would be lost on someone who had not heard of Hannibal, Othello, and Crispus Attucks:

Nigger[7]

> Hannibal. . . Hannibal
> Bangin' thru the Alps
> Licked the proud Roman,
> Ran home with their scalps—
> "Nigger. . . nigger. . . nigger. . ."
> Othello. . . black man
> Mighty in war
> Listened to Iago
> Called his wife a whore
> "Nigger. . . nigger. . . nigger. . . "
> Crispus. . . Attucks
> Bullets in his chest
> Red blood of freedom
> Runnin' down his vest
> "Nigger. . . nigger. . . nigger. . . "
>
> —Frank Horne[7]

A reasonably bright class would deduce from the pattern of the poem that the three were black men and heroes, so a long introduction might not be necessary. Slower groups might be told very briefly who the three men were, to help them understand the poem.

We might note, too, that this poem poses the same problem that *Huckleberry Finn* gives us: the word *nigger*. That offensive word, used here as a refrain, makes the poem not simply a paean in tribute to the accomplishments of these black men, but also a condemnation of racist attitudes that would demean and insult such men and ignore their accomplishments. Like *Huckleberry Finn,* this poem attacks the stupidity and vulgarity of such attitudes; nonetheless, the term is so provocative that teachers who might want to use the text will have to judge their classes cautiously before doing so.

VOICES   The problems of specific poems are not insurmountable for a teacher who is sensitive to both the language and the students. Brief analysis will often suggest a teaching method. Reed's "Lessons of War, Naming of Parts," for instance, has two voices: the drill sergeant's and the recruit's. It does not, however, have the usual signals to indicate who speaks which lines. The voices flow into and out of each other, and the reader must determine who is speaking from what is said:

Naming of Parts[8]

Today we have naming of parts. Yesterday,
We had daily cleaning. And tomorrow morning,
We shall have what to do after firing. But today,
Today we have naming of parts. Japonica
Glistens like coral in all of the neighboring gardens,
    And today we have naming of parts.
This is the lower sling swivel. And this
Is the upper sling swivel, whose use you will see,
When you are given your slings. And this is the piling swivel,
Which in your case you have not got. The branches
Hold in the gardens their silent, eloquent gestures,
    Which in our case we have not got.
This is the safety-catch, which is always released
With an easy flick of the thumb. And please do not let me
See anyone using his finger. You can do it quite easy
If you have any strength in your thumb. The blossoms
Are fragile and motionless, never letting anyone see
    Any of them using their finger.
And this you can see is the bolt. The purpose of this
Is to open the breech, as you see. We can slide it
Rapidly backwards and forwards: we call this
Easing the spring. And rapidly backwards and forwards
The early bees are assaulting and fumbling the flowers
    They call it easing the Spring.
They call it easing the Spring: it is perfectly easy
If you have any strength in your thumb: like the bolt,
And the breech, and the cocking-piece, and the point of balance,
Which in our case we have not got; and the almond-blossom
Silent in all of the gardens and the bees going backwards and forwards,
    For today we have naming of parts.

—Henry Reed

A discussion of responses to the poem may lead students to discover the pattern, but some groups, again, will require more help than others. The help may take the form of questions:

Where do you find the poem confusing?

What do you hear in the poem?

Can you place the images in two groups?

Can you find two lines that sound as if they were spoken by the same person?

The teacher could help more directly by reading the poem aloud, slightly emphasizing the change in voice. Or he might have students read the poem, assigning the sergeant's lines to one reader and the remaining lines to another, though that essentially solves the problem for them.

Each strategy offers the students slightly more help than the one before—the trick is to help enough but not too much. If the students can understand the poem without much assistance, so much the better. Their success will be sufficient reward for the labor required. If the teacher finds herself doing all the work, leading the students through the thinking step by step, she may suspect that either the poem is too difficult or the class too lazy.

Bad Poetry

Bad poetry can be almost as enjoyable as good poetry, though in a slightly different way. The contorted, contrived, and trite can give the reader a satisfying sense of superiority. True, it is a little bloodthirsty to enjoy someone's weakness in this way, but it is pleasant, nonetheless. Contemporary popular magazines are rich with doggerel in praise of God, country, motherhood, fidelity, family life, the democratic way, and assorted other vacuities. Laurence Perrine's *Sound and Sense* contains a chapter entitled "Bad Poetry and Good" that provides some examples. Perrine suggests pairing a good poem with a bad one in order to help students see the sentimentality and the bombast. Clough's "Say Not the Struggle Nought Availeth," for instance, is joined to "The Man Who Thinks He Can" ("If you think you are beaten, you are;/If you think you dare not, you don't. . .," and so on).[9]

Such pairings help the students learn to evaluate and judge. Each poem serves as a base against which the other may be tested: The pretension of one reveals the sincerity of the other, and cliches and borrowed thoughts will seem dimmer and drabber when contrasted with originality and freshness. The distinctions, however, will not always be obvious, especially to immature readers. Some will feel an honest liking for what strikes you as a dismally poor poem. The purpose of these comparisons is not to homogenize the tastes of the students, making them agree with your judgments, but to give them an opportunity to compare the merits of different works. Although glaringly bad poems invite ridicule, it must be engaged in cautiously, so that students will not feel that the disparaging remarks apply to them as well. Intimidated by the severity of the teacher's judgments, they may grow less and less willing to risk their own, and this attitude will isolate them from the poem, preventing them from reading. Perrine warns:

> A final caution to students. In making judgments on literature, always be honest. Do not pretend to like what you really do not like. Do not be afraid to admit a

liking for what you do like. A genuine enthusiasm for the second-rate is much better than false enthusiasm or no enthusiasm at all. Be neither hasty nor timorous in making your judgments. When you have attentively read a poem and thoroughly considered it, decide what you think. Do not hedge, equivocate, or try to find out others' opinions before forming your own. Having formed an opinion and expressed it, do not allow it to petrify. Compare your opinion *then* with the opinions of others; allow yourself to change it when convinced of its errors: in this way you learn. Honesty, courage, and humility are the necessary moral foundations for all genuine literary judgment.[10]

That caution might be extended to the teacher. Do not, by extravagant praise or severe condemnation, lead your students to accept judgments they do not feel. To do so is to encourage intellectual dishonesty, and thus to discourage learning. Instead, share your judgments with them in a way that encourages them to form reasoned judgments of their own.

As a transition from verse to prose, in the form of the short story, let's pause to take a quick look at a simple comparison between a poem and a pamphlet in Workshop #6.

BEAR COUNTRY

Consider this as a way of looking at some of the effects of genre (with a fairly sophisticated group of readers).

This activity involves a bit of forgivable deception. Prepare two different handouts. Do this in landscape format so that, when folded, the instructions for the activity will be on the front panel, page 1. Since the instructions will be the same for both handouts, they should all appear identical to a casual observer. The instructions you give will be something like the following:

As you read the following text, try to observe yourself reading:

What do you feel? What do you think?

What do you find yourself focusing on?

Does your mind wander, and if so, to what does it stray?

What do you experience or get from the text?

Is there anything about the text that bothers you or confuses you?

Try to record your thoughts as you read or immediately after you finish reading so that the sequence of events is fresh in your mind.

The texts on the two handouts, however, will be slightly different. Since they will be on the second panel, page 2, inside the fold, if you're lucky no one will notice that not all students have the same text. The first text is the following poem:

You Are in Bear Country[11]

They've
been here
for thousands of years.
You're
the visitor.
Avoid
encounters. Think ahead.
Keep clear
of berry patches
garbage dumps, carcasses.
On woods walks bring
noisemakers, bells.
Clap hands along the trail
or sing
but in dense bush or by running water
bear may not hear your clatter.
Whatever else
don't whistle. Whistling
is thought by some to imitate
the sound bears make when they
mate.

You need to know there are two
kinds:
ursus arctus horribilis
or grizzly
and ursus americanus
the smaller black
said to be somewhat less likely to
attack.
Alas, a small horribilis
is difficult to distinguish
from a large americanus.

Although
there is no
guaranteed life-saving way
to deal with an aggressive bear
some ploys

have proved more
successful than others.
Running's a poor choice.
Bears can outrun a racehorse.

Once you're face to face
speak softly. Take
off your pack
and set it down
to distract the grizzly.
Meanwhile back
slowly toward a large
sparsely-branched tree
but remember
black bears are agile climbers
in which case
a tree may not offer escape.

As a last resort you can
play dead. Drop
to the ground face down.
In this case
wearing your pack
may shield your body from attack.
Courage. Lie still. Sometimes
your bear may veer away.
If not
bears have been known
to inflict only minor injuries
upon the prone.

Is death
by bear preferred
to death by bomb? Under
these extenuating circumstances
your mind may make absurd
leaps. The answer's yes.
Come on in. Cherish
your wilderness.

—Maxine Kumin

The second text is the poem recast as prose:

You Are in Bear Country

They've been here for thousands of years. You're the visitor. Avoid encounters. Think ahead. Keep clear of berry patches, garbage dumps, carcasses. On woods walks bring noisemakers, bells. Clap hands along the trail or sing but in dense bush or by running water bear may not hear your clatter. Whatever else don't whistle. Whistling is thought by some to imitate the sound bears make when they mate.

You need to know there are two kinds: ursus arctus horribilis or grizzly and ursus americanus the smaller black said to be somewhat less likely to attack. Alas, a small horribilis is difficult to distinguish from a large americanus.

Although there is no guaranteed life-saving way to deal with an aggressive bear some ploys have proved more successful than others. Running's a poor choice. Bears can outrun a racehorse.

Once you're face to face speak softly. Take off your pack and set it down to distract the grizzly. Meanwhile back slowly toward a large sparsely-branched tree but remember black bears are agile climbers in which case a tree may not offer escape.

As a last resort you can play dead. Drop to the ground face down. In this case wearing your pack may shield your body from attack. Courage. Lie still. Sometimes your bear may veer away. If not bears have been known to inflict only minor injuries upon the prone.

Is death by bear preferred to death by bomb? Under these extenuating circumstances your mind may make absurd leaps. The answer's yes. Come on in. Cherish your wilderness.

—Canadian Minister of the Environment

The two texts are identical except for one punctuation mark. Kumin has a note with her poem telling us that it was adapted from a brochure of the Canadian Minister of the Environment. The prose version isn't in that brochure; it is simply the poem recast as prose.

On the third panel, page 3 of the folded sheet, in both versions of the handout, give students some instructions for the reflection and discussion that will follow. The following is an example.

Reflection

1. Now that you've read the text and recorded what happened as you read, think back over the experience. What did you get out of reading the text? What did you feel or think as you read? What did you remember or reflect on when you finished reading?

2. Upon what did you focus most intently as you read? What is the most important thing to come out of your reading?

Discussion

3. Please discuss your reading with your partner. What similarities and differences do you notice in your experiences with the text? Did you do different things with the text, read for different purposes? Was the reading

more pleasant, or annoying, for one than for the other? What accounts—
or what might account—for those differences?

Analysis

4. When we return to the full group, I'll ask you to comment briefly on what transpired in the discussion with your partner. What differences or similarities in the experiences with the text did you notice? Did the discussion, the sharing of the readings, reveal anything about *your* reading or about the texts?

Arrange students with the two versions alternating, so that when you then pair up the students and surreptitiously give them the sheets, one student will have the prose and one the poetry. As you're passing them out, encourage the students to imagine themselves alone in the room for the moment. Discourage them from chatting with, even glancing at, one another, explaining that you want them to have their own, unique encounter with the text before discussing it. You're trying at this point to keep them, from noticing the difference on p. 2. Ask them to read the text in solitude, record their responses, and discuss their readings. Bring the group back together to see what they've observed.

Typically, readers of the prose version report being troubled by the piece. The information didn't seem very helpful and was conveyed in an almost frivolous tone that wasn't appropriate for such a brochure. "Alas, a small horribilis is difficult to distinguish from a large americanus"—what help is that? The last paragraph was most annoying. Why would such a brochure invite you into the park by telling you that "death by bear" is preferred to "death by bomb"? First, isn't the pamphlet supposed to keep you from dying, and second, what does the bomb have to do with anything? They are not pleased.

The readers of the poem, however, didn't find the last paragraph—or, rather, stanza—troubling at all. They found it an invitation to reflect on the risks we have to take to enjoy life. Some talked about diving in waters where sharks may be found, some about parachute jumping—if you aren't willing to take a few risks, they said, you'll miss out on much of this. Furthermore, they found some pleasure in the light touch that annoyed the readers of the prose. "Alas, a small horribilis is difficult to distinguish from a large americanus," condemned as frivolous and inadequate in the prose, was humorous and rhythmic in the poem.

The point of this activity and the reason for inviting all of this conversation is to enable you to say, "The words in the two handouts were exactly the same. So what accounts for these differing reactions?" And the obvious conclusion is that, in addition to our unique perspectives, we have differing expectations of different genres. Thus we tend to read them differently. We *could* have been amused and invited to reflect on risk and adventure by that last paragraph in the prose, but the genre set us up to expect something different and so we chose not to take that path. We *could* have read the poetry and criticized the inadequacy of its guidelines for personal safety in the north woods but, because what we had in our hands was a poem, we chose not to. The choice remains with the reader, but the genres promise us different rewards and push us in different directions.

The Short Story

One advantage of the poem is that it is usually short and compact. The class can cover it in one fifty-minute period, examine its diction and structure, explore the personal associations it evokes, and conclude with a sense of having finished something. Novels, on the other hand, are long. To examine one as if it were a poem, paying close attention to nearly every word, would be impossible—neither time nor the patience of your students would allow it. The short story lies somewhere in between. It repays close analysis, because it must be tightly constructed to be successful, but it is more leisurely than a poem. Not quite so compressed and dense as poetry, the language of the short story often seems more relaxed and comfortable. Reading it is like listening to a friend's account of an interesting event. The short story seems less a formal performance than the poem. At the same time, it is less complete than a novel. We can live in a novel, with its detailed characters and scenes. But we can't live in a short story; it goes by too quickly, always concentrating on the event or idea that sustains it.

Plot

The short story shares the compression of the poem, but it is less the linguistic compression of rich, dense lines than a compression resulting from focus on one event or idea. Compare, for instance, the poem "The Man He Killed," by Thomas Hardy, and the short story "The Sniper," by Liam O'Flaherty. They are both about the same idea—the strange irrationality of killing in warfare—and they are both brief, even for their respective genres. "The Man He Killed" is only twenty lines long, and "The Sniper" would fill no more than four or five pages. But they achieve their effects in different ways.

Hardy contrasts a possibility with a fact. The speaker and his victim might have sat down together for a drink or two had they met under other circumstances; instead, they met on the battlefield and the speaker killed his enemy. The first two stanzas present the alternatives, and in the third the speaker tries to explain why it should have worked out as it did. His first answer—"Because he was my foe"—fails to satisfy him. He tries to undergird it with expressions of assurance—"Just so; my foe of course he was;/That's clear enough; although"—but in that "although" and in the hesitation of the semicolons, his doubt shows itself. His foe was a man like the speaker himself, perhaps caught up in the war for reasons as insubstantial as his own—out of work, little else to do, and so off to war. It is a strange reason for killing a man, but the speaker has no other. In the end he says that war is "quaint and curious," and leaves it at that, trying to resolve his confusion with a label. But the label is inadequate justification for the killing.

How has the poem worked on us? It has given us a likeable fellow, serving for the moment as a soldier, and through him it has given us contrasting images, one of two men chatting amicably over a drink in a cheerful tavern and the other of those same two men trying to kill one another in battle. The first is the speaker's fantasy, and the second his account of what actually happened. The images are brief and compact. The battlefield is not there in gruesome detail, nor are the personalities of the men fully presented. We are neither revolted by the gore of warfare nor distressed by the death of a character we have come to like. Instead, there is a simple contrast between the possibility of friendship and the actuality of killing.

Much lies in the hesitation: "I shot him dead because—." The speaker pauses at that dash, as if uncertain of what is to follow. At the end of the stanza, "although" asks us to pause again and doubt the reason offered. Then, having been asked to doubt, we are given no explanations. The killing is dismissed in vacuous terms, "quaint and curious," and we are left to realize that behind this pleasant but empty-headed speaker there is another presence, one suggesting that the killings are senseless and ridiculous.

Thus a few carefully balanced images set the scene for us. A dash, a conjunction, and "although" suggest an attitude underlying that of the speaker, and expressions like "foe" and "quaint and curious" confirm the presence of that attitude. A very few words have carried us to the perceptions of the last lines.

What about O'Flaherty's short story? It, too, is short. But is it compressed in the same way? Do individual phrases carry as much of the burden as does "quaint and curious" in Hardy's poem? Briefly, the scene for "The Sniper" is Dublin during the Irish civil war. The sniper from whose perspective the story is told discovers another sniper on a nearby rooftop and, after an exchange of fire, kills him, the body falling into the streets below. The victor then descends to the street, curious about the man he has killed, and discovers that it is his brother.

The story buys its effect cheaply, depending as it does on the coincidental relationship between the two men, and one might argue that the word "brother" carries as much weight as the phrase "quaint and curious." Certainly changing the last line, "Then the sniper turned over the dead body and looked into his brother's face," so that it ended with "and looked into the man's face" would drain the story of much of its impact. But the shock of brother finding brother is prepared for not by one carefully balanced inner conversation, such as we found in "The Man He Killed," but by a detailed account of the events leading up to the final scene. We see the sniper first lying on a rooftop, impatient, eager, so restless that he lights a cigarette despite the risk of exposing his location. He is then fired on, and finds and kills two targets of his own. Next he is wounded and has to bind up his wound and plan his escape. Event follows event; details of the setting accumulate along with information about the character. We stay with the man through much of the night, watching the armored car move into position beneath him, watching him kill the soldier and the woman who reveals his hiding place. In Hardy's poem the war is described only briefly: "ranged as infantry,/ And staring face to face, I shot at him as he at me." The short story gives us much more detail:

> Cautiously he raised himself and peered over the parapet. There was a flash and a bullet whizzed over his head. He dropped immediately. He had seen the flash. It came from the opposite side of the street.[12]

The shooting here is described, not merely mentioned, as it is in the poem. We see the movements, hear the bullets, see the flash.

The rhythms of the language follow the events. When events move quickly, the sentences move quickly; the machine gunner looks out of the car and is killed, the woman runs, the sniper fires again, and the woman falls, all in one short paragraph. But when he is wounded and falls back to the roof, six slow paragraphs creep by as he suffers the pain, binds the wound, and reflects on his situation. It is almost as though the writer is not organizing events for us but simply presenting them, allowing us to live through them as though we had been there on the roof. Of course, that's much too simple. The short story writer organizes, as does the poet, but somehow his presence is felt less strongly. Lacking the steadier rhythms of poetry, the prose of the short story seems more colloquial, more like the language of a friend simply telling.

Still, the story is compressed. We know only certain things about the man, the time, and the place; we see the events from only one perspective. And we see only one short episode consisting of the sniper's activities the night he kills his brother. Although the language is not as condensed as that of the poem, the focus of the story results in a similar compression. In the story, the eagerness of the sniper and the violence of the shootings are juxtaposed suddenly with the reminder that men have brothers, that families are torn apart by war. On the one hand are the excitement and savagery of war, on the other the concept of brotherhood and all that it connotes. The story implies a criticism of war much like that of Hardy's poem. People who could be friends (in the poem) or who are brothers (in the story) find themselves killing each other for the vaguest and least satisfying reasons. But while Hardy compresses his condemnation of war and killing into a set of contrasting images, O'Flaherty develops his idea in a carefully selected sequence of events.

The difference, of course, is plot, the core of the short story. Plot is action and movement. If a story is successful, it will be a carefully planned sequence, not a haphazard collection of events. The author's vision will govern what the reader sees. There are, of course, stories in which plot seems nonexistent, but we will ignore these for the moment. In the O'Flaherty story, the plot is simple. It focuses on the excitement and pain of the fighting itself until the last sentence, when the sniper's unexpected discovery suddenly reminds us of another realm of experience. It is the contrast between that last event and those preceding it that raises the questions. It forces us to imagine for ourselves the thoughts and feelings that fill the mind of the sniper as he looks down at his brother.

The compression of the short story lies, then, in the selection and arrangement of events. The author chooses what to include, what to leave out, and what to gloss over based on what she wants the story to say. Students should recognize that these are choices and learn to consider the purpose of each. Such reflection will help them to understand both the craft and the vision of the writer.

Conflict

Plot depends on conflict, which in turn depends on character. The elements of fiction are intertwined. The plot of a story is often most easily discussed in terms of the conflict that arises—the imbalance, the opposition in motives or desires that gives the story its tension and movement. It can be a simple physical conflict, such as one person attempting to rob another, who resists. Or it can be an intellectual or moral struggle—a banker plans a complex embezzlement scheme (the intellectual challenge) and at the same time wrestles with a conscience that condemns the theft (the ethical conflict). But without some sort of conflict, there is no story. Perfect harmony may be pleasant and we may seek it in our own lives, but we won't look for it in a story. It isn't interesting—nothing moves, nothing happens, and there are no surprises. Such a story would find few readers.

In "The Sniper," we witness a gradual change in the nature of the conflict. The conflict moves, as if by steps, more deeply within the character. The struggle is first external, the physical conflict of men fighting. When the sniper is wounded, the struggle becomes internal as he tries to control the pain and continue fighting. Toward the end, the conflict shifts from his body to his mind as he struggles with fear and disgust at having killed his enemy. O'Flaherty does not describe the conflict at the very end—he leaves us to imagine the thoughts and feelings that would accompany the killing of a brother—but the gradual shift from external to internal suggests that the final conflict is deep within the psyche. The killing of a brother must touch some deep, fundamental chord.

Simple classification of the nature of the conflict is an insufficient analysis of the events of a story. To categorize the conflict as man against man, man against nature, man against society, or man against himself is to take only the first halting step toward comprehending it. The reader must further consider what the nature of the conflict reveals about the vision of the writer. Does O'Flaherty see the drama and excitement of war as a screen obscuring much more significant issues? Or could it be that he intends no general condemnation of war, and makes no judgment about the rightness of the Irish civil war, but is simply dramatizing the sort of tragedy that may occur in such a battle? Such questions as these, based on the conflicts within the story, lead us to the crucial issues. The concept of conflict is simply a tool that may help us discuss our responses to the work.

Character

The investigation of conflict leads logically to the question of character. Conflict does not exist without character. A storm at sea may be fierce and tumultuous, but there is no conflict in the scene until we place characters in a boat on the waves and challenge them to survive. *The Perfect Storm* would not have been a very interesting movie if the *Andrea Gale* hadn't stayed out too long on the fishing grounds. "The Sniper," with which we began, may not serve well to illustrate characterization in the short story. Its protagonist, the nameless soldier, is sketchily portrayed. We know only that he looks like a student, that he has a fanatical glint in his eye, that he shoots well, and that he is a Republican rather than a Free Stater. Still, we glimpse his feelings as the story proceeds, and so we may examine the interaction of character and plot.

In fact, the vagueness of the character seems to be consistent with the design of the story. We noted the absence of comments about the war; neither side is depicted as morally superior, and no purpose is given either for the war in general or for the sniper in particular. We don't know what he is fighting for, only that he is fighting. Further, he is essentially indistinguishable from his enemy; both are simply snipers. The lack of detail about both the war and the character suggests that they are not the central issues for the writer. He is apparently not concerned with the particulars of this war, nor does he seem to be interested in the details of this man's life. Instead, perhaps, he wants to represent all wars and all soldiers. Further detail about the character might make him too unique, too unlike you and me, allowing us to set his experience aside from our own. By leaving him largely undefined, O'Flaherty invites us to see him as Everyman, perhaps to imagine ourselves in his role.

Students may notice that O'Flaherty doesn't name either his protagonist or the dead brother. What is the effect of not naming them? One consequence, of course, is to lessen the distinction between them. They are somehow alike. That observation suggests the further question: Are there *any* significant distinctions between them? The only apparent distinction between the two is that they are on different sides in the war, but no importance is attached to that. Neither side is identified as right, or superior, or virtuous; the men are simply enemies. The absence of a distinction between the two men, and the omission of any references to the causes or principles of the war, tends to make the war seem pointless, a meaningless exchange of lives. In that context, not naming the men suggests that the event portrayed here, although it is one specific encounter in a long war, can be generalized to other men. The two snipers, trying to kill each other, may be seen to represent all soldiers who fight, enthusiastically, but without awareness of the tragedies they inflict on others and on themselves. We cannot say, of course, that the writer purposely decided not to name his characters, but we can say that the absence of names enhances the effect of the story by suggesting that all men at war are in one sense killing their brothers.

Thus, even in a story where character seems thin, the characterization may help to indicate the significance of the events. In other stories, characterization may be the reader's dominant concern from the beginning. "The Stone Boy" by Gina Berriault is a good example. A boy, Arnold, shoots and kills his brother in a careless hunting accident. The story focuses on Arnold's strange reaction to the event—he appears cold and unmoved by it—and the effect this reaction has on his parents and other people in the community. Clearly the major concern in the story is character. What accounts for the boy's behavior? Is it natural or unnatural? Are parents and other adults sufficiently understanding? Is the problem one of communication; that is, does Arnold simply find his emotion beyond his ability to express? Is it one of comprehension—does he not understand what has happened? Or is it that he just doesn't care?

"The Sniper" and "The Stone Boy" make an interesting pair, since in both stories one brother kills another. How, we might ask the students, do the two killings differ? How do the reactions of the surviving brothers differ? True, we do not see the reactions of the sniper, but we can imagine them. How would we expect him to react? How do we think O'Flaherty would expect him to react? What clues do we have?

We might also ask students to explore the writers' characterization techniques. Which character do we come to know more fully? Most students will feel somewhat more knowledgeable about Arnold than about the sniper, even if his reactions to the death remain mysterious. How, then, do we come to know him better? How are we shown what he is like? The students may observe that Arnold is carefully described, and his feelings, even those he does not articulate, are presented to us in some spots ("To dispel emphatically his uneasy advantage over his sleeping brother, he threw himself on the hump of Eugie's body"). Moreover, he is represented in his own dialog and in the speech and actions of other characters. Balanced against the sparse characterization in "The Sniper," these techniques add up to a fairly complete description of Arnold.

A reminder: The techniques of characterization are not important by themselves, and they shouldn't be taught in a way that distracts students from the stories. If knowledge of these techniques, as of other technical elements of literature, is acquired during the exploration of responses, however, it may add to the exploration. As students react to Arnold and the people surrounding him, they will seek evidence for their reactions in the text. It's important that they know how to evaluate the evidence they find there.

For instance, a student may conclude that Arnold doesn't care about his brother's death and may point to several remarks that seem to substantiate the observation: "'Not a tear in his eye,' said Andy," and "'He don't give a hoot, is that how it goes?' asked Sullivan." That student needs to realize that the comments of characters in the story are not necessarily accurate and complete. Their points of view should be weighed against information from other sources in the story. Portraying one character through the observations of others is a powerful technique, but in most cases, the judgment of others will not be final or conclusive; it is simply one bit of information to keep in mind.

Berriault gives us no answers about Arnold, but she does carry us through a sequence of events and conversations that offer some insight into his feelings and thoughts. Clearly the most interesting material from which to draw inferences about him is in the last lines. Arnold has come to his mother's door in the middle of the night, presumably to tell her how he feels about killing his brother, and has been sent away with an angry remark. At the story's conclusion his mother asks him what he wanted:

> "I didn't want nothing," he said flatly.
>   Then he went out the door and down the back steps, his legs trembling from the fright his answer gave him.[13]

Why does that simple answer frighten him? What does it imply for his future relations with his family? The answer lies not in one line of the story but in the knowledge of Arnold that accumulates throughout. Our understanding of his character depends on observations and information gathered from every scene.

We began our discussion of the short story with a tentative effort to distinguish it from the poem. It is not, finally, distinguishable from either the poem on one side or the novel on the other. All of them are ranges on one spectrum. We could probably find twenty literary works that could be arranged at equal intervals on a scale, with the lyric poem at one end, the short story somewhere in the middle, and the novel at the other end. The lyric poem might be represented by one of Shakespeare's sonnets, or perhaps by Wordsworth's "My Heart Leaps Up." As we move toward narrative, we would find "The Highwayman" and "The Rime of the Ancient Mariner," poems that tell stories. Somewhere along the line might be Poe's "Fall of the House of Usher," with its sonorous, poetic opening lines, and then less poetic stories like Hemingway's "The Killers." Beyond this short piece we would find stories spanning several episodes, like Chekhov's "The Lady with the Pet Dog." By degrees the stories would lengthen, approaching the complexity of the novel. Henry James' "The Beast in the Jungle" is either a long short story or a short novel. Tolstoy's *The Death of Ivan Ilyich* is longer still. In time we would arrive at *War and Peace*. Beyond that we get to *Ulysses*—are we then circling back toward poetry?

Thus the genres blend together to some degree, sharing techniques and subject matter. As we move off in other directions, too, the transitions are smooth and gradual. Some stories contain mostly dialog, so that they approach the form of the play. Some novels are so full of historical fact or autobiographical detail that they seem to blend history and fiction, or autobiography and fiction, as in the realm of television where the "docudrama" blends documentary and drama.

As we move from the short story to the novel, the blending of genres is obvious. Both are narratives; they seem to differ only in length and scope. But despite their similarities and their common strategies, there are some significant differences between them.

The Novel

In our brief glance at the short story, we mentioned plot, the events that form the foundation of the story; character, the imitation of person through dialog; description; action; and conflict, the energy and purpose in the interaction of character and plot. Much that was said of plot, character, and conflict in the short story applies to the novel. Like the short story, the novel is narrative. Length alone, however, is a significant difference, and affects all of these elements.

Plot provides an example. Short stories tend to emphasize one event, issue, or idea. "The Stone Boy" is about an accidental killing and its aftermath. The later scenes all develop the consequences of the killing. Had the story grown into a novel, we might have followed Arnold through adolescence into maturity, perhaps into old age. Even if the killing remained the most important event in the tale, it is unlikely that it would have occupied our attention throughout the story. A novel is too long to be devoted entirely to one incident, though the writer might often return to the crucial episode, tracing its influence on Arnold's life. The novel has a wider scope than the short story. It usually covers more time, more events, and more characters.

That breadth has several consequences. One is that novels typically convey the impression of reality more effectively than short stories or poems. A poem is clearly a performance, an art form, a verbal dance, and a short story is an episode, a short segment cut out of a larger tapestry. But a novel, especially once we are deeply involved in it, is as rich and full and detailed as life. We learn the characters' habits and their tastes in food, music, and entertainment; we rush through their busy moments and grow bored along with them in the dull moments between; we see their friends and family. We are immersed in detail, just as we are in our own lives. The short story gives us selected detail, just enough to carry the incident narrated. The novel gives us selected detail, too, but it doesn't seem to. It seems to give us everything and thus leaves us with the impression that we are living in the world it creates.

Many readers report a sense of dissociation after finishing a novel that has captivated them. It is, they say, like coming out of one world into another. The room in which they sit seems, for an instant, less real than the imaginary world they have just left. Ask any child what it was like to finish one of the *Harry Potter* books. Ask him why he is so eager for the next one. That desire to live in this imaginary world may be part of the reason for the popularity of series books and sequels; readers may wish to re-enter a world they have come to enjoy. The adolescent wants to go back to Hogwarts; the adult wants to be back in the saddle in one of Louis L'Amour's westerns or hanging out on Travis McGee's boat in John McDonald's series of mysteries. The sense of reality in the novel carries with it a penalty, though, for unsophisticated readers. They may lose track of the patterns and themes in the novel that give it meaning, just as they may lose track of the patterns and themes in their own lives. A poem is clearly and unmistakably a writer's vision, but many novels just seem to happen.

It is important, however, to maintain a sense of the author's intent if one is to learn from a work. Unsophisticated readers, forgetting that the novel is a constructed work of art, may submit it to crude tests, or worse, not question it at all. They may, for example, judge it against their own notion of reality, a perfectly valid way to begin. Finding that they don't know people like the characters portrayed, they may dismiss the work either as idle fantasy or as something irrelevant to their own experience. Or they may accept without adequate reflection the picture the work presents. They may fail to question the heroism or villainy of characters identified as heroes or villains, accepting superficial stereotypes in place of real characters. They may neglect to explore the codes of ethics implicit in a work. They may, in other words, fail to think about the novel as a vision, the product of one writer's reflection and labor. Treated thus, the novel may entertain them, but it loses its power to enrich their thought.

One of our goals must be to encourage reflection on the novel as an art form so that students come to realize that it is a vision of reality and not reality itself. That is perhaps best done by encouraging them to test their own visions against that of the work. They will be willing to respond to questions about the logic of events and the nature of the characters.

Do people behave as these characters behave?

Would you, in similar circumstances, act that way?

Do events really follow one another as these do?

Are these events coincidental, or are there cause-and-effect relationships among them?

Are they exaggerated or diminished by the telling?

Such questions, phrased appropriately for the book and the class, lead almost inevitably to discussion of the form of the novel.

Plot

Questions about the logic of events, for instance, are questions about plot. That is perhaps most easily demonstrated in mystery or adventure novels—Lowry's *The Ghosts of Now* or *The Other Side of the Dark,* for example, or Hahn's *Dead Man in Indian Creek,* Bennett's *The Dangling Witness,* Hillerman's *The Dark Wind,* or perhaps even adult mysteries such as Cross's (Carolyn Heilbrun's) *The Puzzled Heart,* or Forsyth's *The Day of the Jackal.* In these books, the dominant issue is often, "What happens next?" or perhaps "Why did these events happen?" This easily leads to questions not about the events themselves, but about the guiding vision from which they grow: What has the writer told us, and what has she failed to tell us, perhaps intentionally? What scenes or episodes has she emphasized, by giving them a great deal of attention? And finally, how might they be connected to one another? Do they reveal a pattern?

Much of the reading of a novel is a search for patterns in the mass of detail. If no patterns exist, the reader is likely to be unhappy with the work. It will be a shapeless, pointless collection of episodes, and although that may be much like real life, it is not satisfying in fiction. Sometimes, however, an apparent lack of pattern is itself a pattern. A novel like Remarque's *All Quiet on the Western Front* may leave some readers dissatisfied for this reason. *All Quiet on the Western Front* is a war story, but it is not a story of adventure, triumph, or even survival. Raised on the war movies they might see on television, students may expect to read about the excitement of battle or the nobility of fighting for one's country. Instead, they find a series of events that seem loosely strung together. There is a battle here, a gas attack there, an advance that seems to go nowhere, and a retreat. Several events may make a strong and lasting impression, especially the encounter between Paul, the novel's main character, and the French soldier. But the events seem related only because they happen to Paul and his friends—there is no sense of progress in the book. There is simply the constant filth, hunger, and dying.

Finally Paul is killed, on a quiet day with little action anywhere, pointlessly, uselessly, and almost completely unnoticed. Where, the students may ask, has the book taken us? The answers to that question lie in patterns that the students may have observed without realizing their significance. Events in the book do not seem to build on each other as we might expect them to. The battle does not move. We see no strategy, no contest of opposing minds, no brilliance leading to victory or blundering leading to defeat. But there is nonetheless a pattern.

Part of it is in the absence of the perspective that would allow us to see the larger design. We see the war through the eyes of a frontline infantryman; his perceptions fill the book. And what he sees is endless killing without any apparent point, continual suffering, gradual decay of the spirit, and finally his own gloomy death that seems to matter to no one, least of all himself. That pattern, although it doesn't build to a grand climax in which mysteries are solved, wrongs are righted, or justice is satisfied, nevertheless does make a point. It suggests that war, for the footsoldier, is not a noble, exciting, patriotic adventure. The purposes, causes, and ultimate results of the war recede into relative insignificance for him in the face of other matters. He is reduced by war to the point at which death seems a relief.

We aren't trying to provide a comprehensive interpretation of *All Quiet on the Western Front*. The point here is simply that identifying the patterns of events and characters in a novel may help us understand the author's intent.

Theme

The meaning growing out of these relationships among the events and characters in a work is the theme. Theme registers first as a set of impressions, feelings, or thoughts left by the work. As those feelings and thoughts are articulated and clarified, they become a statement of the theme. That statement is the answer to the question, "What's it all about?" or "So what?—why bother reading this?"

The concept of theme poses at least two problems. Students may try to simplify it to one word or a short phrase—in the case of *All Quiet on the Western Front,* "war," or perhaps "War is hell." These may be true enough, but they are not complex enough to do justice to the work. Students may also extend them much further than the work justifies or credit them with more authority than the work merits. Teachers, on the other hand, sometimes divorce the concept of theme from questions of personal significance, asking students to accept a statement bleached of relevance to their own thoughts and lives. An interpretation, whether it owes more to the words on the page or the personal experience that informs the thought, must recognize both the mind that creates it and the text that constrains it.

OVERSIMPLIFICATION   The problem of the oversimplified statement can be frustrating for us. Seeing subtleties that the students miss, aware of implications they have neglected, we may grow impatient with their willingness to accept crude generalizations. We may help them awaken to other possibilities in several ways. One simple technique is to have them compare the statements they have offered. Suppose, for instance, that a reading of *All Quiet on the Western Front* has produced comments like the following:

War is hell.

War is disgusting.

War is unjustifiable.

War is not very exciting.

War hurts young men, not the politicians responsible.

War is degrading.

Asked to identify the similarities and differences among these brief statements, students may discover ideas they did not express at first. For instance, the two statements "War is disgusting" and "War is degrading" are obviously similar. The student who finds war disgusting may point out the mud, the bad food, the lack of sanitation, and the inability to sleep comfortably. The student who finds it degrading, however, may point out the reduction of men to the status of tools, the loss of self-determination, and the obligation to kill other men. Elaboration reveals the differences in the two students' ideas. We could debate which insights are more significant, but it might be more useful to combine the observations of each student into a more complicated statement of the theme. Reducing the meaning of the work to one word obscures what the text has to offer, but drawing contrasts among such statements may encourage students to look for details that will flesh out their interpretations.

Students could, of course, be asked directly to supply such details: Why do you say that the theme of *All Quiet on the Western Front* is "War is hell"? By contrasting the different statements of theme that arise in a group, however, we make use of the students' natural desire to understand one another and explain themselves, as well as their wish to comprehend the text.

Stating the theme trades specificity for control. We must give up a certain amount of detail for the sake of a concise statement. Still, students must recognize that the thematic statement is not an end in itself but a tool useful in thinking about the mass of material the book offers. Its purpose is not to dismiss detail but to organize it. If it is too simplistic to contribute anything to the discussion, then the effort is wasted.

Overextending the theme is a danger related, perhaps, to the tendency to oversimplify. *All Quiet on the Western Front* clearly does not glorify war; it depicts it as dirty, degrading, demoralizing work. But would it be fair to Remarque to assert that he condemns all warfare? He has depicted one war, or, rather, part of one war, from the perspective of a footsoldier, but that is hardly a basis for asserting that he would consider all wars unjustifiable. He has not commented on the purposes of the war—they are beyond the scope of his novel—and though readers may have opinions about the morality of war, and might use *All Quiet on the Western Front* to initiate discussion of those opinions, it would not be legitimate to attribute to Remarque ideas that he did not express. Students must learn to push inferences only as far as the work will carry them, to distinguish between inferences based upon their analysis of the text and assertions that arise from their own beliefs.

INDIVIDUAL RESPONSE AND THEME   The second problem—that of the relevance of personal experience to the discussion of theme—naturally stems from the teacher's desire to train students to read accurately. For this purpose she may insist that they be faithful to the text in forming interpretations. That faithfulness, however, does not require abandoning their own perceptions or ignoring their feelings or associations. Rather, it means defining the relationship between these associations and the text. Statements of theme will thus vary, and the sophisticated reader is likely to accept the validity of many of the variations.

Let's return to "The Stone Boy" to illustrate the point. We might read this as the story of someone unable to cope with his situation. Arnold cannot understand or react to his brother's death; it is as though the event is so far beyond his comprehension that it does not register upon his emotions at all. Because he does not demonstrate the emotional response those around him expect to see, they reject him. This view might lead us to a thematic statement like "You must respond to an event in a socially approved manner, regardless of your real feelings, or you are likely to be ostracized."

That is a reasonable interpretation of the story, although it neglects several particulars. Consider, however, how the thematic impact of the story might differ for someone in circumstances like those of one of the characters. A parent, for instance, might note the importance of the moment Arnold goes to his mother's door and is sent away. He is apparently beginning to react to the killing at that moment, but his mother's rebuff destroys the opportunity, silencing him and isolating him from her. This may lead our reader to include in her thematic summary some reference to the fragility of human relations and the possible catastrophic consequences of even a small gesture of irritation such as the mother commits in her anger and sorrow. That interpretation might borrow strength from the similarities between the mother's lapse and Arnold's. Dragging the rifle through the fence is a small carelessness, resulting, perhaps, from haste or impatience. But its consequences, too, are disastrous. The pattern suggests that very little things—insignificant remarks—moments of slight inattention, might yield horribly bitter fruit. It is a theme that a parent would be interested in; it respects both her unique viewpoint and the content of the story. And it may give the story personal significance by helping her shape her own perceptions and behavior. Good literature ought to do as much for the reader.

Another reader, a teacher, might tend to emphasize the inarticulateness of the characters. Arnold cannot speak of the killing, even to say that he does not understand his own feelings. His parents are unable to help him; their inadequacy is vividly represented by the father's final, feeble remark to the sheriff: "The gun ain't his no more." The sheriff can only say that Arnold is either a moron or reasonable beyond his comprehension, crudely oversimplifying the possible reasons for Arnold's strange behavior. The teacher, aware of the power of language to ferret out information, to express feeling, to shape reasons, to comfort, to strengthen bonds between people, could not help noticing that the characters in this story seem totally incapable of using language for any of these purposes. She might see the failure to communicate as one theme of the story.

Theme is not purely in the work, on the page. It resides in the transaction between the reader and the text. Thus, different readers may see different themes in a work or state the same theme differently. If both teacher and students recognize this, theme can be a useful tool in discussing a work of fiction.

Other Genres

Discussion of genre is exceptionally difficult. The distinctions are subtle and elusive, and a full treatment of them is far beyond the scope of this text. This chapter has described the characteristics and demands of a few genres, as well as some of the concepts useful in discussing them. Teachers who plan to teach works from other genres—drama, epic, essay, or the like—might explain briefly to the class the important features of each. If they keep in mind that their purpose is not to teach the technicalities of genre analysis but to bring student and text together in intellectually and emotionally productive ways, then worries about the technicalities will diminish. They will be able to encourage students to observe the techniques of the writers as they raise and examine questions about human behavior. Knowledge of the genres will develop from and support the search for meaning.

Endnotes

1. Richard Lanham, *Style: An Anti-Textbook* (New Haven, CT: Yale University Press, 1974).

2. Randall Jarell, "Death of the Ball Turret Gunner," in *The Complete Poems* (New York: Farrar, Straus & Giroux, 1969), p. 144.

3. James Dickey, interview in *The Poet's Craft: Interviews* from the New York Quarterly.

4. Stephen Dunn, "Insomnia," in *Local Time* (New York: Quill-William Morrow, 1986), p. 41.

5. John Livinston Lowes, *The Road to Xanadu: A Study in the Ways of the Imagination* ([Rev. ed.] Ed.) Boston, MA: Houghton Mifflin, 1964).

6. Abraham Bernstein, *Teaching English in High School* (New York: Random House, 1961).

7. Frank Horne, "Nigger."

8. Henry Reed, "Naming of Parts", in *Lessons of War* (New York, Chilmark Press, 1970). rpt in *Henry Reed: Collected Poems*, ed. Von Stallsworthy (NY: Oxford Press, 1991), p. 49.

9. Laurence Perrine, *Sound and Sense* (New York: Harcourt, Brace and World, 1956), pp. 214–230.

10. Ibid., pp. 218–219.

11. *Maxine Kumin,* "You Are in Bear Country," in *The Long Approach* (NY: Viking Press, 1986).

12. Liam OFlaherty, "The Sniper," in *Liam O'Flaherty: The Collected Stories*, A. A. Kelly, Ed. (New York: Palgrave Macmillan, 2000), p. 96.

13. Gina Berriault, "The Stone Boy," in *Man in the Fictional Mode*, *Book 3*, Hannah Beate Haupt, Ed (Evanston, IL: McDougal, Littel & Co., 1970).

6 *Literature for Young Adults*

In those days, being restricted to a diet of children's titles, I devoured juvenile adventure stories, science fiction and mysteries. How strange, it seemed to me, that the high-minded librarians refused to stock the Hardy Boys or Tom Corbett, the Space Cadet.[1]

—MICHAEL DIRDA

Later Dirda will say, "To be an indiscriminate reader—as the luckiest young often are—means that the right books are all around you."[2]

The right books aren't necessarily those in the lists of eternal classics, the canon—at least, not for young readers. Perhaps not even the great children's books, those we buy as gifts for our nieces and nephews to entice them to read, will be the right books for a particular child. Dirda, an avid reader who came ultimately to love and write about the great books, reports that "For unknown reasons, I never read, nor cared to read, the standard children's classics. *Charlotte's Web* and *The Wind in the Willows* I would open only as a lucky grown-up."[3] He was lucky to find the books he needed at the time he needed them. They prepared him for the books he would want and need later, when those classics would reward his efforts.

The subject of this chapter is the right books for the students in secondary schools. In the last chapter we discussed the three genres most often taught in high school literature classes. We also mentioned that we would consider two categories—fiction for young adults and viewed literature—apart from the question of genre. Though often overlooked, these categories have special relevance to response-based teaching, since they are the types of literature that tend to attract students outside of class. They are broad enough to require extended treatment, and we will devote a chapter to each. Our topic here is young adult literature, that body of literature that has the best chance of offering the right book at the right time.

Importance of Young Adult Literature

If we are to begin our teaching with students' responses, we need literary works that provoke responses, stimulating students to think, feel, and talk. Without such works, awakening interest in discussion and writing can be very difficult. We're forced to trick students into temporary interest in something that doesn't really appeal to them. Planning becomes a search for games and gimmicks to hold the attention if not engage the mind and heart. Given a text inappropriate for our students, there is little else we can do.

A quick glance at typical secondary school English curricula, however, will suggest that some of the literature has not been chosen primarily for its appeal to students. Senior high school programs, for instance, are often organized historically. British literature is taught in the twelfth grade, beginning with *Beowulf* and "The Seafarer" and continuing as far into the present as time allows. American literature, usually taught in the eleventh grade, begins with sinners dangling above Jonathan Edwards' fiery pit and works its way forward until June or the censor's fiery pit stops it.

This is not to say that the literature found in historically arranged courses is necessarily uninteresting, simply that it was selected for its historical suitability rather than its interest for the students. Historical significance, however, does not guarantee personal significance. Secondary school students may not have the knowledge or interest to appreciate the progress of literary art, and they may not share all the interests and concerns of the writers who have found their way into the standard anthologies. Students who are brought too early to writers they might later appreciate often report their unhappiness. Milton's *Paradise Lost* may simply be lost on young students, and even such an adventure story as "The Rime of the Ancient Mariner," taught too soon, may leave them cold and indifferent.

Many readers can recall responding differently to a work at different times in their lives. Kylene Beers tells of her daughter, moving from one school to another, who was assigned *To Kill a Mockingbird* three years in a row. She didn't mind reading it again because she had enjoyed the book so much the first time, but after her third reading she commented that the new version was much better than the one she had read the year before:

> She had decided that in eighth grade she must have read an abridged version; I wanted to hug her and tell her that when she was in eighth grade, she was abridged.[4]

The new version of *To Kill a Mockingbird* hadn't been revised at all, of course—it was the reader who had been revised by another year of growth.

We can't have exactly the same literary experience twice; having once read we're slightly or dramatically changed by the experience so that re-entering the same text yields a new reading. The Russian poet Marina Tsvetaeva described the phenomenon vividly:

> There are books so alive that you're always afraid that while you weren't reading, the book has gone and changed, has shifted like a river; while you went on living, it went on living too, and like a river moved on and moved away. No one has stepped twice into the same river. But did anyone ever step twice into the same book?[5]

The same, identical text becomes a new book because the reader has become a new reader. Young people might read *Gulliver's Travels* as an exciting fantasy, a strange adventure in an imaginary world. When these same readers have grown and matured, Gulliver is a vastly different character and his adventures assume another meaning. Maturity accounts for the differences in the readings. The difference is in the reader, not in the text. If younger readers were expected to analyze the satire of the work, to read it as a commentary on the social mores of the time, they might respond less sympathetically. *Gulliver's Travels,* however, is one of those rich works that appeal in various ways—it is both an adventure story and a social commentary. Few works are quite as flexible, and I mention *Gulliver's Travels* not because it is typical but because it is atypical.

The difference in our readings of *Gulliver's Travels* as children and as adults indicates the gulf between childhood and maturity and suggests the importance of considering that gulf in planning literature instruction. Try, as a short experiment, the exercise presented in Workshop #6.

REMEMBERED BOOKS

This should take about a week. Spend some time–a few minutes or a few hours–calling to mind some book you enjoyed in childhood but haven't read since. If you have trouble coming up with a title, sort through the boxes of books in the attic, talk with your parents, or wander through the children's books in a nearby library. Something will work to prod your memory. Go back as far into your childhood as you can. You might remember your father reading the *Babar* books to you, or getting *Charlotte's Web* for a birthday, or coming upon *The Velveteen Rabbit* somehow. If you can't get any further into your past than adolescence, that will do. Pick something that stands out in your memory if at all possible. Don't re-read it at this point, however; don't even open it if it's lying there on your own child's nightstand. If she brings it to you and demands that you read it to her at bedtime, tell her . . . well, you'll have to read it to her, but it will short-circuit this experiment.

Having identified such a book, lock yourself away where you won't be disturbed for an hour and reflect on your memories of the book and the experience of hearing it or reading it. Then write about it:

How do you remember the book and the experience?

With what do you associate it—your family, a room, a feeling, a particular person?

What can you remember of the story line and the characters?

What do you recall it meant to you at the time?

Why did you enjoy it?

Why do you still remember it?

Capture as much as you possibly can about your experience with that book. At first, not much may come to mind, but one memory will lead to another and you should be able to fill a page or so. Then file that page away somewhere and don't look at it for three to five days. Forget about the book and the hours you spent writing.

After those several days have passed, find the book. Steal it from your child or borrow it from the library, then read it again. When you've done so, write briefly about your responses to the work *now*. Pretend that you've never seen the book before and are coming to it cold. Forget, insofar as you can, your earlier experience with it:

Do you like the book?

How do you respond to it?

How do you feel about it?

What do you think of it?

Again, follow your thoughts as far as you can, writing as much as you can about today's reading of this text. And now, once again, file this page away for three to five days.

When the time has passed, pull out both sheets—the one about your remembered experience with the book and the one about your recent reading—and compare them. What do they tell you about the text, about you, and about your transactions with the text? Was your second reading as pleasant an experience as you remember your first being? Was it the same experience or noticeably different? Do you observe anything about yourself—how have you changed, and how have your expectations for texts changed? What can you say, as a result of this experiment, about the nature of literary experience?

What this workshop tries to do is to keep the text constant—it hasn't changed—but to change the reader—you *have* changed over the years. Thus the literary experience the text enables is new and different.

If you have students of your own, you might try a similar experiment with them. Choose a short text suitable for them and, near the beginning of the school year, ask them to write a brief response to it. File it away. Then, later in the school year, perhaps a few weeks before the summer break, without reminding them that they've already seen the text, pull it out again (reformat it if you want to make the extra effort to disguise it, but some will recognize it anyway) and once more ask them to write a short response.

Collect those and take a few days to read through the pairs of papers from each student to see what they might reveal, and then return the two responses to the students and ask them to compare them. What do their two short response papers tell them about their growth over the year?

There is, fortunately, a growing body of literature well suited for young adult readers. It has not always been considered respectable, and by many it still is not, but literature written for young adults has, in the past several decades, attracted the attention of many librarians and teachers as well as the students themselves. Writers who did not originally think of themselves as writers for young adults have been drawn into the field by the responsiveness of young adult readers and the encouragement of publishers, who have found a profitable market in readers of middle school, junior high, and high school age. When Robert Cormier was writing *The Chocolate War*, he wasn't thinking of it as a novel for young adults, but, convinced by his publisher that it would be noticed in that market, he agreed to have it billed as a young adult book, and then found himself writing almost exclusively for that age group.[6] That the field of young adult literature has become recognized and significant is indicated by the fact that today we see writers not being pushed toward that arena by their editors, but instead intentionally and purposefully choosing it. Some of our most skillful contemporary writers aim their books at the young adult, including Chris Crutcher, Carolyn Cooney, Walter Dean Myers, Gary Paulsen, and J. K. Rowling, to name a very few.

Others, thought of primarily as writers for adults, may be seen moving from writing for adults to writing for a younger audience. Such prominent and popular writers of adult fiction as Michael Chabon and Carl Hiaasen have both recently published books aimed at the readers still in your classes. Chabon's *Summerland* (2002, Hyperion Books) and Hiaasen's *Hoot* (2002, Knopf) both appeared in the bookstores in 2002. Other books aimed at adults have been discovered by young adult readers. *The Lovely Bones*, by Alice Sebold (2002, Little, Brown Publisher), is an example. Furthermore, schools are beginning to include works of young adult literature in the English program, sometimes as books to be discussed in classes, usually in the middle schools, but more often as supplemental or independent reading. It has become an important body of literature.

Some works have been so well received that they have been recast as movies, perhaps the ultimate compliment for a literary work in this era. Sheila Schwartz's *Like Mother, Like Me* (1984, Bantam); Bette Greene's *Summer of My German Soldier* 11973, Dial); and S.E. Hinton's *The Outsiders* (1967, Viking) were among the first works of this genre to make it to the movie theaters. More recently, Duncan's *I Know What You Did Last Summer* (1973, Little, Brown) joined the ranks of books recast as movies, and Crutcher's *Staying Fat for Sarah Byrnes* (1993, Greenwillow) is likely to join them soon. The first of the Harry Potter series, J. K. Rowling's unbelievably popular books about the schooling of the young wizard, made it very quickly onto the screen, and films are planned for the remainder of the series, even though the books have not yet been written.

Literature for young adults has also begun to attract the attention of scholars Shiela Schwartz's *Teaching Adolescent Literature* (1979, Hayden) was published in 1979, and Ken Donelson and Aleean Pace Nilsen's comprehensive and readable *Literature for Today's Young Adults,* first published in 1980, is now in its sixth edition. Since then, many others have followed, including Althea Reed's *Reaching Adolescents: The Young*

Adult Book and the School (1985, Holt, Rinehart & Winston). Even Zipes *Sticks and Stones*, though its focus is not on pedagogy and it is seldom read by teachers, is a contribution to the study of this body of literature. Literature for young adults is, in other words, now a body of works that merits our attention.

Doing this literature justice in one chapter isn't possible. An historical treatment would require us to include books that might not be as useful to teachers as more recent works, and since our concern in this text is teaching literature, we'll refer those interested in the history to Donelson and Nilsen's scholarly work. A comprehensive survey of the available literature for young adults would fill not a chapter but a large volume, and since it would be immediately out of date we will forego that alternative as well. A close analysis of a few works would be both too narrow and too detailed to be useful. So we'll content ourselves here with examining several works grouped according to two of the most controversial themes in contemporary young adult literature in the hope that addressing themes will suggest patterns in the body of literature and perhaps ways of organizing instruction. It will offer a taste of young adult literature and allow us to make some suggestions about connections between these works and the standard English curriculum

Thematic grouping has at least three serious drawbacks. First, individual works are often hard to categorize. A book may develop many themes, and as we have argued, two readers are likely to see two different themes in the same text. Thus, in a sense, placing a book in a thematic slot means trying to respond and think for someone else. But if we keep in mind that the assignment to categories is simply one reader's judgment, not meant as a substitute for one's own reading of the books, then the arbitrariness of the placement will remain obvious and harmless.

A second drawback lies in the categories themselves. They too will seem arbitrary, and they will be. Countless ways of ordering the material are possible, and each one will incline us to see certain features of the works and neglect others. We might, for instance, tend to overlook a good book that does not fit neatly into one of our categories, just as a biologist discussing cats and dogs may not be happy with the cheetah, which has some features of both. A different set of categories might encourage us to focus on that same book, as the biologist discussing predators that lie in wait and those that chase would use the cheetah as one of his principal illustrations of the latter group. The categories will both emerge from and shape the reading of the works. Again, we should simply remain aware of that to avoid deceiving ourselves into thinking that there is anything inevitable about the way we choose to arrange the literature.

A third drawback of the thematic arrangement is the number of possible categories: sexuality, coming of age, race and ethnic identity, family, alienation, illness, death, suicide, insanity, fantasy, science fiction, gothic romance, the occult, power, independence, handicaps, adventure, westerns, religious experience, violence, humor. . . . The list could go on indefinitely. For brevity's sake we will discuss only two possible groups and only a few of the works that might be placed within each one. We'll then make some suggestions about keeping up with this rapidly growing body of literature, and end by referring you to some useful websites, booklists, and other references.

Sexuality

Someone once commented that if biographers were to do justice to the sexual lives of their subjects, their biographies would have to be two or three times longer than they usually are. Much of that additional text would have to be given to adolescence, when the preoccupation with sexuality seems to be as strong and distracting as it will ever be. As the restraints on writers for adolescents have eased, it is not surprising that many of them have chosen to write about the turmoil of emerging sexuality. Nor is it surprising that some have found their books tucked securely away in a dark corner of the librarian's desk. Sexuality is clearly a sensitive issue no matter how it may be treated, and young adult fiction treats it in a variety of ways.

Consider, for example Judy Blume's *Forever . . .*, a novel that has probably aroused more debate than any other work of young adult fiction dealing with the issue of sex. It was first published in 1975, and it had angered some readers by the time they finished the first sentence. It begins, "Sybil Davison has a genius I. Q. and has been laid by at least six different guys."[7] This sentence was not calculated to slide unnoticed past watchful guardians of youth, virtue, and virginity, whose loud protests alerted young readers to the possibility that there must be something interesting here. There is, as any English teacher knows, no surer way to entice students to read a book than to warn them of its sinful, wicked content. *Forever . . .* became immensely popular.

The book is about a young girl's first sexual experience. Katherine, the protagonist and narrator, meets Michael, they fall in love, their friendship grows and then dies. Much of the book is devoted to the sexuality of the relationship, which is treated frankly and directly. The affair is neither idyllic nor catastrophic, neither glamorous nor sordid, neither solemn nor comical. Blume seems to have taken care to present the story with a minimum of intrusive comment. There is, for instance, no obvious moralizing about the rightness or wrongness of Katherine's sexual involvement. Even her parents, who could so easily be cast in the role of guardians of traditional morality, make no speeches about the virtue of virtue. Although they are appropriately concerned for Katherine's happiness and safety, they seem also to respect her autonomy and integrity. Katherine's mother discusses sex with her openly, if nervously. She advises Katherine to think carefully and act cautiously, but beyond that, she is unwilling to prescribe how her daughter should behave:

> "It's up to you to decide what's right and what's wrong. . . . I'm not going to tell you to go ahead but I'm not going to forbid it either. It's too late for any of that. I expect you to handle it with a sense of responsibility though, either way."[8]

The absence of a strong condemnation of the sexual activity annoys some critics and teachers. They find nothing in the book, either in the beliefs the characters express or in the outcome of events, to frighten young readers about sexuality. Katherine does not get pregnant, does not contract a venereal disease, and is not ostracized by her friends, thrown out of school, or otherwise traumatized by her experience with Michael. The more vehement critics of the book would wish for at least one or two of those misfortunes to punish her affair.

If Blume does not condemn the sexual involvement, neither does she glamorize it. Michael and Katherine's first experiences are clumsy rather than ecstatic. They do have to worry about pregnancy, discovery, and their own ineptness. Their first effort is interrupted by Michael's over-excitement, and they must dress and drive to the drugstore to buy more condoms before they can try again. The evening leaves Michael embarrassed and Katherine disappointed, but relieved:

> "I'm no longer a Virgin. I'll never have to go through the first-time business again and I'm glad—I'm so glad it's over! Still, I can't help feeling let down. Everybody makes such a big thing out of actually doing it. But Michael is probably right— this takes practice."[9]

Her experience is not the fireworks display of old, third-rate romantic films. It is not perfect or otherworldly. But it is a beginning, and they go from there to more satisfactory experiences.

Blume's treatment of sex is balanced. She represents it neither as pure evil nor as pure pleasure, but as a natural though confusing and complicated process. Her failure to condemn angers those who view literature as an instrument for indoctrination rather than an art form to promote thought. They see her unwillingness to condemn as tacit approval, or even advocacy, of sexual experimentation, and they conclude that the book is immoral. It could be argued, however, that *Forever . . .*, by neither condemning nor advocating the activities it recounts, invites the reader to reflect and consider. What it *does* seem to advocate is the sense of responsibility mentioned by Katherine's mother. And Katherine does act responsibly. She is careful and considerate of both Michael and herself; she neither uses him nor is used by him. Ultimately, she is responsible enough to withdraw from the relationship when she decides it can no longer be satisfactory for both of them. But she does not regret it; it has done her no harm and has presumably helped her grow.

Regardless of what the book advocates or fails to advocate, it is likely to provoke thought and discussion. It deals clearly and vividly with an issue that interests almost every adolescent. If our concern is not to shape the attitudes of our students but to teach literature, then we may be able to use students' interest in the sexual content to draw them into the book. Curious about first sexual experiences, the students may be led to look carefully at the characters, examining their motives and behavior. They may wish to consider whether the portrayal is realistic and whether it neglects some aspects of the experience and overemphasizes others. They may know of, or may have experienced, sexual encounters similar to or different from the characters in Blume's story. Their parents may have attitudes toward their children's maturing that can be compared with those of Katherine's parents.

This is not to suggest that such a book as *Forever . . .* should become a tool we use to pry into the private lives of the students or their families. We are teachers and should not become either amateur psychotherapists or voyeurs. Literature *invites* us to reflect on—and perhaps to discuss—issues of personal significance, but it doesn't *demand* that we do so. Students have the right to make their own decisions about what they will make public and what they will withhold. Literature also enables us to discuss private, even intimate, issues without the vulnerability of public disclosure because we can, if we wish, focus on the characters rather than ourselves, discussing *their* choices rather than ours, *their* problems, *their* values, *their* mistakes, rather than ours. At times you may hear such passion in a student's voice when she discusses a situation in a story that you begin to suspect that she is no longer talking about mere images conjured out of ink and paper but about herself, her friends, or her family. That is, quite likely, what is happening. She may be speaking about Katherine but thinking about someone else entirely. Literature enables us to protect ourselves by objectifying our experience, viewing it, or something like it, in the lives of the characters. We can then talk about ourselves *without* talking about ourselves, discuss our fears without betraying them, reflect on our hopes without revealing more than we want to.

If students consider some of the issues a book like *Forever* . . . presents they will be engaging in literary analysis of the most significant sort—analysis inspired by a desire to understand both themselves and the text. To judge the work, after all, requires them to consider their own notions about sexual experience. Blume's novel raises enough of the issues about sexuality, and treats them delicately enough, that it may be considered an invitation to think rather than an effort to indoctrinate.

Another book dealing with adolescent sexuality has been accused of presenting a less balanced view. Ann Head's *Mr. and Mrs. Bo Jo Jones,* written about ten years before Blume's *Forever* . . ., concerns not so much the developing sexuality of the characters as its result: an unwanted pregnancy. Where Blume is direct and explicit in describing Katherine's first sexual experience, Head is roundabout:

> . . . when Bo Jo said, "Let's go have a look at the ocean," I don't even remember feeling daring about it or giving it a thought one way or another. I trusted Bo Jo. I trusted myself. I had no idea that there actually is a point of no return.
> Afterwards I was shattered. And furious with Bo Jo. And furious with myself.[10]

Somewhere in between those two paragraphs is July's first sexual encounter, signaled by the word "afterwards." To realize what has occurred, the reader must pull together several clues, for nowhere up to this point in the story has the narrator referred to sex. She does refer to love and marriage, but she says only that she has strong ideas about them. She speaks of "my downfall" without telling us precisely what it is. Then, in the passage quoted above, she mentions a "point of no return" and says that afterwards she was shattered. For the reader to infer that July's downfall is sex, he must be able to share, at least imaginatively, the attitudes toward sex implicit in her words. He must make the imaginative leap from "shattered" to sexuality. The "mock reader," to borrow Walker Gibson's term for the reader implied by the text,[11] is one who shares July's vision that sex is a downfall, shattering and shameful, too offensive to be spoken of directly. Only that vision organizes and interprets those insubstantial clues.

Some of Head's readers, perhaps more now than in 1967, when the book was first published, find the attitudes it reflects uncomfortable and demeaning. They argue that sex need not be seen as degrading and destructive, that it need not result in pregnancy, as it does in this story, and that it need not be spoken of coyly and obliquely. It does not have to just happen as it does in Head's book; people can judge their own readiness for it and can foresee and control the possible consequences. They may point out that Head's book presents a very narrow view—her characters never consider contraception, or afterwards abortion or adoption. Instead, their path seems preordained: Sex will lead to pregnancy, which will lead to marriage and all the complications it must involve for adolescents. In short, some readers argue that the book sustains an antiquated notion of sex, promoting the foolish belief that carefully cultivated ignorance and abstinence are the best safeguards for the young.

Forever . . . and *Mr. and Mrs. Bo Jo Jones* show dramatically different attitudes toward sexuality, but there are other interesting differences between the two books. The adult characters contrast neatly. In *Forever . . .*, Katherine's mother speaks openly with her about sex, showing respect for Katherine's judgment and responsibility. Her grandmother is also helpful, giving her information about contraception and encouraging her to think. Her parents do not abdicate all responsibility, and late in the novel arrange for Michael and Katherine to be separated for a time, but they do not try to control her completely. The parents in *Mr. and Mrs. Bo Jo Jones,* on the other hand, try repeatedly to engineer their children's lives. July's parents, when they hear that she is pregnant and married, push for annulment of the marriage and adoption for the baby. They decide between themselves, "'Whatever your answer . . . we are agreed that an annulment is still the only solution.'"[12] They are planning for their children, not with them. Katherine's parents, although they have opinions, are willing to discuss them with their daughter. The parents in *Mr. and Mrs. Bo Jo Jones* come to their children with decisions made; they speak to inform or persuade or command, not to discuss.

The differences between the two novels—in the motives and reasoning of the characters, the logic of events, and the relationships—should promote thought about both the fictional worlds and the real world. If the adolescent readers are interested in sexuality, as they usually are, then they are very likely to be interested in the characters and events of these stories. This interest will make them more likely to read sensitively and carefully. Of course, there is some danger that provocative works like *Forever . . .* and *Mr. and Mrs. Bo Jo Jones* will be lost in the discussion they stimulate. The talk can drift from the issues raised by the text to issues and anecdotes in general, growing aimless and shallow. Some of that drift is inevitable in a class that tries to deal with individual students' responses, but too much of it reduces the discussion to cocktail conversation. The teacher must keep in mind that her job is not to teach about sex, but about literature. If sex is an issue in the literature, it must be considered, but the primary point is to teach students to find pleasure and wisdom in reading, to read reflectively and thoughtfully, and to talk and write intelligently about the experience. To do that, they must test the fictional world against their own. If students lose themselves in daydreams and reminiscences, the teacher must encourage them to weigh those thoughts against the work. If the discussion yields only stale arguments and memorized platitudes, then gentle questioning, to raise doubts about prefabricated visions of the world, may be necessary.

Testing one work against another establishes a context in which the encouragement and questioning come more easily. July and Katherine might be compared with one another. How do their attitudes toward sex differ? Do they want the same things out of life? Students may notice, for instance, that July is happy to work as a secretary to put her husband through college, whereas Katherine seems determined to make a life for herself and will not accept a secondary role. Students might be encouraged to improvise, write, or at least imagine short dialogs between the two girls on such topics, trying to capture their attitudes and reveal their differences. Similarly, how do Michael and Bo Jo compare? What are the differences in their attitudes toward sex and toward the girls? Are they both responsible? Are they responsible in the same way? How might each view the actions of the other? How might Michael and July have reacted to one another; how might Bo Jo and Katherine? Would either of these recombinations work? As students discuss these questions we should, of course, encourage them to explain themselves, citing passages that support or contradict their interpretations. Doing so may teach them the habit of providing evidence for their inferences and reasons for their judgments.

More specific questions about choices and decisions might also yield good discussion. For example, the class could be asked how Michael and Katherine might have dealt with pregnancy. Would they have told anyone? How might they break the news to their parents? How might their parents respond? The students might also be encouraged to speculate about the authors. What can they infer about the attitudes of the authors and how those attitudes compare? Students might be asked to write or act out a discussion between the two writers, perhaps with a third student as moderator. If students were to act out such a panel discussion, it would probably run more smoothly if they planned out their questions. They might start with something like, "Do you think that your novels encourage responsible thought and action on the part of adolescents who read them?" or "How would you each defend your novel against a school board that objected to your portrayal of adolescent sexuality?" and move on from there to questions that encourage the students playing the authors to talk about one another's books. Of course, all such suggestions have to be judged in the light of the students. Some groups will be interested in pursuing these questions; some will not.

More recent novels for young adults continue to explore the theme of sexuality, though in some of the more recent novels, the sexual event recedes into the background as the author investigates other complications that arise from it or around it. Rita Williams-Garcia's *Every Time a Rainbow Dies,* published in 2001, is interesting in this context because it treats the protagonist's first sexual experience so casually. It's surprising that this book hasn't raised the hackles of the censors for that reason alone. The young man, Thulani, in love with a beautiful and, for the moment, inaccessible girl, Ysa, is relieved of his virginity by another girl, Julie, in whom he has little interest:

> He ate dinner at Julie's a few times, sometimes with her family, though they were
> seldom home. Her parents worked off-hours, and her brother was in college. Julie

gave him his first kiss, and after a month, a Christmas gift (an ankle bracelet that she pointed to in a store window), she took his virginity in her bedroom while Janine, Mona, and Yvette stood guard downstairs.[13]

The hasty initiation is completed, and the narrative rapidly moves on to other events. There's little reflection on the occasion. Thulani has little to say about it; parents are never around to comment or react (Thulani's mother is dead and his father out of his life); there are no repercussions, no consequences, no major changes in Thulani's character or his situation. Thulani's thoughts remain on Ysa, though he continues to see the other girl. His first sexual experience seems to be about as momentous an occasion as his first ride on the subway.

When he and Ysa later do find themselves together, the event is more fully recounted, and clearly more significant. Nonetheless, that the young man's first sexual experience can be such a minor event in the novel is an indication that times have changed. In *Forever . . .* and in *Bo Jo Jones* it was the central event, the moment around which all other action revolved. Here, in a young adult novel published in 2001, it's a minor event dispensed with in less than a page. That difference alone might be interesting to discuss with a class.

That isn't the case in all of the more recent books, of course. Louise Plummer's *A Dance for Three* (2000, Delacorte Press), for example, considers the plight of a young girl, Hannah, who finds herself pregnant but rejected by the boy who refuses to acknowledge that he is the father. The situation obviously invites comparison with *Bo Jo Jones*, but students might also be interested to compare the relationship of Hannah and her mother, who are forced by the situation to deal with their own tensions, with the relationship between July and her parents, and that between Katherine and hers. Their analysis may suggest to them something about the gradual evolution of attitudes toward sexuality in our society. Jerrie Oughton's *Perfect Family* (2000, Houghton Mifflin) examines a similar plight, but one with a different resolution. In this story, the young girl, Welcome, is also pregnant, but not by the boy she loves. The father in this case is an old friend, and her inability to find any other way to cope with the circumstances leads Welcome to desert them both and run away to hide with relatives.

Delicacy is, of course, demanded. Some students, even entire classes, may be reluctant to talk about these matters, and their reticence should be respected. Literature classes should not intrude on students' privacy. The literary work itself helps guard against intrusiveness by providing other people and events to talk about. Students need not speak of their own attitudes—they can instead explore those of the characters; they don't have to talk about their own experiences—they can instead discuss those recounted by the book. This enables them to discuss delicate matters like sexuality without uncomfortable disclosures about themselves. When we notice students talking about the actions of a fictional character with a conviction that suggests strong personal feelings, although they may never refer to what they, themselves, believe or how they, themselves, would act, we may hope that the talk is helping them to clarify their thinking about their own lives while preserving their safety.

If, however, students are comfortable with the group and confident in their opinions, there is no reason to keep them from speaking of their own beliefs and values. They may want to compare their attitudes with those of the characters, to consider how they would handle problems that arise in the books. Here again, though, delicacy is demanded. We should, if possible, help students avoid revealing thoughts or experiences that may later embarrass them. They will have to continue to work and play with the others in the class, and, as in any social group, they may find the information used maliciously. If we sense that students are speaking too openly, revealing too much about themselves or their families, then we should find some way of tactfully interrupting or diverting the conversation.

A well-timed request to write rather than discuss is often useful in such cases. The energy produced by the discussion can be transferred to the task of writing. Students may not be eager to abandon the ease of talk for the labor of composition, but if they do it they may find that they write with unaccustomed vigor and consider what they have written important. Putting ideas on paper rather than speaking them also allows the students time to decide rationally whether their thoughts should be shared or whether it is wisest to keep them for journal entries and private conversations with their most trusted friends.

Such books as the few we've discussed here have enough merit to stand on their own in the English curriculum, but they might also be grouped with more traditional works. *Forever . . .* and *Mr. and Mrs. Bo Jo Jones* might well be read along with Wharton's *Summer* or Hawthorne's *The Scarlet Letter*—obvious possibilities, since they, too, deal with sexuality. Required reading in some curricula, and much more complex and sophisticated than either of the more contemporary works, *The Scarlet Letter* nonetheless raises many of the same questions:

What is responsible behavior in a society?

How are the experiences of the males different from those of the females in these works?

How completely must an individual conform to the expectations of his society, especially in matters that are largely private?

To what extent do these private matters affect the society as a whole?

How much should a society have to say about the private behavior of its citizens?

Several of these works, and others, might be brought together in various ways. The class might be asked to begin with *Rainbow* or *Forever . . .*, since they are the most contemporary and most explicit and therefore probably most provocative, moving then to *Mr. and Mrs. Bo Jo Jones,* less explicit and contemporary, and ending with *The Scarlet Letter,* the most distant in style and time.

The more recent work is probably the more accessible to the students, dealing as it does with familiar times and places. *The Scarlet Letter,* on the other hand, comes out of another society, with different mores, different values. Such a plan, beginning with the more contemporary and moving back in time, might more effectively lure the students into the reading by giving them the most approachable work first and allowing them to use it as a foundation on which to build their understanding of the more difficult texts.

These works are obviously not equally challenging. *The Scarlet Letter* is a much more difficult text than any of the others, and the objection might be raised that a class capable of reading it would be well beyond the easier books. Nonetheless, they may be worth reading. There is much to be said for spending some of our time reading material that comes easily to us. Not even the most literate adult *always* chooses the most demanding text. Jacques Barzun read mysteries, and you and I have our own taste in books to read on airplanes. If reading is always hard work for our students, they're likely to develop a distaste for the process.

If there isn't time for all of the class to read all of the books, or if it seems desirable for other reasons to separate the class into groups, we might assign each book to a part of the class. Such a strategy would be especially useful if we find ourselves teaching eleventh-graders of such widely varying ability that some would be dismally frustrated by Hawthorne. Obligated by the curriculum to teach *The Scarlet Letter*, we might assign that book to the more capable students and the other books to those less skillful. The groups assigned the young adult texts might be expected to read some, but not all, of *The Scarlet Letter*, so they would have at least some experience with the work. Discussion then might be based on broad questions applicable to each of the works, questions like, "What are the attitudes and values of the book's heroine?" Such a question could well develop out of students' early comments on the works, when they are likely to report approving or disapproving of the heroine's actions. They could be asked to explain further, illustrating with references to the text full enough to be comprehensible to others in the class who have not read the book. The need to explain to those others may help stem a student's tendency to lapse into vagueness and uncertainty.

Discussions among groups that have read different works are difficult to run, but not impossible. We have to judge how much help the students need. Some classes can simply begin to talk about the interesting issues, allowing details of plot and characterization to emerge as they are called for. Others might work better if each group summarizes its book, answering questions about the story line, before they begin to explore the differences in content and style. And all will probably be helped by inferential questions that require them to look closely at both the text and their own experiences. It should not be difficult to conceive of workshop sessions in which students reading different books can come together to discuss a shared issue.

Students in such a heterogeneous class as the one imagined here might, for instance, be asked to choose one or two paragraphs or passages that they think will best characterize the heroine of their novel. Perhaps they could make individual selections at home and bring them in to class the next day, where they could spend a few minutes collaboratively deciding which is the most effective passage. The readers of each book could then be asked to present these to the class and the entire group could then consider what differences and similarities they can infer from the selections.

Such an activity would honor each book, would provide the students with practice citing the text appropriately and choosing passages that make a point, would call upon them to draw inferences from what they find, would require them to explain their analysis to one another, and would invite them to work toward consensus about an aspect of the text.

Another possible arrangement of the three works is to have the class concentrate on one for close reading and analysis in the classroom, and read one or both of the others outside class. As students discuss issues in the main text, they may be asked to consider the same issues in the texts they are reading independently. If a class working on *The Scarlet Letter* discusses the relationship between a social group and an individual within it who does not share its mores or abide by its customs, the students might be asked to consider the relationship between society and the individual in *Rainbow, Mr. and Mrs. Bo Jo Jones,* or *Forever . . .*, perhaps writing a brief paper on the issue. Such a paper would require them to apply the analytic skills they are developing in class to something they have read outside and would thus measure the extent to which they are learning to respond to and analyze literature.

Works of young adult literature taught along with the standard curriculum might make the classics more accessible to students by helping them see through the differences to the fundamental similarities. Hester Prynne may speak differently, wear different clothes, and live in a society with different beliefs, customs, and laws, but her problem is not unlike that faced by many young women today. Students who have considered the issues in the contemporary setting of *Forever . . .* may be more receptive to such a book as *The Scarlet Letter.*

There are few aspects of love and sexuality left unexamined within the collection of good young adult literature today. In *Speak*, for instance, Laurie Halse Anderson (1999, Farrar Straus Giroux) tells the story of Melinda's year in school following her rape by one of the school's most popular boys. Silenced by the trauma, she grows more and more isolated from her classmates until she is finally forced by the desire to protect one of them from the same fate to acknowledge and deal with the event. Aaron Fricke's *Reflections of a Rock Lobster* (1981, Alyson Publications Inc.) is an autobiographical account of growing up homosexual and facing the reactions of others, many of whom refused to tolerate his difference, while Bette Greene's *The Drowning of Stephan Jones* (1991, Bantam) examines even more virulent homophobia. M.E. Kerr's *Hello, I Lied*, (1997, HarperCollins) deals with a young man uncertain of his homosexuality, tempted toward heterosexuality by the arrival of an intriguing girl. Alex Sanchez's *Rainbow Boys* (2001. Simon & Schuster) follows three young men in high school, all of them dealing with complications posed by their homosexuality. Nancy Garden's *Annie on My Mind* (1982, Farrar, Straus, Giroux) is a story of two young women who fall in love and have to consider the consequences of making their lesbianism public. Jacqueline Woodson's *If You Come Softly* (1998, Putnam) tells of an African American girl and a Caucasian boy who are drawn to one another despite the disapproval of those who surround them. And there are many others.

The issues are treated in the short story, too, in collections such as *Love and Sex: Ten Stories of Truth* (Michael Cart, Editor, 2001, Simon & Schuster), and in books that consist of the reflections of adolescents themselves on their own experience of love and sexuality. Ann Turner's *Learning to Swim: A Memoir*, for example, is a collection of poems recounting a neighbor's sexual aggression and its effects on a young girl. Consider her introductory poem, both as a commentary on her experience and a testimony to the power of writing:

Listen[14]

Listen, I am trying
to remember everything
because it keeps coming back
like a skunk dog
on the porch
whining to get in,
and I'm afraid
if I don't let it in
it will never
go away.
This is what I remember:
that hot room,
your strange body,
your hands hurting,
and harsh words in my ears
telling me terrible things
would happen
if I ever
told.
But now you can't
find me or reach me
or hurt me ever
again
and once I tell the words
I am going to kick
you off my porch
and learn to breathe
again.

Things I Have to Tell You: Poems and Writing by Teenage Girls (Betsy Franco, Editor, 2001, Candlewick) offers the perceptions of young girls growing up in this society, while *You Hear Me?: Poems and Writings by Teenage Boys* (2000, Candlewick Press) presents the young boy's point of view. These two anthologies would be a useful resource in a classroom library, giving students the perspectives of others their own age on these significant issues and offering them examples of what their peers have been able to produce. Seeing such writing might inspire them to attempt it themselves; at the very least, it should reveal to them that the writing of imaginative literature is a way of making sense of experience available to us all, and not merely the domain of an intellectual elite. Another very useful collection of poems is one compiled by Naomi S. Nye and Paul B. Janeczko, entitled *I Feel a Little Jumpy around You: A Book of Her Poems and His Poems Collected in Pairs* (1996, Simon & Schuster). They've paired poems, one by a male and one by a female, in such a way that they invite discussion of the issues addressed.

Clearly, many of the young adult books are not likely to be accepted or approved by some adults; equally clearly, they deal with human concerns and confusions faced by a great many of our students. Such books as these offer the students a chance to think through the complications in which life entangles them, to observe how others have dealt with these matters, to articulate their own thoughts and confusions, and perhaps to move closer to some control over their own fate. Even if these texts, and others like them, can't be smuggled into some classrooms, we might still make ourselves aware of them and guide students toward them when it seems appropriate.

We have discussed several works of young adult literature at some length to illustrate their potential and show how they might be related to one another and to other items in the English program. Some schools, of course, won't allow a book like *Forever* . . . even in the library, much less in the classroom. And students uncomfortable with the subject matter should not, of course, be forced to deal with it. Finally, some teachers will find that they can't teach such a book without embarrassment. Recognizing that, they should bypass it for other works. Since schools, students, and teachers differ widely across the country, no recommendations about teaching these books would be suitable in all settings, so it is probably more useful to suggest possible patterns for instruction, indicate the range of material available, and then leave the details to the imagination of each teacher.

Violence

As a society we seem to be more comfortable with violence than with sex. *Lady Chatterley's Lover* must fight its way through the courts; *Forever* . . . is banished from the shelves of middle, junior, and even senior high school libraries; and magazines like *Playboy* come under attack from public prosecutors in relatively cosmopolitan cities like Atlanta; but maiming, raping, torturing, disemboweling, and murdering continue in books and movies with few protests from anyone. The public school English curriculum has never shied away from the violent, even the gruesome. *Hamlet* litters the stage in the final act with four bloody corpses; "The Cask of Amontillado" seals a man live in a tomb; *Beowulf* rips arms off of monsters; *The Red Badge of Courage* slaughters soldiers on the battle field; "The Most Dangerous Game" hunts a man down as if he were an animal; *The Lord of the Flies* transforms a group of schoolboys into savages who torment and kill each other. All that bloodshed and brutality has created barely a ripple compared to the waves of angry objection to books like *Mr. and Mrs. Bo Jo Jones* and *Forever.* . . . Sexuality offends us more than slaughter.

In young adult literature, what violence there is comes close to the adolescent's experience. S.E. Hinton's *The Outsiders* (1967, Viking) deals with the violence of street gangs in a community divided between the affluent and those close to poverty. Kin Platt's *Headman* (1975, Greenwillow), also about gangs, views them from the perspective of a boy who both needs the gang and wants to escape from its influence. *The Chocolate War* (1974, Pantheon) portrays the violence resulting from one young man's resistance to the pressures of his schoolmates. Patricia Dizenzo's *Why Me? The Story of Jenny* (1981, William Morrow) and Sandra Scoppettone's *Happy Endings Are All Alike* (1978, Harper Collins) both consider rape and its effects on the victim. Rita Williams-Garcia's *Every Time a Rainbow Dies* (2001, William Morrow) explores the effects of a violent rape upon both the young girl and a boy, Thulani, who witnesses it and tries, too late and unsuccessfully, to intervene. Lois Duncan's *Killing Mr. Griffin* (1978, Little, Brown) examines the issue of responsibility for a violent act not fully intended by its perpetrators. In all of these stories, as in most of the young adult fiction dealing with violence, the central characters are themselves young adults, and the issues raised are likely to be significant for young adult readers.

Duncan's *Killing Mr. Griffin*, for instance, tells about a group of high school students who decide to frighten their strict and demanding English teacher. Led by the demonic Mark, they agree to kidnap Mr. Griffin and haul him off to a secluded spot in the woods where they will humiliate and terrify him, forcing him to beg for his life. It will be, they think, suitable repayment for his harshness in the classroom. But the plan goes astray. The students fail to account for Mr. Griffin's courage; he refuses to beg for his release despite his helplessness. The kidnappers, after some arguing among themselves, decide to leave him bound and blindfolded, hoping that the long, cold night in the woods will break him. But they have also failed to account for his health, and Mr. Griffin, suffering from a heart condition and unable to take the nitroglycerin on which he depends, dies during the night, turning the kidnapping into murder.

The story raises some interesting questions about violence and responsibility. Are the students equally responsible? Mark is clearly the leader—without him the kidnapping would not have been attempted. Still, all of the group participate willingly in an obviously criminal act resulting in death. Shouldn't they all share equally in the responsibility for that act? And what is it that the students are responsible for? They kill a man, but they did not mean to. They don't shoot him or knife him—they only try to frighten him, and unfortunately he dies. Some readers may argue that his death is not the students' responsibility since it results from the heart problem, of which they are ignorant; others will hold that the kidnapping, which is not beyond their control, puts Mr. Griffin in a situation that causes his death, and that the students are thus guilty of killing him.

The issue is not simple. Readers will have to consider distinctions between "murder" and "killing," examine their notions of "responsibility," and consider the implications of either forgiving the stunt or punishing it. They will have to look closely at the students' relationships among themselves and with Mr. Griffin. The book invites both introspection and analysis. Each reader must ask himself how forgiving he is and how strictly he wishes to hold people accountable for their actions. And as he asks those questions about his own values, he may also examine the text to see how Duncan has influenced him.

Most readers will notice, for instance, that in the beginning of the book Mr. Griffin is little more than tyrannical. He humiliates his students, penalizes them for the slightest errors, and rewards their efforts with only minimal praise and with exhortations to do still better. Those first pages encourage sympathy for the students and anger at Mr. Griffin. But in Chapter 5 Duncan takes us into Mr. Griffin's home. He is now "Brian," not just "Mr. Griffin." We see his wife, who is expecting their first child, and hear them talk about, among other things, his students and his teaching. Mr. Griffin has given up college teaching because he thought he could contribute more to high school students. His strictness is well-meant; he wants his students to succeed, even if his demands make him unpopular. In this setting Brian Griffin is a more likable character—a perfectionist, perhaps, and thus annoying at times, but not the cruel man his students think he is. His wife's perspective helps to soften us:

> . . . it made him suddenly so human, so vulnerable, that she wanted to hug him. It was terrible to be married to a man whose weaknesses were his virtues.[15]

Chapter 5 changes the perspective for the reader. It is not a subtle change—one advantage of adolescent literature is that the books are accessible to students, both in theme and in technique. Students can see the writer's craft here, while in a more subtle work they may have difficulty understanding it even when it is explained to them. Seeing the change in perspective in Chapter 5, students can be led to speculate about its purpose, and should quickly realize that Duncan has complicated matters.[16] There are no good guys and bad guys. Neither Mr. Griffin nor his students (with the possible, and awkward, exception of Mark) can be considered entirely evil or virtuous, and thus judgments about the events in the story require a bit more intellectual labor.

The violence in the book may be examined from several points of view. Its disastrous consequences raise questions about the appropriateness of violence:

Was kidnapping the right tool for accomplishing the students' objectives?

What were their objectives?

Did they hope to improve the situation in Mr. Griffin's classroom, or did they simply want revenge?

If the former, was there a better way for them to proceed?

If the latter, was revenge justified? Had Mr. Griffin done enough to them to warrant a violent response?

Readers may also want to consider the psychological violence of which Mr. Griffin seems to be guilty:

Can he be said to treat his students violently in refusing to tolerate mistakes, punishing even accidental offenses like Jeff's loss of his paper in a windstorm, and forcing Mark to beg to be allowed to retake the course after failing it?

If so, does that in any way justify the students' action? Could another way out of the situation have been found?

Would Mr. Griffin's wife, who exhorted him to offer something besides criticism, have been able to find a better solution?

Should the school's principal have intervened?

Should there be school-wide policies governing such situations?

Students might further speculate about the momentum of violent acts in this book. Mr. Griffin's harsh treatment leads to the kidnapping; the kidnapping becomes a killing; the killing requires a cold-blooded murder to cover it up. Is life really like that, students may ask, and if it is, how does one interrupt the sequence of events before too much damage has been done?

Another issue, related to the question of responsibility, is that of autonomy. Throughout the book characters allow others to make decisions for them. Readers may be asked if there are friends who hold sway over them as Mark does over his friends. Can they be as easily influenced, and if so, why and how? Issues such as these may be too personal and embarrassing to discuss publicly; if so, ask the class to consider them in journal entries. And, of course, the presence of the book and its characters will allow students to discuss the issues without overt reference to themselves or their own situations if they prefer.

Duncan's *Killing Mr. Griffin* is an excellent work dealing with violence and its consequences, but in some ways it is less problematic than other books in this category. Its violent scenes are not especially graphic or shocking—the kidnapping itself, for instance:

> Jeff had the car door open in an instant and had hurled himself upon the thrashing figure. From his position in the backseat, David was holding the bag down with difficulty as the man in front twisted and shoved at it with frantic hands. Jeff grabbed for his wrists and struggled to bring the arms down to the sides, finding it far less easy than he had anticipated.[17]

Although kidnapping *is* a violent act, it isn't particularly gruesome or brutal. Some parents might object that allowing students to read such a passage encourages imitation, but they won't be able to complain about vivid depiction of violence. They will have seen far worse on evening television. But there are novels for young adults that do portray the brutality more graphically. Scoppettone's *Happy Endings Are All Alike,* a book that complicates the lives of librarians and teachers in conservative communities by dealing with both lesbianism and rape, is such a book. The rape scene is gruesome:

> This time he hit her again. The sound of flesh and bone connecting with flesh and bone magnified inside her head to a deafening pitch. The intensity of noise almost obliterated pain. . . .
>
> She saw the fist come toward her. She moved too slowly and it caught her squarely on the bridge of her nose. There was a crunch, then warm, gushing liquid flowed over her lips, chin. Blood. Pain.

Abruptly, painfully, he entered her. She could not help crying out. The knife slid down the side of her neck, cold, pointed. Was she cut?[18]

The vivid narration of events like this one, and the candid, though less graphic depiction of the lesbian relationship, may make the book difficult to discuss in the classroom. Some teachers and students may find addressing such issues in a large group awkward and embarrassing, in which case the book might better be read individually or discussed in small groups.

However it is handled, the book invites us to think about the presence in society of violent and irrational people like the rapist, Mid. It offers some insight into the strange patterns of thought that infect them, and also reminds us that the infection can spread. Mid is clearly a despicable character, capable of feeling that Jaret's homosexuality justifies his brutal rape. His perverted logic may allow students to dismiss him easily, labeling him as evil or sick or demented. But when his thoughts are echoed by the police chief, supposedly a responsible and competent adult, they are harder to forget. Perhaps the most frightening scene in the book is the exchange between the chief and Jaret's parents after the rape:

"He's confessed. Howsoever, there are complications." He took out a handkerchief and mopped his forehead. "This weather," he mumbled.

Kay and Bert exchanged glances. The air conditioning was cooling the room nicely.

Foster cleared his throat. "You see, the Summers boy claims the two girls . . . ah, your daughter and the Danzinger girl, are ah. . . ." He gave an odd, nervous laugh, wiped his hands with the handkerchief. "Ah . . . intimate with each other."

Kay lit a cigarette, bit the inside of her lip.

"I don't see what their relationship has to do with anything."

The chief jerked his head in surprise. "Well, now."

"I mean," Kay went on, "is their relationship supposed to be some sort of defense for him?"

"If I may say so, Mrs. Tyler, you seem to be taking perverted behavior in stride, so to speak."

She glanced at Bert. He looked undone. Back to Foster. "First of all I don't think it's perverted, but that's neither here nor there." She lit a fresh cigarette from the old one. "Secondly, no matter what their relationship is, it has absolutely nothing to do with the fact that Jaret was beaten and raped. Does it?" she challenged him.

Foster shrugged his shoulders. "The Summers kid is gonna say that seeing them . . . you know, intimate and all . . . made him crazy."

"That's absurd," Bert said.

"You may think so, Mr. Tyler, but I guarantee you that this sort of deviant stuff doesn't go over too big in a nice little town like Gardener's Point." He sniffed.

"And rape does?" Bert said.

Foster ignored this. "The thing of it is that the Summers kid is gonna tell if you press charges. And there's something else. The Cross boy says he was intimate with your daughter. She wasn't a virgin," he said righteously.

"So what?" Kay was outraged. "What does that matter?"

Foster went on. "Let me put it to you this way: See, we have a hearing and the judge learns that your girl's not a virgin and on top of that she's a lez. Well he's not gonna think much of her morals. I'm just trying to give you some friendly advice. "

"Are you telling me that this bum, this scum of the earth, is going to get away with what he did if we press charges?" Bert asked.

"Could very well be."[19]

Foster reveals that Jaret's sexual preference and the fact that she is not a virgin are, for him and probably for the court, extenuating circumstances; if they don't fully justify the rape, they at least offer some excuse for it. The fact that he, the police chief, can express such thoughts with no awareness of their irrationality and their vulgar disregard for the individual's rights suggests that Mid is only an extreme instance of something more widespread, something that may contaminate the minds of people who walk among us accepted as normal and rational. Students may need help in seeing the importance of this scene in the book, but it is an excellent passage for teaching them to make significant connections between parts of a literary work.

Thus Scoppettone's book brings violence close to the young reader in two ways. First it shows the adolescent as both the victim and the predator, and second, it suggests that the predator's mentality may be shared to some degree by many others. It is a frightening notion, but students may be able to think of incidents from their own experience that confirm it.

Laurie Halse Anderson's *Speak* takes a different approach to similar violence. In *Speak,* Melinda is raped by a friend at a party. That has happened, however, before the narrative begins. It is, of course, essential to the story, the motivating event, but as the novel opens we are unaware of it and are well into the aftermath. At first we see only Melinda's reluctance to go to school:

It is my first morning of high school. I have seven new notebooks, a skirt I hate, and a stomachache.[20]

Shortly thereafter, still on the first page, we discover that she is not simply reluctant to get back to work after summer vacation, but that something more is going on:

The bus picks up students in groups of four of five. As they walk down the aisle, people who were my middle-school lab partners or gym buddies glare at me. I close my eyes. This is what I've been dreading. As we leave the last stop, I am the only person sitting alone."[21]

Melinda tells us immediately that she is an outcast, but it will be a while before we learn that she has been ostracized for calling the police at a party at the end of the summer, and longer still before we learn why she did so and what it is that has virtually silenced her.

Most of the book is not so much about the rape itself, but about Melinda's subsequent effort to figure out how to cope with all that follows upon it—the rejection by her friends who don't know what happened to her, the silence into which she has retreated, unable to figure out how or with whom to discuss matters, the responsibility she feels for the other girls who might be the rapist's next victims. That is not to say that the rape is insignificant, but Anderson doesn't dwell on it, describe it in detail, or otherwise highlight it. Instead, she concentrates on the social and psychological consequences for her character. The event itself isn't a central scene in the book, as it is in *Happy Endings Are All Alike*; it isn't even witnessed and described by another character as it is in *Rainbow*; nor is it coyly glossed over, as is the sexual encounter in *Mr. and Mrs. Bo Jo Jones*. Still, it is the traumatic moment that catapults Melinda into the circumstances with which she struggles, and through which she grows.

It is inappropriate to draw inferences about the evolution of literature for young adults from a quick comparison of only two books, but it is interesting to consider the implications of the fact that in Scoppettone's 1978 novel the rape itself is prominent and vividly recounted, while in Anderson's 1999 book it doesn't even occur within the time-frame of the novel. Scoppettone builds to the scene of the rape; Anderson places it some three months before *Speak* begins. If your students have read both books, you might invite them to speculate about the impact of these differences upon their readings of the book. "What effect," you might ask, "does the more vivid depiction of the violence achieve?" Students might observe that it focuses their attention on the immediate physical and psychological suffering, that it may anger the reader by showing so clearly the indifference of the rapist to the rights of the victim, and perhaps that it captures the reader as violent scenes often do, attracting and repelling them at the same time.

They might then be asked about the effects Anderson achieves by placing the rape in the background, having it occur off-stage and in the past. "What effect does leaving the violence in the background of the story have upon the reader of *Speak*?" The focus, they may notice, comes to fall upon the difficulties Melinda faces afterwards, her efforts to deal with the adjustments she must make, the social and psychological consequences of the rape and her inability to speak of it, and ultimately her need to confront the event publicly. Anderson invites—and gently urges—her readers not just to consider the inhumanity of the act and be outraged, but also to reflect on all that it demands of the victim afterwards. In that sense, it is a book not so much about either sexuality or violence as about coping and courage.

This is not to say that one book is better than the other. Rather, I hope to point out that in responding to these texts and analyzing what their authors have done and what effects they've worked upon their readers, students might be led to take a more reflective and thoughtful approach to fiction. Some students will likely say that Scoppettone's book is more exciting, that it would make a better movie, that there's more action, more of the dramatic violence that they go to the movies to see. Others may argue that Anderson's book is more thoughtful and reflective, that it encourages us to see how violence affects people for a long time and in subtle, complex ways. The point is not to achieve consensus, but to make our students more aware—aware of what they look for in literature, what writers do to influence them, and how they think and feel about the events and circumstances the books offer us.

Both Scoppettone's and Anderson's books end on a fairly optimistic note. Jaret seems strong enough to cope with the physical violence she has suffered and the psychological violence she will suffer during the trial. In the last line of *Speak* Melinda says, "Let me tell you about it." She is going to speak again.

On the other hand, several of Robert Cormier's books are less hopeful. *The Chocolate War,* one of the best works written for adolescents, depicts the violence of a group toward an individual within it. Set in a Catholic high school, the novel describes the tactics of a secret fraternity and a sadistic teacher who band together during the school's yearly chocolate sale to force students to cooperate with the project. The Vigils, the secret fraternity, and their leader, Archie, devise "assignments" for non-members to carry out. The assignments are pointless stunts, invented primarily for the purpose of exercising power over others. Archie, making one of the assignments, is described as "carried on marvelous waves of power and glory." Jerry, the central character, decides not to submit to that power, not to sell the chocolate, and thus makes himself the target of both the fraternity and the teachers.

The violence Jerry suffers is at first psychological—he is harassed and humiliated—but as he and others resist, matters gradually slip out of control, culminating in a contrived parody of a boxing match arranged by Archie. The savage beating Jerry receives breaks him, and he tries to tell his only remaining friend not to resist as he has tried to:

> He had to tell Goober to play ball, to play football, to run, to make the team, to sell the chocolates, to sell whatever they wanted you to sell, to do whatever they wanted you to do. . . . They tell you to do your thing but they don't mean it. They don't want you to do your thing, not unless it happens to be their thing, too. It's a laugh, Goober, a fake. Don't disturb the universe, Goober, no matter what the posters say.[22]

The book ends with the hero broken, physically and psychologically, and with Archie and Brother Leon triumphant.

The Chocolate War is a study of one young man's effort to assert his autonomy in the face of tremendous pressure to submit. It raises interesting questions about the relationship of the individual to the group, the rationality of human behavior, and the nature and effect of violence. Students might discuss their own values and expectations. Would they, for instance, be willing to stand with someone like Jerry in a confrontation with someone like Brother Leon or Archie? Would they feel capable of standing alone, as Jerry did, in such a situation? Is the right to be who and what you want to be worth the possible suffering? Can connections be made between *The Chocolate War* and their own experiences? Most schools have projects of some sort that students are expected to take part in; have the students felt illegitimate pressure to participate in "voluntary" activities? If so, how did they feel and how did they respond?

Cormier's sharply drawn characters will suggest comparisons, too. Archie, the sadistic manipulator of others, might be compared with Mark in Lois Duncan's *Killing Mr. Griffin,* Urek in Sol Stein's *The Magician* (1971, Delacore), and Jack in William Golding's *Lord of the Flies* (1962, Coward McCann). Brother Leon might be compared with Mr. Hoyt, the headmaster in Kirkwood's *Good Times, Bad Times* (1968, Simon and Schuster). One benefit of such comparisons is that they draw attention to the writer's craft. The class can compare specific paragraphs, observing the prose style, the point of view, and the focus of the various writers. Some authors of young adult fiction books are accomplished stylists—Cormier is one—whereas others border on the illiterate. Direct comparisons, with careful analysis of short passages, will reveal these differences to the students.

Cormier's *Chocolate War* is about violence at home—that is to say, in the school, among people the age of our students. Nolan's *If I Should Die Before I Wake* (1994, Harcourt Brace) begins there and leaps suddenly to violence on a national scale. Hilary, a vicious and angry young girl, has found a place with the Neo-Nazis who, having left her school a few years earlier with insufficient intelligence and character to do anything significant with their lives, entertain themselves by harassing the Jewish citizens in the community, vandalizing their cemetery, and tormenting the Jewish students. The story begins with Hilary in a hospital bed after a motorcycle accident. Ironically, it is the Jewish hospital. At the end of the first chapter, after Hilary's character and anti-Semitic attitude have been well established, we see her spinning off into apparent unconsciousness to emerge, at the beginning of the next chapter, as a young Jewish girl in Poland during the years before World War II.

She is suddenly transformed, through the hallucinatory effects of her injuries and her hospitalization, from a perpetrator of mindless, stupid acts of violence upon a few of her neighbors into one of the millions of victims of the Holocaust, where such viciousness was national policy. The contrast in scale—Hilary's defacing of the town's Jewish cemetery against the murder of millions—is, however, not nearly so powerful as the similarity in attitude and behavior between Hilary and the Nazis brutalizing Poland. In Chapter 1, her friends kidnap Simon, a Jewish student in her school, and stuff him into a gym locker; in Chapter 2 she, in her new identity, is seized by the soldiers, beaten, and forced into slave-labor. Much of the book is about her life as Chana, trying to survive in the ghetto and finally in Auschwitz, but it is also about Hilary, recovering from the accident and gradually coming to learn something about herself, about violence, and about the people around her.

If the reader can suspend disbelief in Nolan's device for a moment, the book may invite her into reflecting upon the attitudes that breed violence and the awful consequences that ensue when those attitudes are shared by a great many others *If I Should Die* essentially plucks a young girl out of contemporary American society and drops her into Poland under the Nazis during the late 1930s. The device invites young readers—who are, after all, roughly the same age if not, we hope, of the same ideology as Hilary—to imagine themselves similarly transported. Perhaps it also suggests that the world Hilary finds herself in could emerge here and now if the attitudes she herself holds at the novel's opening come to prevail. And that suggests the great significance of individual decisions; the forces that subjugated Poland consisted essentially of too many people like Hilary, each one contributing enough so that savagery would triumph. There is, in other words, much to discuss in the book.

And there are, of course, obvious links to a great many other works that are, or might be, employed in the schools. *The Diary of Anne Frank* comes inescapably to mind. Taught often around the eighth grade, it is the work mostly frequently chosen to deal with the Holocaust and it perhaps moves us to that theme from the theme of violence. If we took that path, we might find ourselves reading Lowry's *Number the Stars* (1989, Houghton Mifflin) or Hillesum's *An Interrupted Life: The Diaries of Etty Hillesum, 1941-1943,* (1983, Pantheon) or perhaps viewing movies like *Schindler's List* or *Night and Fog*. On the other hand, we might find ourselves looking at persecution in other times and places. Bette Greene's *The Drowning of Stephan Jones* (1991, Bantam), for instance, tells of the murder of a gay man by a homophobic group similar in some ways to the Neo-Nazis in *If I Should Die*. Many of Chris Crutcher's excellent books deal with violence. *Staying Fat for Sarah Byrnes* (1993, Greenwillow), for instance, deals with the friendship of Eric and Sarah, whose abuse as a child has traumatized her. *Whale Talk* (2001, Greenwillow) tells the story of a young man helping a child suffering from both the racist attitudes and abusive behavior of her adoptive father. The possibilities are infinite.

A great many other works address the issue of violence. Two of Cormier's other books, *I Am the Cheese* (1977, Knopf) and *After the First Death* (1979, Pantheon), deal with the violence of governments against their own citizens. Many works depict the violence of gangs; one of these, Hinton's *The Outsiders* has become a classic contemporary problem novel for adolescents. There are books about violence within the family, war, and violence against nature, as well as mysteries and adventures like Paul Zindel's *The Undertaker's Gone Bananas* (1978, Harper and Row). It is, sadly, a relevant issue in the lives of most of our students.

Characteristics of Young Adult Literature

The corpus of young adult literature is large, diverse, and growing. To generalize about such a massive collection of works may seem foolhardy; still, we can identify characteristics that many of the currently available books share. This may be useful, if only as a crude outline of the field into which we may fit the individual books we encounter.

The literature for young adults is first of all likely to have adolescents as its central characters. As Robert Carlsen says,

> Today's young reader wants what *Seventeenth Summer* gave an earlier generation: an honest view of the adolescent world from the adolescent's point of view; a book

that holds a mirror up to society so that readers can see their own world reflected in it.[23]

The books discussed earlier in this chapter all share this feature, as do some earlier works of literature that, though not written specifically for adolescents, were seized by adolescent readers for their own. *Catcher in the Rye, The Lord of the Flies,* and *A Separate Peace* all focus on adolescent characters.

In many of the books, an adolescent is also the narrator. Duncan's *Killing Mr. Griffin* is necessarily in the third person, since part of the author's strategy is to show the reader a side of Mr. Griffin's life that the students cannot see. However, *Forever . . .* is narrated by the heroine, Katherine, and it seems quite likely that the book's popularity is partly a result of Blume's ability to write convincingly in the young girl's voice. Even those books not narrated in the first person must owe much of their appeal to portraying the thoughts and feelings of the adolescent characters. Young readers, working through the confusing growth of adolescence, are naturally interested in the experiences of others approximately their own age and living through similar stages.

Language

One problem with using an adolescent narrator is adolescent language. In skillfully written books like *Forever . . .*, the problem is minor; the voice Blume has created for her heroine, Katherine, is smooth and palatable. Crutcher's characters find ways of sounding like young adults without employing their more irritating linguistic affectations, such as punctuating their sentences with a ceaseless repetition of the word "like." In some works, however, the voice may be grating:

> If you knew I was a seventeen-year-old handsome guy hacking out this verbose volume of literary ecstasy, you'd probably think I was one of those academic genii who run home after a titillating day at school, panting to commence cello lessons. I regret to inform you, however, that I do not suffer from scholasticism of the brain. In fact, I suffer from it so little I dropped out of my puerile, jerky high school exactly eleven months ago.[24]

Adult readers, and probably many younger readers, too, will find they can tolerate only so much of that sort of prose. Granted, the problem may be more acute for the teacher than for the student, and such extremes may help to create a character; still, the language of some of the books can be a barrier for the teacher beginning to explore this literature.

Even in third-person narratives, where it is not necessary to imitate the adolescent voice, we often find stumbling prose. Stylistic clumsiness, however, may be useful for students who lack confidence with more sophisticated writing. Even a fairly poor student can see the awkwardness in "Another undercurrent that was lingering on was the fact that he felt a lot of guilt that he had put together. . . ."[25] and in "The only thing that was unfortunate was that Bobby had put the stick shift into reverse."[26] Suggesting other phrasing may give students a satisfying sense that they, too, might be able to write. Even our least sophisticated students should be able to come up with something like "A lingering undercurrent was the guilt. . . ." and "Unfortunately, Bobby had shifted into reverse." At the very least, looking at such sentences should remind our students that authors are fallible.

Because the central characters are adolescents, the central concerns in these books are those of adolescence. Even in Cormier's *After the First Death* (1979, Pantheon), which involves kidnapping, murder, and terrorism, the crux of the story is the relationship between father and son and the discovery the son makes about himself—issues significant to most adolescents. In *The Undertaker's Gone Bananas,* essentially a mystery story, the adolescents' relationships with others are a major issue. The content of young adult fiction is now largely unrestricted—homosexuality, suicide, rape, cancer, death, mental illness, child abuse, divorce—but those subjects are usually viewed through the eyes of an adolescent.

There are some interesting exceptions and variations. Alice Childress, in *A Hero Ain't Nothin But a Sandwich* (1973, Coward McCann), uses multiple narrators to tell the story of Benjie's difficulties with drugs. The focus is on Benjie's problems, but we see them from the perspective of others around him as well as from his own. Richard Peck's *New York Time* goes even further from the norm, describing events in the life of a woman in her thirties. If we admit to the category of young adult literature those works of adult fiction that have found popularity with younger readers, the exceptions are more numerous still.

The "problem novel," as our discussion must suggest, has dominated young adult literature. Many students, however, especially middle school students, still seek lighter fiction—the comedy of Richard Peck's *Secrets of the Shopping Mall* (1979, Delacorte), the horror of Joan Aiken's *A Touch of Chill* (1980, Delacorte), or the fantasy of Madeleine L'Engle's *A Wrinkle in Time* (1962, Ariel). Adolescents are reading westerns, detective stories, romances, tales of the occult, and nonfiction as well. Teachers should not forget, in recommending books to students, the wide range available; presenting only books that address problems would narrow the students' conception of literature unnecessarily.

The better young adult literature, despite its adolescent perspective, tries to avoid the simple-minded stereotypes and patterns found in much popular fiction. Teachers are not always tyrannical and uninformed, parents not always domineering and stupid. Good and evil are not so clearly and simplistically delineated. There is, of course, a wide range in the quality of young adult fiction, as there is in adult fiction. Some works, like Cormier's *Chocolate War* and Glendon Swarthout's *Bless the Beasts and Children* (1970, Doubleday), can be expected to survive for a long time; others will disappear quickly and quietly.

Young adult literature is usually short; most of the books run between one hundred and two hundred pages in paperback. As a result, the story usually progresses quickly, a feature that is appreciated by many readers but poses problems for the authors. Fewer characters can be introduced, and they cannot be so fully drawn as in a longer novel. This may tempt the writer to rely more than he might wish on stereotypes or formulas. Description, setting, and background must be handled with economy; digressions, even important ones, must be held to a minimum. Some authors achieve impressive subtleties even within the confines of the short novel. *After the First Death,* for instance, establishes an interesting parallel between the young, innocent boy, sacrificed by his father, and the assassin; both young men strive to satisfy the expectations of mysterious fathers, and both fail. Few writers, however, manage to accomplish what Cormier accomplishes in his books.

Summary and References

Young adult literature is a vast and sprawling collection. This chapter has sought only to introduce it, to discuss a few representative books, and to sketch its general characteristics. Reading several of the books discussed or listed here will provide a taste of the literature. Beyond that, there are several excellent sources of information about literature for young adults:

Books About Young Adult Literature and Writers

G. ROBERT CARLSEN, *Books and the Teenage Reader: A Guide for Teachers, Librarians, and Parents,* Revised Second Edition (New York: Harper & Row, 1980). Aimed at a broad audience, as the subtitle indicates, Carlsen's book discusses the nature of reading, the development of reading interests, and the wide assortment of books—including young adult novels, adult books, classics, and the various genres—useful with young readers. An older text, this is nonetheless a classic, and well worth exploring.

KENNETH L. DONELSON AND ALLEEN PACE NILSEN, *Literature for Today's Young Adults,* Sixth Edition (New York: Allyn & Bacon, 2000). This is an impressive scholarly text discussing the history of literature for young adults, the nature of contemporary works for adolescents, and the issues faced by teachers and librarians who hope to present the literature to their students.

SHEILA SCHWARTZ, *Teaching Adolescent Literature: A Humanistic Approach* (Rochelle Park, NJ: Hayden, 1979). An older work, but still interesting. Schwartz begins with a brief discussion of methodology, and then analyzes a large number of young adult books grouped according to theme.

DANIEL KIRKPATRICK, *Twentieth Century Children's Writers* (Chicago: St. James Press, 1989). This guide presents a brief biography, bibliographies, and an essay of critical evaluation of about six hundred writers of literature for children and adolescents.

Booklists

KYLENE BEERS AND TERI LESESNE (EDITORS) AND COMMITTEE ON THE SENIOR HIGH SCHOOL BOOKLIST, 2001, *Books for You: An Annotated Booklist for Senior High,* 14th Edition (Urbana, IL: NCTE, 2001).

Jean E. Brown and Elsine C. Stephens, *Your Reading: An Annotated Booklist for Middle School and Junior High*, 11th Edition (Urbana, IL: NCTE, 2003).

Journals and Other Publications

Keeping up with adolescent literature is impossible, but there are several publications that may help:

The English Journal. National Council of Teachers of English, 1111 Kenyon Road, Urbana, IL 61801.

Voices from the Middle. National Council of Teachers of English, 1111 Kenyon Road, Urbana, IL 61801.

The ALAN Review. National Council of Teachers of English, 1111 Kenyon Road, Urbana, IL 61801. By the Assembly on Literature for Adolescents.

Best Books for Young Adults. Yearly list from Young Adult Services Division of American Library Association, 50 E. Huron St., Chicago, IL 60601.

Booklist. A magazine devoted to reviewing books for librarians, published by the American Library Association, 50 E. Huron St., Chicago, IL 60601.

Books for the Teen Age. New York Public Library, Fifth Ave. and 42nd St., New York, NY 10018.

Bulletin of the Center for Children's Books. University of Chicago Graduate Library School, University of Chicago Press, 5801 Ellis Ave. Chicago, IL 60637.

Journal of Adolescent and Adult Literacy, International Reading Association, 800 Barksdale Rd., PO Box 8139, Newark, DE 19714-8139.

School Library Journal. R.R. Bowker Company, 1180 Avenue of the Americas, New York, NY 10036

Wilson Library Bulletin. H.W.Wilson Co., 1950 University Ave., Bronx, NY 10452.

The Horn Book. The Horn Book, Inc., Park Square Building, 31 St. James Ave., Boston, MA 92116

Kirkus Review. Kirkus Service, Inc., 200 Park Ave. South, New York, NY 10003.

New York Times Book Review. The New York Times, Times Square, New York, NY 10036.

Voice of Youth Advocates. Scarecrow Press, 4501 Forbes Boulevard, Suite 200, Lanham, MD 20706

Websites

The International Reading Association's lists of Young Adult Choices is released each year at *http://www.reading.org/choices/choices_download.html*

The American Library Association's lists can be found at *http://www.ala.org/yalsa/booklists/bbya*

Consider *http://www.overbooked.org* (which will lead to several other interesting sites) and *http://teenlink.nypl.org* (a site at the New York Public Library).

Most useful to you, however, will be the search engines (Google, Yahoo, Copernic, and so on.) If you start there you won't waste time looking at old links or miss new ones.

A Postscript on Categories and Lists

In this chapter we have looked at two prominent themes in current young adult fiction, discussing several representative works. We could have considered other categories or other works, and any of the works mentioned could have been placed elsewhere. Cormier's *After the First Death,* for instance, mentioned as a book about violence, could have been said to deal with the theme of parent-child relationships; the father, knowing that his son will break quickly under pressure, sends him off to negotiate with terrorists, planted with false information he is expected to reveal. It could as well have been classified with books about self-knowledge or coming of age; the boy discovers that he can't withstand even mild torture and was not expected to be able to, and the knowledge drives him to suicide. Or it could have been grouped with works that investigate the relationship between the individual and his society; here, the boy is sacrificed to protect a secret government project.

Categories, in other words, are arbitrary and contrived, and may as much limit thought about the work as assist it. The various books and articles about young adult literature subdivide it in different ways. Schwartz's *Teaching Adolescent Literature* offers seven categories: The Outsider, The Other, Minorities, Regions and Locales, Teenagers and Sex, Violence: Real and Vicarious, Family Life and Lifestyles, and Science Fiction as Prophecy. Donelson and Nilsen, in *Literature for Today's Young Adults,* in addition to creating chronological categories, offer the following groups: Parent/Child Relationships, Body and Self, Sex and Sex Roles, Friends and Society, Adventure-Romances, Love-Romances, Adventure Stories, Westerns, Mysteries, Stories of the Supernatural, Historical Fiction, Science Fiction, Fantasy, Utopias, Biographies, Quiet Heroes, Heroes in War, Heroes in Sports, Books About the World Around Us, Books About Physical and Mental Health, Books About Sex, Books About Drugs, How To Books, Books About Work, Fun Facts, and The New Journalism. *Your Reading* offers a different set of groups, *Books for You* another, and Carlsen's *Books and the Teenage Reader* still another. The bibliographies in those works are extensive and useful.

Our purpose here is not to argue for a system of organization, but simply to encourage reading some of the young adult literature and considering its possible appeal to secondary school students. You'll be able to figure out how it might work with your students and in your curriculum.

Endnotes

1. Michael Dirda, *An Open Book: Coming of Age in the Heartland* (New York: Norton, 2003), p. 59

2. Ibid., p. 94

3. Ibid.

4. Kylene Beers, "When Kids Can't Read," in *What Teachers Can Do: A Guide for Teachers* (Portsmouth, NH: Heinemann, 2003), p. 117.

5. Marina Tsvetaeva, "Pushkin and Pagachev," 1937; repr. in *A Captive Spirit: Selected Prose*, J. Marin King, Ed. and Trans. (New York: Ardis Publishers, 1980).

6. Ken Donelson and Alleen Pace Nilsen, *Literature for Today's Young Adults*, Sixth Edition (Boston: Allyn & Bacon, 2000), p. 13.

7. Judy Blume, *Forever* . . . (New York: Bradbury Press, 1975), p. 9.

8. Ibid., p. 93.

9. Ibid., p. 116.

10. Ann Head, *Mr. and Mrs. Bo Jo Jones* (New York: New American Library, 1967), pp. 8–9.

11. Walker Gibson, "Authors, Speakers, Readers, and Mock Readers," *College English*, 11, No. 5 (February, 1950), pp. 265–269.

12. Head, p. 47

13. Rita Williams-Garcia, *Every Time a Rainbow Dies* (New York: Harper-Tempest, 2001), pp. 121–122.

14. Ann Warren Turner, *Learning to Swim: A Memoir* (New York: Scholastic, Inc., 2000), pp. 1–2.

15. Lois Duncan, *Killing Mr. Griffin* (New York: Dell, 1978), p. 59

16. If you have the opportunity to use this book, try to interrupt your students' reading of it before they get to Chapter 5. Ask them to record their impressions of several of the characters, making sure that Mr. Griffin is one of them. Don't do much with those very brief essays at the time—just file them away for the moment. Later in the book, perhaps just after Chapter 5, ask them again to jot down their impressions of the characters. Then pull out their first papers and ask them what has happened. The comparison should serve to make them aware of how the author manipulates her readers, pushing them in one direction and then offering new information or another perspective to force them to think through matters once again.

17. Duncan, pp. 69-70.

18. Sandra Scopettone, *Happy Endings Are All Alike* (New York: Dell, 1978), pp. 114–115.

19. Ibid., pp. 160–162.

20. Laurie Halse Anderson, *Speak* (New York: Farrar, Strauss & Giroux, 1999), p. 1.

21. Ibid.

22. Robert Cormier, *The Chocolate War* (New York: Dell, 1974), p. 187.

23. G. Robert Carlsen, *Books and the Teenage Reader: A Guide for Teachers, Librarians, and Parents*, Revised Second Edition (New York: Harper & Row, 1967), p. 59.

24. Paul Zindel, *I Never Loved Your Mind* (New York: Bantam, 1972), p. 1.

25. Paul Zindel, *The Undertaker's Gone Bananas* (New York: Bantam, 1979), p. 45

26. Ibid., p. 151.

7

Visual Literacy

"I f Shakespeare were alive today he'd be turning over in his grave."

It was a comment a friend of mine made as we left a movie one evening and, strangely enough, I understood what he meant despite the Yogi Berra-ish nature of his remark. I could picture Shakespeare, alive, a spinning whirling dervish bouncing off the walls of his sarcophagus, looking just like Yogi, a stocky, unshaven Barishnikov in shin-guards, pirouetting beneath a towering pop foul that he knew was going to come down somewhere between first base and third, but just where that might be he had no idea. It would be impolitic of me to name the movie but I can remember it, probably only because my friend's comment fixed it in mind. It was otherwise eminently forgettable except for a few spectacular explosions and various other pyrotechnic achievements. Had we come in after the opening credits we wouldn't have known whether it was a spy story or a documentary on strip mining. Shakespeare would not have been impressed.

But if he were alive today instead of spinning in his grave, Shakespeare would be in Hollywood writing for the movies, probably teamed up with Spielberg, though Sam Peckinpah would of course handle *Titus Andronicus*.

Film and television are forms of literature. We might quarrel over their merits, arguing that most television and some films are too bad to be called literature, but the same could be said of much of what we find in the bookstores. It may be dangerous to use the term "literature" as a word of praise, reserved for only the best books, the classics, the canon, the texts worthy of study in graduate seminars. To do so is likely to embroil us in endless debate about what merits the label "Literature" and what is mere... well, what should the less laudatory term be? "Fiction"? "Prose"? Truman Capote once responded to a question about a fellow author's books with the caustic comment, "That's not writing; that's typing." Bookstores themselves have made that distinction though somewhat less sarcastically, as we noted in the first pages of this book, labeling one section "Literature" and another "Fiction." Perhaps we should have another section labeled "Typing."

Labeling books that way lends special dignity to those that qualify as "Literature," and at the same time serves the useful purpose of helping people avoid them. But the fact remains that, even if they tiptoe quietly through the literature shelves so that they don't disturb Dostoevsky's slumbers, and breathe a deep sigh of relief when they make it to the friendlier waters of the mere-typing section, the books they find there will provide them with the raw materials of literary experience. Those books will offer stories, characters, conflicts, values, and the other elements that they would have found if they had tripped in the aisle with Shakespeare, Dickens, Welty, Hawthorne, and the other giants. Not as well-written, not as thoughtful, not as demanding, not as rewarding. . . but if those are the books they choose, then those are the books with which they will have what literary experiences they are capable of having. A great many of our students, after they escape our grasp, unless we have managed to persuade them that there are rewards in the more demanding books, will find most of their literary experience in the mere-typing section. They are likely to find even more of their literary experience with film and television.

Again, we can quarrel over their merits, arguing perhaps that film and television don't provide us with the raw material out of which we can shape the sort of literary experience that *Hamlet* and *Moby Dick* sustain, but nonetheless, most of our students will spend more time with *Buffy the Vampire Slayer* and *Dawson's Creek* and whatever replaces them next season, and with *Clueless* and *Dumb and Dumber* and this season's new blockbusters, than they will with Dostoevsky and his shelf-mates.

So perhaps it makes sense for the English curriculum to acknowledge that much of literary experience comes through the visual media and to teach students to think intelligently about it. At the moment, most programs ignore it. We invite students, with our help, to reflect on the visions of human possibilities offered them by the most serious, thoughtful, and respected writers, but we leave them on their own to deal with the dominant literary form of their culture. That neglect may leave them vulnerable to the shaping influence film and television are likely to have. Rather than abandon them to what is, after all, an intensely commercial medium—television shows are clearly, at least in part, tools used to sell products—it would make sense to encourage students to develop the habit of reflecting occasionally upon what they are being offered, what they're being told about the world and their place in it by the shows they watch. And in many ways teaching the visual media isn't all that different from teaching the other literary genres.

The typical movie or television show (excluding, of course, news programs, game shows, and the like) is, after all, basically dramatic fiction, a play in two dimensions, on a huge screen or in a little box. It has characters, as do the novel and the play. It places those characters in some conflict that they must resolve; thus it has a plot, with beginning, middle, and end (except the soap opera, which has only a middle). It is divided into scenes, with some of the same techniques for transition between them that would be found in a stage play. It may develop a theme, or at least focus on some controlling idea. It shares, in brief, many features of fiction and perhaps most features of dramatic literature.

Further, it works upon the reader or viewer as both fiction and drama work. It evokes responses from viewers—sympathy for one character, dislike for another, anxiety in the suspenseful moments, and satisfaction when the tension is resolved. It leaves characters and situations only partially developed, requiring viewers to fill in imaginatively, although of course the visual element is provided. The incompleteness of literature, both visual and printed, is at best a productive ambiguity allowing readers to add something of themselves to the reading, and at worst the shallow stereotyping that provides little unique detail at all. Whether best or worst, however, the technique is virtually the same for the visual and the printed; a representation is offered to the viewers, who flesh it out imaginatively, respond to it, and perhaps think about it.

The visual literature is also as value-laden as the written. Dealing with human life as it does, it cannot be otherwise. It continually reveals its values in its choice of some subjects—crime, violence, romance—rather than others, such as philosophy, art, and scholarship. Further, it probably serves to inculcate those values in its audience, as written literature does, subtly suggesting to the viewers what is important and how they ought to see things. Albert Ellis has pointed out, for instance, that our view of love tends to be closer to the vision offered in popular novels, songs, television commercials, and movies than to the facts of love and marriage as recorded by the sociologists and psychologists. Love, Ellis observes, does not conquer all, as the divorce rate suggests. It must be nurtured and cared for, not simply "fallen into."[1] Yet people tend to accept unreflectively the simpler visions presented in songs, stories, and movies.

This last similarity, the embodiment and communication of values, constitutes the strongest argument for granting film and television a place in the curriculum. Television, especially, is the literature we are immersed in for three to four hours a day, on the average. If film and television do function as written literature does, communicating a vision of the world, and if viewers do absorb from them ideas of good and bad, possible and impossible, true and false, then it is appropriate that the schools teach children to watch them intelligently. At the very least, it seems that we should encourage students to bring some of the skills and dispositions they may develop as they read and analyze written literature to their encounters with the visual literature that will probably occupy so much more of their time and may influence them so subtly. Disparaging the visual media, urging students simply to avoid it, will work about as well as the "Just say no" drug policy proposed by some of our dimmer political figures.

Students are sometimes urged not to waste their time watching television, but the appeal is a moral rather than an intellectual one, usually presented as a premise, not as a reasoned conclusion. It is assumed that television is a waste of time. In the schools, at least, the student sees little or no investigation or questioning of the medium that would lead to that conclusion. Rather, he hears a proclamation, ex-cathedra, condemning the medium for its inadequacies and so he probably suspects that the teacher's motives are to secure more time for the literature she teaches. It is an exhortation easily ignored. And it should be. Children should question a teacher's ungrounded assertions just as they should the messages of television or the enticements of advertising. To accept those messages uncritically is to accept someone else's thinking, to place one's mind in someone else's hands. The schools should work instead to create thinking, skeptical, rational people.

It seems reasonable, then, to invite students to examine the visual media. They fill much of the students' lives anyway, and will continue to do so whether the schools pay attention to them or not. They reflect certain ideas about the world, and thus ought to be thought about rather than simply absorbed. And they are accessible enough that students should be able to understand and analyze them thoroughly.

What, then, should students be expected to learn about the visual media? First, they might analyze their own habits and patterns. If, as we've argued, the experience with a poem is a transaction between a reader and a text, requiring that the reader look at his own responses, his own questions, his own contribution to the event, then the experience with a movie or a television show will be much the same. And it will be the sort of experience students have virtually every day. Film and television are, after all, an important part of almost everyone's life. Even homes without books, newspapers, and indoor plumbing have television, maybe even with cable service. In almost every home, students will find that television is part of the habit and ritual of the day. Second, they might learn that watching film and television can be much like reading a literary work; they can respond to and think about the visual just as they would the written. Third, they may learn something about the technical elements of visual literature and their differences from the techniques of written literature.

Examination of Habits

Let's begin with the first issue, the habits of the students. Were we to investigate their reading habits, we might find a tremendous range. Some students, especially in the middle or junior high schools, are voracious readers, devouring books at a rate they will never again equal as adults. Others may proudly state that they have never read a book and never hope to. Some of those who do read may choose a wide variety of books, while others may stick to books about horses, books by Judy Blume or Gary Paulsen, or some other narrow category.

On the other hand, if we examine the viewing habits of our students (and let us ignore film for the moment), we will find that nearly all spend a fairly large amount of time watching television. There are non-readers, but there seem to be almost no non-viewers. Different students will watch different shows, but they will all watch something. In the late 1970s, the teenage audience watched an average of 3.5 hours per day time, almost eight thousand hours during the six years of secondary school.[2] In the early 1990s, a study by the Yankelovich Youth Monitor and the Corporation for Public Broadcasting concluded that children viewed about 3.1 hours a day.[3] More recently, the Annenberg study concluded that children ages two to seventeen spend about 2.5 hours a day watching television.[4] Television viewing time may be dropping off slightly. On the other hand that study also reports the following:

> In terms of time spent in front of screens, children reportedly spend over four and
> a half hours (281 minutes) watching television or videotapes, playing video games,

using the computer, or browsing the Internet each day. This is up 21 minutes from the time reported spent in front of screens last year.[5]

That's a lot of time. Over the six years of secondary school it amounts to almost 5,500 hours with the television, almost 9,900 hours in front of a screen.

The Television Log

To begin an investigation of the medium, students might be encouraged to assess the role of television in their lives by keeping a log for a week or two. They can devise the log themselves, deciding what information they are interested in obtaining, but it should include the title of the program, its time and station, the nature of the show (comedy, mystery, soap opera), its sponsors, some notes on its content, and their reactions to the show. This sort of information can be analyzed in several ways. The students might begin by summarizing the data across the class to determine the most and least popular shows. They might then examine those lists and speculate about the characteristics of the shows that account for their rank. They might then be asked to watch several shows closely, a few that ranked high in their estimation and several that fared poorly, perhaps armed with a checklist or set of questions, in order to confirm or refute their speculations. The overriding question might be, "What is it that makes a show popular, and what makes it unpopular?"

An exercise such as this is useful practice in gathering and interpreting data, set in the context of the students' own lives rather than the more academic areas to which many assigned research papers lead. Because this research focuses on an aspect of the students' world, it is more likely to stimulate reflection and discussion.

Analyzing tastes and preferences can lead students to insights into themselves, the others in the class, and the medium itself, as do discussions of response to written literature. Why do they watch *Friends*, if they do? They may decide that it's enjoyable for its sheer silliness, its slapstick elements, Joey's ingenuous blundering and silly expressions, and Phoebe's nonsensical remarks. Or they may note that there is something reassuring in the reliability of the friendships portrayed, observing that despite all the petty annoyances with one another, all the little conflicts, all the adolescent intrigue, they can depend on the friends to hang together, to like and support one another, and to show up on time next week. Doubtless they will make many other points about the show. It might help to bring in a tape of one of the shows and watch it together, interrupting it whenever someone wants to point out some feature of the show or the characters that makes it work or weakens it. By noting and examining their reactions, students may come to understand themselves and the show better. If they say simply, "I like the show," or perhaps say nothing at all, but only sit down regularly to stare at it for reasons unexamined, they miss an opportunity to learn something about both themselves and the medium.

They may, of course, resist this invitation to look closely at the experience. We've all heard the plaintive, "Why can't we just enjoy it?" And of course they can and should "just enjoy it" much of the time, as we do. But, we can insist, it's important to understand what it is we're enjoying and how it may be shaping our views of the world and our place in it.

This sort of initial activity might be expanded in any of several ways. They might next do the same sort of analysis with a show that they reject as uninteresting or unsuccessful. Why don't they watch whatever it is they see as a failure? How do they react to it, and what features of the show evoke that reaction? Discussion of these issues should begin to make them more alert to their own reactions and more observant of the strategies employed by the producers, directors, and actors to elicit those reactions. Or they might examine shows they are less enthusiastic about but that might be more popular with their parents, or perhaps with younger children. If *Frasier*, for example, fell into that category, they might compare their responses to it with their responses to the show they prefer. What are the differences? Why does one show appeal to one group, the other show to another? Can they identify differences in the situations portrayed, the issues addressed, the behavior of the characters, or the language employed? It won't be hard for them to note, for example, the differences in the speech patterns of the Crane brothers and those of Joey and Chandler in *Friends*. What effects do those differences have on the students as audience?

In addition to analyzing a few contemporary shows that draw different audiences, they might also be encouraged to look at older shows. They may find that many of the out-of-date shows have little appeal for them, but it might still be valuable for them to consider why those shows were popular in their time. Some they may still enjoy. In *M*A*S*H*, for instance, they may be amused by the interplay of vastly different characters like Colonel Potter, Hawkeye, and Klinger, curious about their ability to work comfortably together, and encouraged by the show's constant message that human life is valuable and its suffering is to be sympathized with and alleviated.

Similarly, hearing such comments made by others might teach students something about their classmates, revealing aspects of their minds and personalities that were hidden in the dimmer light of the daily routine. Such discoveries might show the students new ways of seeing the world. Those who see *M*A*S*H* as a dull war story with not enough fighting and killing may learn from their classmates another way of looking at the show that offers pleasures their own habits of thought have locked out.

The show is obviously before their time. The war in Korea ended before they were born. How, you might ask, does that shape their responses? Is it too old, too distant? The class might be invited to reflect on the choice of setting. Could such a show be set, you might ask, in Afghanistan in 2002 or Iraq in 2004? Students are likely to observe that those events are too recent, still too painful, to be the context for a television comedy—some distance is required before they can become a source of humor. How much time? How much distance?

Such questions lead into the analysis of the relationship between show and audience, raising questions about the producer's expectations of viewers and about the attitudes and values the audience is likely to bring to the show. There are some shows that almost demand such analysis. *All in the Family*, for instance, with Archie as the representative of painfully antiquated notions about virtually everything, dealing with his more progressive daughter and son-in-law, was received in drastically different ways by different segments of its audience. Some viewed Archie as an ironic hero, a humorous fellow betraying archaic and largely discarded notions about politics, race, religion, human rights, and the roles of men and women; others viewed him as a hero, plain and simple, a spokesman for good old American values. That show seemed to arrive at just the right time. A decade earlier, and it might not have lasted a month; a decade later and it might not have evoked much reaction at all.

Similar questions about the relevance of social context might, or course, be raised about other media. Young adult novelist Chris Crutcher, for instance, had to abandon an already completed manuscript of a novel that dealt with a violent incident in a school when Columbine hit the news. Similarly, the release of Arnold Schwarzenegger's movie *Collateral Damage* was delayed for some time when the World Trade Center and the Pentagon were attacked. In both cases, the immediate context simply wasn't appropriate; both novel and movie would have looked exploitive, even though they had been completed before the incidents that would have condemned them had occurred.

The television log kept by the students can serve as the basis for discussion of their responses to what they watch, and that will lead into consideration of many of these issues. If unable to bring television shows into the classroom without difficulty, we can nonetheless begin with the perceptions and reactions of the students, rather than with information on form, production, history, industrial organization, and other technicalities, keeping the focus at first on the students themselves.

Their reactions to the medium will serve as windows into their own minds and those of their classmates. Students may consequently learn something about the group. They might find, for instance, that the boys in the class tend to watch certain shows whereas the girls prefer others. Identifying the distinguishing characteristics of these shows might be revealing. Further, they may think about the shows they watched several years ago and observe something about their own maturing, noticing that they've abandoned some shows and moved on to others. Better still, they might collect data from younger students and compare the interests of the different age groups. Again, the objective is not the list of shows but an analysis of students' reactions and the features of the shows that seem to cause them.

Such analysis should lead fairly smoothly into a discussion of conception and technique. Beginning with their responses, the students can move on to what evoked those responses, and ultimately to analysis of both the medium and of themselves as audience for it. When students have had that experience, they are likely to be less passive and mindless in their viewing.

Television's World View

The public and the press have been concerned for a long time about the effects of television on the young. Violence and sex are the central concerns. The fear is that viewers will imitate the behavior they witness, and the typical response to that fear is condemnation and censorship. For years we've seen complaints about the quality and likely effect of television from such groups as the National Citizens' Committee for Broadcasting, the National Gay Task Force, and Action for Children's

Television. Large or small, rational or not, these groups all want to establish some control over television and thus over the thinking of the people who watch it. And the complaints come from all sides. Most complaints about the violence, predictably, condemn it; the National Rifle Association, however, in amusing contrast, once objected to the content of television broadcasting, criticizing a CBS special, "The Guns of Autumn," which suggested that hunting is not a kind and gentle recreation. It's hard to satisfy the diverse and contentious American public.

The issue is not simple. There is evidence that both children and adults can be influenced by what they watch. The theory that television is cathartic, allowing viewers to release their aggressions vicariously, has been abandoned by most researchers. As Leonard Berkowitz long ago remarked in his opening address to a Media Violence Conference in Stockholm, Sweden, ". . . most authorities are. . . fairly well agreed that the viewers do not discharge their own pent-up aggressive impulses simply through watching other people beat each other up."[6] Berkowitz cites instances in which the fictional violence of television and film has been obviously and directly imitated, and reports research indicating that aggression on film can increase the viewer's willingness to act aggressively and her tendency to see aggression as justified. He points out that even "well socialized, well behaved university students" can be stimulated by violent movies to "stronger attacks upon an available target." "The argument," he says, "by and large, is over. Media violence can have bad effects and can stimulate aggressive behaviour."[7]

The arguments continue, nonetheless. One is over the broadcast industry's responsibility. On the one hand, it is argued that very few people are disturbed enough to be stimulated to violence by watching a violent television program, and those who do are likely to commit violent acts without that added stimulus. Those who hold this position argue that the harm done by censorship will far outweigh the minuscule good achieved. On the other hand, there are those who think the networks should be held legally responsible for acts that can be linked to their shows. An eleven million dollar suit was filed against NBC in 1978, charging it with responsibility for a sexual assault committed in apparent imitation of a scene from the movie *Born Innocent*. Some time later, a lawyer defending a young man accused of murder argued that his client had watched so many violent television shows that his judgment was hopelessly distorted, and that therefore television, and not he, was guilty. The defense was, of course, ludicrous; if successful, it would have effectively relieved everyone of the responsibility for any behavior for which he could find a model. Still, that the argument could be made at all is instructive. It illustrates the difficulty of determining the roles of viewer and medium in shaping behavior and suggests that responsibility is an important issue in the debate.

Rather than argue the appropriateness of public control over the broadcast media, the merits of censorship boards, or even the value of television's image of the world, it seems best to try to define the school's role in teaching about a medium that can influence the viewer's conception of the world and her behavior. In any society that purports to respect freedom of thought, censorship is, of course, intolerable. There is no set of beliefs and values that all citizens will agree on, no code of behavior that everyone will happily abide by, no certified standard of right and wrong that everyone will subscribe to. Lacking that unanimity, we can either impose some standard, censoring and prohibiting whatever departs from it, or accept diversity, arguing for our own views but tolerating or even welcoming those of others. The second alternative seems more promising. The world's experiments with totalitarianism have not been happy ones.

If we are to teach students to deal with diversity of opinion, then we have to confront them with that diversity and encourage them to think about it carefully. In other words, they need to learn to reflect on what they see—something they may rarely do. Watching television is usually a passive activity, often accompanied by other activities, such as eating or doing homework. Most families do not talk much about television, and thus its more subtle messages tend to go unexamined. Although it is potentially our most social form of literature—we can watch it in small groups, discuss it as it is in progress, even, if we bother to tape it, control when and where we watch it, interrupting it if we wish, running the tape back to watch segments again so that we might analyze and discuss—in fact, it seems often to be a solitary activity, with family members scattered from room to room, each with a different television, a different show.

And so we tend to absorb it, giving little thought to what it brings us. Our failure to analyze makes us susceptible to the indirect messages of the medium. John Fiske and John Hartley observe:

> The world of television is clearly different from our real social world, but just as clearly related to it in some ways. We might clarify this relationship by saying that television does not represent the manifest actuality of our society, but rather reflects, symbolically, the structure of values and relationships beneath the surface.[8]

It is this structure of values, and what it may do to the viewer, that concerns George Gerbner and Larry Gross, who discuss the possible long-range effects of television viewing. Their analysis of the content of television programs leads them to the following observations and conclusions:

> Night after night, week after week, stock characters and dramatic patterns convey supposed truths about people, power and issues. . . .
>
> Unlike the real world, where personalities are complex, motives unclear, and outcomes ambiguous, television presents a world of clarity and simplicity. In show after show, rewards and punishments follow quickly and logically. Crises are resolved, problems are solved, and justice, or at least authority, always triumphs. The central characters in these dramas are clearly defined: dedicated or corrupt; selfless or ambitious; efficient or ineffectual. To insure the widest acceptability (or greatest potential profitability), the plot lines follow the most commonly accepted notions of morality and justice, whether or not those notions bear much resemblance to reality.
>
> In order to complete a story entertainingly in only an hour or even half an hour, conflicts on TV are usually personal and solved by action. Since violence is

dramatic, and relatively simple to produce, much of the action tends to be violent. As a result, the stars of prime-time network TV have for years been cowboys, detectives, and others whose lives permit unrestrained action.[9]

Gerbner and Gross also study the views held by the American public and conclude that heavy viewers tend to have distorted notions that can be traced to television. For instance, most leading characters in shows are, quite naturally, American. Heavy viewers are much more likely than others to overestimate what percentage of the world's population lives in the United States. Among occupations, the professions are twice as heavily represented on television as in the real world. Again, heavy viewers asked to estimate the real proportions are much more likely than light viewers to overestimate. Both cases seem to reflect the influence of television's view of the world.

Television not only influences our culture, John Leonard argues, it "is our culture, the only coherence we have going for us, naturally the repository of our symbols, the attic of old histories and hopes, the hinge on the doors of change." It both reflects us and trains us:

> The sitcom, after a lot of thrashing about with events and personalities, instructs the members of its "family" and the rest of us on appropriate behavior, helps them internalize the various decencies, define the wayward virtues, modulate peeves, legislate etiquette, compromise the ineffability of self with clamors of peer groups.
>
> In the Fifties, that flabby decade, the sitcom proposed as a paradigm the incompetent father, the dizzy mother, the innocent child. In the Sixties, it proposed the incompetent father, the dizzy mother, the innocent child, war as a fun thing and young women with supernatural powers (witch, genie, magical nanny, flying nun) who could take care of their men and their children, look cute, and never leave the house. In the Seventies, it proposed the incompetent father, the dizzy mother, innocent child—all sitting around discussing abortion, infidelity, impotence, homosexuality, drug addiction, and death—and the career girl (have talent, need sex). The inability of the American father to lace up the shoes of his own mind without falling off his rocker has been constant, perfectly reflecting and perpetuating our cultural expectations.[10]

If television offers us that sort of perception, then we must teach students to receive it critically and skeptically, not simply to absorb it. Were we to accept uncritically the visions offered us, we would be burdened with a narrow and unrealistic view of the world and of huge groups of people. If we were to impose on the real world the expectations cultivated by television, we would find ourselves committing a serious injustice.

But the stereotypes film and television offer us are not invulnerable. They can be identified, examined, and dealt with. The structure of values Fiske and Hartley refer to may be complex, subtle, and quietly interwoven into the story, but it is not totally inaccessible or fixed. Looking back, we remember a time when television showed women only in the home, or perhaps as teachers or librarians—not in the courtroom, the operating room, or the police car. Similarly, we remember when a black man or woman could be a laborer or a maid, but not a scientist, scholar, or judge. Television reflects and perpetuates the visions of existing culture, but it can't sustain these views in the face of other forces. Now, the demographics of the television world have changed somewhat. *The Cosby Show* put an African American family, headed by two professionals, on the stage, and it was followed by others. It's doubtful that adequate representation of the diversity of the country has been achieved or ever will be, and it's likely that Hispanics and Asian Americans will find themselves on the screen too seldom. Producers have to be convinced that any show they invest in will have a large enough audience to merit the risk developing a show entails, and they won't happily gamble when the potential audience seems to them to be too small.

Television changes quickly in some ways, and it would be difficult to predict the shape of television's world in the future. Whatever it is at any moment, however, students can investigate it fairly easily, using their discussion of preferences as a basis. So the questions for students to address may include "What impressions of the world and what system of values is television promoting?" and "How do your own perceptions and values differ from those you find on television?"

They could begin that analysis by choosing several shows, each to be analyzed by a small group of students. The class might be asked to plan a series of questions, or a checklist of features, to use in the study. Its content would vary according to the interests and sophistication of the class, but it should include questions about the nature of protagonists and antagonists, the patterns in the plot, and the typical outcome. Consider the following very brief set of questions:

1. Who is the protagonist? What are his or her most appealing traits? What are his or her least appealing traits?
2. Who is the antagonist? What are his or her characteristics?
3. What is the central element of conflict in the show? Is it about money, power, love, something else?
4. How is the issue resolved? By fighting, reasoning, chance, something else?

As simple as the list is, it can help to stimulate further investigations. For instance, the description of the protagonist might suggest a second set of questions. If the students' notes show that most of the heroes they observed are male, white, middle-class, single, tall, clean-shaven, with non-routine jobs, they might then look at all the prime time shows and ask the following:

1. What is the hero's gender?
2. What is the hero's race?
3. What is the hero's economic status?
4. What is his employment?
5. What are the hero's physical features?
6. What is the hero's marital status?

The data yielded by this second set of questions might reveal a bias in television's conception of the world. Perhaps the students will discover that most heroes in the adventure shows—the comedies will differ—do share those characteristics they first noticed:

> What, they might be encouraged to ask themselves, does that mean?
>
> Why does that particular image dominate?
>
> Do they find themselves or others emulating the characters they see portrayed?
>
> What might those not cast in the same mold think about the image of the hero?
>
> Are there respectable, happy patterns and personalities not represented?
>
> Would they actually want to live as the television heroes live?

Such questions may lead students to consider several issues, not the least significant of which is the commercial nature of television. One reason for the predominance of certain character types is simply financial. A show is a device that sells a product, and its success is determined by how many people watch the show and may thus be influenced to buy the product. Consequently, shows are designed for wide appeal.

Students might be interested in considering the strategies behind that design. They might, for instance, attempt to infer the audience targeted by the producers of various shows that exhibit different features. Who would they expect to find, for example, in the audiences for *Dawson's Creek*, *Boston Public*, *Six Feet Under*, *Frasier*, *Friends*, *Monk*, and *NYPD Blue*, or some other collection?

> Is it one undifferentiated group or not? How can they tell?
>
> What features of the show itself give them clues?
>
> What can they deduce from the sponsors who pay for it and advertise on it?
>
> What can they learn from interviews with people who consider themselves faithful watchers of one show or another?

Such research is essentially a study of the reading act; they are examining how a text, in this case a visual text, is designed and constructed, and how it is read, or in this case viewed. Such study can only make them more alert and rationale about the medium.

Perhaps they could even design shows and propose them to another group within the class, who would play the role of network or potential sponsor and select those they predict would be financially worth producing. A project of that sort would require students to think about the design of shows. Heroes are created, and actors chosen, to capture the largest possible audience. What features, you may ask your students, would they give the hero of a show intended to attract a certain part of the viewing audience in this country?

It might be easier to start with one show or a small group of shows and analyze the features of their lead characters. You might ask: "What characteristics seem to be presented as good traits in the main characters of [_____]?" Students could then consider whether they respect those characteristics and whether they think many people do. The ruthlessness of the heroes of the old show *Dallas*, for instance— is it to be admired? Is it also present in other shows? Media studies reveal that it is. Police programs, for example, often show their heroes performing in ways that would, in the real world, be considered gross violation of police procedure, though they are dramatic and effective in the fictional world of television. The officers in *NYPD Blue*, for instance, occasionally seem to stray from prescribed police procedure. Do they, too, glorify a kind of ruthlessness? That too makes for good drama, with action and violence, but the good drama may not be exemplary police work. How, we may ask, can we avoid the grip of the conceptions the visual media offer us? Fiske and Hartley, referring to several studies of television and social values, argue that "the main difference between heroes and villains is the greater efficiency of the heroes and the sympathy with which they are presented. Otherwise, there are few clear-cut distinctions, particularly in morality or method."[11] It's a disturbing observation that our heroes and villains are virtually indistinguishable.

Students investigating the values present in the shows they watch may reach similar conclusions. They may wonder how constant, unreflective viewing of shows that promote such values might affect the thinking of the watchers. Could people gradually and unwittingly absorb those same values? You might point out that adults have been killed and injured imitating the reckless driving style of *Smokey and the Bandit* and the *Dukes of Hazzard*, although the stunts are obviously dangerous and clearly demolish the cars used in them. Recent movies like *Ronin* and *Bad Boys* offer even more reckless models for the foolish to imitate. If adults are so easily deceived, how will they fare with more subtle ethical questions? Most adults are bright enough to know that although the recklessness makes for entertaining film, in the world outside the movie set it makes for high insurance bills and time in jail, but how will they fare with slightly more subtle matters?

We have suggested some questions that teachers could ask about heroes on television. You might ask similar questions about the villains. Do they also follow a pattern, and if so, what does that indicate? Or you might ask about typical plots. Is there a pattern? What accounts for it? Students might divide the shows into the genres of police procedurals, detective shows, adventures, situation comedies, and so on and identify repeating patterns in each. Does each genre have its own shape? If that shape is observable, does it vary greatly from show to show or from episode to episode? How well does it conform to the real world? How predictable are the shows? And if they are predictable, then what is their appeal?

Technical Elements

These questions bring us closer and closer to the technical elements in the visual media, so we might now consider how to introduce these elements in the classroom. Once they have analyzed a show in some detail, students might try to invent a story line that would suit the show. In teams, they might design plots consistent with the patterns noted, working with the values they have identified as implicit in the show's content. They could then work together to write dialog and stage directions. If time permits, and if the equipment is available, the scripts might actually be performed and videotaped. This will demand attention to the technical elements of television production- blocking, timing, sound, manipulation of the camera, and the like.

Robert Meadows describes a similar strategy, in which he has students adapt a well-known tale—his examples are "Little Red Riding Hood" and "Goldilocks"—to the format of a television show chosen by the students. He lists six steps: (1) dividing the class into five-person committees, each of which chooses a show; (2) observing and taking notes on the show; (3) writing the script; (4) rehearsing; (5) producing the videotape; and (6) evaluating. The students who undertake this activity, he notes, become more critical and skeptical viewers, more aware of the patterns and stereotypes and sentimental appeals than they were before the activity.[12]

The stories and poems in the literature program are good candidates for this treatment. How, for instance, might "The Most Dangerous Game" be adapted for television? On what shows, if any, would it fit? How would it be different if adapted for different shows? Could Robinson's "Richard Cory" be rewritten for, perhaps, *Six Feet Under*? Could any of Poe's detective stories be used in one of the police series, or any of O'Henry's tales in *Frasier*? Some of Guy de Maupassant's stories found their way into old radio shows; could they be adapted to one of the current television dramas? "The Necklace," for instance,—might that be an episode of *Friends*, with one of the group borrowing some item of fake jewelry, losing it, and trying to figure out how to replace it? Comparisons such as these suggest ways of including television in the context of a traditional literature course.

Other methods will come readily to mind. When analyzing the television hero, for instance, students might be asked about characters in literature they have studied during the year (or any other literature they may have read). Which characters would be most suitable for the lead in a television show or series? Is there one they could propose successfully to the networks? What features would make her popular? How is she like other television heroes? How is she different? The class might even invent a series around such a character, specifying the setting, other regular characters, kinds of episodes, the tone of the show (serious, comic), the established shows with which it would compete, and perhaps even the sort of sponsor it might attract and possible strategies for selling it to a backer. Students might suggest actors who could play the main roles and, if especially sophisticated, even discuss which producers and directors might be interested in the series.

Such close study of television, first identifying its values and then adapting other stories to the established format, will involve students in the technical aspects of the medium. The character's appearance itself is a matter of technique. In a short story we would call it description and ask how it reveals character, attitude, motivation, and status. In the visual media, which usually function without a narrator, we don't read or hear a description; rather, we see the character dressed in certain clothes, walking and speaking in a certain way. These details must reveal character without the intervention of an interpreter. Or rather, the camera serves as interpreter. It must catch expressions and touch on significant features so that they catch our notice. Thus it guides our attention, as the narrator does in a short story. The absence of a narrator accounts for yet another difference between the visual and the written media: Writing is better suited for handling extended thought, whereas the visual media are better for action and movement. Thus a more philosophical work may not translate well to the screen. Long passages of introspection have no vehicle in the visual media; a long monolog disrupts the forward motion of a film and seems out of place. So ideas must somehow be conveyed in the action, or developed in dialog, and that limitation makes film and television less intellectual media than the essay, novel, and short story can be.

But the writer can never convey the violence of a fight, the tumult of a stampede, or the power of a volcano quite so effectively as the film can, with its visual and aural resources. Perhaps it is this fact that has led the visual media to concentrate on violence. A gangster can fill the screen with his brawling for hours, while his potential in the essay might be exhausted after a page or two. Because the visual media are biased in that way, it is even more important that students be trained to see the power of all the media, visual and written. To be immersed in the visual, as so many of the present generation are, is to neglect other important modes of depicting and thinking about the world and its experiences.

As character description is presented visually, so is setting. It is there for us to see, perhaps with the addition of a line in the dialogue to name the city or specify the date. Description and setting are elements in the visual media, just as they are in the written, and although they are achieved in different ways, their principles are the same. Still, the grammar is different. In discussing written literature, we may talk about diction and sentence structure. With film and television, we would talk instead about camera angle, movement, distance from the subject, and focus.

These elements may go virtually unnoticed at first. The film can create the illusion that we are watching real action. A superintendent of schools in a large eastern system once remarked that he'd like to do away with letters of recommendation for prospective teachers because he had to wonder about the motives and biases of the writer. Instead, he wanted videotapes of the candidate teaching a lesson. That, he said, would be like having the person actually there in front of him. Then, he thought, he wouldn't have to worry about interpreting a text. He was laboring under the illusion—or perhaps delusion is the proper term—that the film provided direct and immediate contact with reality itself, that all he had to do was observe. If an educated adult can be so naive about the shaping effects of camera angle, timing of cuts, selection of the central subject in the shot, quality of the sound recording, and all the other elements that shape what finally appears on the screen, and ultimately how we respond to it, then we may expect our students to be almost as naive.

But they can learn to look for those elements in both film and television by noting their responses and then trying to see how those responses were achieved. The most dramatic moments are the most accessible. Suspense and fright are emotions whose source is easily analyzed, and the analysis will introduce students to the methods of the visual media.

Students may even be able to reconstruct from memory the techniques of especially powerful scenes. In *Psycho*, the ominous presence of the stuffed animals; the quiet, eerie voice of the innkeeper; the peephole into the motel room adjoining the office; the dark, looming mansion; the long period of near silence leading up to the killing; and finally the killer's silhouette through the shower curtain all contribute to the building tension. From other films, students may recall brightly lit shots of the unsuspecting victim alternating with dimly lit shots, perhaps of only the killer's feet steadily and quietly approaching. The cuts may grow gradually more rapid to suggest the imminence of the crime and heighten still further the tension of the audience. The discussion of scenes like these will call attention to the use of sound, light, and movement, both by the actors and by the camera. It will invite comment on the camera operator's selection of her subject (only the feet of the stalking killer), on the editor's timing of cuts (slow in one scene and quick in another), and on other aspects of filming.

If films can be obtained for use in the class, the study can be much more vivid and lively. Students can time scenes to note the pacing of different events—the violent scenes with many cuts, perhaps so rapid that images remain on the screen for less than a second, and the leisurely scene-setting shots with fewer cuts and gentler transitions.

For these purposes it might be useful to distinguish between film and television. Although similar, they have some important differences, and pacing is a case in point. Television pacing is bound by certain external constraints. The show is limited, for one thing, to a specific length. On the major networks, the time is cut into half-hour units, and shows are planned to fit neatly into one or several of those units. Further, the program must accommodate regular breaks for commercials. The script must divide neatly and logically into scenes so that the audience will not feel disrupted by the advertising.

The students' efforts to write scripts suitable for television will tell them much about the difficulties of the medium. They may notice that the necessity of dividing the show into segments severely limits them. They cannot write scenes that require a steady building of tension longer than the twelve minutes or so between commercials. Watching a movie not made for television but shown on television interrupted by soap, new cars, used cars, dishwashers, and announcements of forthcoming shows reveals the same problem. The movie, originally edited without the constraint of commercial interruptions often fits badly when re-edited to fit into the small, regular slots. Breaks often come at inopportune moments, disrupting the flow of the story.

Comparing television and film will reveal other technical differences. Film, because of the large screen, is able to handle wide vistas and huge battlefield scenes. On the small screen, such images are much less impressive. A lone rider, moving slowly along a ridge in the distance, seems on the movie screen diminished by the grandeur of the country; on the television he may be only a speck moving through a blur. Television, on the other hand, is intimate. It is in the home, accessible and controllable. The viewer can alter the volume, tune the picture, and discuss the show with others while it is in progress. And television seems to deal intimately with its subject matter. Much of the drama on television takes place inside a room. That seems to be the perspective television manages well. Have students, if they can tolerate it, spend a minute or two watching how a soap opera is staged, with all of its intimate close-ups. Students may note other points of comparison.

In both film and television, as in writing, focus is an important issue. In a short story we may be shown an event through its effect on one of the characters. Similarly, a scene in a film may focus on some minor character whose reaction shows us the significance of the event or tells something about the main character. Thus awe in the faces of the office-workers informs us that the person walking through is a powerful figure in the company; silence falling over a saloon tells us that the man who has just entered is to be feared; terror in the faces of the victims suggests the horrible visage of the monster, and so on. Focus falls temporarily on someone other than the main character, describing through effect rather than directly. Focus is a tool of both writers and directors.

Similarly, both the written and the visual media can show much through details. In Shirley Jackson's short story "After You, My Dear Alphonse," the little offers that Johnny's mother makes to Boyd reveal her prejudice, or at any rate, her stereotyping of Boyd. In *Psycho*, the fly sitting unharmed on Perkins' hand at the end of the film suggests the depth of his psychosis. In both cases much is done with little, and so sensitivity to details is very important for the reader and the viewer.

Films based on literary works are useful for comparing visual and written literature. Many have been made especially for use in the classroom. More recently, commercial television has begun to adapt classics and contemporary literature into short television movies for young viewers. Such items offer both a second look at the work itself and a glimpse into the nature of each medium. Films made as pedagogic tools are often unsatisfying—a mixture of drama and lecture, they leave the viewer with the feeling that she has tasted the story but not digested it. But the films and television specials that attempt to recreate a work and not just teach about it provide an interesting chance to see how written and visual media treat the same story. Even such a program as the cartoon show *The Simpsons* often alludes in clever ways to works of literature that we find in the English curriculum.

Recently, there has been a great deal of cross-fertilization between print and visual media. Whereas in the past books were made into films, now we also find films made into books, films made into television series, and television series made into books. Some works are now available in several media, providing interesting possibilities for teaching. Let's look at one such pair, the film *Death Wish*, which we discussed briefly in Chapter 2, and the novel from which it was made.

A comparison of the film and the book will reveal both technical and conceptual differences. One obvious difference is in the portrayal of the killers. In the book they remain faceless, unidentified, part of the mass of New York's humanity. In the film they are shown clearly; the camera comes close to the dirty, leering faces, and we hear the quiet, sadistic voices. Their repulsiveness is nearly tangible.

Why that difference? Why would the writer choose one strategy and the director another? Part of the answer may be the different potential of the two media.

Film, with its strong visual impact, can shock and repel us quickly. It can tell us much about the characters through their dress, expressions, and bearing. In *Death Wish* the film, we quickly see that the killers are corrupt and sadistic, without redeeming features. In print, it would take longer to convey that repugnance. The writer, Brian Garfield, is not interested in looking into the killers' minds or explaining their degeneracy; he is concerned with the consequences of their actions on the main character, Paul Benjamin, whose wife and daughter they assault. In the film they can appear, be clearly identified as villains, and vanish quickly; in the book, they might take more time and trouble than they are worth. Further, they might arouse our own hatred enough to interfere with our perception of Benjamin's response. Better, perhaps, to treat them as Garfield does, as menacing apparitions, hovering, ominous, but never clearly seen and confronted.

So, at any rate, might the discussion go. Students could also consider the effect of having the villains remain faceless in the movie too, or of making them full characters in the novel. The difference between the two works is crucial and easily traced throughout.

Another difference, perhaps related, is in the transformation of Benjamin himself. In the novel he changes gradually. His unfocused anger seeks out objects and begins to find them. The first is an addict who tries to rob him late at night on the streets—a fairly clear instance of self-defense. We are almost satisfied that he acted appropriately to the threat. But it is also something more. Benjamin has thrown himself in the addict's way, seeking an excuse to satisfy his rage, taking a misplaced revenge for the deaths of his wife and daughter.

His second killing is slightly different. He finds a man robbing a drunk in the park and confronts him. When the man flees, Benjamin stops him and shoots him while his hands are raised in surrender. The killing is clearly not self-defense this time; it is not even a defense of the drunkard. The victim has been stopped from committing a crime, but he is no longer a threat—he has given up. Benjamin is satisfied with less justification for this killing than for the first.

The deterioration continues. Two teenage boys prepare to strip his car, and he shoots them from hiding. This time he doesn't even confront his victims. Then he kills a man stealing a television set from an apartment. The crimes grow less threatening and further removed from him, but they still provoke him to kill. Finally, he murders three of four teenagers he finds throwing bricks at a passing subway train.

At the beginning of the novel, Benjamin is a justifiably angry man who unfortunately has no target for his anger. By the end, he is one of the predators, corrupted by the tragedy he has suffered and by his unsatisfied desire for vengeance. When he kills his first victim, he is still a hero; when he kills his last, he has been transformed into someone disturbingly like the savages he hunts.

The movie follows a different path. There is no gradual change in the encounters here; each one seems justified and laudable. Benjamin begins as a hero and ends as a larger hero. The public applauds his one-man war against crime, and the papers report decreasing street crime as the vigilante begins to intimidate the criminals. The ineffectiveness of the police serves as background and contrast to his efficiency.

He becomes a contemporary Robin Hood, defending the weak in a society with too many predators and too few police. Finally he is forced to leave town, but he leaves in triumph. In the final scene, arriving in a new city, he helps a young girl who has been knocked down by one of the local ruffians, and with his final gesture, a finger pointed like a gun at the culprit, shows his intention to continue his private war.

The book chronicles Benjamin's deterioration from victim to killer; the film chronicles his resurrection from victim to killer. It is an interesting contrast—the same story presenting two opposing visions. Garfield himself has repudiated the film:

> The movie was all right, but it wasn't my book and there wasn't anything I could do about it. I had written about a man whose rage turned into paranoia. He ended up shooting unarmed teenagers on the street because he didn't like their looks. It's what I saw as the ultimate result of the vigilante mentality.
>
> In the movie, they made him into a white knight, cleaning up New York City without regard to what's right or wrong or what's legal.[13]

The contrast, although it may be less obvious to young students than to more experienced readers, is probably sharp enough to be sensed, and that feeling may lead students to try to specify the difference. It may suggest questions like those we have discussed: How do the killings differ between novel and film? How does the main character differ? The answers will call attention to both the technique and the artistic conception of each work. Pairing books and films allows for this sort of investigation. Just as students might compare how two poems treat one theme, so might they compare the different treatments of one story in two media, print and film.

Other potentially interesting pairings are possible. The film *M*A*S*H* might be compared with the television show. The television show *Star Trek* might be compared with the books based on it, with the film, or perhaps with the movie *Star Wars*, which is in some ways similar. For the lower grades, where something like *Death Wish* would be inappropriate, the books in Laura Ingalls Wilder's *Little House* series might be compared with the television show *Little House on the Prairie*. The Harry Potter books might be compared with the movies made from them. So, too, could the Tolkien books and movies be examined. And of course, every so often a story will show up in the form of a television episode or a children's special, or, like *Roots*, a special with wider appeal.

It seems appropriate for the English teacher to encourage intelligent viewing of film and television. They are similar enough to the printed literature from which they have sprung that dealing with them should not be difficult. The basic strategy is the same: Begin with responses, look for the sources of those responses in the person and in the work, compare responses to clarify and enrich them, and compare works to see still other features.

There will, of course, be problems. One is obtaining films, or arranging for the classes to see them at a theater. Some students will be unable to watch a particular show that you want to discuss, either because parents forbid it or because they insist on watching something else. There is the problem of having to discuss something from memory or notes without being able to refer directly to it. That, however, might be seen as an opportunity rather than a disadvantage because it might motivate students to learn to take careful notes as they watch.

Then there is the problem of censorship, as absurd as it may seem in a modern democracy. Predictably, the movies made from the Harry Potter books have been condemned for the witchcraft and magic they portray. In many communities, the showing of a film like *Death Wish* would be considered grounds for firing a teacher. These communities are willing to gamble that keeping children ignorant will keep them pure and safe. This idea seems to be persistent, as efforts increase to pull books off library shelves, close movie theaters, and harass magazine publishers, and teachers will have to deal as best they can.

Teachers who hope to incorporate some film and television into English courses will have to note these problems, consider the nature of the community and school, and perhaps get the advice and support of supervisors and principals if possible. At the very least, they should probably communicate with parents, telling them about purposes and plans for including the visual media. Informing them may forestall some problems and even win allies for teachers, although it will also alert the budding censor to the opportunity for more meddling in the academic process. One further purpose of informing parents is to gently encourage a change in the patterns of viewing in the homes of your students. Television is discussed in few families. Both children and adults sit in front of the set, absorb what it presents, and then go about their business, never analyzing what they have seen. Suggesting to the parents that television may have a subtle influence on the ideas of its viewers, and that it is useful to help students learn to resist and control that influence, may draw them into the circle. They may agree to watch with their children occasionally, reflecting on the questions teacher and students have devised and offering their own responses and judgments. Ideally, students and their parents might develop the habit of talking about shows, trading reactions and opinions. That habit might help sustain the goals of the instruction after the students have left your class.

If we were deliriously optimistic, we might even hope that some parents would read with their children and discuss the books with them, but we should probably be pleased if they sit around for a few minutes discussing an episode of *Friends*. At the very least, some parents might begin to think about the education their children are receiving and participate in it in some small way.

Special Courses

We have not discussed special courses in film and television since we have been most concerned with how they function as literature and with their place in the literature curriculum. Special courses are possible, however, though they may require extra funding and other assistance. Film courses need films, which have to be rented and shipped. They also require adjustments in the schedule—one class period is usually not long enough. Block scheduling, if it happens to be in place in your school, may help somewhat. Television courses, unless they depend on memory and note-taking, will require video equipment and tapes of the shows to be discussed. If there is sufficient interest among students and teachers, however, and if the climate in the school and the community is favorable, such courses can be very good, generating a great deal of enthusiasm and hard work.

Courses in television production or film-making can be especially valuable. In preparing a show or film, students will have to exercise many of the skills English courses are expected to teach. They will have to talk among themselves, negotiating their ideas, predicting, and planning. They will have to write letters asking for information or permission, scripts, programs, advertisements, and production schedules. And that work will be in the context of a real activity, not to satisfy some arbitrary assignment or invented task. If the equipment can be obtained, such courses are excellent additions to the curriculum.

The Industry

Intensive courses would also allow time to investigate another side of the media—the commercial side. Although knowledge of the industry behind film and television isn't necessary to intelligent viewing, the industry is fascinating, and students may want to know more about it. Almost inevitably, discussion of film and television leads to talk about money, about the advertisers who control so much of what happens and about the people involved in the business. An awareness of that huge and complicated industry is useful in understanding the visual media, its motivations, and its effects upon the public.

Endnotes

1. Albert Ellis, *The American Sexual Tragedy* (New York: Twayne Publishers, 1954), p. 98.

2. D.F. Roberts, "One Highly Attracted Public," in *TV and Human Behavior*, G. Comstock, Ed. (New York: Columbia University Press, 197), pp. 173–287.

3. *Kids and Television in the Nineties: Responses from the Youth Monitor*. CPB Research Notes, No. 64 (ERIC) ED402903, November, 1993.

4. Emory H. Woodard, IV, *Media in the Home 2000: The Fifth Annual Survey of Parents and Children*. (The Annenberg Public Policy Center of the University of Pennsylvania, 2000), p. 19.

5. Ibid.

6. Leonard Berkowitz, Opening Speech to the Medial Violence Symposium in Report from a Media Violence Symposium in Stockholm, April 25th, 1974 (Stockholm, Sweden: University of Stockholm, September 1974), pp. 1–3.

7. Berkowitz, p. 10

8. John Fiske and John Hartley, *Reading Television* (London: Methuen, 1978), p. 24.

9. George Gerbner and Larry Gross, "The Scary World of TV's Heavy Viewer," *Psychology Today*, 9, No. 11 (April 1976), 44.

10. John Leonard, "And a Picture Tube Shall Lead Them," *Playboy*, 23, No. 6 (June 1976), p. 204.

11. Fiske and Hartley, p. 29

12. Robert Meadows, "Get Smart: Let TV Work for You," *English Journal*, 56, No. 2 (1976), 121–124.

13. Brian Garfield, quoted in Terry Brewster, "Best-Selling Author Believes in Taking a Quick Write," *Friends*, Volume 37, No. 10 (1980), p. 12.

8

The Literature Curriculum

Literature has been in trouble ever since Plato banned the poets from his ideal society. Plato thought that, because they dealt in fictions, poets could contribute little to the pursuit of truth and virtue and were probably a threat to the morality of a society's youth. Many people still share Plato's fears, and others who don't are nonetheless unsure that literature serves any valuable purpose. It may be harmless amusement, they might think, but little more—it is surely not a serious, useful study, like mathematics, biology, engineering, or economics. Even those who teach it are sometimes vague about its value, making for it nebulous and unconvincing claims. In some ways it is surprising that a subject so weakly supported should be as firmly entrenched in the curriculum as literature seems to be.

Its place in the curriculum is at once tenuous and secure. In the elementary grades, what literature there is comes to students through the reading program, often presented in the form of basal reading texts that may or may not contain good literature. Some teachers and schools have expanded that to include much of the excellent children's literature now available, and to experiment with book clubs, independent reading groups, and literature circles, but the early grades often focus on *reading*. In the secondary grades, however, literature seems secure. It is taught from seventh through twelfth grade as a major part of the English program in most schools. Although some protest that too much of the English program is devoted to literature and more time should be spent teaching writing, few have openly suggested that literature is frivolous and not worth teaching at all. They may not know why it's there, and may not see it as a serious endeavor, but it has been there so long that they are willing to assume that surely someone, somewhere, must know why we teach it.

On the other hand, there are many who take literature seriously enough to wish to control its effect on students. Such people sense that literature might not be simply irrelevant and harmless, but that it might actually influence its readers and, unwilling to put any faith in students' ability to manage that influence intelligently, try to manage it for them by determining what they may and may not read.

However, despite literature's ubiquity in the schools and the love and fear with which it is regarded, its role in the curriculum has never been satisfactorily defined by most schools and many teachers. Other disciplines have, in this era, a more apparent purpose. Science contributes to progress and to comfort and security; it is clearly valuable. Mathematics supports all of the sciences as well as business and industry; it, too, is clearly practical and useful. This is a scientific, mathematical, pragmatic era. The nation's health is measured by its production, its economy, and its military and political stature rather than by its accomplishments in art, music, dance, and theater. Literature's role in such an era may be hard to identify, and may seem peripheral, at best.

Literature does not, after all, contribute to the common good in any *tangible* way. It does not make its readers healthy, secure, or rich; it doesn't put food on the table, shelter the homeless, build bridges, prevent traffic jams; it doesn't conquer disease, settle international conflict, or solve economic problems. In these pragmatic times, literature seems to make few pragmatic contributions. I recall being asked by an older student during my first year at college what I intended to choose as my major. "English," I told him, and he replied, "Ah, and what are you going to do with that—look upon life with a broader perspective?" His mildly sarcastic remark troubled me. That "broader perspective" he disparaged seemed a worthwhile objective; on the other hand, I couldn't see why anyone would pay me a living wage for having it. I couldn't articulate, for him or for myself, just what contribution such training would enable me to make to the betterment of the world.

Asked what literature can do for the student, the teacher often has only the vaguest, most abstract, and most unconvincing answers. "It will enrich their lives," we might answer, or "It will invite them to reflect on life's difficult questions." Or we might propose that the study of literature "will acquaint students with their cultural heritage," which sounds like a good thing to be doing. All of those assertions, however, carry little weight with someone who wants to know how those students are going to earn a living with that enrichment, those reflections, that cultural awareness. All of those arguments have a hollow ring in a culture dominated by the sciences, a culture that judges success in terms of productivity and acquisition.

That the English program has suffered from this pragmatism and emphasis on science became obvious in the 1960s, when the nation started setting aside funds for basic educational research. In 1961 the government divided up 561 million dollars—71 percent went to the physical sciences, 26 percent to the biological sciences, 2 percent to the psychological sciences, 1 percent to the social sciences, and nothing to the humanities.[1] The Russians had jumped out into the lead and English presumably could contribute little to catching up, little to the national defense. We didn't need a broader perspective on the Russians—we needed to beat them. Literature, perhaps literacy in general, was not worth a chunk of the budget; it was not practical. Now, it would seem obvious to those of us who have gone into the teaching of the English language arts that literacy *does* contribute to the national security, since the ability to read and write, and thus to think, is fundamental to almost every other intellectual achievement, but the reluctance of politicians to invest much in literature teaching isn't surprising.

The History

The problem is much older than the 1960s; it dates back to the time English entered the curriculum. English is not as old a subject as many of its teachers imagine, having secured a place in the curriculum only around the late 1800s, or early 1900s. Arthur Applebee, summarizing the early history of English teaching in the schools, observes:

> By 1865, schools and colleges recognized a variety of loosely related minor studies of the vernacular—rhetoric, oratory, spelling, grammar, literary history, and reading all had their places, often conflicting with one another for attention. Though many of these studies made use of literary selections, literary study in its own right had yet to find a place or a justification. Rhetorical and grammatical studies often included literary texts, but instruction was designed and carried out in the service of composition, not literature. Literary history, though the schools called it the teaching of literature, was biographical in emphasis and often involved no literature at all.[2]

Literature in the late nineteenth century was not the central element in the curriculum that it is now. It came in gradually, competing for a place with older pedagogic traditions. Of these, in the colleges at least, rhetoric and oratory dominated. They were the significant studies in schools intent on educating future ministers and bureaucrats. Of the related disciplines, classical studies had perhaps the most influence on literature teaching. The classics were studied first for their historical significance and second as a rigorous mental discipline that toughened the sinews of the mind.

As English studies gradually entered the curriculum, they were shaped by the tradition that had emphasized the classics, rhetoric, and oratory. Literature was seen in this context and became a subject to study and know in the same way that the classics were studied and known. The emphasis fell on information, knowledge *about* the literature rather than sensitive reading of the literary works themselves. By 1870 the emphasis on information in literary studies was well established. Such study of the facts about literature remains an element in high school instruction to the present day, though the justification has changed from mental discipline to knowledge of our literary heritage.[3]

As the schools moved into the twentieth century, it became apparent that their role was changing somewhat. By the turn of the century not all high school students were college-bound; a great many were going directly to work. The formal, classical training that prepared them for college did not prepare them as well for blacksmithing, bartending, and bricklaying. Pressure to reform the English curriculum ultimately yielded several results; one of the most important was the *Bureau of Education Bulletin Number Two,* compiled by James F. Hosic, a founder of the National Council of Teachers of English.

The report, issued in 1917, was the work of a joint committee formed by the Commission on the Reorganization of Secondary Education (a commission of the

National Education Association) and the National Council of Teachers of English (NCTE). It expressed the committee's concern about the growing number of students who did not go on to college, for whom the high school curriculum seemed less and less suitable. For some time the curriculum had been strongly influenced by college entrance criteria, through such organizations as the National Conference on Uniform Entrance Requirements. Hosic and his committee thought that the molding of the high school curriculum by the colleges had produced some unfortunate results. He concluded:

> The English course as a whole tended to formality, scholasticism, and overmaturity, and needed to be vitalized, redirected, and definitely related to the life of the present.[4]

The committee recommended that the English program more carefully consider students' needs. Planning, they thought, should focus somewhat less on scholarship and somewhat more on the psychology and the needs of the student. English should be thought of as a tool for effective living so that students would be prepared, not just for the academic life, but for life in whatever role they might have to play.

Unfortunately, the concept of English as a social instrument did not grant literature a very dignified place. Hosic suggested distinguishing between "English for work" and "English for leisure," the first to teach composition and the second to teach literature.[5] Hosic had granted literature a place in the program, but only as recreation or entertainment. He demoted the reading of literature from the serious, scholarly, but doubtfully relevant pursuit of knowledge to a mere source of amusement.

This new conception of the English program had the virtue of being somewhat more consistent with the needs and interests of the students. It recognized that a great many of them would not become ministers or scholars, but would simply need to speak and read and write competently, and it encouraged teachers to respect those needs. In treating English as a set of skills to be developed, rather than a body of facts to be memorized, it began the transition from a curriculum focused on the discipline to one focused on the student.

But along with that virtue—that it considered the students' needs—it had the great defect of conceiving of literature as little more than a pastime. It was "English for leisure," nothing more. That was to say, essentially, that literature had no serious contribution to make to the students. It was fine for the scholars in their towers, and it was fine for helping while away the otherwise boring evening hours before the proliferation of television sets, but that was about all.

The "life-adjustment" principle was to dominate in the schools for several decades, exemplified, for English teachers, by the NCTE's *Experience Curriculum in English*. This curriculum was devoted to relevance, with little concern for significance. It taught telephone manners and how to write thank-you notes, and proposed model units in which, for example, such a purpose as the provision of milk and other needs for the children of an indigent family dominates the work of a group for weeks, subject-matter divisions being ignored and any material used whenever it serves the group purposes.[6]

Such an activity had obvious merit, and might well find a place today, especially in the interdisciplinary programs attempted by the middle schools, but it reveals that the discipline had moved far away from rigorous study of the classics. English was now a social tool, a collection of skills for getting along well in the world.

The Basic Issues Conference

This state of affairs persisted until the late 1950s. Then, in 1957, the Russians launched Sputnik and precipitated a flurry of activity in the United States. People became worried about the educational system that had failed to produce scientists skillful enough to stay ahead of the Russians. In 1959, the Modern Language Association, the College English Association, and the National Council of Teachers of English met together in a Basic Issues Conference to reassess the state of the art in English teaching. They asked:

> Has the fundamental liberal discipline of English been displaced, at some levels of schooling, by ad hoc training in how to write a letter, how to give a radio speech, manners, dating, telephoning, vocational guidance? Can agreement be reached upon a body of knowledge and set of skills as standard at certain points in the curriculum, making due allowances for flexibility of planning, individual differences, and patterns of growth? This issue seems crucial to this entire document, and to any serious approach to the problem. Unless we can find an answer to it, we must resign ourselves to an unhappy future in which the present curricular disorder persists and the whole liberal discipline of English continues to disintegrate and lose its character.[7]

Project English

The Basic Issues Conference marked the beginning of a swing away from the life-adjustment curriculum and back toward a more rigorous academic approach. The laxity of the curriculum had become distressing, especially when national security came into doubt. The money that was poured into curriculum development over the next decade went to projects characterized by close attention to the discipline. Albert R. Kitzhaber, who directed one of the most productive of the twelve Project English Curriculum Centers during the 1960s, foretold the direction English curriculum planning would take when he observed that one respect in which the English curriculum is particularly vulnerable is its almost complete failure to reflect the present state of knowledge in the disciplines from which it draws its proper substance—philology and linguistics, rhetoric, logic, and the critical study of literature.[8]

The life-adjustment era had overcome the sterility of the classical approach of the late 1800s, but at the cost of losing its scholarly grounding. It had become insubstantial, almost trivial, and those who worked on the English curriculum during the 1960s tried hard to re-establish a respectable foundation. Predictably, the English curricula produced by the Project English Centers were serious, scholarly affairs. The Oregon Curriculum Center, for instance, produced a series of six massive anthologies, concerned more with the literary heritage, its great works and its body of scholarship, than with the students' telephone manners. The Nebraska curriculum was similarly demanding. Carnegie-Mellon's was almost oppressively weighty and solemn, with no illustrations at all, no break in the page after page of dense text—no one would accuse it of catering to its students or seeking to make English too light, too relevant, or too easy. So English once again reversed its field, rejecting the life-adjustment approach and turning to the scholarly disciplines to structure its curriculum.

This academic era, however, proved to be very brief. Late in the 1960s it was disrupted suddenly by the conclusions of the Dartmouth Seminar. Held in 1966 and attended by about fifty prominent English educators from the United States, Britain, and Canada, this meeting cast serious doubts on the direction taken by many of the Project English Centers and acquainted the representatives from the United States with the fundamentally different philosophy then current in England.

The British educators were concerned not so much with rigor and intellectually demanding labor in their schools as with making the work personally significant to the students. They spoke, for instance, of encouraging students to respond to the literature read rather than having them analyze it. John Dixon, in *Growth Through English,* one of the two major summaries of the Dartmouth Conference, says,

> The essential talk that springs from literature is talk about experience—as *we* know it, as *he* [the student] sees it (correcting our partiality and his; exploring the fullness of his vision, and ours). Conversely, only in a classroom where talk explores experience is literature drawn into the dialogue—otherwise it has no place. The demand for interpretation—was it this or that he meant?—arises in the course of such talk: otherwise it is a dead hand.[9]

Since Sputnik, U. S. schools had been encouraged to demand rigorous work and impose high standards of scholarship. Now, at Dartmouth, the British recommendations seemed to contradict that philosophy. James Britton, in the opening paper for the Literature Study Group, rejected the notion that our purposes in the schools include the "driving out of bad currency"—that is, correcting the child's taste for inferior literature—and argued that we should be trying instead to awaken his appetite for better works. He argued further against the dominance of the critics, who represent, of course, high standards of literary performance:

> The point at which critical statements can be of help to a student is . . . a difficult one to determine. It is even more important, however, to consider the manner in

which such help is offered. The voice of the critic must not be allowed to seem the voice of authority; more harm has probably been done to the cause of literature by this means than by any other. It is all too easy for the immature student, feeling that his own responses are unacceptable, to disown them and profess instead the opinions of respected critics. And to many teachers, with their eyes on what may rightly go on in other parts of the curriculum, this looks like good teaching. It may of course be the best kind of preparation for an ill-conceived examination, and this may be the real root of the trouble.[10]

The Dartmouth Conference precipitated a great deal of heated debate among educators alert enough to hear about it. It suggested a set of criteria for English teaching different from those the Project English curriculum planners had had in mind. They had been concerned with intellect; Dartmouth suggested more concern for emotion. They had been thinking of the discipline; Dartmouth suggested that they think of the child. The question of purpose was not so simple or dichotomous as that, but emphasis did seem to be shifting once again from the subject to the student, as it had in the first part of the century under the guidance of Hosic and others.

James E. Miller summarizes this evolution of English curriculum. There have been four stages, he says: the Authoritarian, the Progressive, the Academic, and the Humanitarian:

> The first of these stages, the Authoritarian, we identify with the arid classicism and rote learning of the nineteenth century; the second, the Progressive, with John Deweyism (something different from the real Dewey), indiscriminate permissiveness, and social adjustment, all running deep into the twentieth century. In more recent times we have been witness to a revolution in our schools which we may, for convenience, date from Russia's Sputnik launching in 1957, and which I have arbitrarily designated Academic. . . .
>
> We are now. . . on the threshold of the fourth stage [1967], which I call the Humanitarian. If we pause for a moment and glance backward, we note that the stages I have described are not clearly defined historical periods but merely the slow swinging of a pendulum between two poles of emphasis which may be variously described as substance and psychology, subject matter and student, or intellectuality and society.[11]

We are now either well into Miller's fourth period, or—more likely—beyond it to a fifth, and a great many conflicting pressures weigh on the schools. The humanism evident in the recommendations of the Dartmouth Seminar still runs strong, but it has been countered by the back-to-basics movement, which espoused the teaching of the least significant language skills in ways least likely to help students and virtually certain to alienate and humiliate them. More recently, the concentration on testing has worked its insidious effects on the schools, driving out many students, abusing those who remain, reducing instruction in literature and writing to mind-numbing skill-based test-preparation in some areas, but at the same time giving politicians and the press lots of material for speeches and editorials. The "No Child Left Behind Act," perpetrated upon suffering schools and innocent children in 2001, is probably the epitome of such nonsense, legislating policies and programs nationwide (which were then virtually ignored in budget requests) based on narrowly identified and poorly interpreted "scientific research."

Whether "Humanitarian" will remain the best term to describe this era in English education remains to be seen. The significant point to be observed in this brief history is that the vacillation back and forth from student-centered to discipline-centered has not settled upon a conception of literature adequate to support the curriculum. And yet, in those two poles of the pendulum swing, the two crucial elements of such a conception are apparent.

Conceptions of the Literature Curriculum

A vision of the curriculum that somehow integrates the two poles between which we have been swinging might reduce the uncertainty about the fundamental purposes and appropriate focus of the literature curriculum that has always created problems with planning. In the concluding chapter of his history of English teaching, Applebee identified some of the remaining and persistent defects of the English curriculum:

> Teachers of literature have never successfully resisted the pressure to formulate their subject as a body of knowledge to be imparted.[12]
>
> The acknowledged goals of the teaching of literature are in conflict with the emphasis on specific knowledge or content.[13]
>
> There is a need to reconceptualize the "literary heritage" and its implications for patterns of teaching.[14]

These are, of course, the very problems that have plagued us from the first. They betray the inadequate conception of literature upon which curricula have been built.

Consider first the consequences of thinking of our subject as simply a "body of knowledge to be imparted." If what we are teaching is a "body of knowledge," then we naturally seek a pattern suitable to that body of knowledge. What sort of knowledge do we have about literature? What leaps first to mind is the rich historical data accumulated over several centuries of scholarship. We know dates and places, trends and influences. We know which earlier writers have influenced which later writers. We have identified literary epochs and their characteristics. We have documented the emergence and decline of genres. So, conceived as a body of information, the literature curriculum tends to become a course in literary history or genre, as many high school literature textbooks show.

For example, a typical curriculum—and there are exceptions—will focus on American literature in the eleventh grade and British literature in the twelfth. Those textbooks, and therefore the courses, are most often arranged chronologically. As a result, the class is likely to concentrate on historical matters, examining the literature in terms of periods, dates, major authors, major works, and so on. The organization of the course predisposes the teacher to focus on information, a pattern inherited from literature's first days in the curriculum.

In the lower grades, where the students may be more resistant to studying the history of an art form, that chronological arrangement is less palatable. The tenth grade text, therefore, is probably organized by genre, with a section for the short story, one for poetry, one for drama—perhaps even one for the short novel. The concept here is slightly different. The literature is arranged to yield not historical information but technical information about the distinguishing characteristics of the genres. Unfortunately, this pattern is even less likely than the historical to appeal to young students. Below the tenth-grade level, in the middle school and junior high, the texts are likely to be organized around themes, probably a much more sensible pattern if the themes are well-chosen.

This common curricular design confirms the history Applebee has traced and the problems he has identified. In this arrangement, especially in the upper grades, literature is knowledge—information to acquire, remember, and be tested on.

The Literary Heritage

The usual justification for such a curriculum is that students need to become familiar with their literary heritage. The literary heritage model for the literature curriculum is appealing. It suggests that the students will be immersed in great traditions and profit from the best the culture has to offer. The belief in teaching the literary heritage implies a faith that it will produce good results of some sort for the students. Exactly what these results are is often left unspecified. Generally they seem to include moral and intellectual effects such as making students better people and clearer thinkers, and social or cultural effects such as producing a sense of common experience and thought.

Here let us simply observe that literature's moral purpose is either a justification for teaching it or a reason to attack it. Literature's contribution to moral development could be viewed simplistically as didactic and prescriptive—it *gives* students their moral sense. If we take that position, then it is imperative that we choose only the *right* literature, the works that will mold our students properly, yielding only moral and upstanding citizens. Such a stance assumes that students *can* be so molded, and leads, of course, to unending debate about the stamp with which we hope to imprint our students—will it be yours or will it be mine? Or, frightening thought, will it be that of someone from out of town?

On the other hand, granting students more individual freedom and responsibility, we may instead see literature as *suggesting* moral visions for them to consider and to either accept or reject. Seen this way, literature is an invitation to observe and reflect, to consider how different writers from different places, times, cultures, religions, and individual circumstances, have viewed the world; and to assume the responsibility ourselves of shaping our values and beliefs.

Even among those who favor the teaching of literature, the didactic view has been inadequate. It assumes that the text will work upon the student rather than the other way around. Thus it emphasizes *extracting* from the work rather than *transacting* with it. It asks students to remember the text so that they may be guided by it, and it strives for the right interpretation. *Aesop's Fables* are the perfect texts for such an approach; they tell a story and provide the moral, the lesson to be carried home from school so that when the student's mother asks what she learned that day she can report succinctly "Slow and steady wins the race," or "A bird in the hand is worth two in the bush," or whatever it was that today's fable taught. Such a curriculum would focus on the works themselves rather than on how the individual reader might interact with them because it assumes that the student, the reader, is simply the receptacle into which the text pours its wisdom. Designers of such a curriculum would try to identify those books that would best shape the students, best mold them in the desired image, best represent the heritage they share, and best represent the history from which they have come. Applebee warns, however, that

> Any definition of a literary heritage in terms of specific books or authors distorts the cultural significance of a literary tradition by failing to recognize that what the Great Books offer is a continuing dialogue on the moral and philosophical questions central to the culture itself.[15]

To think of the literature curriculum simply as a list of titles is to miss the central issue. The heritage is not the bibliography itself, but the rich history of evolving perceptions and ideas that the literary works contain. Ronald LaConte, describing how he was misled by his efforts to teach the literary heritage, says:

> The problem, of course, is that I was viewing the literary heritage as a body of *works*, classic pieces of literature to be studied and mastered. It's a view that continues to be very popular. One of the glaring ironies of most courses in the humanities is that they have so little to do with humans. They tend to be concerned with the form, style, historical sequence, and even a bit with the content of the *works*, but seldom do students experience a genuine feeling of identification, of sharing with other humans a "shock of recognition."[16]

A literature course conceived as a repository of the great works is likely to be more like a walk through a graveyard, admiring the tombstones in hushed reverence, than an encounter with the minds of great writers and thinkers. This is not to suggest that the great works do not belong in the curriculum, but simply that they should not be approached with awe and handled with kid gloves. Unless the students see them as exchanges with another mind about significant issues, the great works will be little more than great burdens.

LaConte offered another criticism of the typical literary heritage course: its "narrow ethnic focus."[17] He noted that the literature program closely examines the British heritage but seldom gives much attention to the other cultures that have influenced American life. In recent years many programs have partially corrected that problem by offering courses in world literature and by better representing the literature of minority groups. More teachers are coming out of programs that do acquaint them with the broader range of contemporary literature from various ethnic or cultural groups. And almost all modern literature textbook series make an effort to fairly represent the diversity of the society, though they are faced with the complex problem of selection and the simple problem of weight. The publishers may find new stories and poems to better represent Hispanic, Asian, Native American, and all the other groups that compose twenty-first century American society, but sooner or later "The Rime of the Ancient Mariner" or some other treasured piece is going to have to go or the books will be crippling for the poor students to lug around. Despite the progress that has been made, few curricula are committed to covering the range and variety of thought and perception throughout the world. Our concept of heritage still tends to be strongly nationalistic.

Competence

The Mandel collection in which LaConte's essay appears proposed two other models for the English curriculum. Each deserves some attention. The competence model, immensely popular with those educators committed to segmenting, measuring, and record-keeping, proposes that we think of the subject as a set of behaviors engaged in by students, and thus subdivide the discipline into its smallest discrete units. Advocates of this model argue that specifying the behaviors to be produced gives teaching precision. It enables teachers to plan thoroughly, with a clear sense of purpose and direction, and easily judge the effectiveness of their instruction. It also, unfortunately, inclines them to see English as a collection of separate skills and activities, without regard for the broader though less specific goals of literature teaching. This conception of the curriculum is, of course, perfectly suited to the heavy emphasis on testing and measuring that is currently strangling literature instruction—and probably every other academic discipline as well—throughout the country.

It is unlikely that the significant goals for the literature program can be expressed in lists of behavioral objectives, as the profession once tried to do, or in lists of "academic knowledge and skills," as some systems are trying to do today, because it is unlikely that the effects of reading can be measured in the behavior of students. Literature acts on the mind and the emotions, but how its effects may show themselves is uncertain. Whether they will be seen at all by outside observers is questionable; that they can be produced on demand in the classroom, by each of thirty or forty students, seems unlikely.

Some behaviors, of course, can be elicited in this way. We can insist that students learn to spell William's last name "Shakespeare" (or "Shakespere" or "Shakspeare" or however we may prefer), and if we are sufficiently resolute, we can force most students to show that they have learned it. We could even browbeat them into learning to spell the names of Macbeth, Banquo, MacDuff, and a few other characters so that we can then produce a test that will give us the opportunity to measure their knowledge generating high scores and low, averages, medians, standard deviations, and all sorts of other statistical marvels. We could even manage to do this with more sophisticated literary issues than spelling. But can we get them to demonstrate that reading *Macbeth* has helped to shape their understanding of power or temptation or ambition or that *Romeo and Juliet* has helped them better understand the complex relationships between parents and children? Some will reflect on those issues and speak and write about them willingly. Others, equally affected by the reading, may be unable or unwilling to demonstrate, on demand, that it has done so. Others may find that their reading exerts its influence on them later, perhaps many years later. And, most important of all, this particular work may not be appropriate for this particular student at the moment we offer it to him. We have all had the experience of reading a *great* book or a *great* poem and finding ourselves untouched. Of the poems my favorite poets have written, those poets I return to regularly, many leave me cold, uninterested, unmoved. To ask me to demonstrate deep reflection or to engage in serious analysis of those texts would be like asking me to demonstrate how I would savor a meal consisting of dishes I didn't like so that you could measure my ability to appreciate the culinary arts. To limit our teaching to those behaviors we can observe and measure is to disregard most of the substance of literature. Moffett warns:

> In insisting that desirable behaviors be *observable,* the behavioral approach rules out a great deal of learning—too much to merely mention in a cautionary note prefacing the goals. Consider, for example, what may be happening in a more taciturn member of a discussion group. The effects of certain reading, acting, and writing on a student's social, emotional, and cognitive growth tend of course to be long-range and inextricable. Although it helps to acknowledge that many of these effects will occur years later and often out of school, in practice these effects will either not be observed by evaluators or be falsely attributed to more recent school treatment—or, most likely, be ignored because they cannot be causally traced.[18]

Curricula planned with this model in mind tend to contain long lists of skills and activities. A great many systems have a list of what they may call the "Essential Knowledge and Skills" or the "Academic Knowledge and Skills" for each of the disciplines, including English. Such lists may be helpful in reminding us of all that we need to teach, but in many cases the philosophy that guides them seems deficient. It seldom addresses the major issue: Why does the student study literature? What can it do for her? What contribution does it make to her life? Competence curricula are often very explicit about what is to be learned and how it should be evaluated, but they fail to examine the broader goals of the literature program. Reducing the literature program to a list of activities and objectives, practical as that may seem, obscures and interferes with the more important purposes for teaching literature.

If, as we have argued, reading helps the student create his world—that part of it, at least, that is symbolic, emotional, aesthetic, and intellectual—then literature is too vast and imprecise a study to submit to the shackles of a competence-based program. Analysis of the various skills and behaviors involved in studying literature may contribute valuable information about the activities possible in the classroom, but unless the fundamental purpose of teaching is kept clearly in mind and allowed to govern the teaching, the value of literature will be as well concealed behind the lists of competences as it has been in the past behind lists of information.

Process

Barrett J. Mandel, in his introduction, speaks of the process model as the "inside out" of the competence model:

> Whereas the competencies approach advocates the introduction of concepts and skills at the appropriate time so that students can master them, the process approach advocates the creation of an environment in which students can "discover" what has heretofore been unknown to them.
>
> For the teacher of process education, the paradigm means the natural, inevitable flowering of an individual's skills and concepts under the guidance of teachers who pose questions that are open-ended and provocative. Needless to say, the "non-teaching" done by process teachers requires great sensitivity, knowledge of cognitive levels, and patience.[19]

As we might gather from Mandel's description, the process model offers limited guidance for curriculum design. In advocating the "natural flowering" of the student's abilities and suggesting open-ended investigation, this model declines to specify exactly what is to be learned and when. Instead, the teacher must become aware of the possibilities and then capitalize on the opportunities that arise.

Such a model relies heavily on the skill of the teacher. If she is good, with thorough knowledge of her subject and insight into the students, then the process model allows her the freedom to respond to the moment, to explore possibilities as they arise in class. It also *demands* that she do so, because it does not give her a reassuring list of objectives or activities to follow. It is based on the belief that the natural processes of learning and growing will provide better guidance, if the teacher trains herself to watch them. As Barbara and Gene Stanford remark, ". . . the process curriculum tends to value the internal judgments about growth made by the individual learner more than external standards established by society."[20] It is a model that has been explored and enriched by the work of such people as Nanci Atwell, with her emphasis on the classroom as a workshop; Steve Zemelman and Harvey Daniels, with their emphasis upon on the communal nature of writing; and, of course, Louise Rosenblatt, with her emphasis upon the transaction between the reader and the text.

The pre-eminent concern of those teaching in this model is the natural growth of the child. Rather than seek the structures of curriculum in the discipline itself, teachers drawn to the process model seek them in the psychology of the child, in the interests, problems, and behavior patterns that emerge. The Stanfords note of the typical process curriculum that it is often organized into integrated units relating to the developmental tasks of adolescence. Thematic units derived from the tasks seem to be more helpful to students than units focusing on isolated skills drawn from the domains of composition, vocabulary development, or public speaking.[21]

The Stanfords suggest units on such topics as "identity, woman and man, dealing with conflicts, death, communication, generations, values, loneliness, love, and planning for the future."[22] Their suggestions are reminiscent of what we saw in *An Experience Curriculum in English:* units designed with more attention to the students than to the discipline of English. Such units could have great merit, but they might easily become indulgent, relying too heavily on students' ability to decide what they need. As the Stanfords themselves caution, total student freedom is not the ideal; planning that draws on the best that both students and teacher can offer will be more productive. Clearly students have a great deal to offer, and unless they are somehow involved in planning their work, many opportunities will be lost. But they cannot precisely foresee their adult needs, and although the teacher's guesses about the future may also be far off, his advantage in age, experience, and training should not be overlooked.

One curious thing about the essays in Mandel's collection is that, regardless of which model is being promoted, the writer takes steps to qualify it. Those writing about the competence model warn that curricula can become trivial unless planners carefully attend to some of the larger, unmeasurable goals of teaching. Those writing about the process model want to remind the reader not to neglect the demands of the discipline—students do, after all, have to learn to do more than attend to their own emotions. Those writing about the literary heritage do not want classwork to become so academic that it is removed from the issues that preoccupy adolescents. It is as though all are seeking some sort of middle ground that will accommodate the focus of each model. Obviously, students do need to develop the skills that the competence model might teach them; obviously, they should come to understand the cultural tradition that permeates and shapes their lives; obviously, the uniqueness of each student should be taken into account, as the process model suggests. Each pattern offers something valuable. We should not be required to choose between them, perhaps, but rather should be allowed to benefit from what each has to offer.

Recent Confusions

Since early in the 1990s, roughly, the conversation about curriculum (though the word seems to be less often used) has focused most intently on the early grades, has become more strident, and has taken the form of a pitched battle between those who hold out for "direct instruction" and those who lean toward "whole language." Direct-instruction advocates typically argue for rigidly structured teaching focused on sound-letter correspondence, phonics, word recognition, decoding, and the like. They hope to teach kids to read by drilling them systematically and intensively on skills. Whole language proponents, on the other hand, prefer a view of reading as meaning-making and thus ask students to use language for authentic and valued purposes, much as adults do, acknowledging the students' differing interests and abilities, encouraging them to identify and pursue reading that matters to them, giving them choices about books and writing tasks, and in general attempting to create authentic experiences in which the child's linguistic abilities might naturally develop.

Although this battle is being waged mostly around reading instruction in the elementary schools, it merits some attention in a discussion of middle and secondary education because it will shape our conversation at these upper grades, too, first of all because it will establish a pattern for thinking about instruction, encouraging us to think in terms of discrete skills or behaviors and distracting us from theory, research, and philosophy to issues of politics, religion, and money.

The curricular conversation turned nasty when the federal government, instead of letting educators continue their work of sorting out strategies and approaches, decided to join in the debate, taking the side of the direct-instruction advocates and throwing its influence and its money toward them. Politicians saw the opportunity to win favor with some constituencies by coming down on the side of God, morality, phonics, discipline, and good grammar; religious fundamentalists saw the opportunity to seize a bit more control of a few more minds by mandating texts and ways of dealing with them; and corporations saw the veins of gold in the scripted programs they could create and the tests they could sell to evaluate the poor students who would have to suffer through them. Several reports[23] precipitated a running controversy between proponents of decoding, phonics-based and word-recognition reading instruction, represented by Marilyn Adams[23a] and Reid Lyon, for example, and those who defend the more integrated, natural approach, represented by Ken and Yetta Goodman, Richard Allington, and many others.

Ken Goodman, in one of the most compact discussions of this complex matter, reviews some of the research documenting the power of whole language approaches and sketches the loose alliance among the political far right, religious fundamentalists, and some of the corporations involved in testing and publishing. He points out that "the NAEP evidence provides robust support for the effectiveness of whole language. It's clear from the data that the attacks on whole language are not based on any demonstrable failure."[24] On the contrary, twenty years of research and teacher experience have documented the power of such approaches, and he asks the logical question, "So what *is* motivating the attacks?" He then proceeds to argue convincingly that the attacks are driven by the political, economic, and religious agenda of various groups rather than by educational philosophy or principle.

Most telling, perhaps, are the economic issues. Goodman points out, for instance, that "Several people who are authors of Distar and Open Court (both published by SRA/McGraw Hill) have played key advisory roles or have actually been on the payroll of states whose legislation and/or regulations they have advised or controlled."[25] In a similar essay, Richard Arlington points out that many publishers made money "by ignoring scientific evidence at the behest of ideological policy mandates."[26] In the current debate in literacy circles about curricular matters, some concerned parties seem driven by matters other than educational philosophy or research. So appalled is Goodman by what he has observed that he concludes, "The underlying objective of those who attack whole language is to bring down public education itself."[27]

The point here is not to enter the heated debates over primary and elementary instruction—they are much too complicated to address adequately in a few paragraphs—but rather to indicate that, as Francis R. A. Peterson says, "the 'reading wars' have moved into the political arena. In some sense, disagreements about the nature of reading instruction have become yet another front in America's culture wars."[28] Clearly the war has to be fought or education will slip into the hands of the far-right, the fundamentalists, and those who can profit by manipulating public policy to their own ends, but we won't fight it here. While the battle is raging we need to continue searching for a vision of literature instruction that might enable us to organize our work, plan our units and our lessons, and perhaps suggest paths out of the controversy.

The reconciliation of the three conceptions of curriculum Mandel identified—and perhaps of the two camps at war today—might be found in Rosenblatt's ideas and the patterns of instruction discussed earlier. Her theory respects and addresses the text, the reader, and the act of reading. Her conception of the poem as a transaction between the reader and the text justifies equal attention to the student and the discipline and the meeting of the two. Student-centered curricula tend to focus too intently on the students, whereas discipline-centered curricula overemphasize the subject matter. By promoting one element above the other, both fail to hit the mark. But if we look instead at the *transaction* between reader and text, between individual and culture, we might achieve a literature program combining the best elements of the various approaches to curriculum design.

Transactional Model

What such a curriculum might look like is difficult to predict. In order to be responsive to the changing student body, it would have to remain flexible. It would have to develop over time and be contributed to by a large group of students, teachers, and scholars. It could never be as tidy and complete as some of the curricula planned in other models—too much of what it holds important is unpredictable, perhaps even inarticulable. Though textbooks may be designed to support it, they can never contain it or prescribe it. Still, some of its important features may be foreseen.

It would, following Applebee's suggestion, conceive of the literary heritage as more than a list of great books. It would try to focus on the great issues that inspired the great books, and it would attempt to raise those issues at times in the student's development when she is likely to be interested in them, insofar as something as idiosyncratic as that can be predicted.

The "great issues" approach itself is not a new one. The Carnegie-Mellon project English program, for instance, was predicated on the belief that "literature is mankind's record, expressed in verbal art forms, of what it is like to be alive. . . . The writer of literature deals with universal concerns of every age and every culture. . . ."[29] In fact, most of the Project English Centers tried to develop curriculum along thematic lines, and the themes often seem to represent the great cultural issues. The University of Nebraska Center organized its literature program around such themes as "The Hero" for the eighth grade and "Man and Nature, Society, and Moral Law" for the tenth. The eleventh grade addressed three themes in American literature: individualism and nature, sin and loneliness, and American materialism.

But as G. Robert Carlsen and James Crow point out in their assessment of the Centers as a whole:

> for the most part the Centers have been concerned almost exclusively with the content of English and only incidentally with methodology. Perhaps the strangest omission of all is the lack of concern for the learner and how he learns. . . . Many of the Centers make highly questionable assumptions about children and the learning process. . . . The programs are distinguished by their serious and humorless intensity.[30]

They suffered, in other words, from too much attention to the demands of the discipline and too little attention to the needs of the students. They may have conceived of the literature in terms of the great cultural questions, but they failed to bring it to bear on the students' lives. There are ways to correlate those broad cultural concerns with the students' development, so that each can be addressed when students are most likely to be receptive and in a manner that is likely to interest them. We do know something about how children mature, and it is possible that that information could be brought to bear on the curriculum.

We know, for instance, a fair amount about patterns of reading interest. G. Robert Carlsen's studies have contributed much to our knowledge of the developmental patterns in adolescent reading, but, although his perceptions have been confirmed and only slightly modified by subsequent studies, that knowledge has not been employed effectively in curriculum development. Carlsen concluded that the reading interests of adolescents fall into three stages. The first, which he labels "Early Adolescence," about age eleven to fourteen, is characterized by an interest in animal stories, adventures, mysteries, the supernatural, sports, coming of age in different cultures, stories about the home and family life, slapstick, stories set in the past, and fantasy. "Middle Adolescence," roughly age fifteen to sixteen, typically selects nonfiction adventure, longer historical novels, mystical romances, and stories of adolescent life. "Late Adolescence," about age seventeen to eighteen, is the period of transition to adult reading. The issues for this age group are the search for personal values, social questions, strange experiences and unusual circumstances, and the transition to adult roles.[31]

Carlsen also identifies some issues students are typically not interested in reading about:

> Generally, the concerns of the great middle-aged section of the population have little appeal. Teens rarely care to read about characters who are middle-aged unless, as in spy stories, the individuals are highly romanticized and lead lives of incredible adventure. They are not interested in the character who has had to compromise with life or who is bowed down by the humdrum. Clyde Griffith in *An American Tragedy,* though young, is branded despicable by the young reader and not worth reading about. . . . Books about the wealthy usually have little attraction for the young. Wealth is tolerated only in a historical romance or story of intrigue.

Nor do teenage readers care for stories of the industrial or political world or the trials and tribulations of marriages.[32]

Carlsen's analysis of the stages of reading interest isn't sufficient foundation for an entire literature curriculum, but it might well serve as a starting point. Teachers might begin, for instance, by trying to correlate these stages of development with some of the great cultural issues. There is little agreement, of course, on what those issues are, but any formulation acceptable to the planners will do—it can always be modified in the light of further research or reflection. The Stanfords' set of themes might be a suitable place to begin.

LaConte suggests that the themes identified be stated as polarities—opposites that represent a range of human experience. The example he develops in his essay has clear potential for correlation with the stages of reading interest Carlsen identifies:

> By carefully framing polarities and thematic questions to take into account the maturity and interest of the students, we could fashion a program of "developmental exploration" in which students confront more sophisticated and intellectually challenging questions at each grade level. For example, within our loyalty-treachery polarity, the student might start in the seventh grade by exploring the question "How are animals loyal to humans?" and end in the twelfth grade by exploring the question "How can the state betray the individual?"[33]

The question he suggests for the seventh grade fits neatly into Carlsen's pattern—it would allow the students to read animal stories, which Carlsen tells us they are likely to enjoy—and yet the unit would be chosen for its theme, not simply to cater to the students' interests. Similarly, the question suggested for the twelfth grade, involving the relationship between an individual and the state, fits in with the transition to adult roles. Significant literary works could be chosen for each topic. Instruction could be designed to encourage and enrich the transactions the students could have with the texts. In such a curriculum the students would be discussing issues, not simply isolated works.

Such a curriculum plan would be imprecise, of course; it would have to remain responsive to the unique interests, needs, and abilities of the students who show up for class, and thus there would have to be plenty of opportunities for teachers to modify what they do, select other works than those suggested by the master plan, and take more time or less with activities. Still, the example from LaConte's proposal illustrates the possibility of developing curricula that are both academically sound—that is, concerned with significant ideas and literary works—and psychologically sound—that is, based on the maturity and interests of the child.

LaConte goes on to discuss some of the issues curriculum planners must consider. One is the question of selection: How should works be chosen for each of the central themes? LaConte suggests that the works chosen should represent different answers given to the question during different historical periods. He recommends a "three-tiered structure of past, present, and future,"[34] rather than the traditional chronological organization of the literature course. Students can learn to see attitudes and ideas as socially created, evolving constructs by observing their evolution through the past and speculating about their evolution in the future.

He also offers some advice about course organization, suggesting a balance between control and freedom. He identifies two basic approaches to planning a thematic curriculum—demonstrative and exploratory—and cautions against relying too heavily on either:

> While demonstrative organization lends itself to a tighter structure and control, exploratory organization affords far richer teaching opportunities. The demonstrative approach can too easily become moral indoctrination, using both literature and theme as object lessons in a particular point of view. The exploratory approach, on the other hand, can degenerate into totally uncontrolled bull sessions with both literature and theme being lost in verbal meandering.[35]

The balance he recommends between the two accommodates both discipline and student. It allows the teacher to decide on some of the issues to be addressed and some of the works to be considered, drawing on her knowledge of the literature, but it also asks her to observe the students and respond to their interests and the relevant digressions they may introduce. That balance would respect Rosenblatt's transactional theory, keeping its focus on the transaction, the meeting of reader and text.

Young Adult Literature in the Curriculum

The thematic structure would also provide a basis for including young adult literature in the curriculum. If our purpose is to structure a dialog about important ideas rather than to teach a prescribed reading list, the bibliography for a course need not be limited to works that have achieved high stature in the eyes of the academic community. Two criteria apply in this curriculum. One, of course, is literary merit and significance; the other is suitability for the group of students being taught. Until recently, most literature curricula and secondary school literature textbooks, especially in the upper grades, have considered the first of those criteria but neglected the second. And, of course, constrained as they inevitably were by their very format—weighty, hard-bound anthologies of short texts surrounded by recommendations for teaching—the textbook series could do little more than suggest works of young adult literature to supplement their instruction and perhaps provide a few sets of selected texts. Publishers of textbook series couldn't build their programs around young adult novels. Nonetheless, as we explored in some detail in Chapter 6, those works are very suitable for the students we face. An energetic and hardworking teacher might be able to craft his instruction around a core group of novels, some adolescent and some adult, probably canonical; a teacher less imaginative or more tightly constrained by a prescribed curriculum or textbook might be able to enrich the instruction with well-chosen young adult novels; and a teacher less confident in her ability to identify worthy goals, choose appropriate materials, and design effective strategies might prefer to rely on the plan laid out for her in a series, only occasionally venturing out to try her hand with a book of her own choosing. However it happens, young adult literature should find a place in the English program.

Young adult literature clearly appeals to secondary school students, but some of its critics consider it a sad compromise with immature taste and cheap popular culture. Much young adult literature, to the contrary, is exceptionally good. Regardless of whether we agree with that judgment, however, in a curriculum based on the transaction between the reader and the work, the immaturity of students' taste and the deficiencies of popular culture are easy to accept: the first because it is natural—the students are adolescents and thus may be expected to have adolescent tastes—and the second because even shallowness (and, as we've argued before, much of adolescent literature is *not* shallow) may serve a purpose in the classroom, if only to offer simpler and clearer examples of literary strategies, successes, and failures. If we want young students to deal with the theme of survival, they'll grasp it more clearly in Scott O'Grady's *Basher Five-Two* (1998, Yearling), with Captain O'Grady struggling to stay alive after crashing behind enemy lines, than they will in Theodore Dreiser's *Sister Carrie* (1900, Doubleday) a much more complex tale of the struggle to survive in American society. If we want them to be alert to strategies of storytelling and plot development, they'll be better able to analyze those features in T. A. Barron's *The Fires of Merlin* (1998, Philomel Books) than in Lord Alfred Tennyson's *Idylls of the King* (1859). Just as a beginning guitarist will have a more musical experience with a simple folk song than with Bach's "Jesu, Joy of Man's Desiring," so will a young reader have a more satisfactory literary experience with an accessible text than with one whose complexity and sophistication overwhelm him. Students will come to perceive, through both natural maturation and experience in the classroom, what literature is more likely to reward their efforts.

That isn't to suggest that curriculum should rely solely on the students' natural development. If we could do that, schools would be unnecessary. But ignoring the natural patterns of development is equally foolish. If a young girl prefers Janet Dailey to Emily Brontë, to insist that she change her mind is probably a waste of effort. Better to examine the works students are willing to read, questioning and responding to them, and let their virtues and defects emerge in the process. This is the proper attitude for an intellectual dialog, in any case—one of questioning and openness to experience, rather than reliance on accepted authorities. If students learn to explore texts and readings while dealing with books of lesser merit, they *are,* nonetheless, learning the process. They will be able to apply it later to books of greater sophistication and maturity.

Besides, arguing about the greatness or lack thereof in a particular work may be entertaining, but it's probably little more than that. To argue for the greatness of a particular work is to argue for a personal perception. We may address the text and pretend that we are talking only about observable features of the work, but we are also, almost inevitably, talking about *our* reactions to those features, about the impression they have made upon us, about how we have read, responded, and interpreted, about how we have valued or rejected aspects of the writer's vision. The value of a work for any one reader depends on the quality of his own transaction with the text. We can claim that some texts are more likely, because of certain demonstrable features, to sustain a rewarding transaction. Too often, however, teachers assume that their experience, training, and age give them the authority to judge a reader's transactions with a text, and they use their own readings as the benchmark. A young reader is unlikely to read a text in the same way as the older, more experienced reader. Too seldom do we take into account the vast difference between our own situations and abilities and those of the students. Texts that are powerful for an adult may not have the same effect on adolescent readers. There are very few twelfth-graders who, on the basis of their own experience with the work, will assert that *The Faerie Queen* is a great piece of literature.

The suggestion that adolescent literature be granted a place in the literature curriculum is not a compromise. It doesn't weaken the curriculum by displacing the great works. Rather, it strengthens it by offering students the emotional and intellectual experiences of significant reading—the same sorts of experiences that skilled adults may have with the established great books of the culture. It invites them to participate at their own level in the ongoing dialog about the major issues of human life.

Other Considerations

In addition to the matters discussed above, planners of literature curricula might keep several other points in mind. We've suggested that they watch their natural tendency to think of curriculum in terms of lists of works and think instead of the issues— the emotion and thought—that inspire the works, so that they might involve students in the cultural dialog. Essentially, we've suggested that planners consider both the student and the work, focusing on the transaction between the two. Even when the transaction between reader and text is foremost in the teacher's mind, however, there may be dogmatic insistence on one mode of thought, usually interpretation.

The transaction between work and reader, however, may take various shapes. It may, of course, be an act of interpretation and inference. The reader may grow curious about the intentions of the author and want to speculate about her intent and assumptions. Or the reader may even become intrigued by the technical workings of a piece and want to discuss how the author achieved his effects. Such a reading may seem highly intellectual, with little of the personal response that we argued for earlier in the book. There is no reason, however, to deny the legitimacy of a response simply because it is analytical and rational.

On the other extreme, the student's response may wander far away from, or even resist any connection with, the work read. The student's train of thought may stray so far from the work that it seems totally irrelevant. Although that sort of response is clearly not a close reading of the text, it, too, is legitimate. It is one of the possible satisfactions to be derived from reading. What, after all, are we likely to do with a reading of Robert Frost's "The Secret Sits"?

> We dance round in a ring and suppose,
> While the Secret sits in the middle and knows.[35]

This seems to be a poem that invites us to wander and roam, perhaps far from the text, far from Frost's reflections. What is the Secret? How can we know? What did Frost have in mind when he wrote the poem? Interesting questions, perhaps, and there may be ways to address them, but the answers surely don't lie within the text itself. Frost doesn't give us many clues. He's vague from the first word, "We." Who is he referring to? Americans, since he was one? New Englanders?—he was one of those, too. All of his readers? Perhaps just poets? Maybe just male poets? In a student's paper you'd circle that "We" and write a caustic remark about pronoun reference, but we—that is to say "we teachers," to make the reference less ambiguous here—allow Frost liberties we don't grant our students. And then we come to the "Secret." Capitalized, but why? What, or who, is the Secret? Frost doesn't say.

So if this poem works for its reader, it probably does so *because* the reader strays and wanders. We all have questions we wonder about without ever coming to a satisfactory conclusion. They may be vast and cosmic—Is there a god?—or they may be more mundane—How do I get my students to do their homework? But whatever they are, they intrigue or plague us and we dance round them in the late hours of the night, feeling all the while that there must be some answer, that someone must know, that we are close—but not quite there—to an answer. This poem probably works for a reader—if it does work—because it allows her to reflect and wonder and speculate about her own doubts and confusions. If she doggedly sets out to pry loose from these two lines clear and certain knowledge of Frost's secret, she's likely to find herself faced either with frustration on the one hand, or a difficult dissertation topic on the other.

Both ends of the spectrum should be respected in the classroom—the interpretive and the expressive. One we may perhaps call *self-bound*, the other *text-bound*. The one is introspective and self-satisfying, the other may ignore the self for the pleasures of investigating something in the text. Students should broaden their repertoire, learning to experience the literature in various ways. If they remain totally self-bound, they are trapped within their own minds, unable to compare their perceptions with others. If they are entirely text-bound, they may not have the satisfaction of finding personal connections with the works they read. Either extreme is a handicap. A good literature curriculum would ask its teachers to remain alert to this issue, perhaps by keeping some record of the range of students' responses and working to help them expand it.

Furthermore, students should learn that the different approaches to the text call for different sorts of elaboration and development. The self-expressive, in which the student speaks of his feelings or of his own thoughts, or perhaps tells something of his own story, is likely to lead him into narrative or poetry. He is not, in this case, building an argument so much as he is reporting something about himself, his own attitudes and values, perhaps his own uncertainties and confusions. When making assertions about himself, the student is the supreme authority (which doesn't necessarily mean that he is truthful in his assertions or that he is perceptive). On the other hand, if he wishes to speak about the text, attributing to it certain characteristics and discussing its merits, or about the writer, evaluating his vision, logic, or truthfulness, then he is committed to making an argument, to compiling evidence and drawing from it reasonable conclusions. When he chooses an efferent stance, he obligates himself to a different form of discourse.

Just as the curriculum should discuss the relationship between students and the literary work, it should also draw attention to the relationships among the people involved. We have described the appropriate relationship between the teacher and the class. It is not that of the captain to his troops or the informed to the ignorant; it is rather that of the more experienced and wise to the somewhat less experienced and less wise. The teacher can offer the benefits of broader reading, but she cannot give students *the* reading, the final, authoritative, correct reading. That can be achieved, if at all, only by the individual for the individual.

Both teacher and students must provide information in the classroom. The teacher, of course, gives information about books, about techniques, and about her own reading. But the students, too, have very important information to offer, without which the literature course cannot succeed. This includes information about their interests, their reactions to the works read, and their opinions of the responses and interpretations of others. The curriculum must specify an exchange of information in the classroom. Without it, the teacher will know very little about the students' transaction with the text, and thus about the literature they create in the act of reading.

The curriculum should also address the relationship among the students, for their exchanges can contribute a great deal to the development of literary insight. They can offer much that the teacher might not, since they are closer in age and experience. Their common ground may allow them to help each other understand the literature and themselves. Students are a resource too seldom used in the schools.

Planning the Literature Curriculum

Implicit in much of this chapter is the idea that a variety of people need to be involved in the complex and time-consuming work of planning a literature curriculum. Obviously the teachers need to be involved, though in many school systems they are not. They know the students and thus have essential information to offer. They also know the constraints under which they work, constraints that are often hard to imagine. They will know, for instance, what it is like to try to teach 150 or even 200 students a day. To expect a teacher to give effective instruction in composition and literature to more than twenty or twenty-five students a day is absurd; to give him 100 students a day should be considered criminal. The literature teacher is charged with helping students formulate their ideas of the world, of their own potential, and of the relationships among people, and yet he is asked to work with huge groups of students. Teachers will know what limitations these impossible class loads and other circumstances in their own classrooms impose on them and will be able to anticipate the problems and suggest the necessary compromises for the curriculum.

Clearly, also, for the reasons discussed earlier, students need to be included. They, too, have valuable information to offer. How they can be involved is, of course, a matter for each school or system to decide. In some small schools, they might actually be able to participate as members of planning committees, discussing the purposes of the literature program, the criteria for selecting books, and all the other issues. If that is too formal or elaborate, they might occasionally be asked to comment on texts and activities. If that is too time-consuming, they should at least be observed. Much can be learned by watching as they engage in small-group discussions. Do they seem interested in the text? Do they raise good questions? What do they catch and what do they miss as they talk? Much can be learned from fairly simple anecdotal notes taken during an activity in which the teacher is a bystander or taken soon after a lesson in which the teacher is actively participating.

Parents also need to be involved, or at least informed. They often labor under misconceptions about the curriculum, especially about the English program. They are even less well-informed than most school administrators about the appropriate purposes of teaching literature and composition and may believe that literature should be used to implant values rather than to investigate them, that teaching grammar will improve students' writing, that books containing profanity or dealing with sex will poison their children's minds, or other such nonsense. Asking for parents to participate in curricular decisions can be dangerous because it may be an opening wedge for those who want to impose their misunderstandings about language learning on teachers or who want to control curriculum for their own purposes. Still, they do have a stake in the school and thus need to have a voice. Allowing it to be heard may enable us to educate parents about education and help them change their expectations of schools and teachers.

School administrators should also be involved, though in a subordinate role. The administrators responsible for handling money will need to be kept informed of plans made for the curriculum so that, in their enthusiasm, planners don't spend more than the system has. Those charged with scheduling and related duties will also need to know what the English curriculum becomes so that they can offer the necessary support.

Finally, someone should serve as supervisor of English to coordinate the task of curriculum planning. The knowledge of teachers, students, and scholars has to be synthesized. The various people who have insights to offer the schools too often remain isolated and ignorant of each other's work. Teachers are uninformed about educational research or literary theory, critics fail to understand the minds and emotions of young children, and students too seldom know the goals of the teachers or grasp the significance of their own labors. The task of coordinating a curriculum development project is formidable.

A Final Word on the Shape of the Curriculum

The curriculum should be an evolving, changing document, rather than something rigid and unbending. Guides written over a three-year period, printed, bound, distributed, and then untouched for the next ten years are of dubious value. Too few people participate in their conception and birth, and over too short a time. It would be much more helpful to conceive of the curriculum guide as a file drawer with a philosophy, a file drawer filled with units of instruction, bibliographies, and articles, supported by a bookshelf containing significant texts and journals. During each year, in an ideal world, a committee with rotating membership could assess the value of the materials, the effectiveness of the teaching, and the ideas emerging in the journals, and then work during the summer to reformulate aspects of the literature program.

In a school operating this way, the curriculum would be alive, changing and growing as the students and teachers change, responding to developments in literary theory and educational research. The staff would continually redesign and evaluate the curriculum, and would thus feel a sense of ownership and responsibility for it. Because of that responsibility, they would be motivated to continue reading and learning, and thus might continue to find the satisfactions for which they entered the profession.

Endnotes

1. Albert R. Kitzhaber, "Project English and Curriculum Reform," in *Iowa English Yearbook*, Number 9 (Fall 1964), p. 4.

2. Arthur N. Applebee, *Tradition and Reform in the Teaching of English: A History* (Urbana, IL: National Council of Teachers of English, 1974), pp. 13–14.

3. Ibid., p. 11.

4. James F. Hosic, Ed., "Reorganization of English in Secondary Schools," in *United States Bureau of Education Bulletin Number 2* (U.S. Government Printing Office, 1917,) p. 14.

5. Ibid., pp. 129–130.

6. *An Experience Curriculum in English*, National Council of Teachers of English Curriculum Commission (New York: Appleton-Century, 1935), pp. 10–11.

7. George Winchester Stone, Jr., Ed., *Issues, Problems, and Approaches in the Teaching of English* (New York: Holt, Rinehart and Winston, 1964), p. 7.

8. Kitzhaber, p. 6.

9. John Dixon, *Growth Through English* (London: Oxford University Press, 1967), p. 60.

10. James Britton, "Response to Literature," in *Response to Literature*, James R. Squire, Ed. (Champaign, IL: National Council of Teachers of English, 1968) p. 6.

11. James E. Miller, Jr., "Literature in the Revitalized Curriculum," *NASSP Bulletin*, No. 38 (April 1967), pp. 25–26.

12. Applebee, p. 245.

13. Ibid., p. 246.

14. Ibid., p. 247.

15. Ibid., p. 248.

16. Ronald LaConte, "A Literary Heritage Paradigm for Secondary English," in *Three Language-Arts Curriculum Models: Pre-Kindergarten Through College,* Barrett J. Mandel, Ed. (Urbana, IL: National Council of Teachers of English, 1980), p. 126.

17. Ibid.

18. James Moffett, *Coming on Center: English Education in Evolution* (Montclair, NJ: Boynton/Cook, 1981), p. 13.

19. Barrett J. Mandel, *Three Language-Arts Curriculum Models: Pre-Kindergarten Through College* (Urbana, IL: National Council of Teachers of English, 1980), p. 7.

20. Barbara Stanford and Gene Stanford, "Process Curriculum for High School Students," in *Three Language-Arts Curriculum Models: Pre-Kindergarten Through College,* Barrett J. Mandel, Ed. (Urbana, IL: National Council of Teachers of English, 1980), pp. 139–140.

21. Ibid. p. 152.

22. Ibid., p. 153.

23. National Academy of Education, Commission on Reading, Richard C. Anderson, and National Institute of Education (U.S.). 1985. *Becoming a Nation of Readers: The Report of the Commission on Reading.* (Washington, DC: National Academy of Education, National Institute of Education, Center for the Study of Reading, 1985).

23a. Adams, Marilyn Jager, 1990. *Beginning to Read: Thinking and Learning About Print.* (Cambridge, MA: MIT Press, 1990).

24. Kenneth Goodman, "Who's Afraid of Whole Language: Politics, Paradigms, Pedagogy, and the Press," *In Defense of Good Teaching* (York, ME: Stenhouse Publishers), p. 3–38. Quote from p. 6.

25. Goodman, p.35

26. Richard L. Arlington, "Troubling Times: A Short Historical Perspective," in *Big Brother and the National Reading Curriculum: How Ideology Trumped Research* (Portsmouth, NH, Heinemann, 2002) p. 5.

27. Goodman, p. 35.

28. Francis R. A. Peterson, "The Politics of Phonics," in *Big Brother and the National Reading Curriculum: How Ideology Trumped Research* (Portsmouth, NH: Heinemann, 2002), pp. 157–194. Quote from p. 184.

29. Erwin R. Steinberg, Robert C. Slack, Beekman W. Cottrell, and Lois S. Josephs, "The Overall Plan of the Curriculum Study Center at Carnegie-Mellon University," in *English Education Today*, Lois S. Josephs and Erwin R. Steinberg, Eds. (New York: Noble and Noble, 1970), p. 61.

30. G. Robert Carlsen and James Crow, "Project English Curriculum Centers," *English Journal*, 56, No. 7 (October, 1967), pp. 991–992.

31. G. Robert Carlsen, "Books and the Teenage Reader: A Guide for Teachers," *Librarians, and Parents*, Revised Second Edition (New York: Harper and Row, 1980), pp. 35–42.

32. Ibid., pp. 42–43.

33. LaConte, p. 135.

34. Ibid., p. 132.

35. Ibid., p. 131.

36. Robert Frost, "The Secret Sits," in *A Witness Tree* (New York: Henry Holt, 1942).

9 *Evaluation and Testing*

On a recent visit to a high school in a large southern city, I fell into conversation with an English teacher who was lamenting the problems her school and its students were facing. "We bring in about 900 freshman," she said, "and four years later graduate about 300 seniors." The discrepancy astounded me as much as it depressed her. It seemed incomprehensible that so many students could wander off, take jobs, join the military, or find some other way of getting by, but she assured me that her numbers were more or less accurate. How, I asked, could you lose 600 students, two-thirds of your incoming class, in four years? "We test 'em right out the door," she said.

She went on to tell me that the system's high-stakes tests were terrifying many of the kids who cared about themselves and their futures, and leaving others apathetic and indifferent. Convinced that they could not succeed on the tests, many of them just gave up, shut down, hung around school for awhile until they couldn't take the boredom any longer or the school couldn't tolerate their dead weight, and then dropped out. Many, she said, left shortly before the big testing weeks, and many left immediately after them, as if to escape the pain of hearing the results. Not only did the kids face these major examinations, but they also had to deal with countless smaller ones—there were thirty or forty "test days" in her school's academic calendar, she reported. Of course, there were other factors at play, she admitted, but the tests, she was convinced, drove more students out of the schools than anything else.

If that's true, it's sadly ironic. In the interests of improving education, of making the schools accountable so that our students will emerge from them better-educated, stronger, more competent, more confident, better citizens, better able to manage and enjoy their lives and contribute to society, we've settled on a strategy that frightens and humiliates them, persuades them that they are incompetent and uneducable, distracts them from the pleasures and pains of learning to the fear and embarrassment of constant assessing, and drives them from the relative safety of the schools onto the streets or into menial jobs that their neglected education barely qualifies them to perform.

As a way of improving teaching and learning, we could hardly find a worse approach than testing in general, and high-stakes testing in particular. That's especially true with literature.

Testing and the Discipline

Literature, because it is the meeting of reader and text, is a difficult subject to test. If we could establish the one right reading of a work, as the New Critics tried to do, or if we believed that information about literature is of primary importance, as do some of those inclined toward an historical approach, or if we were satisfied with comprehension questions, as the writers of some basal readers seem to be, then assessing the learning of literature would be easy. We could ignore the aesthetic and concentrate on the efferent. Tests would be simple to design, administer, and grade, and we could all feel confident that we know how we are doing. But if reading is the idiosyncratic experience that Louise Rosenblatt and others believe it to be, matters are not quite so simple.

Testing is easiest when we have clear standards for performance and acceptable units of measurement. In the 100-yard dash, faster is better. We agree that seconds and fractions thereof are the units of measurement, we post a reliable observer at the finish line, fire off the pistol, and shortly thereafter we know who gets the A, who gets the B, and so on. There are, of course, aspects of English that can be accurately measured, too. We can agree on the spellings of words, give students a list on Monday, test them on Friday, and again we know who gets the A and who the F. We might even be able to agree on most of the principles of punctuation and test them, though there's much that depends on individual sense of rhythm. We can also assess the students' knowledge of a body of facts—names, dates, titles, and the like. Thus it is that English has been plagued by a swarm of inappropriate tests and measurements. The teaching profession has succumbed to the temptation to measure what it can, and because we tend to teach what we know will be measured, this has been much to the detriment of students and the discipline.

The problem is, of course, that the essential matters are not easily tested or measured. Spelling and punctuation are useful skills, but they are obviously superficial; they pale into insignificance beside the ability to create, to imagine, to relate one thought to another, to organize, to reason, or to catch the nuances of English prose. Information about literature is also interesting, perhaps even important, but unless students can read sensitively, respond, and consider and compare their responses, the information is just so much useless baggage. But inventing, reasoning, responding, and reflecting do not lend themselves readily to testing, especially testing that is economical and efficient and that yields precise and manageable numbers. So schools often compromise, testing what seems testable, and hoping for the best with the remainder of the discipline.

The consequences of that compromise are predictable. What is tested becomes the most important part of the curriculum, and what is not tested is neglected. In some school systems where serious efforts were made to design assessments that asked students to write, teachers began to make serious efforts to teach writing. But assessments of writing are difficult and expensive; kids have to be given circumstances conducive to writing, they have to be given several opportunities, ideally with different modes, and then trained readers have to be brought together to read all those essays, discuss their standards and procedures, and arrive at scores. It costs a lot of money to test that way. So a great many schools moved away from such elaborate evaluation plans, hoping that simpler tests, tests that could be machine-scored, might at least give them some indication of the students' relative abilities. After all, they reasoned, if a student can identify the subject and the verb in a sentence he's given, then perhaps he'll be able to put one of each in a sentence of his own. So those systems are tempted to reduce their writing instruction to the testable basic skills of spelling, punctuation, grammar, and usage; skills often assumed by the gullible public to be the equivalent of writing. Similarly, they are tempted to abandon literature to teach comprehension, vocabulary, identifying words in context, or any of the other testable aspects of reading. Education is thus reshaped, inappropriately, by the pressures of the tests. Elements of the discipline rise to prominence or fade into obscurity not because of their level of importance but because they are easy or difficult to test.

One frequent objection to the approach to literature teaching this book suggests is that it would make testing difficult or impossible. "How," we are asked, "can you test response?" Clearly it *is* difficult to test, in any traditional sense, the students' unique and changing transactions with the literature. But that difficulty does not reduce the importance of those transactions or increase the importance of abilities more easily tested. Too often, the schools conclude that *testing* something insignificant is more important than *teaching* something significant. Form, then, outweighs substance, and the rituals of the institution undermine its purposes. Education then becomes silly—a pointless game whose significance and pleasure have been lost, where achieving the scores becomes more important than achieving the results those scores are supposed to represent. One principal in a large city school, when offered help with the reading program, responded, "We don't have time for that—we have to get these kids ready for the test." Given more time to reflect he might have worded his comment differently, but that he could say, in essence, "Teaching them to score well on the test is more important than teaching them to read" indicates just how corrosive the effect of testing can be. Teachers may rightly object that testing is an obligation forced on them by administrators and by tradition and that there's little they can do about it. Nonetheless, it remains their job to fight its influence and keep in mind the purposes for which they teach literature.

Testing and the Student

The obsession with testing not only tends to distort our vision of the discipline, but it also confuses students about their role in the educational process. By giving the responsibility for evaluation to the teacher, continual testing suggests to students that they are not the ultimate judges of their own thoughts and emotions, as they must be. Of course, externally imposed assessments are surely appropriate and necessary in some situations, when there are clear standards of correctness or when someone must be certified to do a particular job. Surgeons, pilots, electricians, and plumbers have to perform certain specified tasks accurately and reliably. We can specify what those tasks are, teach them, and make reasonable judgments about the skill with which students are able to perform them. Prospective airline pilots, for instance, can be tested on the skills and knowledge they are expected to have, and clearly they *should* be tested to improve the odds that the public will survive their professional services. I don't want to fly with the pilot who cut class the day they studied landing. I'd even prefer not to fly with the one who gets landings right 80 percent of the time. Not everyone should be allowed to fly a 747 (not, in any case, a 747 on which I am a passenger). But everyone should be allowed to read, write, speak, listen, think, and attempt to sort out his or her life, which is the domain of the English classroom.

Literature is more personal, variable, and idiosyncratic than plumbing and wiring and landing planes. We can test the electrician by plugging in the toaster and seeing if anything catches fire or blows up, but to test someone's reading of a literary work we would have to know her better than she is likely to know herself. We would have to understand the interplay of events in her life—the works she has read, the people she has met, and her thoughts and feelings about these experiences. Without that knowledge and insight, we are unqualified to judge her transaction with the work.

We can judge some of it, of course. A misunderstood word, for instance, is fairly easy to detect. If the text reads "proscribe" and the student reads "prescribe," anyone who knows the two words can point out the error and help the reader correct it. But the more subtle and more essential matters are not so manageable. Consider, for example, the difficulties of testing the last several weeks of work on *Romeo and Juliet*. You have in your classroom, let's say, a boy and girl who think they are deeply and eternally in love, a boy and a girl who have just parted ways angrily, a few students who feel that their parents are controlling their every decision and a few from broken families or without parents to offer any council at all, a couple of kids who are beginning to question their sexual identity, and several who fear that they are so unattractive that they'll never find a boyfriend or girlfriend. You also have a student or two hoping for a career onstage or in the movies and a few so shy that the idea of performing terrifies them. Toss in one or two, for good measure, who are in trouble with the law for gang-related activities, and several football players so worried about their place on the team that you have no idea how *Romeo and Juliet* might touch them. How do you devise an easily graded test on the play that takes into account the disparate readings and responses these thirty students will have had? Could we come up with fifty multiple-choice questions that respect their individual and unique transactions with Shakespeare's play, that acknowledge their differing perspectives, that allow them to identify with the characters or dislike them, to approve their decisions and choices or condemn them, to accept their values or reject them? Only one of the five alternative answers to each of our test questions can be correct, of course. . . . Could we come up with even ten such questions?

If we can't, and if we absolutely must have that fifty-question test so that we can generate defensible numerical scores, then we're faced with the unhappy obligation to focus our test questions on those matters to which there are right answers:

Romeo is in love with:

A. Capulet

B. Mercutio

C. Juliet

D. Benvolio

E. Hamlet

Coming up with fifty such questions should be fairly easily, if tedious. Scoring the tests will be even easier, if no less tedious. Unfortunately, it reduces the play to little more than a source of irrelevant details to be memorized Thursday, recalled Friday for the exam, and forgotten on Saturday.

Questions of values and beliefs, and judgments about the significance of a literary work for the student, aren't testable in this simple and efficient way. They probably aren't really testable at all because only the student himself can decide what he has made of the text, how it speaks to him, how it informs his thinking about issues that matter to him, how it contributes to his intellectual, aesthetic, emotional, and social growth. And these are, of course, the significant issues in literature.

To say that these more difficult and interesting matters should not be tested is not to suggest that they should go unexamined, or that the teacher should have no role in their examination. The teacher's help in evaluating beliefs, ideas, and judgments is extremely important. But responsibility for evaluation must lie primarily with the student, since he is the only one with access to the necessary information. He alone knows whether he has thought carefully and honestly; he alone can know what issues matter most to him, what he believes, or what memories are triggered by a literary work. Such reflection can only be elicited in a classroom that manages to awaken the student's interest in the literature and its effects, that succeeds in revealing the connections between the text and the reader, and that values self-discovery. One serious problem with testing is that it often substitutes for this sort of evaluation, just as grades have come to substitute for evaluative comment. Students, rather than ask themselves what questions the reading of this poem has awakened for them, what insights they've found into their own lives, what they've learned about classmates through the discussion, and other such interesting evaluative questions, learn to ask only "Is this going to be on the test?" or "What grade did I get?"

Grading

It's curious that our educational system has managed to convince so many people that something as ephemeral as a grade actually has meaning. Students will listen impatiently to careful explanations of their abilities and their weaknesses, and then demand, "But what did I get?" as if the letter grade says more than the most elaborate statements about their work. Even some parents, after a lengthy and detailed commentary on their child's work, feel sadly uninformed about what the child is accomplishing until the explanation is reduced to a single letter selected from the first five of the alphabet.

This astounding preference for meaningless simplicity over meaningful complexity would be unfathomable anywhere else but school. A pilot in training, having some difficulty with her landings, would not be satisfied to hear that her efforts were worth a "C." Not even refining the system so that we could say she had earned a "C−" or a "C+," or changing the letter into a number—79—would satisfy her, though such pseudo-precision might delude the naive. She would want to know instead what she was doing right, what she was doing wrong, and how she could improve. To substitute a grade for an evaluation in the lesson on landings would be obviously foolish. And yet, in learning language, a much more complicated task than learning to land an airplane, we are often content with the simple letter grade.

The problem is not simply that the grade doesn't inform; rather, it misinforms, deceives, and demeans. It pretends to the precision of mathematics though it is at best only impression and judgment. In so doing, it conceals information that might be useful to students (and parents), offers them an empty symbol as substitute, and reduces them to the stature of objects to be measured and sorted.

Reliance on testing encourages students to look to someone else for final judgments even on important matters. Student come to believe that they must obtain answers from an authority rather than formulate the answers themselves. They are thus likely to pester the teacher for explanations and interpretations—"We've talked about the poem, shooting the bull for forty-five minutes, Mr. Probst; now will you please just tell us what it really means?" Students who develop this attitude are insulated from the literature and themselves. By looking outside rather than in, they learn to avoid intelligent reading. Testing thus cultivates dependence, discouraging intellectual responsibility and self-reliance.

Epistemology

Perhaps the most serious problem with extensive testing is that it distorts the students' conception of knowledge. Knowledge becomes what the teacher knows, or what lies in the books. It is some *thing*, out there in the world, waiting to be found. Such an idea is destructive; it leads students to assume that they have no role in making knowledge and to wait for knowledge to be given to them. That puts them at the mercy of those who will be happy to choose what to offer them as knowledge: politicians, cult-leaders, advertisers, or anyone else who might see profit in manipulating people who are trained to accept what they're told.

Knowledge is not such a simple matter. It cannot be bought and sold; rather, it must be made. It is the product of the mind's interaction with the world. As such, it changes and grows. David Bleich asserts that "the purpose of pedagogical institutions from the nursery through the university is to synthesize knowledge rather than to pass it along."[1] If knowledge is simply out there to be found, there is no possibility for progress—we can only know what someone else already knows. But if knowledge is created, there can be new knowledge, new ways of seeing, thinking, and behaving, and we are not limited to what we now have. To convince students that knowledge is something they can be given ready-made is to trap them, to discourage them from thinking and exploring, to make them gullible.

A belief that much knowledge is to be created by the individual seems especially appropriate in the realm of imaginative literature, so much of which is about unique and infinitely variable human experience. Granted there is much that has to be socially or collaboratively decided—we do need to come to some joint decisions about what is required of pilots and surgeons—but those matters that literature addresses—love, hate, good, evil, and the other grand unanswerable questions—are for the individual to decide. Denise Levertov writes of the act of reading literature in her poem, "The Secret."

The Secret[2]

Two girls discover
the secret of life
in a sudden line of
poetry.

I who don't know the
secret wrote
the line. They
told me

(through a third person)
they had found it
but not what it was,
not even

what line it was. No doubt
by now, more than a week
later, they have forgotten
the secret,

the line, the name of
the poem. I love them for
finding what
I can't find,

and for loving me
for the line I wrote:
and for forgetting it
so that

a thousand times, till death
finds them, they may
discover it again, in other
lines.

in other
happenings. And for
wanting to know it,
for

assuming there is
such a secret, yes,
for that
most of all.

—Denise Levertov

Two readers of her poem, she tells us, have found the "secret of life" in one of her poems. But she, herself, doesn't know what that secret is. She didn't hide it there for them to find. She has no idea what it is. She isn't, you'll notice, saying that they saw her point, that they grasped her purpose, that they deduced what she wanted them to deduce or inferred what she set them up to infer, that they now possess the wisdom she hoped to convey, that they got her point, that they see what she wanted them to see. They see what she, herself, cannot see. Nor is she complaining that they have read something into her poem that she didn't say, that they are putting words into her mouth, that they are imposing on her poem a meaning that it won't bear and that she didn't intend. She is simply, and happily, saying that they found something in her poem that she hadn't put there.

She is even content that they're going to lose that secret now that they've found it. You'd think that, having found something so grand as "the secret of life," you'd want to hang onto it and file it away carefully so that you could get back to it when you might need it, but no, they're going to lose it if they haven't lost it already, and that's fine with her. They'll find it again, she says, in other poems and in other events. This is not the sort of finding that you engage in when you retrieve your keys from under the sofa cushion. Rather, this finding is an act of creating. Levertov didn't hide the secret like an Easter egg; she wrote a poem, and two readers created the secret—their secret—in the creative act of reading. Levertov doesn't even know what it is; she is simply happy to have learned, through that "third person" (who had to be an English teacher), that the secret had been found.

If we were that "third person," that English teacher, with thirty kids in our class, several of whom had discovered the secret of life in a text we'd taught, while others had not had so momentous an encounter simply because the text didn't touch them just as many texts don't touch us, no matter what good readers we may be, how would we design a suitable test, easily graded, quantifiable, and justifiable to students, parents, and administrators? How would we test the "knowledge" students gathered when not even the author herself knows what that knowledge is?

Forced to devise a test—again, an easily graded test yielding the numbers that allow sorting and ranking—for our session on "The Secret," we'd have to ignore the "secret of life" the girls found and focus instead on whatever there is in the text that can be remembered or forgotten, about which we can write questions that can be answered correctly or incorrectly. We could ask how many girls there were, how long it had been since they discovered the secret (or was it since the poet learned of their discovery?), if they'll ever find it again, why the poet loves them. . . . But none of those questions deal with the literary experience those two readers had; all of them distract us from the heart of the matter, which is the transaction between reader and text.

Students learn quickly, if we test on such trivial matters, that the literary experience doesn't count; what matters are the details. They begin to confuse information with knowledge. You don't get an A for discovering the secret of life; you get an A for recalling accurately that there were two girls and not three. If we do that often enough we achieve the effect casually alluded to in a short review of Linda Davis' *Badge of Courage: The Life of Stephen Crane*:

> Most Americans encountered Stephen Crane in high school, when some teacher assigned *The Red Badge of Courage* in lit class. But the novel's vivid power was easily

lost in the anxiety over pop quizzes and theme papers, and few of us ever both-
ered to read Crane again.[3]

Most appalling about that brief quote is the casual acceptance of these consequences. It is as if to say, "What more could we expect? That's just the way English
classes are. The pop quiz is more important than the power of the novel."

My colleague from Chapter 1, who announced to me, "I only read trash," was
saying essentially the same thing. If we concentrate exclusively on the efferent reading, on the testable, then we are sacrificing the heart and core of our discipline.
That was not what I went into teaching to accomplish.

It is natural, in a scientific era, to imagine that all knowledge is to be found in
the physical world. The impressive knowledge today is that of physicists designing
powerful weapons and biologists developing potent drugs, and the source of that
sort of knowledge *is* the physical world. Its criteria are objective, drawn from scientific method and statistical analysis. The knowledge literature deals with, however, is different. It has to do with the individual and his interactions with the world,
and thus it has a personal element. To know about the issues of great literature—
love, death, justice, and so on—we must pay attention to our own uniqueness as
well as to the observable data of the outside world. We do not weigh and measure
these elements as we weigh and measure the raw materials of science, and yet knowledge of them is obviously important. Literature's knowledge is different from that
of physics and biology, harder to parcel out into questions on an exam, but it is no
less significant.

Alternatives

None of this argument against testing and its effects should be construed as an argument against evaluation. Instead, it is an argument against the form evaluation has
taken in too many schools. Evaluation has become something the teacher does *to*
the students, rather than with them, something imposed rather than shared. But at
its best it could be a cooperative venture in which teacher and student share impressions and help each other understand what has happened in the reading of the
literature.

The pattern of evaluation should grow logically out of our concern for students' responses to the literature and their analysis of them. At the end of a unit the
teacher might ask students questions like the following:

Did you enjoy reading the work? Can you identify why you did or did not?

Did the literary work offer any new insight or point of view? If so, did it lead
    you to a change in your own thinking? If not, did it confirm thoughts or
    opinions you already held?

Did the discussion reveal anything about the work, about your classmates, or about
    yourself?

Such questions ask students to evaluate their own transaction with the text and
with other students. They focus on the experience of reading and discussing rather
than on the work read. Further, they ask students to watch for changes, suggesting

that growth is more important than correctness. They do not, by focusing exclusively on details of the text as many examinations do, declare the students' opinions, feelings, and thoughts irrelevant.

Questions like these could be handled in several different ways. They could be discussed openly in class. If the teacher senses that some students have profited from reading the work and might be willing to talk about their experience, then open discussion might be the most effective way of assessing the group's efforts. Those students who did enjoy the work and think carefully about it would illustrate some of the possibilities for meaningful reading, though of course they should not be identified as models to imitate—that would effectively silence them. Those who didn't get as much from the works could at least see what might happen if the next selection works better for them.

Students might sometimes be asked to reply to evaluation questions in writing so that the teacher can review them for insight into the students' minds. Over time, she may be able to note patterns in the students' reactions and take them into account in her planning. Perhaps a class continually expresses frustration with the literature selected, reporting that the works give them no pleasure and stimulate little thought. That information could prompt the teacher to review her selection of material and her methods of instruction. Perhaps one student reveals hostility toward adults or toward the authority of the school. The teacher might then choose works that would invite discussion of the relationships between adults and children and the problems of achieving autonomy. The replies of some students may suggest lines of inquiry that had not occurred to the teacher as she read the work herself or even as she discussed it with her class. Private evaluations may reveal some of the thoughts and feelings that the students were unwilling to articulate before the entire group.

You do, of course, need to analyze the comments students make in these evaluations and in their other work, both written and oral. You need some way to determine how the students are progressing. One possibility is to devise a general checklist for the students' work that touches on the major issues. Such a list might be set up as a worksheet for anecdotal records and include questions or issues that interest you. Every few weeks, during a class when the students are writing or otherwise engaged, you might pull out a notebook in which you had such a sheet for each student and flip through the pages entering reflections that come to mind about the students' work. You'll find that you have much to say about some students and nothing about others, which will serve as a reminder to watch them more closely or try harder to draw them out. You may discover that some students are making an impression by the sheer quantity of their talk rather than by its thoughtfulness. The questions suggested here are hardly complete and may not be the ones you'd use, but they are meant simply to suggest criteria that teachers might devise.

Consider a possible checklist like the one shown in Figure 9–1 and a hypothetical student whose work we analyze using it. One Friday, when the class is tied up with other matters, we jot down some notes about her work during the previous week or two.

We'll probably seldom have even these few notes on all our students, given the typical full day of the English teacher, but perhaps they'll indicate how such an anecdotal record system might help. These notes, for instance, might give us some direction

Student's Name: Jane Eyre	Notes
1. Does the student seem willing to express responses to a work, or is she cautious and constrained?	Seldom has much to say about a text, though she sometimes jumps in to answer questions of a factual nature.
2. Does the student ever change her mind, or is she intransigent?	Stubborn yesterday—finally did express an opinion and then clung to it tenaciously, ignoring all others. Noticed this before. Seems utterly unwilling to consider other possibilities and never changes her mind about anything. Many of the students share this problem—they don't listen to one another or if they do it's for the purpose of arguing.
3. Does the student participate in discussions, listening to others, considering ideas offered, and presenting her own thoughts?	Her mind is usually elsewhere, though she sometimes follows the exchanges when they get heated.
4. Does the student distinguish between the thoughts and feelings she brings to a literary work and those that can be reasonably attributed to the text?	Hard to tell, but when she speaks out it is usually to express a strong feeling—seldom lets it lead into analyzing what the text or another student has presented.
5. Is the student able to distinguish between fact, inference, and opinion in the reading of a literary work?	No clue—have to devise some way of figuring this out.
6. Is the student able to relate the literary work to other human experience, especially her own—that is, can she generalize and abstract?	Occasionally provoked by a text to talk about her own experience, but the text is always a point of departure and she seldom refers back to it once she's off on her own story.
7. Does the student accept the responsibility for making meaning out of the literature and the discussions? Or does she depend on others to tell her what works mean?	Almost never—she sometimes uses it as a springboard for her own proclamations, but takes no responsibility beyond taking notes if I talk too much.
8. Does the student perceive differences and similarities in the visions offered by different literary works, or is she unaware of the subtleties?	She never ties two works of literature together. It is as if each is a separate entity to be read and forgotten.
9. Other observations	Seems a loner, isolated, few friends.

FIGURE 9–1

with this student. For the first question we note that she seldom expresses a response but will sometimes answer questions of fact. That suggests that we might push a bit harder to get her (and possibly the rest of the class) to articulate and explain the effect a text has had upon her. It's very easy for students to wait for the simple, factual question, shoot their hands into the air, answer it, and hope they're off the hook for the rest of the period.

Perhaps your observation might suggest to you that, instead of the pop quiz asking for a few details from the most recently read chapter, you might instead ask for five minutes of writing designed to elicit more than recall. Your assignment, though it would have to be worded appropriately for your students, might be something like the following:

1. In several sentences, state your response to the reading. Did you like it or not; did it awaken any feelings (anxiety, curiosity, anger, boredom, something else); did it raise any questions; did it make you expect anything to come in future chapters? This paragraph is about *you*, your reactions to the text. Think about how you felt and what you thought as you read the chapter.
2. Then, in several more sentences, tell me what one or two features of the chapter made you feel or think as you do. Was it something a character did or said, something about the situation, something about the language? This paragraph is about the text and how it had the effect on you that you described in the first paragraph.

This assignment might achieve several purposes. First, by breaking the task into two parts, one of which is specifically to do what the student (Jane) has not been doing, it might encourage her to reflect on and try to state her response to the reading. Second, it would allow her to talk about the details from the text, which she seems willing at least occasionally to do. Third, if you need—or have been required to have—some sort of policing quiz to determine whether students have done their homework, this will serve that purpose without reducing the text to nothing more than a list of details to be memorized. The students won't be able to write these two short paragraphs if they spent the previous night at the local video arcade instead of at their desks. Fourth, although the activity may be specifically tailored to help Jane move forward, it isn't a bad experience for the rest of the students. If you have no notes that day on the child sitting next to Jane, he won't be harmed by this activity, although it was devised with someone else in mind. Tomorrow, perhaps, or next week, you'll notice something about his performance that will suggest some other activity, and Jane will, presumably, profit from that, as well. Fifth, it is a quiz that might sustain discussion for the rest of the period.

It's probable that you'll find yourself making very similar comments about several students. Question #2 in our notes on Jane, for instance, reveals that if she ever does express an opinion or make an observation she holds to it regardless of other students' insights or objections. It also reminds us that others in the class have the same problem. That refusal to change one's mind is not an uncommon problem for students trained in classes that emphasize correctness. Basal readers, with their several comprehension questions following each reading assignment, could not be better designed to persuade students that being right matters more than anything else. When you find a pattern emerging, it might suggest the focus for subsequent lessons. Let's say, for example, that you do notice in your anecdotal notes on several of your students this same reluctance to listen to one another, this same resistance to considering other readings. That evaluation would suggest that you might devise an activity whose purpose is to encourage close attention to other readings. Consider this workshop as a possibility:

PAIRED READINGS

This is an effort to have students concentrate on the *reading* rather than simply on the text, and to *collaborate* in making sense out of a text. It asks students to work in pairs with two poems. Explain that for the first poem one student will be the *reader* and the other the *interviewer*. When they move on to the second poem, the roles will be reversed.

Choose two poems, perhaps thematically related, divide the class into pairs, and give the students instructions like the following, worded suitably for your group:

For this reading we'll divide the class into pairs, each of which will be given two short texts. Each of you will serve once as *reader* and once as *interviewer*. Here's the plan:

1. Decide quickly which of you will first be the *interviewer* and which the *reader*. Both should then glance quickly through the first text to get a rough idea of what it's about.

2. The *reader* should then read the text, talking about it aloud—but not too loud—as he or she goes. The *reader* should make any comments that come to mind—memories that arise, feelings evoked, problems or confusions with the text itself, anything. The *interviewer* should take notes, as thoroughly as possible, on everything the *reader* says, but should do so without interrupting. The *interviewer's* focus should be on capturing what the *reader* reports about his or her reading, not on correcting, explaining, or debating.

3. Next, take a few minutes for the *interviewer* to read over the notes and frame a few questions or comments. There may be something the *interviewer* didn't quite catch, or a story that merits elaboration, or a point that the *reader* needs to explain a bit more. While the *interviewer* is reviewing his or her notes and formulating questions and comments, the *reader* should read over the poem again,

4. The *interviewer* then should ask his or her questions and make comments. The purpose of these questions and comments is to start a conversation, so feel free to follow the talk wherever it takes you.

or

The interviewer goes through his or her notes, circling the three to five most interesting, problematic, or confusing points. Comment on or ask a question about each, again taking notes on the replies.

5. When the conversation seems to wane (and if time allows), the *reader* then reads the text aloud again, commenting further, while the *interviewer* once again takes notes, looking especially for anything new that comes up. After the second reading, the *interviewer* should again share his or her observations and ask questions, hoping to continue the conversation.

6. The *interviewer* then reports to the reader, discussing the reading, telling the reader anything interesting he or she observed, wondered about, or speculated, saying whatever he or she can about the *reader's* reading of the text. Note that this is a report, not an evaluation, and it should lead to some conversation. When the discussion is finished, the *interviewer* should turn all the notes over to the *reader*, who will file them away for the moment.

7. *Reader* and *interviewer* now trade roles and run through Steps 1 through 5 again, using the other text.

8. Each student should now take the notes his or her partner has created and, using them, write a page or so about his or her reading of the text.

There are several purposes for the pattern. One is simply to slow down the reading, encouraging productive pauses. There is little for the *reader* to do while his partner is reflecting on the notes he's taken and preparing his question, and so he has time to re-read the text. A second purpose is to provide helpful responses—prods, questions, reactions—that might stimulate further thought about the reading. And the third purpose, the one suggested by the anecdotal notes on our hypothetical student, is to encourage some collegiality among students, to force them to listen to one another, and to cast them into the role of helper for one another, while giving them some guidance in that role.

These activities, all involving reading texts while working in pairs, require close attention not to the teacher's lecture, but to the responses of another student to the text. The structure demands that students attend to one another, and might have the desired effect, over time, of increasing their willingness to listen closely to what others have to say.

If the purpose of evaluation is not to rank and sort and grade but rather to help the teacher understand what the students are doing well and might be doing better, then these brief anecdotal notes are likely to be a more useful evaluative tool than most other quizzes and tests.

If the record sheet illustrated above is too ominous and overwhelming, with a separate sheet for each student and all those empty blocks staring at us, waiting to be filled in, then a simpler, less demanding strategy may be called for. Perhaps a record sheet for each class so that you can periodically make notes on the group as a whole would suffice to give you some information about the class. Or, if we wanted to be able to do a rapid assessment of individual students, we might devise a list of descriptors arranged as dichotomous pairs. The first, for example, might simply be:

This student seems:

open _____ closed

Others might be:

This student:

speaks willingly _____ speaks reluctantly

enjoys the reading _____ dislikes the reading

relates work to self _____ remains distant

listens to others _____ refuses to hear other ideas

is rational _____ is emotional

Locating students on each continuum may give the teacher some rough clues about their habits and inclinations.

If might occasionally be valuable, too, to have students write briefly about themselves as readers, something along the lines of a "Reader's Autobiography," perhaps. You might suggest the following:

Describe yourself as a reader. What do you like to read; what do you not enjoy?

Of the works we have read so far, which were the most enjoyable and which the least?

How do you prefer to study a work—do you like free and open discussions of texts, do you prefer to learn about writers, do you like small-group tasks or whole-class work?

Were there any authors that you especially liked (or disliked) and why?

Have you noticed any changes in yourself as a reader over the last several months?

A brief—very brief—paper on such questions, written at the beginning and end of the school year, and perhaps several times in between, might serve as a record of their development in their own words. Michael Dirda says, in the preface to *An Open Book: Coming of Age in the Heartland*, "Most of all, I wanted these pages to celebrate the joy that books brought to my young self and to record how I discovered them, what I felt, and how they shaped my character."[4] We may not get such a tribute to books from many of our students, but if they grow more aware of what they like and what they reject, and of how they prefer to deal with books, they will have profited.

All of the information gathered from such evaluative strategies can be equally valuable to both teacher and student. For the teacher it can suggest directions for the future; for the student it is a record of her own development. In a set of evaluations collected over the course of a school year, the student may be able to see changes in her behavior and in her patterns of response. She may note that interests died away and were replaced by others, that some confusions were clarified, and that other issues about which she had once had firm convictions became ambiguous and frustrating. She may discover that her later entries reveal concerns that never surfaced early in the year. The evaluations, which she has written herself, though the teacher will have spoken with her about them and perhaps added comments, may provide concrete evidence of the effects of literature on her life, just as slashes on a tree give evidence of physical growth.

Evaluating Writing About Literature

Much of our evaluation in the literature classroom is of the student's writing. We may value discussion highly, but it's tough, without an assistant charged with the task of observing and taking notes, to develop a persuasive record of the student's work. Papers, however, can be collected in a portfolio over the course of a year and provide concrete documentation of at least one aspect of the student's performance. If these papers are to tell us anything about the student's transaction with literary texts, however, we have to look at them not just for their virtues and flaws as compositions, but for what they reveal about what the student can do with the texts he reads.

If transactions with texts are as potentially rich and complex as Louise Rosenblatt and others have argued they are, then the essays we invite our students to write have to allow that richness to emerge. Summaries of works won't do; those they can parrot from any of several brands of *Notes*, the pulp-paper substitutes for literary experience that students who want to avoid reading buy so that they can memorize enough information to convince the teacher that they've actually read the work. Nor will formal analyses, distant and cold and impersonal, work. Instead, the essays must give students the chance to explore the range of transactions with texts, respecting their own perspective and experience, attending to elements of the text, and taking into consideration the responses and readings of others—their classmates, at least, and perhaps also critics and scholars.

It might be possible in a literature course to ask students to write a variety of papers that would cover many of the possibilities. We could, for instance, tell students at the beginning of the course that we intended to ask them to compile a portfolio of essays by the end of the semester that would include at least one paper in each of several categories. Hypothetically, those papers might be:

1. a paper telling a story of one's own, called to mind by one of the texts read during the course
2. a paper solving a problem posed by one of the texts or interpreting a difficult text
3. a paper drawing inferences about the assumptions or values of the author as they are revealed in a text
4. a paper discussing another student's reading of a text
5. a paper discussing the relationship between a text read in class and any other piece (in any genre, including film and television) called to mind by the text

A set of assignments like this would give students a chance to tell their own stories, giving them some opportunity to write, and not simply read, the genre of the short story (Essay #1). Rosenblatt has suggested that "one of the best ways of helping students to gain the appreciation of literary form and artistry is to encourage them to engage in such imaginative writing."[5]

Essay #2 would ask them to focus in one paper on aspects of the text, interpreting it, analyzing it, trying to resolve ambiguities, solve problems, or explain effects. In Essay #3 they'd be asked to concentrate on the author, drawing inferences about his or her intent or purpose, values, or beliefs. In Essay #4 they would be expected to focus on someone else's reading of a work, reminding them that texts come to life only when they are read, and they are read by unique and differing individuals. And finally, in Essay #5 they'd be asked to bring the text to bear upon another text, comparing them in whatever way seemed productive.

Students wouldn't necessarily all have to write the same paper at the same time, unless allowing them to choose creates too much confusion for you and the class. If it's manageable, you might, after finishing *Huckleberry Finn*, follow the leads students have given in the discussions and encourage one student to write about his own encounter with racial prejudice (Essay #1), another student to write about *Huck Finn* and *The Invisible Man* (Essay #5), another to interview the classmate who reacted violently to Twain's use of the word "nigger" and write about his reaction to the novel (Essay #4), and so on. The student's obligation would be to make sure that by the end of the course she'd chosen topics that fit each of the five categories, to insure that she'd had experience with various ways of thinking about texts.

How then would we evaluate those papers? Dan Kirby and Tom Liner suggest a rubric that might help.[6] They urge us to develop an evaluation guide, based on the nature of the paper, that invites teachers to offer useful commentary and advice to the student writer. Figure 9–2 provides a sample, based on their model, with a few hypothetical remarks entered.

I'd prefer such a scoring guide without the last two columns, but I've included them just to indicate that it might be possible to adapt a guide that I hope encourages us to say something useful to students about their work so that it is also a scoring

Aspects of Papers:	Poor		Average		Excellent		Weight	Score
Scores:	1	2	3	4	5	6	% #	
Paper explains the issues addressed and justifies the attention to them.			You've told me clearly enough what issue you're addressing, but you haven't explained why it's significant. Why should a reader of your paper, or of this book, be interested in the writer's assumptions about these matters? 4				4	16
Paper analyzes the values of the author, citing the text.					You've shown very clearly how you've drawn your inferences about the author's position on these matters—it's a very good analysis. 5		4	20
Paper expresses the writer's own perspective on relevant issues and connects it to the text.	You say very little about your own position. What do you believe, and how does it shape your assessment of the writer's beliefs? 2						4	8
Paper is logical and coherent.			Except for your reluctance to tell us where you stand, you do organize your points clearly enough.4				3	12
Paper is grammatical and well-written.					Your paper is correct but you might want to take more risks. Virtually every sentence is the same length, same structure. Let's work on variety in the future. 5		2	10
Final Comments on Student's Paper: You seem to stay very distant from the work you're writing about, as if you don't want to express yourself. I know there's safety in removing yourself from the arena, but literature is about human experience and should touch us directly. For readers to understand your paper, you have to let them know something about yourself. Try to be more willing to take a stand, to let us know what you think and how your feel about what you're reading.							Total Score: 66 of 102	

FIGURE 9–2 *Essay Assignment: A paper drawing inferences about the assumptions or values of the author as they are revealed in a text.*

system. If we are required to grade students on their writing rather than evaluate it and help them with it, then we might be able to do so in this way, attaching the numbers to real comments, hoping we can keep the focus on aspects of the essays, but keeping the numbers handy if we have to defend ourselves to parents or administrators.

These scoring guides, tailored to the individual assignments, all of which would be designed to encourage and respect individual response to texts, might give us some basis for evaluating work, selecting texts, and devising writing assignments.

Evaluating Discussion

The heart of literature is, or ought to be, conversation. Of all the activities in a classroom, discussion must be the hardest to assess. Papers hold still for us—we can read them, one at a time, at our own pace, making the comments and suggestions that we think will be most helpful for the students. If we have to grade them, we can devise a relatively defensible scheme for generating the required letters or numbers. We can specify criteria, even weight various aspects of the essays, and satisfy ourselves, many administrators, some parents, and even a few students that we've been fair and objective. But discussion is harder to deal with. I once had a teacher who counted the number of times we contributed, entering a check beside our names in his grade book for each answer or comment we offered, occasionally giving us a ✓+ if the remark was unusually sharp or insightful. Even in the tenth grade we knew that he was rewarding the glib, that sheer quantity was what mattered, so those who were willing to play the game spoke up as often as they could, regardless of whether they really had anything to say. It was the oral equivalent of giving ten pages to the teacher who had asked for a five-page essay, of having twenty footnotes in your research paper when you were required to have at least ten. Again, the demand for quantification was undermining the educational process.

We do need, however, some way of encouraging students to take the classroom conversation seriously, and in the school culture where the most often asked question is "Will this be on the test?" if it isn't assessed in some way, it isn't likely to be valued. If the teacher values conversation about literary experience, she's likely to have to figure out some way of evaluating it, not only to know how well things are going, but also to justify the time spent talking to her students.

Here again, some sort of record-keeping system might help, if it's kept simple enough so that it doesn't overwhelm us. There's so little time available in the school day for anything but dealing with the students that I'm reluctant to suggest one more task. Nonetheless, a simple checksheet might help us here, too. We might, for instance, try to articulate for ourselves and our students just what it is that we're hoping for in classroom conversation about literature. We might come up with a list of those features and use it occasionally as a tool to evaluate either the entire class or individual students. The sheet might look something like the one shown in Figure 9–3.

Criteria for the Evaluation of Discussion	
The student/class. . . .	Notes:
1. comes prepared to engage in the work of the classroom, having read, written in the journal, conducted interviews, or sought out information or experience necessary for participation in the discussion	
2. supports the ongoing discourse of the classroom, by contributing to the discussion, by listening attentively to the offerings of others, and/or by helping, when necessary, to draw others into the discussion	
3. accepts responsibility for the success of the discussion by refraining from sarcasm or insult that silences others and by tolerating digressions from his or her immediate concerns	
4. is willing to probe and question, to speculate, and to take risks	
5. tolerates the missteps, meanderings, and recursiveness typical of discussion and explores the possibilities in ideas offered	
6. attempts to build upon and extend the thoughts of others	
7. questions others, exploring the potential of their contributions, and offers clarification and elaboration upon his or her own ideas when necessary	
8. assumes some of the work necessary to maintain discussion and push it along (i.e., helps by summarizing issues, raising questions, extracting significant points, making connections, and setting an agenda)	
9. assumes the responsibility for independent and individual summary and closure	
10. looks for connections between texts, the ideas offered by other students, and experiences outside the classroom	
11. acknowledges the structure of the discussion and abides by the patterns implicit in it (for example, brainstorming, storytelling, responding, and problem-solving all imply different sorts of discussion)	

FIGURE 9–3

These may not, of course, be the criteria you have for discussions in your classroom, but some such list might help you to explain to students what you're hoping for and might help you show students what they're doing well or poorly. Had I had such a list, it would have been immensely helpful to me in dealing with a few cynical and sarcastic students I once had in a very bright twelfth-grade class. I might have been able to pull out this list and explain to those kids that despite their wit and brilliance and impeccable prose style, they were not "listening attentively to the offerings of others" (#2), not "refraining from sarcasm or insult" (#3), not "tolerating the missteps, meanderings, and recursiveness typical of discussion" (#5), and in general not "supporting the ongoing discourse of the classroom" (#2 again). If I'd had to, I could have decided to enter a weekly grade based on these criteria and used it to shape the behavior of the more recalcitrant but still grade-conscious troublemakers. "Your last paper," I might have said, "merits publication in *PMLA* and might even win a Nobel Prize, so it gets an A+. Your performance in our discussions, however, is worth roughly a D−, so you're hanging in with a weak C at the moment."

The grade, of course, is not the point. In fact, it's a dismal distraction from the point, which is good conversation about significant ideas. But we are saddled with grades and grading, and until the schools evolve further and they are forever banished we'll have to cope with them, and when we can, use them to our advantage.

The Range of an Evaluation Program

Alan Purves, in an essay on testing competence in reading, suggests a distinction useful in discussing evaluation:

> Research has shown that there may be quite individual responses—perceptions, feelings, attitudes—to a piece of writing, but at the same time there are certain shared perceptions. . . . These shared perceptions can be thought of as the *meaning,* and the particular or individual understanding as the *significance.*[7]

Both need to be considered in evaluating what's transpiring with our students.

In another essay,[8] perhaps the most complete and thorough analysis of the problems of evaluation in literature, Purves lists various aspects of literature instruction falling in the general categories of "Content" and "Behavior," be considered. Purves subdivides the category of "Content" into Literary Works, Contextual Information, Literary Theory, and Cultural Information. These categories are further subdivided. Under Literary Works, he lists genres to be taught, including both the traditional (poetry, drama, fiction, and nonfiction) and movies, television, and other mass media. Contextual Information includes biographical and historical knowledge. Literary Theory refers to literary terminology and critical approaches, and Cultural Information to knowledge of the dominant myths and metaphors of a culture.

The category "Behavior" is a checklist of those behaviors that might be elicited from students. These fall into three broad categories of Knowledge, Response, and Participation. Knowledge in this context means applying information. It is further subdivided into the various sorts of information one might apply in discussing literature: knowledge of specific works, biographical information, terminology, and so on. Response is divided into several categories, including recreating the work, expressing feelings, interpreting and judging, and analyzing the work and its parts. Participation deals with the willingness to respond.

Such checklists will help teachers evaluate both students and programs. Analyzing a curriculum might reveal, for instance, that poetry is overemphasized or that novels are neglected. Either might be an imbalance in the curriculum. Or the analysis might indicate that media other than the printed word have been ignored. These "literatures" could be important, and the teacher might take steps to include them.

Evaluating a student's work against this sort of checklist might reveal that the student is extremely reluctant to express responses, preferring the security of impersonal intellectual discussion. Other students might gladly talk about their feelings and opinions but shy away from the demanding work of reasoning about the texts they read or considering the ideas of others in the group. Neither extreme is desirable; each allows students to avoid an important aspect of the literary experience and of their own development. An evaluation scheme similar to Purves' checklists of content and behavior might reveal these imbalances in the literature program and in the growth of the students.

Of course, such an evaluation scheme would not have the comforting but false precision of testing programs based entirely on the content of the literature. Nor would it be easy to apply and grade. A teacher cannot, for example, give a ten-question multiple-choice test to judge the student's satisfaction in responding. That is a matter that he must assess continually, taking into consideration the interaction between the student and her classmates, how much the student seems to have liked the works read, and countless other variables. Still, it is worth assessing, because so much of the student's enjoyment of literature depends on her ability and willingness to respond to what she reads.

George Hillocks, Jr. analyzes the possible content of the literature program in a slightly different way, focusing on comprehension skills. He suggests that there is a hierarchy of skills, and that students who have trouble with questions at one level of the hierarchy will have a great deal more difficulty at the higher levels. The levels Hillocks proposes are these:

Literal Level of Comprehension
1. basic stated information—information that is prominent and important in the text
2. key detail—important to the plot, but less prominently presented
3. stated relationship—a relationship, often causal, between bits of information

Inferential Level of Comprehension
4. simple implied relationships—relationships not stated in the text
5. complex implied relationships—require inferences drawn from many pieces of information
6. author's generalization—inferences about the author's vision drawn from the total work
7. structural generalizations—require an analysis of the work's structure, and an explanation of how it works[9]

Hillocks proposes the hierarchy as an organizing principle for evaluation. He points out its obvious advantages over assessments using simplistic readability scores, observing that

Readability scores are universally based on measures of vocabulary difficulty and aspects of sentence length. They necessarily ignore what might be called the *inferential load* of a work.[10]

They make the further error of assuming that longer words are more difficult than shorter words, although it is obvious that words like *love, peace, justice, honor, good,* and the like are more difficult than *television, rocketship, automobile, and hamburger.* Length and difficulty do not always correspond.

Hillocks suggests developing an inventory based on his hierarchy and administering it at the beginning of the school year. The results serve, he says,

> to define and predict, in fairly specific terms, the comprehension levels of specific students and groups of students and, therefore, provide a guide for deciding how to begin the term's literature program.[11]

A second inventory given at the end of the term would indicate something about the progress made in between. On comparable inventories, students should presumably perform better at the end of the term than they did at the beginning, if we accept the hierarchy as our set of goals for instruction. But although Hillocks' scheme is excellent as far as it goes, it neglects important elements in reading. It assesses only the skills of comprehension and analysis, which are, of course, very important. The development of these skills, however, is closely tied to the student's capacity for responding to the work, which Hillocks' scheme does not examine.

Purves' taxonomy suggests attention to both the literary work and the student in testing—a balanced approach to a difficult task. Ginn and Company's *Responding,* one of the most interesting and creative literature textbook series ever published, applied such a taxonomy in its evaluation plan. Charles Cooper and Alan Purves use a content-behavior grid; in the cells created by the intersection of content and behavior they suggest strategies for assessment. Those strategies include traditional tests as well as a variety of other devices.

One, which they call "The Attitude-Sort," assesses students' attitudes on four factors: willingness to respond, value placed on books and writers, importance given to personal engagement with literary works, and willingness to analyze literature.[12] It consists of thirty-two statements, which students are asked to judge according to how much they are like their own opinions. This activity yields a rough picture of the students' attitudes toward the study of literature, and might, if conducted at the beginning and end of a year or semester, indicate changes in those attitudes. A similar tool is the Likert-Scale, consisting of statements that the student evaluates on a five-point scale from "strongly agree" to "strongly disagree." Such instruments may be designed by individual teachers or school systems to reflect what they consider most important in literature instruction, or they may be borrowed from sources like *A Guide to Evaluation.*

Cooper and Purves also recommend various shorter assessments, including two for students' perceptions of a class period, several for their perceptions of the class as a whole, one for their perceptions of the teacher, and one for their observations about the work of a group.[13] Although most of these do not deal specifically with literature teaching, they may still be useful, especially if modified slightly to suit a particular course or lesson or perhaps simply recast to sound more like the teacher. If students are involved in evaluating the ongoing work of the class, they are more likely to commit themselves to the work.

The Uniqueness of the Discipline

The teacher of literature has a problem. She works in a time when measurement is worshiped, objectivity is a virtue, and the educational system is under attack. She wants to defend her profession and its accomplishments, yet she can't use the sorts of objective tools that yield proof acceptable to the public. Knowledge of literature is simply not testable in any of the traditional ways. To test it is to subvert it, forcing it into a mold that it does not fit.

Tests that deny the personal and idiosyncratic element in literary knowledge or patterns of evaluation that locate authority in the teacher rather than in the student or that presume to establish an objective standard for understanding or appreciating literature will inevitably do more harm than good. It is still possible, of course, to assess and evaluate. But if the evaluations are to have any value for the student, they must respect her autonomy and individuality.

Endnotes

1. David Bleich, *Subjective Criticism* (Baltimore, MD: Johns Hopkins University Press, 1978), p. 133.

2. Denise Levertov, "The Secret" in *O Taste and See* (Norfolk, CT: New Directions Books, 1962).

3. Unattributed review, *American Way*, 31, No. 16, (August 15, 1998), p. 94.

4. Michael Dirda, *An Open Book: Coming of Age in the Hear and Now* (New York: Norton, 2003), p. 15.

5. Louise M. Rosenblatt, *Literature as Exploration*, Third Edition (New York: Noble and Noble, 1968), p. 48.

6. Daniel Kirby, Dawn Lotta Kirby, and Tom Liner, *Inside Out: Strategies for Teaching Writing*, Third Edition (Portsmouth, NH: Heinemann, 2003).

7. Alan Purves, "Competency in Reading," in *The Nature and Measurement of Competency in English*, Charles R. Cooper, Ed. (Urbana, IL: National Council of Teachers of English, 1981), p. 75.

8. Alan Purves, "Evaluation of Learning in Literature," in *Handbook on Formative and Summative Evaluation of Student Learning*, Benjamin S. Bloom, I, Thomas Hastings,

and George F. Madaus, Eds. (New York: McGraw-Hill Book Company,
697–766.

9. George Hillocks, Jr., "Toward a Hierarchy of Skills in the Comprehens
erature," *English Journal*, 69, No. 3 (March 1980), 54–59.

10. Ibid., p. 59

11. Ibid.

12. Charles R. Cooper and Alan C. Purves, *A Guide to Evaluation* (Boston: Ginn
and Company, 1973), p. 22; this manual accompanies Ginn's *Responding* series.

13. They cite two sources for these instruments: Alfred H. Gorman's *Teachers and
Learners: The Interactive Process of Education* (Boston: Allyn and Bacon, 1969), and Robert
Fox et al., *Diagnosing Classroom Learning Environments* (Chicago: Science Research
Associates, Inc., 1966).

BIBLIOGRAPHY

Bibliography on Literary Theory and Literature Teaching

Thematic Issues

"Close-Up: Adolescent Literature." 1975. *English Journal* 64(February).

"EJ Forum: Reader-Response Criticism and Classroom Imperative." 1993. *English Journal* 82(March): 13.

"Enlarging the Range of Response." 1977. *English Journal* 66(February).

"The Lure of Young Adult Literature." 2001. *English Journal* 90(May).

"Multicultural Literature." 1977. *English Journal* 66(March).

"Talking Literature." 2003. *English Journal* 93(September).

"The World of Literature." 2002. *English Journal* 91(May).

"Young Adult Literature." 1984. *English Journal* 73(November).

"Young Adult Literature." 1997. *English Journal* 86(March).

Articles and Books

ABAIR, JACQUELINE M., and ALICE CROSS. 1999. "Patterns in American Literature." *English Journal* 88(July): 83-87.

ABBS, PETER. 1976. *Root and Blossom: The Philosophy Practice and Politics of English Teaching.* London: Heinemann.

ABRAHAMSON, RICHARD F. 1997. "Collected Wisdom: The Best Articles Ever Written on Young Adult Literature and Teen Reading." *English Journal* 86(March): 50–54.

ACKERMAN, JAMES S., and JANE STOUDER HAWLEY. 1967. *On Teaching the Bible as Literature: A Guide to Selected Biblical Narratives for Secondary Schools.* Bloomington, IN: Indiana University Press.

ADDINGTON, A. H. 2001. "Talking About Literature in University Book Club and Seminar Settings." *Research in the Teaching of English* 36: 212–248.

ADDISON, CATHERINE. 1994. "Once Upon a Time: A Reader-Response to Prosody." *College English* 56(October): 655–679.

ADLER, RICHARD. 1974. "Answering the Unanswered Question," in *Re-Vision: Classroom Practices in Teaching English, 1974-1975,* Allen Berger and Blanche Hope Smith. ed. Urbana, IL: National Council of Teachers of English.

ADLER-KASSNER, LINDA, and SHERRY LINKON. 1997-1998. "Reading Popular Culture." *Reader: Essays in Reader-Oriented Theory, Criticism, and Pedagogy* 38–39(Fall-Spring).

ALBRIGHT, JAMES, KIRAN PUROHIT, and CHRISTOPHER WALSH. 2002. "Louise Rosenblatt Seeks Qtaznboi@Aol.Com for LTR: Using Chat Rooms in Interdisciplinary Middle School Classrooms." *Journal of Adolescent & Adult Literacy* 45 (May): 692.

ALIAGA-BUCHENAU, ANA-ISABEL. 2004. *The 'Dangerous' Potential of Reading: Readers and the Negotiation of Power in Nineteenth-Century Narratives.* New York: Routledge.

ALLINGTON, RICHARD. 2002. "Troubling Times: A Short Historical Perspective," in *Big Brother and the National Reading Curriculum; How Ideology Trumped Research,* Richard L. Allington, ed. Portsmouth, NH: Heinemann.

ALTER, ROBERT. 1996. *The Pleasures of Reading: In an Ideological Age.* New York: W. W. Norton.

ANATOL, GISELLE LIZA, ed. 2003. *Reading Harry Potter: Critical Essays.* Westport, CT: Praeger.

ANDERSON, PHILIP M. 1986. "The Past Is Now: Approaches to the Secondary School Literature Curriculum." *English Journal* 75(December): 19–22.

ANDRASICK, KATHLEEN DUDDEN. 1990. *Opening Texts: Using Writing to Teach Literature.* Portsmouth, NH: Boynton/Cook—Heinemann.

ANDREWS, LARRY. 1977. "Responses to Literature: Enlarging the Range." *English Journal* 66(February): 60–62.

———. 1974. "Responses to Literature: In Tennis the Service Is Crucial." *English Journal* 63(February): 44–46.

ANGEL, ANN. 2003. "The Voices of Cultural Assimilation in Current Young Adult Novels." *ALAN Review* 30(Winter): 52–55.

ANN, WILDER, and ALAN B. TEASLEY. 2001. "If You Want Resources About Ya Literature This Is Your Shopping List (a Resource List for High School Teachers and Librarians)." *ALAN Review* 29(Fall): 28–31.

ANONYMOUS. 1997. "Reader Response." *Mosaic: A Journal for the Interdisciplinary Study of Literature* 30(December): 125.

ANSON, CHRIS M. "Book Lists, Cultural Literacy, and the Stagnation of Discourse." *English Journal* 77(February 1988): 14–18.

APPLEBEE, ARTHUR N. 1978. *The Child's Concept of Story.* Chicago, IL: University of Chicago Press.

———. "Stability and Change in the High-School Canon." *English Journal* 81(September 1992): 27–32.

———. 1994. "Toward Thoughtful Curriculum: Fostering Discipline-Based Conversation." *English Journal* 83(March): 45.

————. 1974. *Tradition and Reform in the Teaching of English: A History.* Urbana, IL: National Council of Teachers of English.

APPLEMAN, DEBORAH. 2000. *Critical Encounters in High School English: Teaching Literary Theory to Adolescents.* New York and Urbana, IL: Teachers College Press and National Council of Teachers of English.

APPLEYARD, J. A. 1990. *Becoming a Reader : The Experience of Fiction from Childhood to Adulthood.* Cambridge [England]; New York: Cambridge University Press.

ASH, BARBARA HOETKER. "Reading Assigned Literature in a Reading Workshop." *English Journal* 79(January 1990): 77–79.

————. 1992. "Student-Made Questions: One Way into a Literary Text." *English Journal* 81(September): 61.

ASHLEY, BOB. 1997. *Reading Popular Narrative : A Source Book.* Rev. and Exp. Ed. London; New York: Leicester University Press.

ASSELIN, MARLENE. 2000. "Reader Response in Literature and Reading Instruction." *Teacher Librarian* 27(April): 62–64.

ATHANASES, STEVEN Z. 1988. "Developing a Classroom Community of Interpreters." *English Journal* 77(January): 45–48.

————. 1998. "Diverse Learners, Diverse Texts: Exploring Identity and Difference through Literary Encounters." *Journal of Literacy Research* 30(June): 273–296.

————. 1996. "A Gay-Themed Lesson in an Ethnic Literature Curriculum: Tenth Graders' Response to 'Dear Anita.'" *Harvard Educational Review* 66(Summer): 231–256.

————. 2003. "Thematic Study of Literature: Middle School Teachers, Professional Development, and Educational Reform." *English Education* 35(January): 107–121.

BANCROFT, MICHAEL A. 1994. "Why Literature in the High School Curriculum?" *English Journal*(August) 83: 83.

BARKER, ANDREW P. 1989. "A Gradual Approach to Feminism in the American-Literature Classroom." *English Journal* 78(October): 39–44.

BARTON, BOB, and DAVID BOOTH. 1990. *Stories in the Classroom: Storytelling, Reading Aloud and Roleplaying with Children.* Portsmouth, NH: Heinemann Educational Books.

BEACH, RICHARD. "Attitudes, Social Conventions, and Response to Literature." *Journal of Research and Development in Education* 16: 47–54.

————. 1998. "Constructing Real and Text Worlds in Responding to Literature." *Theory into Practice* 37(Summer): 176–185.

BEACH, RICHARD. "1987. Developmental Differences in Response to a Story." *Research in the Teaching of English* 21(October): 286–297.

————. 2000. "Studying Responses within Activity Systems." *Reader: Essays in Reader-Oriented Theory, Criticism, and Pedagogy* 43(Spring): 20–24.

————. 1993. *A Teacher's Introduction to Reader-Response Theories, NCTE Teacher's Introduction Series.* Urbana, IL: National Council of Teachers of English.

BEACH, RICHARD, et al., eds. 1992. *Multidisciplinary Perspectives on Literacy Research.* Urbana, IL: National Council of Teachers of English.

BEACH, RICHARD, and JAMES MARSHALL. 1991. *Teaching Literature in the Secondary School*. New York: Harcourt Brace Jovanovich, Inc.

BEAN, THOMAS W., PAUL CANTU VALERIO, HELEN MONEY SENIOR, and FERN WHITE. 1999. "Secondary English Students' Engagement in Reading and Writing About a Multicultural Novel." *Journal of Educational Research* 93(September/October): 32–39.

BEAN, THOMAS W., and KAREN MONI. 2003. "Developing Students' Critical Literacy: Exploring Identity Construction in Young Adult Fiction." *Journal of Adolescent & Adult Literacy* 46(May): 638–648.

BEAN, THOMAS W, and NICOLE RIGONI. 2001. "Exploring the Intergenerational Dialogue Journal Discussion of a Multicultural Young Adult Novel." *Reading Research Quarterly* 36(July-September): 232.

BEAVEN, MARY. 1972. "Responses of Adolescents to Feminine Characters in Literature." *Research in the Teaching of English* 6(Spring): 48–68.

BEEHLER, SHARON A. "Close Vs. Closed Reading: Interpreting the Clues." *English Journal* 77(October 1988): 39–43.

BEERS, KYLENE. 1999. "Literature: Our Way In." *Voices from the Middle* 7(September): 9–15.

———. 2003. *When Kids Can't Read, What Teachers Can Do: A Guide for Teachers*. Portsmouth, NH: Heinemann.

BEERS, KYLENE, and ROBERT E. PROBST. 1998. "Classroom Talk About Literature: The Social Dimensions of a Solitary Act." *Voices From the Middle* 16(April): 16–20.

BEERS, KYLENE, and BARBARA G. SAMUELS, eds. 1998. *Into Focus: Understanding and Creating Middle School Readers*. Norwood, MA: Christopher-Gordon.

BENNETT, R. SEBASTIAN. 1994. "A Consideration of Reader-Response Literary Criticism in the Creative Writing Classroom." *The Arkansas Review: A Journal of Criticism* 3(Spring): 22–27.

BENNETT, ROBERT A. VERDA EVANS, and EDWARD I. GORDON, eds. 1979. *Types of Literature*. Lexington, MA: Ginn and Company.

BENTON, MICHAEL. 2000. "Canons Ancient and Modern: The Texts We Teach." *Educational Review* 52(November): 269–275.

———. 1985. *Teaching Literature: Nine to Fourteen*. London: Oxford University Press.

BERG, TEMMA F. 2000. "Reader, Readers, Reading." *Reader: Essays in Reader-Oriented Theory, Criticism, and Pedagogy* 43(Spring): 25–30.

BERGSTROM, ROBERT R. 1983. "Discovery of Meaning: Development of Formal Thought in the Teaching of Literature." *College English* 45(December): 745–755.

BERKOWITZ, LEONARD. 1974. "Opening Speech to the Media Violence Symposium'" in *Report from a Media Violence Symposium in Stockholm, April 25th, 1974*. Stockholm, Sweden. University of Stockholm.

BERNSTEIN, ABRAHAM. 1961. *Teaching English in High School*. New York: Random House.

BETTELHEIM, BRUNO. 1976. *The Uses of Enchantment: The Meaning and Importance of Fairy Tales*. New York: Knopf.

BLAIR, LINDA. "Developing Students Voices with Multicultural Literature." *English Journal* 80(December 1991): 24–28.

BLAKE, BRETT ELIZABETH. 1998. "'Critical' Reader Response in an Urban Classroom: Creating Cultural Texts to Engage Diverse Readers." *Theory into Practice* 37(Summer): 238–243.

BLAKE, ROBERT W., ed. 1989. *Reading, Writing and Interpreting Literature: Pedagogy, Positions and Research.* Brockport, NY: New York State English Council.

BLAKE, ROBERT W., ed. 1990. *Whole Language: Explorations and Applications.* Brockport, NY: New York State English Council.

BLAKE, ROBERT W., and ANNA LUNN. 1986. "Responding to Poetry: High School Students Read Poetry." *English Journal* 75(February): 68-73.

BLAU, SHERIDAN D. 2003. *The Literature Workshop.* Portsmouth, NH: Heinemann.

BLEICH, DAVID. 1971. "Bases of Learning from Literature." *College English* 33(October): 32–45.

———. 2000. "The Changing Reader." *Reader: Essays in Reader-Oriented Theory, Criticism, and Pedagogy* 43(Spring): 31–32.

———. 1995. "Collaboration and the Pedagogy of Disclosure." *College English* 57(January): 43.

———. 1969. "Emotional Origins of Literary Meaning." *College English* 31(October): 30–40.

———. 1975. *Readings and Feelings: An Introduction to Subjective Criticism.* Urbana, IL: National Council of Teachers of English.

———. 1975. "The Subjective Character of Critical Interpretation." *College English* 36(March): 739–755.

———. 1978. *Subjective Criticism.* Baltimore, MD: Johns Hopkins University Press.

———. 1976. "The Subjective Paradigm in Science Psychology and Criticism." *New Literary History* 7(Winter): 313–334.

BLODGETT, E. D., BARBARA BELYEA, ESTELLE DANSEREAU, and CALGARY INSTITUTE FOR THE HUMANITIES. 1984. *Driving Home : A Dialogue between Writers and Readers: Essays.* Waterloo, Ontario, Canada: Wilfrid Laurier University Press for the Calgary Institute for the Humanities.

BLOOM, BENJAMIN S., J. THOMAS HASTINGS, and GEORGE F. MADAUS, eds. 1971. *Handbook on Formative and Summative Evaluation of Student Learning.* New York: McGraw-Hill Book Company.

BLOOM, HAROLD, and OTHERS. 1979. *Deconstruction and Criticism.* New York: Continuum.

BOTTOMS, DAVID. 1983. "Sign for My Father, Who Stressed the Bunt," in David Bottoms, *In a U-Haul North of Damascus.* New York: William Morrow.

BLUNT, JEAN. 1977. "Response to Reading: How Some Young Readers Describe the Process." *English in Education* 11: 32–41.

BOMER, RANDY. 1995. *Time for Meaning: Crafting Literate Lives in Middle and High School.* Portsmouth, NH: Heinemann.

———. 1998. "Transactional Heat and Light: More Explicit Literacy Learning." *Language Arts* 76(September): 11.

BOND, TERESA FLUTH. 2001. "Giving Them Free Rein: Connections in Student-Led Book Groups." *Reading Teacher* 54(March): 574–585.

BOOTH, WAYNE C. 1988. *The Vocation of a Teacher.* Chicago, IL: University of Chicago Press.

BORTOLUSSI, MARISA, and PETER DIXON. 1996. "The Effects of Formal Training on Literary Reception." *Poetics: Journal of Empirical Research on Culture, the Media and the Arts* 23(May): 471–487.

———. 2003. *Psychonarratology: Foundations for the Empirical Study of Literary Response.* New York: Cambridge University Press.

BOYD, FENICE B. 2002. "Conditions, Concessions, and the Many Tender Mercies of Learning through Multicultural Literature." *Reading Research and Instruction* 42(Fall): 58.

BOYER, JAY. 1985. "Technology and the Future of Entertainment in America: A Calculus for Poets." *English Journal* 74(November): 35–45.

BOYLE, PRISCILLA K. 2000. "In Praise of Reader-Response: Validating Student Voices in the Literature Classroom." *Teaching English in the Two-Year College* 27(March): 315–319.

BRACHER, MARK. 1990. "Ideology and Audience Response to Death in Keats's 'to Autumn'." *Studies in Romanticism* 29(Winter): 633.

BRADFORD, KENNETH. 1986. "To Be or Not to Be: Issues on Changes in Literature Anthologies." *English Journal* 75(October): 52–56.

BRANNON, LIL, and C. H. KNOBLAUCH. 1982. "On Students' Rights to Their Own Texts: A Model of Teacher Response." *Research in the Teaching of English* 33(May): 157-166.

BREWBAKER, JAMES M. 1992. "Because a Book Can't Have Smells, Sound, Light, 'the Book Needs You'—*The Winter Room* by Gary Paulsen." *English Journal* 81(February): 87.

BRITTON, JAMES. 1983. "A Quiet Form of Research." *English Journal* 72(April): 89–92.

BROWN, BILL, and OTHERS. 1986. "The Censoring of 'The Lottery'." *English Journal* 75(February): 64–67.

BROWN, DONNA M. 2003. "Fundamentals of Literature: Teaching High School Students with Special Needs." *English Journal* 92(March): 42–46.

BROWN, THOMAS MARY GALLAGHER, and ROSEMARY TURNER. 1975. *Teaching Secondary English: Alternative Approaches.* Columbus, OH: Charles E. Merrill.

BROZO, WILLIAM G. 2002. *To Be a Boy, to Be a Reader: Engaging Teen and Preteen Boys in Active Literacy.* Newark, DE: International Reading Association.

BRUCE, HEATHER E. 2003. "Engaging Adolescent Readers-the Value of Contemporary Literary Theories." *English Journal* 92(July): 90.

BRUNER, JEROME. 1990. *Acts of Meaning.* Cambridge, MA: Harvard University Press.

———. 1986. *Actual Minds, Possible Worlds.* Cambridge, MA: Harvard University Press.

BRUSHWOOD, JOHN S. 1992. "Writerly Novels/Readerly Responses." *Latin American Literary Review* 20(July): 23.

BURKE, KENNETH. 1957. *The Philosophy of Literary Form.* New York: Vintage.

BURTON, DWIGHT L. 1970. *Literature Study in the High Schools.* Third Ed. New York: Holt, Rinehart & Winston.

———. 1980. "Literature Study Today: An Attempt to Be Objective." *English Journal* 69(May): 30–33.

———. 1974. "Well, Where Are We in Teaching Literature?" *English Journal* 63(February): 28–33.

BURTON, DWIGHT L., and OTHERS. 1975. *Teaching English Today.* Boston, MA: Houghton Mifflin.

BUSHMAN, JOHN. 2001. *Using Young Adult Literature in the English Classroom.* Upper Saddle River, NJ: Merrill Prentice Hall.

CÆALINESCU, MATEI. 1993. *Rereading.* New Haven. CT: Yale University Press.

CAIN, WILLIAM E. 1984. *The Crisis in Criticism: Theory, Literature, and Reform in English Studies.* Baltimore, MD: Johns Hopkins University-Press.

CAPLAN, NIGEL A. 2004. "Revisiting the Diary: Rereading Anne Frank's Rewriting." *The Lion and the Unicorn* 28(January): 77.

CARAHER, BRIAN G. 1998. "Beyond Poststructuralism: The Speculations of Theory and the Experience of Reading." *Criticism* 40(Summer): 455.

CAREY-WEBB, ALLEN. 2001. *Literature and Lives : A Response-Based, Cultural Studies Approach to Teaching English.* Urbana, IL: National Council of Teachers of English.

CARICO, KATHLEEN M. 2001. "Negotiating Meaning in Classroom Literature Discussions." *Journal of Adolescent & Adult Literacy* 44(March): 510-518.

Carlsen, G. Robert. 1980. *Books and the Teenage Reader: A Guide for Teachers, Librarians and Parents.* Second Revised Ed. New York: Harper & Row.

CARLSEN, G. ROBERT and JAMES CROW, 1967. "Project English Curriculum Centers," *English Journal,* 56, No. 7(October), pp. 991–992.

CARPENTER, CAROLE H. 1996. "Enlisting Children's Literature in the Goals of Multiculturalism." *Mosaic : a Journal for the Interdisciplinary Study of Literature* 29(September): 53.

CARROLL, PAMELA S. 1994. "Metamorphosis: One Teacher's Change/One Class' Reaction." *English Journal* 83(October): 22.

———. 1997. "Today's Teens, Their Problems, and Their Literature: Revisiting G. Robert Carlsen's Books and the Teenage Reader Thirty Years Later." *English Journal* 86(March): 25–34.

———, ed. 1999. *Using Literature to Help Troubled Teens Cope with Societal Issues.* Westport, CT: Greenwood Press.

CARTER, BETTY. 1994. *Best Books for Young Adults: The Selections, the History, the Romance.* Chicago, IL: American Library Association.

CARTER, BETTY, SALLY ESTES, and LINDA WADDLE, 2000, *Best Books for Young Adults.* Chicago, IL: American Library Association.

CASTAGNA, EDWIN. 1982. *Caught in the Act: The Decisive Reading of Some Notable Men and Women and Its Influence on Their Actions and Attitudes.* Metuchen, NJ: Scarecrow Press.

CAWELTI, JOHN G. 1976. *Adventure, Mystery, and Romance.* Chicago, IL: University of Chicago Press.

CERRA, KATHIE KRIEGER, SUSAN WATTS-TAFFE, and SUSAN ROSE. 1997. "Fostering Reader Response and Developing Comprehension Strategies in Deaf and Hard of Hearing Children." *American Annals of the Deaf* 142(December): 379.

CHAMPAGNE, ROLAND A. 1984. *Literary History in the Wake of Roland Barthes: Re-Defining the Myths of Reading.* Birmingham, AL: Summa Publications.

CHANDLER, KELLY. 1999. "Reading Relationships: Parents, Adolescents, and Popular Fiction by Stephen King." *Journal of Adolescent & Adult Literacy* 43(November): 228–240.

CHAPLIN, M.T. 1982. "Rosenblatt Revisited: The Transaction between Reader and Text." *Journal of Reading* 26: 150–154.

CHASE, NANCY D., and CYNTHIA R. HYND. 1987. "Reader Response: An Alternative Way to Teach Students to Think About Text." *Journal of Reading* 30(March): 530–540.

CHEU, HOI. 2001. "There Is No Class in This Text: From Reader-Response to Bibliotherapy." *Textual Studies in Canada* (June): 37.

CHEW, CHARLES R., Roseanne Y. DeFabio, and Patricia Honsbury. 1986. *Reader Response in the Classroom.* New York: New York State English Council.

CHINN, CLARK A, RICHARD C ANDERSON, and MARTHA A WAGGONER. 2001. "Patterns of Discourse in Two Kinds of Literature Discussion." *Reading Research Quarterly* 36(October-December): 378.

CHRISTIAN, L. K. 1984. *Becoming a Woman through Romance: Adolescent Novels and the Ideology of Femininity, Dissertation Abstracts International.* 45, 05A, Ann Arbor, Michigan.

CHRISTIAN-SMITH, L. U. "Gender, Popular Culture, and Curriculum: Adolescent Romance Novels as Gender Text." *Curriculum Inquiry* 17: 365–406.

CHU, MEEI-LING LIAW. 1995. "Reader Response to Interactive Computer Books: Examining Literary Responses in a Non-Traditional Reading Setting." *Reading Research and Instruction* 34(June): 352–366.

CHURCH, G.W., and I. THOMPSON. 1997. "The Significance of Louise Rosenblatt on the Field of Teaching Literature: Interpreting Textual Data in Writing Research." *Inquiry* 1: 71–77.

CISNEROS, SANDRA. 1992. "Eleven," *Woman Hollering Creek and Other Stories.* New York: Vintage.

CLIFFORD, JOHN, ed. 1990. *The Experience of Reading: Louise Rosenblatt and Reader-Response Theory.* Portsmouth, NH: Heinemann-Boynton/Cook.

———. 1986. "A Response Pedagogy for Noncanonical Literature." *Reader, Essays in Reader-Oriented Theory, Criticism, and Pedagogy* 37(Spring): 48–61.

———. 1979. "Transactional Teaching and the Literary Experience." *English Journal* 68(November): 36-39.

CLIFFORD, JOHN, and JOHN SCHILB, eds. 1994. *Writing Theory and Critical Theory, Research and Scholarship in Composition,* Third Edition. New York: Modern Language Association of America.

CLINE, RUTH, and WILLIAM McBRIDE. 1983. *A Guide to Literature for Young Adults.* Glenview, IL: Scott, Foresman.

CLOSE, ELIZABETH EGAN. "Literature Discussion: A Classroom Environment for Thinking and Sharing." *English Journal* 81(September 1992): 65–71.

COEN, STANLEY J. 1994. *Between Author and Reader: A Psychoanalytic Approach to Writing and Reading, Psychoanalysis and Culture.* New York: Columbia University Press.

COLES, ROBERT. 1989. *The Call of Stories: Teaching and the Moral Imagination.* Boston. MA: Houghton Mifflin.

COMMEYRAS, MICHELLE, and GEORGIANA SUMNER. 1996. *Student-Posed Questions for Literature-Based Discussion.* Washington, DC: National Reading Research Center, U.S. Dept. of Education, Office of Educational Research and Improvement: [For sale by the U.S. G.P.O., Supt. of Docs.].

CONNELL, JEANNE M. 2000. "Aesthetic Experiences in the School Curriculum: Assessing the Value of Rosenblatt's Transactional Theory." *Journal of Aesthetic Education* 34: 27–35.

———. 2001. "Restoring Aesthetic Experiences in the School Curriculum: The Legacy of Rosenblatt's Transactional Theory from Literature as Exploration." *Educational Foundations* 15: 39–56.

CONNOLLY, BILL, and MICHAEL W. SMITH. 2002. "Teachers and Students Talk About Talk: Class Discussion and the Way It Should Be." *Journal of Adolescent & Adult Literacy* 46(September): 16–26.

CONNOR, JULIA JOHNSON. 2003. "'The Textbooks Never Said Anything About...' Adolescents Respond to the Middle Passage: White Ships/Black Cargo." *Journal of Adolescent & Adult Literacy* 47(November): 240.

COOPER, CHARLES R. 1972. *Measuring Growth in Appreciation of Literature.* Newark, DE: International Reading Association.

———, ed. 1972. *Measuring Growth in Appreciation of Literature.* Lexington, MA: Ginn and Company.

———, ed. 1984. *Researching Response to Literature and the Teaching of Literature: Points of Departure.* Norwood, NJ: Ablex Publishing Corporation.

COOPER, CHARLES R., and ALAN PURVES. 1973. *A Guide to Evaluation for Responding.* Lexington, MA: Ginn.

COOPER, CHARLES R., ed. 1981. *The Nature and Measurement of Competency in English.* 1981 Urbana, IL: National Council of Teachers of English.

CORCORAN, BILL, and EMRYS EVANS. 1987. *Readers, Texts, Teachers.* Upper Montclair, NJ: Boynton/Cook.

COX, CAROLE, and JOYCE E. MANY. "Toward an Understanding of the Aesthetic Response to Literature." *Language Arts* 69(January 1992): 28–35.

COX, MITCH. 1988. "Revising the Literature Curriculum for a Pluralist Society." *English Journal* 77(October): 30.

CRAGO, H. 1982. "The Reader in the Reader: An Experiment in Personal Responses and Literary Criticism." *Signal* 39.

CRANNY-FRANCIS, ANNE. 1992. *Engendered Fiction: Analysing Gender in the Production and Reception of Texts, Communication and Culture Series.* Kensington, NSW, Australia and Portland, OR: NSWU Press.

CREBER, J. W. PATRICK. 1965. *Sense and Sensitivity: The Philosophy and Practice of English Teaching.* London: University of London Press.

CRONE-BLEVINS, DEBORAH E. 2002. "The Art of Response." *English Journal* 91(July): 93–98.

CULLER, JONATHAN. 1981. *The Pursuit of Signs: Semiotics, Literature, Deconstruction.* Ithaca, NY: Cornell University Press.

———. 1975. *Structuralist Poetics: Structuralism, Linguistics, and the Study of Literature.* Ithaca, NY: Cornell University Press.

CULP, MARY BETH. 1985. "Literature's Influence on Young Adult Attitudes Values and Behavior , 1975–1984." *English Journal* 74(December): 31–35.

CURRIE, DAWN. 1999. *Girl Talk: Adolescent Magazines and Their Readers.* Toronto; Buffalo, NY: University of Toronto Press.

CUSSLER, ELIZABETH B. "Art in the Literature Class." *English Journal* 78(March 1989): 24–27.

DANIELS, HARVEY. 2002. "Expository Text in Literature Circles." *Voices from the Middle* 9(May): 7–14.

———. 2002. *Literature Circles: Voice and Choice in Book Clubs and Reading Groups.* Portland, ME: Stenhouse Publishers; Markham, Ont, and Pembroke Publishers.

———. 1994. "Pacesetter English: Let Them Eat Standards." *English Journal* 83(November): 44.

DARLINGTON, SONYA. 1994. "Reader-Response: A Visual and Aesthetic Experience." *Reader: Essays in Reader-Oriented Theory, Criticism, and Pedagogy* 31(Spring): 11–26.

DAVIDSON, CATHY N., ed. 1989. *Reading in America: Literature & Social History.* Baltimore, MD: Johns Hopkins University Press.

DAVIS, TODD F., and KENNETH WOMACK. 2002. *Formalist Criticism and Reader-Response Theory.* Houndmills, Basingstoke, Hampshire; New York: Palgrave.

DAVIS, WALTER A. 1978. *The Act of Interpretation.* Chicago, IL: University of Chicago Press.

DE MAN, PAUL. 1978. *Allegories of Reading: Figural Language in Rousseau, Nietzsche, Rilke, and Proust.* New Haven, CT: Yale University Press.

DEBLASE, GINA. 2003. "Acknowledging Agency While Accommodating Romance: Girls Negotiating Meaning in Literacy Transactions." *Journal of Adolescent & Adult Literacy* 46(May): 624–635.

DELFATTORE, JOAN. 1992. *What Johnny Shouldn't Read: Textbook Censorship in America.* New Haven, CT: Yale University Press.

DERRIDA, JACQUES. 1974. *Of Grammatology.* Baltimore, MD: Johns Hopkins University Press.

———. 1978. *Writing and Difference.* Chicago, IL: University of Chicago Press.

DESTIGTER, TODD. 2003. "'Why Did You Teach Us This?': Becoming Unstuck from Familiar Perspectives." *English Education* 35(July): 322.

DEVINE, C. MAURY, CLAUDIA M. DISSEL, and KIM D. PARRISH, eds. 1986. *The Harvard Guide to Influential Books: 113 Distinguished Harvard Professors Discuss the Books That Have Helped to Shape Their Thinking.* New York: Harper & Row.

DIAS, PATRICK. 1987. *Making Sense of Poetry: Patterns in the Process.* Winnepeg, Canada: Canadian Council of Teachers of English.

DIAS, PATRICK, and MICHAEL HAYHOE. 1988. *Developing Response to Poetry.* Milton Keynes: Open University Press.

DICKEY, JAMES. 1974. "Interview in The Poet's Craft." *The Craft of Poetry: Interviews from the New York Quarterly.* Garden City, NY: Doubleday.

DILLARD, ANNIE. 1982. *Living by Fiction.* New York: Harper & Row.

DILLON, GEORGE L. 1978. *Languages Processing and the Reading of Literature.* Bloomington, IN: Indiana University Press.

DILWORTH, COLLETT B. 1982. "Empirical Research in the Literature Class." *English Journal* 71(March): 95–97.

———. 1977. "The Reader as Poet: A Strategy for Creative Reading." *English Journal* 66(February): 43–47.

DIONISIO, MARIE. "Responding to Literary Elements through Mini-Lessons and Dialogue Journals." *English Journal* 80(January 1991): 40–44.

DIPARDO, ANNE, and PAT SCHNACK. 2004. "Expanding the Web of Meaning: Thought and Emotion in an Intergenerational Reading and Writing Program." *Reading Research Quarterly* 39(January-March): 14.

DIRDA, MICHAEL. 2003. *An Open Book: Coming of Age in the Heartland.* New York: Norton.

DIXON, JOHN. 1967. *Growth Through English.* London: Oxford University Press.

DIXON, JOHN, and JOHN BROWN. 1987. *Response to Literature.* Winnepeg, Canada: Canadian Council of Teachers of English.

———. 1984, 1985. *Responses to Literature: What Is Being Assessed?* London: Schools Council Publications.

DONELSON, KEN. 1985. "A Brief Bibliography on Censorship." *English Journal* 74(January): 34–37.

———. 1974. "Censorship in the 1970's." *English Journal* 63(February): 47–51.

DONELSON, KEN. 1997. "'Filth' and 'Pure Filth' in Our Schools-Censorship of Classroom Books in the Last Ten Years." *English Journal* 86(February): 21–25.

DONELSON, KENNETH L., and ALLEEN PACE NILSEN. 2001. *Literature for Today's Young Adults.* Sixth Ed. New York: Addison-Wesley Longman.

DONOGHUE, DENIS. 1998. *The Practice of Reading.* New Haven, CT: Yale University Press.

DORFMAN, ARIEL. 1983. *The Empire's Old Clothes: What the Lone Ranger, Babar, and Other Innocent Heroes Do to Our Minds.* New York: Pantheon.

DOVE, GEORGE N. 1997. *The Reader and the Detective Story.* Bowling Green, OH: Bowling Green State University Popular Press.

DOYLE, ROBERT P. 2000. *Banned Books: 2000 Resource Book.* Chicago, IL: American Library Association.

DREHER, STEPHEN. 2003. "A Novel Idea: Reading Aloud in a High School English Classroom." *English Journal* 93(September): 50–53.

DRESSEL, JANICE HARTWICK. 2003. *Teaching and Learning About Multicultural Literature: Students Reading Outside Their Culture in a Middle School Classroom.* Newark, DE: International Reading Association.

DRESSMAN, MARK, and JOAN PARKER WEBSTER. 2001. "Retracing Rosenblatt: A Textual Archaeology." *Research in the Teaching of English* 36(August): 110–145.

DUKE, CHARLES R. 1977. "The Case of the Divorced Reader." *English Journal* 66(February): 33–36.

DUNN, STEPHEN. 1986. *Local Time.* New York: Quill-William Morrow.

DUNNING, STEPHEN, and ALAN B. HOWES. 1975. *Literature for Adolescents: Teaching Poems, Stories, Novels, and Plays.* Glenview, IL: Scott, Foresman.

DURANTE, ROBERT. 2001. *The Dialectic of Self and Story: Reading and Storytelling in Contemporary American Fiction.* New York: Routledge.

EAGLETON, TERRY. 1983. *Literary Theory: An Introduction.* Minneapolis, MN: University of Minnesota Press.

EBERLY, ROSA A. 2000. *Citizen Critics: Literary Public Spheres, History of Communication.* Urbana, IL: University of Illinois Press.

ECO, UMBERTO. 1994. *The Limits of Interpretation.* First Midland Book Ed. Bloomington, IN: Indiana University Press.

———. 1979. *The Role of the Reader: Explorations in the Semiotics of Texts.* Bloomington, IN: Indiana University Press.

EDWARDS, MARGARET A. 1974. *The Fair Garden and the Swarm of Beasts: The Library and the Young Adult.* New York: Hawthorn.

EEDS, MARYANN. "Grand Conversations: An Exploration of Meaning Construction in Literature Study Groups." *Research in the Teaching of English* 23(February, 1989): 4–29.

EGAWA, KATHY. 1991. "Harnessing the Power of Language: First Graders' Literature Engagement with Owl Moon." *Language Arts* 67: 582–589.

EGOFF, SHEILA, A G. T. STUBBS, and L. F. ASHLEY, eds. 1969. *Only Connect: Readings on Children's Literature.* New York: Oxford University Press.

ELKIN, DEBORAH. 1976. *Teaching Literature: Designs for Cognitive Development.* Columbus, OH: Charles E. Merrill.

ELLIS, ALBERT. 1954. *The American Sexual Tragedy.* New York: Twayne Publishers.

ELLIS, W. GEIGER. 1985. "Adolescent Literature: Changes Cycles Constancy." *English Journal* 74(March): 94–98.

———. 1987. "'What Are You Teaching?' 'Literature'." *English Journal* 76(March): 108–112.

ERICSON, BONNIE. 1997. "Making Literature Meaningful for All Students: Practice Meets Theory in Reader Response." *English Journal* 86(October): 100.

———, ed. 2001. *Teaching Reading in High School English Classes.* Urbana, IL: National Council of Teachers of English.

ERLICH, VICTOR. 1975. "Reading Conscious and Unconscious." *College English* 36(March): 766–775.

ESROCK, ELLEN J. 1994. *The Reader's Eye: Visual Imaging as Reader Response.* Baltimore, MD: Johns Hopkins University Press.

EVANS, R. 1982. "The Question About Literature." *English Journal* 71(February): 56–60.

FAGAN, EDWARD R. 1964. *Field: A Process for Teaching Literature.* University Park, PA: Pennsylvania State University Press.

FAIRBROTHER, ANNE. 1998. "Check out the Real America: Many Hued Many Tongued and Many Storied." *English Journal* 88(November): 57–61.

FARRELL, EDMUND J. 1981. "Literature in Crisis." *English Journal* 70(January): 13–18.

FARRELL, EDMUND J., and James R. Squire, eds. 1990. *Transactions with Literature: A Fifty-Year Perspective.* Urbana, IL: National Council of Teachers of English.

FAUST, MARK A. 2000. "Reconstructing Familiar Metaphors: John Dewey and Louise Rosenblatt on Literary Art as Experience." *Research in the Teaching of English* 35(August): 9–34.

———. 1992. "Ways of Reading and 'the Use of Force'." *English Journal* 81(November): 44.

FAUST, MARK A., and Nancy Glenzer. 2000. "'I Could Read Those Parts over and over': Eighth Graders Rereading to Enhance Enjoyment and Learning with Literature." *Journal of Adolescent & Adult Literacy* 44(November): 234–240.

FAVAT, ANDRE. 1977. *Child and Tale: The Origins of Interest.* Urbana, IL: National Council of Teachers of English.

FEAGIN, SUSAN L. 1996. *Reading with Feeling: The Aesthetics of Appreciation.* Ithaca, NY: Cornell University Press.

FETTERLEY, JUDITH, and NETLIBRARY INC. *The Resisting Reader a Feminist Approach to American Fiction.* Indiana University Press 1978 [cited].

FILLION, BRYANT. 1981. "Reading as Inquiry: An Approach to Literature Learning." *English Journal* 70(January): 39–44.

FINDER, MORRIS. 1985. "Five Questions for the Study of Literature." *English Journal* 74(February): 61–62.

FISH, STANLEY. 1980. *Is There a Text in This Class? The Authority of Interpretive Communities.* Cambridge, MA: Harvard University Press.

FISKE, JOHN and JOHN HARTLEY. 1978. *Reading Television.* London: Methuen.

FLOOD, JAMES, and DIANE LAPP. 1988. "A Reader-Response Approach to the Teaching of Literature." *Reading Research and Instruction* 27(Summer): 61–66.

FLYNN, ELIZABETH A. 1983. "Composing Responses to Literary Texts: A Process Approach." *College Composition and Communication* 34(October): 342–348.

———. 1999. "'Reader Response' in the Nineties." *Reader: Essays in Reader-Oriented Theory, Criticism, and Pedagogy* 41(Spring): 74–89.

FLYNN, ELIZABETH A., and Patrocinio P. Schweickart, eds. 1986. *Gender and Reading: Essays on Readers, Texts, and Contexts.* Baltimore, MD: Johns Hopkins University Press.

FOKKEMA, D.W., and ELRUD KUNNE-IBSCH. 1978. *Theories of Literature in the Twentieth Century: Structuralism, Marxism, Aesthetics of Response, Semiotics.* London: C. Hurst.

FOLTA, B. "Effects of Three Approaches to Teaching Poetry to Sixth Grade Students." *Research in the Teaching of English* 15(1981): 149–161.

FONES, DEBORAH. 2001. "Blocking Them in to Free Them to Act: Using Writing Frames to Shape Boys' Responses to Literature in the Secondary School." *English in Education* 35(Autumn): 21–31.

FOSTER, HAROLD M. 1995. "A Book, a Place, a Time: Using Young Adult Novels in a Reading Workshop." *English Journal* 84(September): 115.

———. 1997. "Embracing All but My Life by Gerda Weissmann Klein." English Journal 86(December): 56–60.

FOSTER, HAROLD M. 1999. "Reflections on the Past, Directions for the Future." *Voices From the Middle* 7(December): 4.

FOWLER, LOIS JOSEPHS, and KATHLEEN MCCORMICK. 1986. "The Expectant Reader in Theory and Practice." *English Journal* 75(October): 45–48.

FOWLER, MARY ELIZABETH. 1965. *Teaching Language, Composition, and Literature.* New York: McGraw-Hill.

FOWLER, ROGER. 1981. *Literature as Social Discourse: The Practice of Linguistic Criticism.* Bloomington, IN: Indiana University Press.

FRANK, JOHN PAUL, and ROBERT F. HOGAN. 1966. *Obscenity, the Law, and the English Teacher.* Champaign, IL: National Council of Teachers of English.

FREEDMAN, LAUREN, and HOLLY JOHNSON. 2000-2001. "Who's Protecting Whom? I Hadn't Meant to Tell You This, a Case in Point in Confronting Self-Censorship in the Choice of Young Adult Literature." *Journal of Adolescent & Adult Literacy* 44(December/January): 356–370.

FREEDMAN, SAMUEL G. 1990. *Small Victories: The Real World of a Teacher, Her Students, and Their High School.* New York: Harper and Row, Publishers.

FREUND, ELIZABETH. 1987. *The Return of the Reader: Reader Response Criticism.* London: Methuen.

FRITH, G. 1979. "Reading and Response: Some Questions and No Answers." *English in Education* 13: 30–31.

FROST, ROBERT. 1942. *A Witness Tree.* New York: Henry Holt.

FRY, D. 1985. *Children Talk About Books: Seeing Themselves as Readers.* Milton Keynes: Open University Press.

FRYE, NORTHROP. 1972. *On Teaching Literature.* New York: Harcourt Brace Jovanovich.

FUCHS, LUCY. 1987. *Serving Adolescents' Reading Interests through Young Adult Literature.* Bloomington, IN: Phi Delta Kappa Educational Foundation.

FURST, LILIAN R. 1992. *Through the Lens of the Reader: Explorations of European Narrative.* Albany, NY: State University of New York Press.

GALDA, LEE. 1982. "Assuming the Spectator Stance: An Examination of the Responses of Three Young Readers." *Research in the Teaching of English* 16(February): 1-20.

———. 1988. "Readers, Texts and Contexts: A Response-Based View of Literature in the Classroom." *New Advocate* 1(Spring): 92–102.

GALDA, LEE, and LAUREN AIMONETTE LIANG. 2003. "Literature as Experience or Looking for Facts: Stance in the Classroom." *Reading Research Quarterly* 38(April–June): 268.

GALEF, DAVID. 1998. *Second Thoughts: A Focus on Rereading.* Detroit, MI: Wayne State University Press.

GALLO, DONALD R. 1992. *Authors' Insights: Turning Teenagers into Readers and Writers.* Portsmouth, NH: Boynton/Cook.

GARDNER, HOWARD. 1973. *The Arts and Human Development.* New York: John Wiley.

GARDNER, JOHN. 1985. *The Art of Fiction: Notes on Craft for Young Writers.* New York: Vintage.

GARDNER, JOHN. 1978. *On Moral Fiction.* New York: Basic Books.

GARFIELD, BRIAN. 1980. quoted in Terry Brewster, "Best-Selling Author Believes in Taking a Quick Write," *Friends,* 37(10): 12.

GARRETT-PETTS, W. F. 1988. "Exploring an Interpretive Community: Reader Response to Canadian Prairie Literature." *College English* 50(December): 920.

GARVIN, HARRY R. 1976. *Phenomenology, Structuralism, Semiology.* Lewisburg, PA: Bucknell University Press.

GAVELEK, JAMES R., and TAFFY E. RAPHAEL. 1996. "Changing Talk About Text: New Roles for Teachers and Students." *Language Arts* 73(March): 182.

GEORGE, MARSHALL A. 2001. "What's the Big Idea? Integrating Young Adult Literature in the Middle School." *English Journal* 90(January): 74–81.

GERBNER, GEORGE and LARRY GROSS. 1976. "The Scary World of TV's Heavy Viewer," *Psychology Today,* 9(11): 44.

GERE, ANNE RUGGLES, and PETER SHAHEEN, eds. 2001. "Making American Literatures in High School and College." *Classroom Practices in Teaching English,* Vol. 31. Urbana, IL: National Council of Teachers of English.

GERRIG, RICHARD J. 1993. *Experiencing Narrative Worlds: On the Psychological Activities of Reading.* New Haven, CT: Yale University Press.

GIBSON, WALKER. 1950. "Authors, Speakers, Readers, and Mock Readers," *College English* 11(5): 265–269.

GILLES, CAROL. 1989. "Reading, Writing, and Talking: Using Literature Study Groups." *English Journal* 78(January): 38–41.

GILLES, CAROL, and JEAN DICKINSON. 2000. "Rejoining the Literacy Club: Valuing Middle-Grade Readers." *Language Arts* 77(July): 512.

GILLESPIE, JOHN THOMAS, and CORINNE J. NADEN. 1997. *Characters in Young Adult Literature.* Detroit, MI: Gale Research.

GILLIS, CANDIDA. 2002. "Multiple Voices, Multiple Genres: Fiction for Young Adults." *English Journal* 92(November): 52–59.

GLASGOW, JACQUELINE N. 2002. "Radical Change in Young Adult Literature Informs the Multigenre Paper." *English Journal* 92(November): 41–51.

GLATTHORN, ALLAN A. 1977. "Censorship and the Classroom Teacher." *English Journal* 66(February): 12–14.

GLOVERSMITH, FRANK. 1984. *The Theory of Reading.* Totowa, NJ: Sussex Harvester Press.

GOODMAN, KENNETH. 1998. "Who's Afraid of Whole Language: Politics, Paradigms, Pedagogy, and the Press," in *Defense of Good Teaching*. York, MA: Stenhouse Publishers).

GORDON, EDWARD J. 1965. *Writing and Literature in the Secondary School*. New York: Holt, Rinehart & Winston.

GORDON, EDWARD J., and EDWARD S. NOYES, eds. 1960. *Essays on the Teaching of English: Reports of the Yale Conferences on the Teaching of English*. New York: Appleton-Century-Crofts.

GORDON, HEATHER G. 2000. "Using a Reader Response Journal." *Teaching English in the Two-Year College* 28(September): 41–43.

GORGA CUKRAS, GRACE-ANN. 2000. "Empowering Students through Literature." *Adult Basic Education* 10(Spring): 21–30.

GOULD, CHRISTOPHER, and KATHLEEN GOULD. 1986. "College Anthologies of Readings and Assumptions About Literacy." *College Composition and Communication* 37(May): 204–211.

GOULD, JAMES A. and JOHN J. IORIO, eds. 1972. *Love, Sex, and Identity*. San Francisco: Boyd and Fraser.

GRAHAM, JOAN, and ROBERT E. PROBST. "Eliciting Response to Literature." *Kentucky English Bulletin* 32(Fall 1982): 30–46.

GRAHAM, JOAN WYNNE. 1985. *The Effects of Reading Ethnic Literature on the Attitudes of Adolescents*. Atlanta, GA: Georgia State University.

GREENBLATT, STEPHEN J. 1981. *Allegory and Representation*. Baltimore, MD: Johns Hopkins University Press.

GRIFFITH, PETER. 1987. *Literary Theory and English Teaching*. London: Open University Press.

GRUGEON, ELIZABETH, and PETER WALDEN. 1978. *Literature and Learning*. London: Ward Lock.

GUICE, SHERRY. 2000. "The Second Time Around: Returning to the Classroom after Ten Years." *English Journal* 89(March): 122.

GUISE, CAROLYN, and TERESA PENPRASE. 1974. "Psychological Literature: Human Behavior in the Classroom." *English Journal* 63(February): 72–75.

GULESIAN, MARK, and STEPHANIE MCCONACHIE. 1985. "Personal Response to Literature in Anthologies." *English Journal* 74(January): 86–88.

GUTH, HANS P. 1973. English for a New Generation. New York: McGraw-Hill.

———. 1964. *English Today and Tomorrow: A Guide for Teachers of English*. Englewood Cliffs, NJ: Prentice-Hall.

GUTH, HANS P., ROBERT BOYNTON, and JAMES SQUIRE. "A Symposium/the Textbook Gap: A Teacher-Author-Publisher Dialogue." *English Journal* 78(October 1989): 14–21.

HAMEL, FRED L. 2003. "Teacher Understanding of Student Understanding: Revising the Gap between Teacher Conceptions and Students' Ways with Literature." *Research in the Teaching of English* 38(August): 49–84.

HAMILTON, GREG. 2003. "English in the City." *English Journal* 93(September): 100–104.

————. 2002. "Mapping a History of Adolescence and Literature for Adolescents." *ALAN Review* 29(Winter): 57–62.

HAMILTON, JOHN MAXWELL. 2000. *Casanova Was a Book Lover: And Other Naked Truths and Provocative Curiosities About the Writing, Selling, and Reading of Books.* Baton Rouge, LA: Louisiana State University Press.

HANCOCK, MARJORIE R. 2000. *A Celebration of Literature and Response: Children, Books, and Teachers in K-8 Classrooms.* Upper Saddle River, NJ: Merrill.

————. "Literature Response Journals: Insights Beyond the Printed Page." Language Arts 69(January 1992): 36–43.

HANSSON, GUNNAR. "Some Types of Research on Response to Literature." *Research in the Teaching of English* 7(Fall, 1973): 260–284.

HARARI, JOSUE, ed. 1979. *Textual Strategies: Perspectives in Post-Structuralist Criticism.* Ithaca: Cornell University Press.

HARDING, D. W. 1968. "Practice at Liking: A Study in Experimental Aesthetics." *British Psychological Society Bulletin* 21: 310.

————. "Psychological Processes in the Reading of Fiction." *British Journal of Aesthetics* 20(1962): 133–147.

HARMS, JEANNE MCLAIN. 1982. *Comprehension and Literature.* Dubuque, Iowa: Kendall/Hunt Publishing Co.

HAROUTUNIAN-GORDON, SOPHIE. 1991. *Turning the Soul: Teaching through Conversation in the High School.* Chicago, IL: University of Chicago Press.

HARPER, H. 1990. "Theory into Practice: Literacy and the State: A Comparison of Hirsch, Rosenblatt and Giroux." *English Quarterly* 22: 169–175.

HARRIS, WENDELL V. 1986. "Toward an Ecological Criticism: Contextual Versus Unconditioned Literary Theory." *College English* 48(February): 116–131.

HARTMAN, GEOFFREY H. 1980. *Criticism in the Wilderness.* New Haven, CT: Yale University Press.

————. 1975. *The Fate of Reading.* Chicago, IL: University of Chicago Press.

HAUPT, HANNAH BEATE. 1970. *Man in the Fictional Mode,* Book 3, ed.(Evanston, IL: McDougal, Littell & Co.).

HAYHOE, MICHAEL, and STEPHEN PARKER, eds. 1990. *Reading and Response.* Milton Keynes: Open University Press.

HAYHOE, MIKE, and S. PARKER. 1984. *Working with Fiction.* London: Edward Arnold.

HAZARD, PAUL. 1983. *Books, Children, and Men.* Boston, MA: Horn Book.

HEIKINEN, DENISE. 1998. "Selected Bibliography of Books on Reading Published in the Past Five Years." *Reader: Essays in Reader-Oriented Theory, Criticism, and Pedagogy* 40(Fall): 79–84.

HENLY, CAROLYN P. 1993. "Reader-Response Theory as Antidote to Controversy: Teaching the Bluest Eye." *English Journal* 82(March): 14.

HENNEBERG, SUSAN. 1996. "Dimensions of Failure in Reader Response." *English Journal* 85(March): 21.

HENRY, GEORGE. 1974. *Teaching Reading as Concept Development: Emphasis on Affective Thinking.* Newark, DE: International Reading Association.

HENRY, JUDITH. 2000. *Overheard at the Bookstore.* New York: Universe.

HEPLER, SUSAN INGRID, and MARIA SALVADORE. 2003. *Books Your Kids Will Talk About!* Washington, DC: National Education Association.

HERALD, DIANA TIXIER. 2003. *Teen Genreflecting: A Guide to Reading Interests.* Westport, CT: Libraries Unlimited.

HERNADI, PAUL, ed. 1982. *The Horizon of Literature.* Lincoln, NE: University of Nebraska Press.

———. 1981. *What Is Criticism?* Bloomington, IN: Indiana University Press.

———. 1978. *What Is Literature?* Bloomington, IN: Indiana University Press.

HERZ, SARAH. 1996. *From Hinton to Hamlet: Building Bridges between Young Adult Literature and the Classics.* Westport, CT: Greenwood Press.

HERZ, SARAH K., and DONALD R. GALLO. 1996. *From Hinton to Hamlet: Building Bridges between Young Adult Literature and the Classics.* Westport, CT: Greenwood Press.

HEYD, SUZANNE H, and MARY H SAWYER. 1997. "Educational Reform: A Drama in Three Acts." *English Journal* 86(September): 43.

HICKMAN, JANE. 1980. "Children's Response to Literature: What Happens in the Classroom." *Language Arts* 57: 524–529.

———. 1981. "A New Perspective on Response to Literature: Research in an Elementary School Setting." *Research in the Teaching of English* 15: 343–354.

HILL, MARGARET H. 2002. "Stolen Lives/Found Opportunities." *Voices From the Middle* 10: 35.

HILLOCKS, JR., GEORGE. 1980. "Toward a Hierarchy of Skills in the Comprehension of Literature." *English Journal* 69(March): 54–59.

HILLOCKS, JR., GEORGE, and OTHERS. 1971. *The Dynamics of English Instruction: Grades Seven-Twelve.* New York: Random House.

HINES, MARY BETH, and DEBORAH APPLEMAN. 2000. "Multiple Ways of Knowing in Literature Classrooms." *English Education* 32(January): 141.

HIPPLE, THEODORE W. 1973. *Readings for Teaching English in Secondary Schools.* New York: Macmillan.

———. 1973. *Teaching English in Secondary Schools.* New York: Macmillan.

HIRVELA, ALAN. 1996. "Reader-Response Theory and ELT." *ELT Journal* 50(April): 127–134.

HOETKER, JAMES. 1982. "A Theory of Talking About Theories of Reading." *College English* 44(February): 175–181.

HOLBROOK, DAVID, ed. 1967. *English for Maturity: English in the Secondary School.* Second Ed. London: Cambridge University Press.

———. 1968. *English for the Rejected: Training Literacy in the Lower Streams of the Secondary School.* London: Cambridge University Press.

———. 1967. *The Exploring Word: Creative Disciplines in the Education of Teachers of English.* London: Cambridge University Press.

HOLLAND, NORMAN N. 1975. *5 Readers Reading.* New Haven, CT: Yale University Press.

———. 1968. *The Dynamics of Literary Response.* New York: Oxford University Press.

————. 1973. *Poems in Persons: An Introduction to the Psychoanalysis of Literature*. New York: Norton.

————. 1994. "Reader-Response Already Is Cognitive Criticism." *Stanford Humanities* Review 4(Spring): 65-66.

————. 1998. "Reader-Response Criticism." *International Journal of Psycho-Analysis* 79(December): 1203–1211.

————. 1999. "The Story of a Psychoanalytic Critic." *American Imago* 56 (Fall): 245.

HOLLAND, NORMAN N. 1976. "Transactive Criticism: Re-Creation through Identity." *Criticism* 18(Fall): 334-352.

————. 1977. "Transactive Teaching: Cordelia's Death." *College English* 39(November): 276–285.

————. 1975. "Unity Identity Text Self." *PMLA* 90(October): 813–822.

————. 2002. "Where Is a Text? A Neurological View." *New Literary History* 33(Winter): 21.

HOLLAND, NORMAN N., and MURRAY SCHWARTZ. 1975. "The Delphi Seminar." *College English* 36(March): 789-800.

HOLLEY, PAM SPENCER. 1994. *What Do Young Adults Read Next?: A Reader's Guide to Fiction for Young Adults*. Detroit, MI: Gale Research.

HOLT, JANICE, and BARBARA HALLIWILL BELL. 2000. "Good Books, Good Talk, Good Readers." *Primary Voices K–6* 9(August): 3.

HOLUB, ROBERT C. 1992. *Crossing Borders: Reception Theory, Poststructuralism, Deconstruction*. Madison, WI: University of Wisconsin Press.

————. 1984. *Reception Theory: A Critical Introduction*. London ; New York: Methuen.

HOOK, J. N. 1997. "The Underlying Purpose in Teaching English." *English Journal* 86(February): 13.

HOOK, J. N., and WILLIAM H. EVANS. 1982. *The Teaching of High School* English. Fifth Ed. *New York: John Wiley*.

HORNER, W. B. 1983. *Composition and Literature: Bridging the Gap*. Chicago, IL: University of Chicago Press.

HOSIC, JAMES F. ed., 1917. "Reorganization of English in Secondary Schools," in *United States Bureau of Education Bulletin No. 2*(U. S. Government Printing Office)

HOWARD, JUDITH A., and Carolyn Allen. 1989. "Making Meaning: Revealing Attributions through Analyses of Readers' Responses." *Social Psychology Quarterly* 52(December): 280.

HOWELL, SUZANNE. 1977. "Unlocking the Box: An Experiment in Literary Response." *English Journal* 66(February): 37–42.

HUGHES, TED. 1960. *New and Selected Poems,* New York: Harper & Row.

HUNSBERGER, MARGARET, and GEORGE DONALD LABERCANE. 2002. *Making Meaning in the Response-Based Classroom*. Boston, MA: Allyn and Bacon

HUNT, RUSSELL. 2000. "Reading Reader, Reading Readers." *Reader: Essays in Reader-Oriented Theory, Criticism, and Pedagogy* 43(Spring): 47–51.

HUNT, RUSSELL A. 1982. "Toward a Process-Intervention Model in Literature Teaching." *College English* 44(April): 345–357.

HUNT, RUSSELL A., and D. Vipond. "Crash-Testing a Transactional Model of Literary Learning." *Reader* 14: 23–39.

HUTCHINSON, JAMIE, ed. 1996. *Teaching Literature in Middle School: Fiction, Standards Consensus Series.* Urbana, IL: National Council of Teachers of English.

HUTCHISON, LAURA. 1993. "Homelessness and Reader-Response: Writing with a Social Consciousness." *English Journal* 82(February): 66.

HYNDS, SUSAN. 1989. "Bringing Life to Literature and Literature to Life: Social Constructs and Contexts of Four Adolescent Readers." *Research in the Teaching of English* 23: 30–61.

HYNDS, SUSAN D. 1985. "Interpersonal Cognitive Complexity and the Literary Response Processes of Adolescent Readers." *Research in the Teaching of English* 19(December): 386–402.

HYNDS, SUSAN D., DEBORAH APPLEMAN, and RUTH VINZ. 1997. "Walking Our Talk: Between Response and Responsibility in the Literature Classroom/Response—(Re)Membering Others and Ourselves." *English Education* 29(December): 272.

INGARDEN, ROMAN. 1973. *The Cognition of the Literary Work of Art.* Evanston, IL: Northwestern University Press.

———. 1973. *The Literary Work of Art: An Investigation on the Borderlines of Ontology, Logic, and the Theory of Literature.* Evanston, IL: Northwestern University Press.

ISER, WOLFGANG. 1978. *The Act of Reading: A Theory of Aesthetic Response.* Baltimore, MD: Johns Hopkins University Press.

———. 1974. *The Implied Reader: Patterns of Communication in Prose Fiction from Bunyan to Beckett.* Baltimore, MD: Johns Hopkins University Press.

———. 1972. "The Reading Process: A Phenomenological Approach," *New Literary History,* 3(2): 280.

JACKSON, D. 1980. "First Encounters: The Importance of Initial Responses to Literature." *Children's Literature in Education* 11: 149–160.

JACKSON, H. J. 2001. *Marginalia: Readers Writing in Books.* New Haven, CT: Yale University Press.

JACOBSEN, MARY. 1982. "Looking for Literary Space: The Willing Suspension of Disbelief Re-Visited." *Research in the Teaching of English* 16(February): 21–38.

JAGO, CAROL. 2002. *Sandra Cisneros in the Classroom: 'Do Not Forget to Reach,' the NCTE High School Literature Series.* Urbana, IL: National Council of Teachers of English.

———. 2002. "Standards in California: A Magical Realist View." *Voices From the Middle* 10 (September): 27.

JAMESON, FREDRIC. 1981. *The Political Unconscious: Narrative as a Socially Symbolic Act.* Ithaca, NY: Cornell University Press.

JARRELL, RANDALL. 1969. *The Complete Poems.* New York: Farrar, Straus & Giroux.

JAUSS, HANS ROBERT. 1982. *Aesthetic Experience and Literary Hermeneutics.* Minneapolis, MN: University of Minnesota Press.

———. 1982. *Toward an Aesthetic of Reception.* Minneapolis, MN: University of Minnesota Press.

JENKINSON, EDWARD B. 1979. *Censors in the Classroom: The Mind Benders.* Carbondale, IL: Southern Illinois University Press.

———. 1985. "Protecting Holden Caulfield and His Friends from the Censors." *English Journal* 74(January): 2633.

JENKINSON, EDWARD B., and PHILIP B. DAGHLIAN. 1968. *Teaching Literature in Grades Ten through Twelve.* Bloomington, IN: Indiana University Press.

JENKINSON, EDWARD B., and JANE STOUDER HAWLEY. 1967. *On Teaching Literature: Essays for Secondary School Teachers.* Bloomington, IN: Indiana University Press.

JENKINSON, EDWARD B., and JANE STOUDER HAWLEY. 1967. *Teaching Literature in Grades Seven through Nine.* Bloomington, IN: Indiana University Press.

JENSEN, MARGARET M. 2002. *The Open Book: Creative Misreading in the Works of Selected Modern Writers.* 1st Ed. New York: Palgrave.

JOBE, LINDA G, and CAROL A POPE. 2002. "The English Methods Class Matters: Professor D and the Student Teachers." *Reading Research and Instruction* 42(Fall): 1.

JOHANNESSEN, LARRY R. 2001. "Enhancing Response to Literature through character Analysis." *Clearing House* 74(January-February): 145–150.

———. 2003. "Strategies for Initiating Authentic Discussion." *English Journal* 93(September): 73–79.

JOHNSTON, ALLAN. 2001. "Reader Response and Its Discontents." In *Proceedings of the Midwest Philosophy of Education Society, 1999–2000,* edited by M. A. Oliker. Chicago: Midwest Philosophy of Education Society, 55–64.

JONES, DONALD. *Medical Aid and Other Poems* (Lincoln, NE: University of Nebraska Press, 1967)

JUDY, STEPHEN N. 1980. *The Abcs of Literacy: A Guide for Parents and Educators.* New York: Oxford University Press.

———. 1981. *Explorations in the Teaching of English. Second Ed.* New York: Harper & Row.

———. 1979. *Teaching English: Reflections on the State of the Art.* Rochelle Park, NJ: Hayden.

JUDY, STEPHEN N., and SUSAN J. JUDY. 1979. *The English Teacher's Handbook: Ideas and Resources for Teaching English.* Cambridge, MA: Winthrop.

KAMPF, LOUIS, and PAUL LAUTER, eds. 1970. *The Politics of Literature: Dissenting Essays on the Teaching of English.* New York: Vintage.

KAROLIDES, NICHOLAS J. 1997. *Reader Response in Elementary Classrooms: Quest and Discovery.* Mahwah, NJ: L. Erlbaum Associates, Publishers.

———. 1992. *Reader Response in the Classroom: Evoking and Interpreting Meaning in Literature.* New York: Longman.

———. 1999. "Theory and Practice: An Interview with Louise M. Rosenblatt." *Language Arts* 77: 158–170.

KEARNS, MICHAEL. 2000. "Empirical Studies in the Reading of Narrative? Sadly, Not Yet." *Reader: Essays in Reader-Oriented Theory,* Criticism, and Pedagogy 43(Spring): 52–56.

KEATING, ANALOUISE. 2000. "Reading's Transformational Potential." *Reader: Essays in Reader-Oriented Theory, Criticism, and Pedagogy* 43(Spring): 57–59.

KELLER, BETSY. 1997. "Rereading Flaubert: Toward a Dialogue between First-and-Second-Language Literature Teaching Practices." *Publications of the Modern Language Association of America* 112(January): 56.

KELLY, PATRICIA P., and ROBERT C. SMALL, eds. 1999. *Two Decades of the Alan Review.* Urbana, IL: National Council of Teachers of English.

KENNEDY, MICHAEL. "Creating Classroom Plays from Adolescent Novels." *English Journal* 76(September 1987): 63-65.

KERSCHNER, LINDA MILANESE. 2002. "Teaching World Literature: Preparing Global Citizens." *English Journal* 91(May): 76–81.

KINTGEN, EUGENE R. 1983. *The Perception of Poetry.* Bloomington, IN: Indiana University Press.

KINTGEN, EUGENE R., and NORMAN HOLLAND. 1984. "Carlos Reads a Poem." *College English* 46(February): 478–492.

KIRBY, DANIEL, DAWN LATTA KIRBY and TOM LINER. 2003. *Inside Out: Strategies for Teaching Writing.* Third Ed. Portsmouth, NH: Heinemann.

KITZHABER, ALBERT R. "Project English and Curriculum Reform," in *Iowa English Yearbook,* 9(Fall 1964).

KNAPP, JOHN V. 2002. "Teaching Poetry Via Hei (Hypothesis-Experiment-Instruction)." *Journal of Adolescent & Adult Literacy* 45(May): 718.

KNICKERBOCKER, JOAN L., and JAMES RYCIK. 2002. "Growing into Literature: Adolescents' Literary Interpretation and Appreciation." *Journal of Adolescent & Adult Literacy* 46(November): 196–208.

KOOY, MARY, and JAN WELLS. 1996. *Reading Response Logs: Inviting Students to Explore Novels, Short Stories, Plays, Poetry, and More.* Portsmouth, NH: Heinemann.

KRUEGER, ELLEN, and MARY T. CHRISTEL. 2001. *Seeing and Believing; How to Teach Media Literacy in the English Classroom.* Portsmouth, NH: Boynton/Cook Publishers-Heinemann.

KUMIN, MAXINE. 1986. *The Long Approach.* New York: Viking Press.

KUTENPLON, DEBORAH, and ELLEN OLMSTEAD. 1996. *Young Adult Fiction by African American Writers, 1968-1993: A Critical and Annotated Guide.* New York: Garland Publishers.

LaCONTE, RONALD T. 1971. *Challenge and Change in the Teaching of English.* A. Daigon, ed. Boston, MA: Allyn and Bacon.

LAIRD, CHARLTON. 1970. *And Gladly Teche: Notes on Instructing the Natives in the Native Tongue.* Englewood Cliffs, NJ: Prentice-Hall.

LANDRY, MAUREEN, and et al. 1982. "Reality-Fantasy Discriminations in Literature: A Developmental Study." *Research in the Teaching of English* 16 (February): 39–52.

LANGER, JUDITH A. 1995. *Envisioning Literature: Literary Understanding and Literature Instruction.* New York: Teachers College Press.

———. 1998. "Thinking and Doing Literature: An Eight-Year Study." *English Journal* 87(February): 16.

LANHAM, RICHARD. 1974. *Style: An Anti-textbook.* New Haven, CT: Yale University Press.

LASKY, KATHRYN. 1996. *Memoirs of a Bookbat.* Harcourt Brace Paperback Ed. San Diego, CA: Harcourt Brace.

LEAL, DOROTHY J. 1999. "Engaging Student's Minds and Hearts: Authentic Student Assessment of Character Traits in Literature." *Journal of Adolescent & Adult Literacy* 43(November): 240–249 IL- 243 charts, 241 diagram.

LEE, HELEN C. 1973. *A Humanistic Approach to Teaching Secondary School English.* Columbus, OH: Charles E. Merrill.

LEE, VALERIE. 1986. "Responses of White Students to Ethnic Literature: One Teacher's Experience." *Reader, Essays in Reader-Oriented Theory, Criticism, and Pedagogy* (Spring): 24–33.

LEGUIN, URSULA K. 1985. "She Unnames Them," *The New Yorker,* January 21, p. 27.

LEHMAN, KIMBERLY T. 2001. "A Classic Solution to Teaching Classics to Contemporary Students." *English Journal* 91(November): 110.

LEHR, SUSAN S. 1995. *Battling Dragons: Issues and Controversy in Children's Literature.* Portsmouth, NH: Heinemann.

LEHR, SUSAN S., and DEBORAH L. THOMPSON. 2000. "The Dynamic Nature of Response: Children Reading and Responding to Maniac Magee and the Friendship." *Reading Teacher* 53(March): 480–494.

LENSKI, SUSAN DAVIS. 2001. "Intertextual Connections During Discussions About Literature." *Reading Psychology* 22(October): 313.

LENTRICCHIA, FRANK. 1980. *After the New Criticism.* Chicago, IL: University of Chicago Press.

———. 1983. *Criticism and Social Change.* Chicago, IL: University of Chicago Press.

LENZ, MILLICENT, and RAMONA MAHOOD, eds. 1980. *Young Adult Literature: Background and Criticism.* Chicago, IL: American Library Association.

LEONARD, JOHN. 1976. "And a Picture Tube Shall Lead Them," *Playboy* 23(6): 204.

LESESNE, TERI S. "Developing Lifetime Readers: Suggestions from Fifty Years of Research." *English Journal* 80 (October 1991): 61–64.

LESSER, SIMON. 1957. *Fiction and the Unconscious.* Chicago, IL: University of Chicago Press.

LEVERTOV, DENISE. 1962. *"The Secret": O Taste and See.* Norfolk, CT: New Directions Books.

LEVY, ANITA. 1999. *Reproductive Urges: Popular Novel-Reading, Sexuality, and the English Nation.* Philadelphia, PA: University of Pennsylvania Press.

LEWIS, CYNTHIA. 1999. "Teaching Literature to Adolescents." *Reading Research Quarterly* 34(January–March): 114.

LEWIS, FELICE FLANERY. 1976. *Literature, Obscenity, and Law.* Carbondale, IL: Southern Illinois University Press.

LIAW, MEEI-LING. 2001. "Exploring Literary Responses in an EFL Classroom." *Foreign Language Annals* 34(January–February): 35–45.

LIFFORD, JEAN, BARBARA BYRON, JEAN ECKBLAD, and CAROL ZIEMIAN. 2000. "Reading, Responding, Reflecting." *English Journal* 89(March): 46.

LINDBLOM, KENNETH. 2003. "Teaching English in the World." *English Journal* 93(September): 96–99.

LITTMAN, LINDA L. 2003. "'Old Dogs, New Tricks': Intersections of the Personal, the Pedagogical, the Professional." *English Journal* 93(November): 61.

LOEB, JEFF. 1998. "'a Blind Man's Ditch': Suppression of the Imagination in the Quest for Test Scores." *English Journal* 87(March): 21–27.

LOTT, SANDRA WARD, Maureen S. G. Hawkins, and Norman McMillan. 1993. *Global Perspectives on Teaching Literature: Shared Visions and Distinctive Visions.* Urbana, IL: National Council of Teachers of English.

LOWERY, RUTH McKOY. 2003. "Dreams of Possibilities: Linking Poetry to Our Lives." *ALAN Review* 30(Winter): 49–51.

LOWES, JOHN LIVINGSTON. 1964. *The Road to Xanadu; a Study in the Ways of the Imagination.* [Rev. ed.] Ed. Boston,: Houghton Mifflin.

LYONS, MARTYN. 2001. *Readers and Society in Nineteenth-Century France: Workers, Women, Peasants.* Houndmills, Basingstoke, Hampshire; New York, NY: Palgrave.

MACFARLANE-HOUSEL, DOREEN. 1984. "Literature: High School," in *Twenty Teachers,* K. Macrorie, ed. New York: Oxford University Press.

MACHOR, JAMES L., ed. 1993. *Readers in History: Nineteenth-Century American Literature and the Contexts of Response.* Baltimore, MD: Johns Hopkins University Press.

MAILLOUX, STEVEN. 1982. *Interpretive Conventions: The Reader in the Study of American Fiction.* Ithaca, NY: Cornell University Press.

MAILLOUX, STEVEN. 1977. "Reader-Response Criticism?" *Genre* 10(Fall): 413–431.

———. 1981. *Theories of Reading, Looking, and Listening.* Lewisburg, PA: Bucknell University Press.

MALLICK, DAVID, PETER MOSS, and IAN HANSEN, eds. 1980, 1982. *New Essays in the Teaching of Literature: Proceedings of the Literature Commission of the Third International Conference on the Teaching of English.* Norwood, South Australia: Australian Association for the Teaching of English.

MANDEL, BARRETT JOHN. 1970. *Literature and the English Department.* Urbana, IL: National Council of Teachers of English.

———. 1979. "Text and Context in the Teaching of Literature." *English Journal* 68(December): 40–44.

MANDEL, BARRETT J., ed. 1980. *Three Language-Arts Curriculum Models: Pre-Kindergarten through College.* Urbana, IL: National Council of Teachers of English.

MANGUEL, ALBERTO. 1996. A History of Reading. New York, NY: Viking.

MANY, JOYCE, and CAROLE COX, eds. 1992. *Reader Stance and Literary Understanding: Exploring the Theories, Research, and Practice.* Norwood, NJ: Ablex Pub. Corp.

MARHAFER, DAVID J. 1988. "Reading a Poem by Dickinson: A Psychological Approach." *English Journal* 77(January): 59.

MARSHALL, JAMES D. "The Effects of Writing on Students' Understanding of Literary Texts." *Research in the Teaching of English* 21: 30–63.

MARSHALL, JOANNE M. 2003. "Critically Thinking About Harry Potter: A Framework for Discussing Controversial Works in the English Classroom." *ALAN Review 30(Winter): 16–19.*

MARTIN, BILL. 1992. "Literature and Teaching: Getting Our Knowledge into Our Bones." *English Journal* 81(September): 56.

MARTIN, PATRICIA. 1993. "'Capture Silk': Reading Aloud Together." *English Journal* 82 (December): 16.

MARTINEZ, MIRIAM G., and LEA M. MCGEE. 2000. "Children's Literature and Reading Instruction: Past, Present, and Future." *Reading Research Quarterly* 35 (January–March): 154.

MARTÍN-RODRÍGUEZ, MANUEL M. 2003. *Life in Search of Readers: Reading (in) Chicano Literature.* Albuquerque, NM: University of New Mexico Press.

MATHIS, JANELLE B. 2001. "Respond to Stories with Stories: Teachers Discuss Multicultural Children's Literature." *Social Studies* 92(July/August): 155.

MATTHEWS, RENE, and ROBIN CHANDLER. 1998. "Using Reader Response to Teach ŒBeloved' in a High School American Studies Classroom." *English Journal* 88(November): 85–92.

MCCANN, THOMAS M., and JOSEPH M. FLANAGAN. 2002. "A Tempest Project: Shakespeare and Critical Conflicts." *English Journal* 92(September): 29–35.

MCCLARAN, NANCY. 1978. "Infusion of Values Education into Contemporary American Literature." *English Journal* 67(February): 56–60.

MCCORMICK, KATHLEEN. 1985. "Theory in the Reader: Bleich, Holland, and Beyond." *College English* 47(December): 836–850.

MCCROSSAN, JOHN ANTHONY. 2000. *Books and Reading in the Lives of Notable Americans: A Biographical Sourcebook.* Westport, CT: Greenwood Press.

MCGINLEY, WILLIAM, KATANNA CONLEY, and JOHN WESLEY WHITE. 2000. "Pedagogy for a Few: Book Club Discussion Guides and the Modern Book Industry as Literature Teacher." *Journal of Adolescent & Adult Literacy* 44(November): 204–215.

MCGUIRE, RICHARD L. 1973. *Passionate Attention: An Introduction to Literary Study.* New York: Norton.

MCHENRY, ELIZABETH. 2002. *Forgotten Readers: Recovering the Lost History of African American Literary Societies.* Durham, NC: Duke University Press.

MCMAHON, ROBERT. 2002. *Thinking About Literature: New Ideas for High School Teachers.* Portsmouth, NH: Heinemann.

MCMILLIN, TRACY SCOTT. 2000. *Our Preposterous Use of Literature: Emerson and the Nature of Reading.* Urbana, IL: University of Illinois Press.

MEACHAM, SHUAIB J., and EDWARD BUENDIA. 1999. "Modernism, Postmodernism, and Post-Structuralism and Their Impact on Literacy." *Language Arts* 76(July): 510.

MEADE, RICHARD A., and JR. ROBERT C. SMALL. 1973. *Literature for Adolescents: Selection and Use.* Columbus, OH. Charles E. Merrill.

MEADOWS, ROBERT. 1976. "Get Smart: Let TV Work for You," *English Journal* 56(2): 121–124.

MEEK, MARGARET, AIDAN WARLOW, and GRISELDA BARTON. 1977. *Cool Web: The Pattern of Children's Reading.* New York: Atheneum.

MIALL, DAVID S. 1985. "The Structure of Response: A Repertory Grid Study of a Poem." *Research in the Teaching of English* 19 (October): 254–268.

MIALL, DAVID S., and DON KUIKEN. 1999. "What Is Literariness? Three Components of Literary Reading." *Discourse Processes: A Multidisciplinary Journal* 28: 121–138.

MIGUEZ, SONJA. 1997. "Using the Reader-Response Approach in the Classroom: An Analysis of Hemingway's 'a Clean, Well-Lighted Place'." *Louisiana English Journal, New Series* 4: 76–79.

MILBURN, MICHAEL. 2001. "Lighting the Flame: Teaching High School Students to Love, Not Loathe, Literature." *English Journal* 91 (November): 90–95.

MILLER, BRUCE E. 1980. *Teaching the Art of Literature.* Urbana, IL: National Council of Teachers of English.

MILLER, J. HILLIS. 1982. *Fiction and Repetition.* Cambridge, MA: Harvard University Press.

———. 2002. *On Literature.* London; New York: Routledge.

MILLER, JR., JAMES E. "1967. Literature in the Revitalized Curriculum," *NASSP Bulletin* 38(April): 25–26.

MILLER, JANET L. 2000. "English Education in-the-Making." *English Education* 33(October): 34.

MILLER, SUZANNE M., and SHARON LEGGE. 1999. "Supporting Possible Worlds: Transforming Literature Teaching and Learning through Conversations in the Narrative Mode." *Research in the Teaching of English* 34(August): 10–64.

MOFFETT, JAMES. 1988. *Storm in the Mountains: A Case Study of Censorship, Conflict, and Consciousness.* Carbondale, IL: Southern Illinois University Press.

MOFFETT, JAMES. 1981. *Coming on Center: English Education in Evolution.* Montclair, NJ: Boynton/Cook.

MONSEAU, VIRGINIA. 1996. *Responding to Young Adult Literature.* Portsmouth, NH: Boynton/Cook.

MOORE, DAVID W., and THOMAS W. BEAN. 1999. "Adolescent Literacy: A Position Statement." *Journal of Adolescent & Adult Literacy* 43 (September): 97–110.

MOORE, JOHN NOELL. 1997. *Interpreting Young Adult Literature: Literary Theory in the Secondary Classroom.* Portsmouth, NH: Boynton/Cook.

———. 2002. "Practicing Poetry: Teaching to Learn and Learning to Teach." *English Journal* 91(January): 44–50.

MORAN, CHARLES, and ELIZABETH F. PENFIELD, eds. 1990. *Conversations: Contemporary Critical Theory and the Teaching of Literature.* Urbana, IL: National Council of Teachers of English.

MORSE, J. MITCHELL. 1972. *The Irrelevant English Teacher.* Philadelphia, PA: Temple University Press.

———. 1976. *Prejudice and Literature.* Philadelphia, PA: Temple University Press.

MOUR, STANLEY I. 1977. "Censorship and the Schools: A Different Perspective." *English Journal* 66(February): 18–20.

MULDOON, PHYLLIS A. "Challenging Students to Think: Shaping Questions, Building Community." *English Journal* 79(April 1990): 34–40.

———. 1991. "Citizenship as Shared Inquiry: Literature Study and the Democratic Mind." *English Journal* 80(November): 61–68.

MUMFORD, JAY C, and JOHN KNOX. 1999. "Reader Response." *National Forum* 79(Summer): 43.

MURPHY, ELAINE. 2001. "In Search of Literature for the Twenty-First Century." *English Journal* 90(January): 110–115.

MURPHY, GERALDINE. 1968. *The Study of Literature in High School.* Waltham, MA: Ginn.

MURPHY, SANDRA. 1998. "Remembering That Reading Is 'a Way of Happening'." *Clearing House* 72(November–December): 89–96.

MURRAY, ROBIN. 2000. "Textual Authority, Reader Authority, and Social Authority: Reconfiguring Literature and Experience in a Reader-Response Context." *Readerly/Writerly Texts: Essays on Literature, Literary/Textual Criticism, and Pedagogy* 8(Spring–Winter): 9–21.

MURRAY-ORR, ANNE. 2002. "Book Conversations as Acts of Caring." *Curriculum & Teaching Dialogue* 4: 89.

MYERS, KRIS L. "Twenty (Better) Questions." *English Journal* 77(January 1988): 64–65.

NAFISI, AZAR. 2004. *Reading Lolita in Tehran: A Memoir in Books.* New York, NY: Random House.

NAIPAUL, VIDIADHAR SURAJPRASAD. 2000. *Reading & Writing: A Personal Account.* New York: New York Review of Books.

NANCE, MARY MOORE. 2000. *Finding a (W)Hole in the Text: A Case Study of Four Readers Reading.* Alberta, Canada: University of Calgary.

NARVAEZ, DARCIA. 2002. "Does Reading Moral Stories Build Character?" *Educational Psychology Review* 14(June): 155.

NATIONAL COUNCIL OF TEACHERS OF ENGLISH CURRICULUM COMMISSION. 1935. *An Experience Curriculum in English.* New York: Appleton-Century.

NATIONAL COUNCIL OF TEACHERS OF ENGLISH. 1995. *Teaching Literature in High School: The Novel, Standards Consensus Series.* Urbana, IL: National Council of Teachers of English.

———. 1996. *Teaching Literature in Middle School: Fiction, Standards Consensus Series.* Urbana, IL: National Council of Teachers of English.

NELL, VICTOR. 1988. Lost in a Book: The Psychology of Reading for Pleasure. New Haven, CT: Yale University Press.

———. "The Psychology of Reading for Pleasure: Needs and Gratifications." *Reading Research Quarterly* 23(1988): 6–40.

NELMS, BEN F., ed. 1988. *Literature in the Classroom: Readers, Texts, and Contexts.* Urbana, IL: National Council of Teachers of English.

NEUMANN, BONNIE H., and HELEN M. MCDONNELL, eds. 1996, *Teaching the Short Story: A Guide to Using Stories from around the World.* Urbana, IL: National Council of Teachers of English.

NEVIL, DANA A. 1999. *Students' Transactions with Multicultural Poetry in the High School Classroom: A Case Study.* Atlanta: Georgia State University Press.

NEWELL, GEORGE E., and RUSSEL K. DURST, eds. 1993. *Exploring Texts: The Role of Discussion and Writing in the Teaching and Learning of Literature.* Norwood, MA: Christopher-Gordon.

NEWELL, GEORGE. E., and R. A. Holt. 1997. "Autonomy and Obligation in the Teaching of Literature: Teachers Classroom Curriculum and Departmental Consensus." *English Education* 29: 18–37.

NEWELL, GEORGE E., and MARCIA SWEET. 1999. "'Headed into More and More Important Things': Transforming a World Literature Curriculum." *English Journal* 88 (May): 38–44.

NILSEN, ALLEEN PACE. 1997. "Readers Responding: Creative Writing and Ya Literature." *English Journal* 86(March): 81-86.

NILSEN, ALLEEN PACE, and KENNETH L. DONELSON. 2001. *Literature for Today's Young Adults.* Sixth Ed. New York: Longman.

NORRIS, CHRISTOPHER. 1982. *Deconstruction: Theory and Practice.* London: Methuen.

NYSTRAND, MARTIN, ADAM GAMORAN, and MARY JO HECK. "Using Small Groups for Response to and Thinking About Literature." *English Journal* 82(January 1993): 14–22.

OBBINK, LAURA APOL. 1992. "Feminist Theory in the Classroom: Choices, Questions, Voices." *English Journal* 81(November): 38–43.

OBOLER, ELI M. 1981. *Censorship and Education.* New York: H. W. Wilson.

ODELL, LEE, and CHARLES COOPER. 1976. "Describing Responses to Works of Fiction." *Research in the Teaching of English* 10 (1976): 203–225.

O'DONNELL-ALLEN, CINDY, and BUD HUNT. 2001. "Reading Adolescents: Book Clubs for Ya Readers." *English Journal* 90(January): 82–89.

O'DONNELL-ALLEN, CINDY, and PETER SMAGORINSKY. 1999. "Gender Roles: Listening to Classroom Talk About Literary Characters." *English Journal* 88(January): 35–42.

LIAM O'FLAHERTY, 2000. "The Sniper," in *Liam O'Flaherty: The Collected Stories, A. A. Kelly,* ed. New York: Palgrave Macmillan, p. 96.

OLIVER, MARY. 1986. *Dream Work.* New York, NY: Atlantic Monthly Press.

OLSTER, STACEY MICHELE. 2003. *The Trash Phenomenon: Contemporary Literature, Popular Culture, and the Making of the American Century.* Athens, GA: University of Georgia Press.

ONG, WALTER J. 1982. *Orality and Literacy.* London: Methuen.

———. 1967. *The Presence of the Word.* New Haven, CT: Yale University Press.

OSEN, DIANE, ed. 2002. *The Book That Changed My Life: Interviews with National Book Award Winners and Finalists.* New York: Modern Library.

O'SHEA, CATHERINE, and MARGARET EGAN. 1978. "A Primer of Drama Techniques for Teaching Literature." *English Journal* 67(February): 51–55.

PACE, BARBARA G. 2003. "Resistance and Response: Deconstructing Community Standards in a Literature Class." *Journal of Adolescent & Adult Literacy* 46(February): 408–412.

PACE, BARBARA G., and JANE S. TOWNSEND. 1999. "Gender Roles: Listening to Classroom Talk About Literary Characters." *English Journal* 88(January): 43–49.

PADEN, FRANCES FREEMAN. 1978. "Theater Games and the Teaching of English." *English Journal* 67(February): 46–50.

PAREKH, PUSHPA NAIDU. 1998. "Poetry as Performance: Hopkins and Reader-Response." *Studies: An Irish Quarterly Review* 87(Summer): 183–189.

PARKER, JR. ROBERT P., and MAXINE E. DALY. 1973. *Teaching English in the Secondary School.* New York: The Free Press.

PARR, SUSAN RESNECK. 1989. *The Moral of the Story: Literature, Values, and American Education.* New York: Teachers College Press.

PATTERSON, ANNABEL M. 1993. *Reading between the Lines.* Madison, WI: University of Wisconsin Press.

PEARSON, P. DAVID, REBECCA BARR, MICHAEL L. KAMIL, and PETER B. MOSENTHAL, eds. 2000. *Handbook of Reading Research.* Vol. 3. Mahwah, NJ: L. Erlbaum.

PECK, DAVID R. 1989. *Novels of Initiation: A Guidebook for Teaching Literature to Adolescents.* New York: Teachers College, Columbia University.

PENNINGTON, JOHN. 2000. "Exorcising Gender: Resisting Readers in Ursula K. Le Guin's Left Hand of Darkness." *Extrapolation: A Journal of Science Fiction and Fantasy* 41(Winter): 351–358.

PERL, SONDRA. 1994. "Composing Texts, Composing Lives." *Harvard Educational Review* 64(Winter): 427.

PERRINE, LAURENCE. 1956. *Sound and Sense.* New York: Harcourt, Brace and World.

PETERSEN, BRUCE T. 1982. "Writing About Responses: A Unified Model of Reading, Interpretation, and Composition." *College English* 44(September): 459–468.

PETROSKY, ANTHONY R. 1976. "The Effects of Reality Perception and Fantasy on Response to Literature: Two Case Studies." *Research in the Teaching of English* 10: 239–258.

———. 1982. "From Story to Essay: Reading and Writing." *College Composition and Communication* 33(February): 19–36.

PETROSKY, ANTHONY R., and CHARLES COOPER. 1978. "Evaluating the Results of Classroom Literary Study." *English Journal* 67(October): 96–99.

PHELAN, JAMES. 2000. "Authorial Readers, Flesh and Blood Readers, and the Recursiveness of Rhetorical Reading." *Reader: Essays in Reader-Oriented Theory, Criticism, and Pedagogy* 43(Spring): 65–69.

PHELAN, JAMES. 1993. "Toward a Rhetorical Reader-Response Criticism: The Difficult, the Stubborn, and the Ending of Beloved." *Modern Fiction Studies* 39(Fall): 709.

PIKE, MARK. 2000. "Keen Readers: Adolescents and Pre-Twentieth Century Poetry." *Educational Review* 52(February): 13–29.

PIRIE, BRUCE. 1997. *Reshaping High School English.* Urbana, IL: National Council of Teachers of English.

POE, ELIZABETH. 1988. "Student Responses to Don Gallo's Sixteen." *English Journal* 77(January): 68–70.

POLLARD, D E B. 1992. "Literature and Representation: A Note." *British Journal of Aesthetics* 32(April): 166.

PRADL, GORDON M. 1987. "Close Encounters of the First Kind: Teaching the Poem at the Point of Utterance." *English Journal* 76(February): 66–69.

———. 1996. "Reading and Democracy: The Enduring Influence of Louise Rosenblatt." *New Advocate* 9: 9–22.

PRATT, MARY LOUISE. 1977. *Toward a Speech Act Theory of Literary Discourse.* Bloomington, IN: Indiana University Press.

PREST, P., and J. PREST. 1988. "Theory into Practice: Clarifying Our Intentions: Some Thoughts on the Application of Rosenblatt's Transactional Theory of Reading in the Classroom." *English Quarterly* 21: 127–133.

PRITCHARD, RUIE JANE. 1993. "Developing Writing Prompts for Reading Response and Analysis." *English Journal* 82(March): 24.

PROBST, ROBERT E. 1987. "Adolescent Literature and the English Curriculum." *English Journal* 76(March): 26–30.

———. 2001. "Adolescent Literature and the Teaching of Literature," in *Instructional Practices for Literacy Teacher-Educators,* J. E. Many, ed. Mahwah, NJ: Lawrence Erlbaum Associates.

———. 1984. "Communication." in *The Clearing House: A Closer Look,* R. B. Shuman, ed. Washington, DC: Heldref Publications.

———. 1984. "Concepts and Uncertainty." In *Communication Theory and Interpersonal Interaction: Volume Ii of Studies in Communication (Selected Proceedings from the Fourth International Conference on Culture and Communication),* S. Thomas, ed. Norwood, NJ: Ablex Publishing Company.

———. 1988. "Dialogue with a Text." *English Journal* 77: 32–38.

———. 2001. "Difficult Days, Difficult Texts." *Voices From the Middle* 9 (December): 50–53.

———. 1983. "Film, Television, and Reality." *English Journal* 72(January): 86–89.

———. 1992. "Five Kinds of Literary Knowing," in *Literature Instruction: A Focus on Student Response,* J. A. Langer, ed. Urbana, IL: National Council of Teachers of English.

———. 1999. "A Miscellaneous, Undeveloped, Untested Collection of Ideas for Using the Letter in Literature Classes." *English in Texas* 29(Fall/Winter): 14–15.

———. 1974. "Literature," in *Creative Approaches to the Teaching of English: Secondary,* R. B. Shuman, ed. Itasca, IL: F. E. Peacock Publishers.

———. 1990. "Literature and Literacy," in *On Literacy and Its Teaching: Issues in English Education,* G. E. Hawisher and A. O. Soter, ed. Albany, NY: State University of New York Press.

———. 1990. "Literature as Exploration and the Classroom," in *Transactions with Literature: A Fifty-Year Perspective. For Louise M. Rosenblatt,* J. R. Squire and E. Farrell, ed. Urbana, IL: National Council of Teachers of English.

———. 2000. "Literature as Invitation." *Voices From the Middle* 8(December): 7–15.

———. 1986. "Mom, Wolfgang, and Me: Adolescent Literature, Critical Theory, and the English Classroom." *English Journal* 75 (October): 33–39.

———. 1982. "On Censorship." *Georgia Journal of Reading* 7 (Spring): 5.

———. 1994. "Reader Response Theory and the Problem of Meaning," in *Inspiring Literacy: Literature for Children and Young Adults,* S. Sebesta and K. Donelson, eds. New Brunswick, NJ: Transaction Publishers.

———. 1994. "Reader-Response Curriculum," in *Encyclopedia of English Studies and Language Arts,* A. C. Purves, ed. Urbana, IL: National Council of Teachers of English and Scholastic Inc.

———. 1994. "Reader-Response Theory and the English Curriculum," *English Journal* 83(March): 37–44.

———. 1997. "Reader-Response Theory in the Middle Grades," in *Into Focus: Understanding and Creating Middle School Readers,* K. Beers and B. Samuels, ed. Norwood, MA: Christopher-Gordon.

———. 1988. "Readers and Literary Texts," in *Literature in the Classroom: Readers, Texts, and Contexts,* B. F. Nelms, ed. Urbana, IL: National Council of Teachers of English.

———. 2003. "Response to Literature," in *Handbook of Research on Teaching the English Language Arts,* J. R. Squire, J. Flood, D. Lapp, and J. Jensen, eds. New York: Macmillan Publishing Company.

———. 1989. "The River and Its Banks: Response and Analysis in the Teaching of Literature," in *Passages to Literature: Essays on Teaching in Australia, Canada, England, the United States, and Wales,* J. O. B. Milner and L. F. M. Milner, eds. Urbana, IL: National Council of Teachers of English.

———. 1994. "Teaching What We Cannot Know." *Voices From the Middle* 1(September): 7–11.

———. 1986. "Three Relationships in the Teaching of Literature." *English Journal* 75(January): 60–68.

———. 1989. "Transactional Theory and Response to Student Writing," in *Writing and Response: Theory, Practice, and Research*, C. M. Anson, ed. Urbana, IL: National Council of Teachers of English.

———. 1988. "Transactional Theory in the Teaching of Literature." *Journal of Reading* 31(January): 378–381.

———. 1972. "Visual to Verbal." *English Journal* 61 (January): 71–75.

———. 1991. "Writing from, of, and About Literature," in *Reader Response in the Classroom: Evoking and Interpreting Meaning in Literature,* N. Karolides, ed. New York: Longman Press.

PROBST, ROBERT E., and JOAN W. GRAHAM. 1982. "Eliciting Response to Literature." *Kentucky English Bulletin* (Special Issue on "The Responding Reader") 32(Fall): 30–46.

PROTHEROUGH, ROBERT. 1983. *Developing Response to Fiction.* Milton Keynes: Open University Press

———. 1986. *Teaching Literature for Examinations.* Milton Keynes: Open University Press.

PURVES, ALAN C. 1968. *Elements of Writing About a Literary Work: A Study of Response to Literature.* Urbana, IL: National Council of Teachers of English.

————, ed. 1971. *Evaluation of Learning in Literature*, B. Bloom, et al, eds., in *Handbook on Formative and Summative Evaluation of Student Learning.* New York: McGraw-Hill.

————. 1972. *How Porcupines Make Love: Notes on a Response-Centered Curriculum.* Lexington, MA: Xerox.

————. 1991. *The Idea of Difficulty in Literature, Suny Series, Literacy, Culture, and Learning.* Albany, NY: State University of New York Press.

————. 1973. *Literature Education in 10 Countries.* New York: John Wiley.

————. 1980. "Putting Readers in Their Places: Some Alternatives to Cloning Stanley Fish." *College English* 42(March): 228–236.

————. 1981. *Reading and Literature: American Achievement in International Perspective.* Urbana, IL: National Council of Teachers of English.

————. 1981. "The State of Research in Teaching Literature." *English Journal* 70 (March): 82–84.

————. 1969. "Structure and Sequence in Literary Study." *Journal of Aesthetic Education* 3: 103–117.

————. 1979. "That Sunny Dome: Those Caves of Ice: A Model for Research in Reader Response." *College English* 40(March): 802–812.

PURVES, ALAN C., and RICHARD BEACH. 1981. *Literature and the Reader.* Urbana, IL: National Council of Teachers of English.

PURVES, ALAN C., and DIANNE L. MONSON. 1984. *Experiencing Children's Literature.* Glenview, IL: Scott, Foresman.

PURVES, ALAN C., and NATIONAL COUNCIL OF TEACHERS OF ENGLISH. 1994. *Encyclopedia of English Studies and Language Arts : A Project of the National Council of Teachers of English.* New York: Scholastic.

PURVES, ALAN C., Theresa Rogers, and Anna O. Soter. 1990. *How Porcupines Make Love II: Teaching a Response-Centered Literature Curriculum.* New York: Longman.

————. 1995. *How Porcupines Make Love III : Readers, Texts, Cultures in the Response-Based Literature Classroom.* White Plains, NY: Longman Publishers USA.

QUEENAN, MARGARET LALLY. 1996. "Whole Language Is Not a Room Arrangement; It's a Controversy." *English Journal* 85(February): 26.

RABIN, SYDELL. 1990. "Literature Study Groups: Teachers, Texts, and Readers." *English Journal* 79(November): 41–46.

RABINOWITZ, PETER J., and MICHAEL W. SMITH. 1998. *Authorizing Readers: Resistance and Respect in the Teaching of Literature.* Urbana, IL: National Council of Teachers of English.

REED, ARTHEA J. S. 1985. *Reaching Adolescents: The Young Adult Book and the School.* New York: Holt, Rinehart & Winston.

REED, HENRY. 1970. *Lessons of War* (New York: Chilmark Press).

REICHERT, JOHN. 1977. *Making Sense of Literature.* Chicago, IL: University of Chicago Press.

REID, I. 1984. *The Making of Literature: Texts, Contexts and Classroom Practices.* Norwood, South Australia: Australian Association for the Teaching of English.

REISSMAN, ROSE C. 1994. "Leaving out to Pull In: Using Reader Response to Teach Multicultural Literature." *English Journal* 83 (February): 20.

RICHARDSON, ALAN. 1994. *Literature, Education, and Romanticism: Reading as Social Practice, 1780-1832.* Cambridge; New York: Cambridge University Press.

RICHARDSON, BRIAN. 1997. "The Other Reader's Response: On Multiple, Divided, and Oppositional Audiences." *Criticism* 39(Winter): 31.

RIFFATERRE, MICHAEL. 1978. *Semiotics of Poetry.* Bloomington, IN: Indiana University Press.

ROBBINS, SARAH. 1993. "(De)Constructing Monday Morning: Conversations About Teacher/Authority." *English Journal* 82(February): 21.

ROBERTS, D. F. 1978. "One Highly Attracted Public," in *TV and Human Behavior,* G. Comstock, ed. New York: Columbia University Press.

ROBERTS, SHERRON KILLINGSWORTH. 1998. "Using Literature Study Groups to Construct Meaning in an Undergraduate Reading Course." *Journal of Teacher Education* 49(November/December): 366.

RODRIGUEZ, WILLIAM ROBERT. 1985. "Three Approaches to Writing the First Poem." *English Journal* 74(April): 33–37.

ROGERS, THERESA, and ANNA O. SOTER, eds. 1997. *Reading Across Cultures: Teaching Literature in a Diverse Society.* New York: Teachers College Press.

ROMANO, TOM. 1995. *Writing with Passion: Life Stories, Multiple Genres.* Portsmouth, NH: Heinemann.

ROMERO, PATRICIA ANN, and DON ZANCANELLA. 1990. "Expanding the Circle: Hispanic Voices in American Literature." *English Journal* 79(January): 24–29.

ROSENBLATT, LOUISE M. 1956. "Acid Test in Teaching Literature." *English Journal* 45(February): 66–74.

———. 1981. "Act I, Scene 1: Enter the Reader." *Literature in Performance: A Journal of Literary and Performing Art* 1(April): 13-23.

———. 1986. "The Aesthetic Transaction." *Journal of Aesthetic Education* 20(December): 122–128.

———. 1995. "Continuing the Conversation: A Clarification." *Research in the Teaching of English* 29(October): 349–354.

———. 1962. "The Genesis of Pater's Marius the Epicurean." *Comparative Literature* 14(Summer): 242–260.

———. 1981. *The Journey Itself.* New York School of Library Service, Columbia University.

———. 1985. "Language, Literature, and Values," in *Language, Schooling, and Society,* S. N. Tchudi, ed. Upper Montclair, NJ: Boynton/Cook.

———. 1931. "L'idee De L'art Pour L'art: Dans La Litterature Anglaise Pendant La Periode Victorienne," in *Bibliotheque De La Revue De Litterature Comparee,* F. Baldensperger and P. Hazare, ed. Paris: Librairie Ancienne Honore Champion.

———. 1982. "The Literary Transaction: Evocation and Response." *Theory into Practice* 21(Autumn): 268–277.

———. 1970. "Literature and the Invisible Reader," in *The Promise of English,* J. E. Miller, Jr., ed. Champaign, IL: National Council of Teachers of English.

———. 1995. *Literature as Exploration.* Fifth Ed. New York: Modern Language Association.

———. 1991. "Literature—S.O.S.!" *Language Arts* 68(October): 444.

———. 1994. "On the (Pendulum) Swinging Eighties," in *Writing Theory and Critical Theory,* J. Clifford and J. Schilb, eds. New York: Modern Language Association.

———. 1981. "On the Aesthetic as the Basic Model of the Reading Process." *Bucknell Review: A Scholarly Journal of Letters, Arts and Sciences* 26: 17–32.

———. 1969. "Pattern and Process—a Polemic." *English Journal* 58(October): 1005–1012.

———. 1964. "The Poem as Event." *College English* 26: 123–128.

———. 1994. "The Quest for 'the Poem Itself'." *Contexts for Criticism,* edited by D. Keesey. Mountain View, CA: Mayfield Publishing Company: 129–136.

———. 1978. *The Reader, the Text, the Poem: The Transactional Theory of the Literary Work.* Carbondale, IL: Southern Illinois University Press.

———. 1998. "Readers, Texts, Authors." *Transactions of the Charles S. Peirce Society* 34(Fall): 885–922.

———. 1983. "The Reading Transaction: What For?" In *Developing Literacy: Young Children's Use of Language,* R. P. Parker, F. A. Davis and J. F. Cassidy, ed. Newark, DE: International Reading Association.

———. 1963. *Research Development Seminar in the Teaching of English , New York University, February 27–March 2.* New York: New York University.

———. 1946. "Toward a Cultural Approach to Literature." *College English* 7(May): 459–466.

———. 1969. "Towards a Transactional Theory of Reading." *Journal of Reading Behavior* 1(Winter): 31–49.

———. 1984. "The Transactional Theory of the Literary Work: Implications for Research." *Researching Response to Literature and the Teaching of Literature: Points of Departure*: 33–53.

———. 1993. "The Transactional Theory: Against Dualisms." *College English* 55 (April): 377–387.

———. 1985. "Viewpoints: Transaction Versus Interaction—a Terminological Rescue Operation." *Research in the Teaching of English* 19(February): 96–107.

———. 1980. "What Facts Does This Poem Teach You?" *Language Arts* 57(April): 386–394.

———. 1978. "Whitman's Democratic Vistas and the New 'Ethnicity'." *The Yale Review: A National Quarterly* 67: 187–204.

———. 1989. "Writing and Reading: The Transactional Theory." In *Reading and Writing Connections,* edited by J. M. Mason. Boston: Allyn and Bacon, 153–176.

ROSENBLATT, LOUISE M., and OTHERS. 1942. "English in Wartime: A Symposium by College Teachers." *College English* 3(February): 495–502.

ROUSE, JOHN. 1983. "An Erotics of Teaching." *College English* 45(October): 535–548.

ROUTH, JANE, and JANET WOLFF, eds. 1977. *The Sociology of Literature: Theoretical Approaches.* Keele, England: University of Keele.

ROWLAND, WILLIAM G. 1996. *Literature and the Marketplace: Romantic Writers and Their Audiences in Great Britain and the United States.* Lincoln, NE: University of Nebraska Press.

RUBIN, DONALD L, TERESA HAFER, and KEVIN ARATA. 2000. "Reading and Listening to Oral-Based Versus Literate-Based Discourse." *Communication Education* 49(April): 121.

RUDDELL, ROBERT B., et al., eds. 1994. *Theoretical Models and Processes of Reading.* Fourth Ed. Newark, DE: International Reading Association.

RUNKLE, DANIELLE R. 2000. "Effectively Using Journals to Respond to Literature." *Schools in the Middle* 9(April): 35.

RUSSELL, DAVID H. 1970. *The Dynamics of Reading.* Waltham, MA: Ginn.

RYAN, BARBARA, and AMY M. THOMAS, eds. 2002. *Reading Acts: U. S. Readers' Interactions with Literature, 1800-1950.* Knoxville, TN: University of Tennessee Press.

RYAN, MARIE-LAURE. 2001. *Narrative as Virtual Reality: Immersion and Interactivity in Literature and Electronic Media.* Baltimore, MD: Johns Hopkins University Press.

SAID, EDWARD. 1975. *Beginnings: Intention and Method.* New York: Basic Books.

SALE, ROGER. 1978. *Fairy Tales and After: From Snow White to E. B. White.* Cambridge, MA: Harvard University Press.

SALVNER, GARY M. 2001. "Lessons and Lives: Why Young Adult Literature Matters." *ALAN Review* 28(Spring–Summer): 9–13.

SAMPSON, G. P., and N. CARLMAN. 1982. "A Heirarchy of Student Responses to Literature." *English Journal* 71(January): 54–57.

SAMUELS, BARBARA G. 1983. "Young Adult Novels in the Classroom." *English Journal* 72(April): 86–88.

SAMUELS, BARBARA G., G. Kylene Beers, National Council of Teachers of English, and Committee on the Junior High and Middle School Booklist. 1996. *Your Reading: An Annotated Booklist for Middle School and Junior High.* Urbana, IL: National Council of Teachers of English.

SAUER, EDWIN H. 1961. *English in the Secondary School.* New York: Holt, Rinehart & Winston.

SAWYER, WALTER. 2004. *Growing up with Literature.* Clifton Park, NY: Thomson/Delmar Learning.

SCALES, PAT. 2001. *Teaching Banned Books: 12 Guides for Young Readers.* Chicago, IL: American Library Association.

SCANLON, PATRICK M. 1986. "Reading Literature with Structur(Alism)E." *English Journal* 75(October): 57–59.

SCHAARS, M. J. 1988. "Teaching My Antonia with Guidance from Rosenblatt." *English Journal* 77: 54-58.

SCHELHAAS, DAVID. 1994. "The Dangerous Safety of Fiction." *English Journal* 83 (February): 51.

SCHILB, JOHN. 1986. "Canonical Theories and Noncanonical Literature: Steps toward a Pedagogy." *Reader, Essays in Reader-Oriented Theory, Criticism, and Pedagogy* (Spring): 3–23.

SCHOLES, ROBERT E. 2001. *The Crafty Reader.* New Haven, CT: Yale University Press.

————. 1989. *Protocols of Reading.* New Haven, CT: Yale University Press.

————. 1982. *Semiotics and Interpretation.* New Haven, CT: Yale University Press.

————. 1974. *Structuralism in Literature: An Introduction.* New Haven, CT: Yale University Press.

————. 1985. *Textual Power: Literary Theory and the Teaching of English.* New Haven, CT: Yale University Press.

SCHWARTZ, MURRAY. 1975. "Where Is Literature?" *College English* 36(March): 756–765.

SCHWARTZ, SHEILA. 1979. *Teaching Adolescent Literature: A Humanistic Approach.* Rochelle Park, NJ: Hayden.

SCHWEICKART, PATROCINIO P. 2000. "Reading as Communicative Action." *Reader: Essays in Reader-Oriented Theory, Criticism, and Pedagogy* 43 (Spring): 70–75.

SEBESTA, SAM LEATON, and KENNETH L. DONELSON. 1993. *Inspiring Literacy: Literature for Children and Young Adults.* New Brunswick, NJ: Transaction Publishers.

SHAFER, GREGORY. 2000. "Prime Time Literature in the High School." *English Journal* 90(November): 93.

————. 1997. "Reader Response Makes History." *English Journal* 86(November): 65.

SHAPIRO, STEVEN G. 1992. "Teaching Modernism and Postmodernism in a Values Elective." *English Journal* 81(January): 60.

SHELLEY, ANNE CROUT. 1998. "Teaching the Classics in High School." *Journal of Adolescent & Adult Literacy* 41(February): 386–388.

SHERIDAN, DANIEL. 1993. "Writing in Response to Literature: The Paper of Many Parts." *English Journal* 82(October): 58.

SHORT, KATHY G., GLORIA KAUFFMAN, and LESLIE H. KAHN. 2000. "'I Just Need to Draw': Responding to Literature across Multiple Sign Systems." *Reading Teacher* 54 (October): 160–172.

SHOSH, JOSEPH M. 2000. "Much Ado About Negotiation." *English Journal* 89 (July): 72.

SHULL, ELLEN M. 1989. "The Reader, the Text, the Poem—and the Film." *English Journal* 78(December): 53.

SHUMAN, R. BAIRD, ed. 1981. *Education in the 80s: English.* Washington, DC: National Education Association.

————. 1984. "Keeping Current in Critical Theory." *English Journal* 73(October): 59–63.

————. 1993. "The Past as Present: Reader Response and Literary Study." *English Journal* 82(September): 30.

SHWARTZ, RONALD B., ed. 1999. *For the Love of Books: 115 Celebrated Writers on the Books They Love Most.* New York: Grosset/Putnam.

SIJIE, DAI. 2001. *Balzac and the Little Chinese Seamstress,* I. Rilke, Trans. New York: Alfred A. Knopf.

SIMMONS, JAY. 2003. "Responders Are Taught Not Born." *Journal of Adolescent & Adult Literacy* 46(May): 684–693.

SIMMONS, JOHN S. 1970. *Teaching English in Today's High Schools,* D. L. Burton, ed. Second Ed. New York: Holt, Rinehart & Winston.

SIMMONS, JOHN S., ROBERT E. SHAFER, and GAIL B. WEST. 1976. *Decisions About the Teaching of English*. Boston, MA: Allyn and Bacon.

SIPE, REBECCA. 2003. "It's About Passion . . . And Staying Professionally Alive." *English Journal* 92(July): 20.

SIPE, REBECCA BOWERS. 2002. "Growing Professionally, Leading the Way." *English Journal* 91(July): 12.

SLATOFF, WALTER J. 1970. *With Respect to Readers*. Ithaca, NY: Cornell University Press.

SLIGHTS, WILLIAM W. E. 2001. *Managing Readers: Printed Marginalia in English Renaissance Books*. Ann Arbor, MI: University of Michigan Press.

SMAGORINSKY, PETER. 2002. "Growth through English Revisited." *English Journal* 91(July): 23.

———. 2001. "If Meaning Is Constructed, What Is It Made From? Toward a Cultural Theory of Reading." *Review of Educational Research* 71(Spring): 133.

SMAGORINSKY, PETER, and JOHN COPPOCK. 1994. "Exploring an Evocation of a Literary Work: Processes and Possibilities of an Artistic Response to Literature." *Reader: Essays in Reader-Oriented Theory, Criticism, and Pedagogy* 32(Fall): 61–73.

SMAGORINSKY, PETER, and CINDY O'DONNELL-ALLEN. 1998. "Reading as Mediated and Mediating Action: Composing Meaning for Literature through Multimedia Interpretive Texts." *Reading Research Quarterly* 33(April–June): 198.

SMITH, BARBARA HERRNSTEIN. 1978. *On the Margins of Discourse*. Chicago, IL: University of Chicago Press.

SMITH, FRANK. 1979. *Reading without Nonsense*. New York: Teachers College Press.

SMITH, KAREN. 2001. "Critical Conversations in Difficult Times." *English Education* 33 (January): 153.

SORENSEN, DIANA. 1986. *The Reader and the Text: Interpretive Strategies for Latin American Literatures, Purdue University Monographs in Romance Languages*. Vol. 5, No. 18. Amsterdam. Philadelphia, PA: Benjamins.

SOTER, ANNA O. 1999. *Young Adult Literature and the New Literary Theories Developing Critical Readers in Middle School*. New York: Teachers College Press.

SPIEGEL, DIXIE LEE. 1998. "Reader Response Approaches and the Growth of Readers." *Language Arts* 76(September): 41.

———. 1996. "The Role of Trust in Reader-Response Groups." *Language Arts* 73(September): 332.

SPOLSKY, ELLEN. 1990. *The Uses of Adversity: Failure and Accommodation in Reader Response*. Lewisburg, PA; Bucknell University Press.

SQUIRE, JAMES R. 1985. "The Current Crisis in Literary Education." *English Journal* 74(December): 10–21.

———. 1968. *Response to Literature*. Urbana, IL: National Council of Teachers of English.

———. 1969. *Teaching Language and Literature: Grades Seven-Twelve*. Second Ed. New York: Harcourt Brace Jovanovich.

SQUIRE, JAMES R., ed. 1977. *The Teaching of English: The Seventy-Sixth Yearbook of the National Society for the Study of Education*. Chicago, IL: University of Chicago Press.

STEIG, MICHAEL. 1989. *Stories of Reading: Subjectivity and Literary Understanding*. Baltimore, MD: Johns Hopkins University Press.

STEINBERG, ERWIN R., ROBERT C. SLACK, BEEKMAN W. COTTRELL, and LOIS S. JOSEPHS, 1970. "The Overall Plan of the Curriculum Study Center at Carnegie-Mellon University," in *English Education Today*, Lois S. Josephs and Erwin R. Steinberg, eds. New York: Noble and Noble.

STEINER, GEORGE. 1979. "'Critic'/'Reader'." *New Literary History* 10(Spring): 423–452.

STEPHENS, ELAINE C. 1998. *United in Diversity: Using Multicultural Young Adult Literature in the Classroom*, J. E. Brown, ed. Urbana, IL: National Council of Teachers of English.

STERN, BARBARA B. 1989. "Literary Critism and Consumer Research: Overview and Illustration." *Journal of Consumer Research* 16(December): 322.

———. 1989. "Literary Critism and Consumer Research: Overview and Illustration." *Journal of Consumer Research* 16(December): 322.

STILL, KIMBERLY. 1997. "Whole Language? Portfolios? Reader Response?...Help!" *English Journal* 86(November): 19.

STILLINGER, JACK. 1997. "Multiple Readers, Multiple Texts, Multiple Keats." *Journal of English and Germanic Philology* 96(October): 545.

STONE, JR., GEORGE WINCHESTER. 1964. *Issues, Problems, and Approaches in the Teaching of English*. New York: Holt, Rinehart & Winston.

STOVER, LOIS T. 1997. "What's New in Young Adult Literature for High School Students?" *English Journal* 86(March): 55–62.

STOVER, LOIS T. 1996. *Young Adult Literature: The Heart of the Middle School*. Portsmouth, NH: Boynton/Cook Publishers.

STOWE, WILLIAM W. 1986. "Popular Fiction as Liberal Art." *College English* 48(November): 646–663.

STRATTA, LESLIE, JOHN DIXON, and ANDREW WILKINSON. 1973. *Patterns of Language: Explorations of the Teaching of English*. London: Heinemann.

STRELKA, JOSEPH P. 1973. *Literary Criticism and Psychology (Yearbook of Comparative Criticism)*. Vol. VII. University Park, PA: Pennsylvania State University Press.

———. 1973. *Literary Criticism and Sociology (Yearbook of Comparative Criticism)*. Vol. V. University Park, PA: Pennsylvania State University Press.

STRINGER, SHARON A, and BILL MOLLINEAUX. 2003. "Removing the Word 'Reluctant' from 'Reluctant Reader'." *English Journal* 92(March): 71.

SUBLETTE, JACK R. 1982. "Back to Basics in Literature; Where and Why?" *English Journal* 71(October): 32–35.

SULEIMAN, SUSAN R., and INGE CROSMAN, eds. 1980. *The Reader in the Text: Essays on Audience and Interpretation*. Princeton, NJ: Princeton University Press.

SULLIVAN, CHARLES WILLIAM, ed. 1999. *Young Adult Science Fiction*. Westport, CT: Greenwood Press.

SULLIVAN, EDWARD T. 2002. *Reaching Reluctant Young Adult Readers: A Handbook for Librarians and Teachers.* Lanham, MD: Scarecrow Press.

SULLIVAN, MICHAEL. 2003. *Connecting Boys with Books: What Libraries Can Do.* Chicago, IL: American Library Association.

SULLIVAN, PATRICK. 2002. "'Reception Moments' Modern Literary Theory and the Teaching of Literature." *Journal of Adolescent & Adult Literacy* 45 (April): 568–577.

SUMARA, DENNIS J. 1996. *Private Readings in Public: Schooling the Literary Imagination.* New York: Peter Lang.

SUSAN, HYNDS, and DEBORAH APPLEMAN. 1997. "Walking Our Talk: Between Response and Responsibility in the Literature Classroom." *English Education* 29 (December): 272–296.

SWEETKIND, MORRIS. 1964. *Teaching Poetry in the High School.* New York: Macmillian.

SWENSON, KAREN. 1999. "Pockets," in *A Daughter's Latitude: New & Selected Poems.* Port Townsend, WA: Copper Canyon Press, p. 88.

SWIRSKI, PETER. 1994. "Iser's Theory of Aesthetic Response: A Brief Critique." *Reader: Essays in Reader-Oriented Theory, Criticism, and Pedagogy* 32 (Fall): 1–15.

SYMONS, ANN, and CHARLES HARMON. 1995. *Protecting the Right to Read: A How-to-Do-It Manual for School and Public Librarians.* New York: Neal-Schuman Publishers.

TABERS-KWAK, LINDA, and TIMOTHY U KAUFMAN. 2002. "Shakespeare through the Lens of a New Age." *English Journal* 92 (September): 69.

TANNER, STEPHEN L. 1986. "Education by Criticism." *English Journal* 75 (October): 22-26.

TATE, GARY. 1995. "Notes on the Dying of a Conversation." *College English* 57 (March): 303.

THIMMESCH, NICK, ed. 1984. *Aliteracy, People Who Can Read but Won't.* Washington, DC: American Enterprise Institute for Policy Research.

THOMPSON, DENYS, ed. 1969. *Directions in the Teaching of English.* London: Cambridge University Press.

THOMPSON, JACK. 1986. *Understanding Teenagers Reading: Reading Processes and the Teaching of Literature.* Australia: Croom Helm.

TIERNEY, ROBERT J., PATRICIA L. ANDERS, and JUDY NICHOLS MITCHELL, eds. 1987. *Understanding Readers' Understanding: Theory and Practice.* Hillsdale, NJ: Lawrence Erlbaum Associates.

TODOROV, TZVETAN. 1981. *Introduction to Poetics.* Minneapolis, MN: University of Minnesota Press.

———. 1977. *The Poetics of Prose.* Ithaca, NY: Cornell University Press.

TOMPKINS, JANE. 1980. *Reader-Response Criticism: From Formalism to Poststructuralism.* Baltimore, MD: Johns Hopkins University Press.

TORBE, M. 1974. "Modes of Response." *English in Education* 8: 21–32.

TRAVERS, D. M. 1984. "The Poetry Teacher: Behavior and Attitudes." *Research in the Teaching of English* 18: 367–384.

TSVETAEVA, MARINA and J. MARIN KING, ed. and trans. 1980. *Marina Tsvetaeva: A Captive Spirit: Selected Prose.* New York: Ardis Publishers.

TUCKER, LOIS P. 2000. "Liberating Students through Reader-Response Pedagogy in the Introductory Literature Course." *Teaching English in the Two-Year College* 28(December): 199–206.

URKOWITZ, STEVEN. 1984. *Literature—College in Twenty Teachers,* K. Macrorie, ed. New York: Oxford University Press.

VANDERGRIFT, KAY E., ed. 1996. *Mosaics of Meaning: Enhancing the Intellectual Life of Young Adults through Story.* Lanham, MD: Scarecrow Press.

———. 1996. *Ways of Knowing: Literature and the Intellectual Life of Children.* Lanham, MD: Scarecrow Press.

VICE, SUE. 1989. "Reviews—the Return of the Reader: Reader-Response Criticism (New Accents) by Elizabeth Freund." *Notes and Queries* 36(March): 136.

VINE, HAROLD A. JR., and Mark A. Faust. 1992. "Situating Readers: Introduction and Invitation." *English Journal* 81(November): 62.

VINZ, RUTH, and DAN KIRBY. 1988. "New Views of Readers and Texts." *English Journal* 77(January): 90.

VOGEL, MARK, and DON ZANCANELLA. 1991. "The Story World of Adolescents in and out of the Classroom." *English Journal* 80(October): 54–60.

WALKER, MICHELLE. 1997. "Authentic Assessment in the Literature Classroom." *English Journal* 86(January): 69–75.

WALLOWITZ, LARAINE. 2004. "Reading as Resistance: Gendered Messages in Literature and Media." *English Journal* 93(January): 26.

WARAWA, BONNIE. 1988. "Classroom Inquiry: Learning About Learning." English Journal 77(February): 30–33.

WARAWA, BONNIE. 1989. "Write Me the Story: Responding to Literature through Storytelling." *English Journal* 78(February): 48–50.

WAXMAN, BARBARA FREY. 2000. "Reader-Response Theory, Social Criticism, and Personal Writing." *Reader: Essays in Reader-Oriented Theory, Criticism, and Pedagogy* 43(Spring): 76–79.

WEAVER, CONSTANCE. 1985. "Parallels between New Paradigms in Science and in Reading and Literary Theories: An Essay Review." *Research in the Teaching of English* 19(October): 298n316.

WEBB, AGNES J. 1982. "Transactions with Literary Texts: Conversations in Classrooms." *English Journal* 71(March): 56–60.

WELLEK, RENE and AUSTIN WARREN. 1942. *Theory of Literature.* New York: Harcourt, Brace and World.

WERDERICH, DONNA E. 2002. "Individualized Responses: Using Journal Letters as a Vehicle for Differentiated Reading Instruction." *Journal of Adolescent & Adult Literacy* 45(May): 746.

WEST, MARK I. 1997. *Trust Your Children: Voices against Censorship in Children's Literature.* Second Ed. New York: Neal-Schuman Publishers.

WHITEHEAD, FRANK. 1966. *The Disappearing Dais: A Study of the Principles and Practice of English Teaching.* London: Chatto and Windus.

WILHELM, JEFF. 2001. "Getting Kids into the Reading Game: You Gotta Know the Rules." *Voices From the Middle* 8(May): 25.

WILHELM, JEFFREY D. 1997. *'You Gotta Be the Book': Teaching Engaged and Reflective Reading with Adolescents*. New York: Teachers College Press.

WILKINSON, PHYLLIS A, and ELISSA KIDO. 1997. "Literature and Cultural Awareness: Voices from the Journey." *Language Arts* 74(April): 255.

WILLINSKY, J. 1988. "Recalling the Moral Force of Literature in Education." *Journal of Educational Thought* 22: 118–132.

WILSON, L. 1981. "The Reader's Contribution in the Literary Experience: Interview with Louise Rosenblatt." *English Quarterly* 14: 3–12.

WILSON, R. N. 1956. "Literary Experience and Personality." *Journal of Aesthetics and Literary Criticism* 15: 47–57.

WOOD, SUSAN NELSON. 2001. "Bringing Us the Way to Know: The Novels of Gary Paulsen." *English Journal* 90(January): 67–72.

WOODARD, IV. EMORY H. 2000. *Media in the Home 2000: The Fifth Annual Survey of Parents and Children*. Philadelphia, PA: The Annenberg Public Policy Center of the University of Pennsylvania.

WORKMAN, BROOKE. 1985. "The Natural: The English Teacher as Humanities Teacher." *English Journal* 74(November): 28–30.

———. 1983. *Writing Seminars in the Content Area: In Search of Hemingway, Salinger, and Steinbeck*. Urbana, IL: National Council of Teachers of English.

WORTHINGTON, PEPPER. 1985. "Writing a Rationale for a Controversial Common Reading Book: Alice Walker's the Color Purple." *English Journal* 74(January): 48–52.

WRIGHT, TERENCE R. 1995. "Reader-Response under Review: Art, Game, or Science?" *Style* 29(Winter): 529–548.

YOUNG, RICHARD, ed. 1981. *Untying the Text: A Post-Structuralist Reader*. London: Routledge and Kegan Paul.

ZAHARIAS, JANE A. 1986. "The Effects of Genre and Tone on Undergraduate Students' Preferred Patterns of Response to Two Short Stories and Two Poems." *Research in the Teaching of English* 20(February): 56–68.

ZANARINI, ANNA. 2001. "Who Dun It? Mysteries." *Voices from the Middle* 9(December): 85–87.

ZANCANELLA, DON. 1992. "The Influence of State-Mandated Testing on Teachers of Literature." *Educational Evaluation and Policy Analysis* 14(Fall): 283–295.

———. 1991. "Teachers Reading/Readers Teaching: Five Teachers' Personal Approaches to Literature and Their Teaching of Literature." *Research in the Teaching of English* 25(February): 5–32.

ZARRILLO, J. 1991. "Theory Becomes Practice: Aesthetic Teaching with Literature." *New Advocate* 4: 221–234.

ZIGO, DIANE, and MICHAEL T. MOORE. 2002. "Accountability and Teacher Education: Just Like Everyone Else—Teaching to the Test?" *English Education* 34(January): 137.

ZIPES, JACK DAVID. 2001. *Sticks and Stones: The Troublesome Success of Children's Literature from Slovenly Peter to Harry Potter*. New York: Routledge.

ZIRINSKY, DRIEK, and SHIRLEY RAU. 2001. *A Classroom of Teenaged Readers: Nurturing Reading Processes in Senior High English*. New York: Longman.

ZOREDA, MARGARET LEE. 1997. *La Lectura Literaria Como Arte De 'Performance': La Teoria Transaccional De Louise Rosenblatt Y Sus Implicaciones Pedagogicas (the Use of Literature as Performance Art: The Transactional Theory of Louise Rosenblatt and Its Pedagogical Implications)*. Mexico.

ZYNGIER, SONIA, and TANIA M. G. SHEPHERD. 2003. "What Is Literature, Really? A Corpus-Driven Study of Students' Statements." *Style* 37(Spring): 14.

INDEX

If I Should Die Before I Wake (Nolan), 173–174
If You Come Softly (Woodson), 163
Imagination, 48, 247
    other readers, imagined dialog with, 13–14
    of viewer, 184
Important word, passage, or feature, identification
    of, 85–86
Inferential level of comprehension, 252–253
Information
    about literature, 117, 226, 232, 238, 251, 252
    from students, 226
"Insomnia" (Dunn), 122
Interpretation of text, 54–55, 95–96, 102, 209,
    224–226
    group discussion and, 12–14, 24
    nature of, 26–27
    perfect reading of text (See Perfect reader)
    theme statement and individual response,
        144–146
Interrupted Life, An: The Diaries of Etty Hillesum, 174
Introspection. See Self-definition
Inverted word order, 124–125
Iorio, John J., 113
Iser, Wolfgang, 16–18, 22, 24

Jackson, Shirley, 198
Janeczko, Paul B., 165
Jarrell, Randall, 119–121
Jauss, Hans Robert, 16, 25–27
Jones, Donald, 44–52, 54, 72
Journals, young adult literature, 178
"Journey, The" (Oliver), 10–11

Kerr, M. E., 163
Killing Mr. Griffin (Duncan), 23, 166–168, 173, 175
Kirby, Dan, 247
Kirkpatrick, Daniel, 177
Kirkwood, 173
Kitzhaber, Albert R., 208
Knowledge
    in Bleich's theory, 12–14
    literature as body of knowledge, 34–35, 206,
        211–214, 251
    testing and, 236–239
"Kong at the Seaside" (Zweig), 44
"Kubla Khan" (Coleridge), 121–123
Kumin, Maxine, 130–133

LaConte, Ronald, 213, 221–222
Lanham, Richard, 118

Learning to Swim: A Memoir (Turner), 164
LeGuin, Ursula K., 41–43
L'Engle, Madeleine, 176
Leonard, John, 191
Lesesne, Teri, 177
Levertov, Denise, 237–238
Like Mother, Like Me (Schwartz), 153
Liner, Tom, 247
Linguistic control, 53
"Listen" (Turner), 164
Listening skills, 88
Literal level of comprehension, 252
Literary heritage, 212–214
Literature
    fiction differentiated from, 1–4
    film and television as, 182–185
    purpose in teaching of, 32–33
    research compared to, 103–104
    social purpose of, 25–26
    uniqueness of discipline, 33–44
Literature for Today's Young Adults (Donelson and
    Nilsen), 153, 154, 177, 179
Little House on the Prairie, 200
Longfellow, Henry Wadsworth, 106–110
Lord of the Flies (Golding), 173, 175
Love, Sex, and Identity, 113
Love, texts on, 110–113
Love and Sex: Ten Stories of Truth (Cart, ed.), 163–164
Lovely Bones, The (Sebold), 153
Lowes, John Livingston, 123
Lowry, Lois, 174
Lyon, Reid, 218

Magicia, The (Stein), 173
Mailloux, Steven, 5
"Man He Killed, The" (Hardy), 134–136
Mandel, Barrett J., 214, 216, 217, 219
Marginalia to capture readings, 37–44
M★A★S★H, 187, 200
Maupassant, Guy de, 195
Meadows, Robert, 195
Metaphors, 124
Miller, James E., 210
Moffett, James, 215
Moral purpose of literature, 212–213. See also Values
Morse, J. Mitchell, 56–57
Mr. and Mrs. Bo Jo Jones (Head), 157–163, 165, 171

"Naming of Parts" (Reed), 96–97, 127–128
National Council of Teachers of English, 207, 208